HITTER

HITTER

The Life and Turmoils of Ted Williams

ED LINN

A HARVEST BOOK

HARCOURT BRACE & COMPANY

San Diego   New York   London

Library of Congress Cataloging-in-Publication Data
Linn, Edward.
Hitter: the life and turmoils of Ted Williams/Ed Linn. — 1st Harvest ed.
p. cm. — (A Harvest book)
ISBN 0-15-600091-1
1. Williams, Ted, 1918– . 2. Baseball players — United States —
Biography. 3. Boston Red Sox (Baseball team) — History. I. Title.
GV865.W5L48 1994
796.357'092 — dc20 93-42460

Designed by Lori McThomas
Printed in the United States of America

First Harvest edition 1994
CDE

*To my lifetime collaborator, Ruth,
and to our own Kids, Hildy, Michael,
and our dearly beloved David*

Contents

Contents

Appendixes

I

Hitter

He was a legendary figure around the San Diego playgrounds long before he entered high school. The kid with the perfect swing. The kid who could hit a ball higher and farther than any of the most powerful adults in town. And who could not only lecture the other kids on the proper technique of hitting but could tell them after watching the opposing pitcher warm up exactly how he was going to pitch to them.

How did he know what he knew? How did he know these things at the age of ten or eleven? Big-league baseball ended at the Mississippi River. The Pacific Coast League stretched only from Seattle to Los Angeles. San Diego, with a population of something like 150,000, was little more than a naval base down in the boondocks.

There was no television to provide an eager kid with expert commentary, complete with replay, on how the battle between the pitcher and the hitter works. There were not even any games to listen to on the radio.

How did a kid growing up in San Diego in the 1930s come to understand the intricacies not only of the battle but of the war?

The explanation of the kids who grew up with him is that there is no explanation. "When it came to hitting, he was a genius." Geniuses don't have to learn; geniuses know. Einstein knew. Mozart knew. Ted Williams knew.

Don't tell that to Ted Williams. "I can tell you exactly when it started," he says. "It wasn't when I was ten or eleven. It happened when I was twelve. I had never followed major-league baseball. The only players I had ever heard of were Ruth and Gehrig. And then I read that Bill Terry had hit .400, and that really excited me. Four hundred! I don't think I even knew what you had to do to hit .400, but I could tell that it was something wonderful. I knew I wanted to do that, too. Hit .400. I was so excited that even though it was dark out—I've never told this to anybody before—I got my little bat, ran out to our little backyard, and began to swing."

And continued to swing every night. Hour after hour, the little boy, alone at home, out in the tiny backyard, swinging by the light of the moon. ("The yard was always cluttered, and so tiny that I'd have to clear a space for myself in the dark.") Over and over and over. *Whoooosh . . . whoooosh . . . whooooosh.* "There were two things I concentrated on. First, I wanted to have a great-looking swing. That was important to me, everybody wants to look good. Second, I wanted to visualize what I was doing. And I always visualized myself in the Polo Grounds, because that's where Bill Terry played." Men on first and second, two out, high inside fast ball. See the ball, see the swing, see the bat hitting the ball, see the long, high fly arcing out toward the right-field bleacher. *Whoooosh . . . whoooosh . . . whoooosh. Whoooosh.*

"I was playing in a sandlot game, and I heard a man say, 'Gee, that kid has quick wrists.' And I thought, *If you think I'm quick with my wrists now, just wait awhile.*"

Something else to visualize. Be quick, be quick, be quick. "In my mind it wasn't a snap. I always visualized it as a push. Push straight out to get the bat started, with the snap of the wrists coming at the end."

There was one other thing about the hitting stroke he was perfecting. He was not thinking in terms of just hitting the ball; he was thinking in terms of hitting the lower half of the ball with a slight uppercut swing. At the age of twelve, Ted Williams was quite consciously developing a home-run swing. "I was in the Polo Grounds. I was swinging the bat at an imaginary pitch. I would say, *High inside, fly ball to right. Low outside, line drive to left field.* Never did I think of hitting a ball on the ground. I wanted to be the hitter who could hit every pitch out of the park, and it just seemed natural that if you want to swing up and hit the ball in the air, you had to hit it on the lower half. I didn't really visualize it as swinging that much up, though. I'd just think in terms of picking the ball up."

All his years of studying hitting as no man has ever studied hitting before have served only to confirm what the twelve-year-old boy had somehow been able to figure out in his backyard. "All you have to do is look at a good swing from the top side and you'll see it's as much a push as anything, because you don't make a circle with your hand.

4

You go from your letters to pushing straight out. But your body is rotating with it, and you get in that point in the hitting zone, your hips are rotating to maintain that power stroke. That's the power position. I've got pictures upon pictures that I can show you."

The quickness, too: "To be quick meant to be quick with the hips and everything else. Quick is one thing. Powerful quickness is what you have to have in hitting. And that comes from the hitting stroke. Two inches is quick, but nothing's there. You have to have a two-foot length of stroke to build up enough energy to get the power you want. So it isn't just quickness, it's a quickness of two feet or a foot and a half to get your bat into that hitting zone with quickness and speed and weight."

There was one phase of his thinking about which he eventually came to have second thoughts. "I think a real good hitter can occasionally hit a pitch that isn't a home-run pitch for him out of the park. But to think in those terms is not real good." But that was a matter of philosophy that had nothing to do with the essential principle of lifting the ball in the air by hitting the lower half with a slight uppercut swing. "More outs are made on the ground. I never realized it then. I just wanted to hit the ball in the air because extra-base hits are in the air."

By the time he was in high school, he was hitting those long high drives out of the park. And was already expounding on the necessity of hitting the bottom half of the ball to teammates who were more than satisfied when they were able to hit the ball at all.

Okay, so it turns out that he has a superhuman pair of eyes. When Ted took his physical for the Naval Reserve in World War II, his eyes tested at 20/10 and were so exceptional in every regard that the examining doctor called in his colleagues to take a look for themselves. His reflexes were so extraordinary that he set records in gunnery that have never been equaled.

"He told me he could sometimes see the ball hit the bat," one of his high-school teammates remembers.

"He told me he actually saw the ball flatten against the bat a number of times," says another.

A born hitter, as Ted Williams was to read a thousand—ten

thousand—times. Oh, yeah? What about all that practice, he wanted to ask. What about all that swinging of the bat, which had started in a less-programmed manner at the age of six.

What about all that thinking? And analyzing? What about all that dedication?

Is it possible—hear me out on this—is it possible that a young boy who is focused entirely on hitting a baseball from his earliest memory, who is swinging the bat in that totally obsessed and concentrated way all the time he is growing up, is also developing the physical attributes that are essential to the achievement of his goal?

Can you will the body, if you start young enough, to adapt to the needs of your desire? Or, to put it another way, does the body, that incredible self-regenerating engine, design itself, in its developing stages, to meet the demands that are being placed on it?

Don't laugh. Anybody who has written about basketball is aware that basketball stars have tended to have the same kind of obsession. The youthful Oscar Robertson, carrying a basketball around with him, dribbling it under the table during dinner, suddenly sprouts, during his year of natural growth, not from five-feet-six to an expected six-one, but to six-five. With a basketball player, one could argue, there is another factor; there is all the jumping and stretching he does while playing the game. But that also makes the point, doesn't it? The youthful Ted Williams is not only thinking baseball and swinging a bat; in the congenial San Diego clime, he is playing baseball twelve months a year.

Will the eyes sharpen to the point at which they can follow the ball into the bat? Will the reflexes become so sharp that when put to the test in a rolling, diving plane they will rip the target sleeve to shreds?

"Why does the apple fall from the tree?" asks Leo Tolstoy in *War and Peace*. "Is it because the fruit has grown too heavy for the branch to hold; or is it because a sudden breeze has shaken the apple loose from the bough? Or is it because there is a little boy waiting under the tree with cupped hands?"

Or, to return to the original thesis, is it genius, which is by definition one of the mysteries of life?

II

Ted and Me

To grow up in Boston in the late 1930s and on through the '40s was to come face to face with one of the phenomena of American life—and probably of all truly civilized societies—THE HERO. Read no sarcasm into that, please. The vast majority of us cannot aspire to be great scholars, statesmen, doctors, or even certified public accountants. The road to glory, for those of us who dwelt in the streets, was in the broad field of entertainment. The young boy could aspire to be a great athlete; the young girl could dream of becoming a singer or an actress. So what could be more natural than that the athlete or the actress would become the hero and heroine of the sprawling populace. If the choices have expanded a great deal in the ensuing years, especially for women, I would doubt whether it is appreciably different today.

Ted Williams was THE HERO, bigger than life, stranger than fiction, able to hit balls over tall buildings on a single bounce. And handsome, too. As he grew older and pinned a double dose of wartime ribbons as a Marine pilot to his chest, there developed an inevitable comparison to John Wayne.

It didn't matter whether you worshiped him or deplored him, the point is that you knew T. Williams was in town. The first question you asked every morning was "What did Ted do?" Only after that question had been answered did you ask, "How did the Red Sox make out?"

He was variously known as the Kid, the Splendid Splinter, Teddy, or, in the shorthand of Dave Egan, the wickedly acerbic columnist of the *Boston Record*, T. Wms. Esq., which—it was understood—was quite literally cutting him down to size. Egan's shorthand, as Ted came to know only too well, would always be a short jab to the short ribs.

Joe DiMaggio may have been a hero of equal stature around the rest of the country, but his impact in New York could not compare with Williams's impact in Boston. The New York players got more national publicity because New York, even more then than now, was the unchallenged center of the communications industry. But the New York scene was so vast and varied, the movers and shakers so abundant, that no individual personality, let alone any individual athlete, could dominate that city the way Ted Williams dominated Boston.

It was not that Boston had been bereft of workaday sports heroes before the coming of THE HERO either. We had the championship Bruins featuring the ''Kraut Line'' (Milt Schmidt, Bobby Bauer, and Woody Dumart), which may have been the greatest hockey line of all time, plus Eddie Shore, who was indubitably the greatest defenseman. In football, Boston College, with Frank Leahy as head coach, had ignited the town. In 1939, Ted's first year with the Sox, Boston College had a couple of local-boy All-Americans in its triple-threat halfback, Charley O'Rourke, and end Gene Goodreault.

As for the Red Sox themselves, owner Tom Yawkey had brought in some of the most powerful names from the rest of the league, swaddled in banknotes and complacency. The team Williams joined had Jimmy Foxx, Joe Cronin, and Lefty Grove, all of whom had come to Boston with one foot already in the Hall of Fame. The only fault that could be found with our team of all-stars was that it was having all sorts of trouble winning ball games. When the Sox bought Ted Williams from San Diego, in December 1937, they had just finished a most uninspiring fifth. A year earlier, they had not even been able to win half their games.

I can remember the first time I ever heard—or, rather, saw—Ted Williams's name. I was thirteen. I see before me now, as clearly as in a mirror, a picture at the bottom of the sports page of the old *Boston Post*. It shows a tall, skinny kid with an unbelievably long neck posed in the follow-through of a wind-around swing. The caption identifies him as a sensational nineteen-year-old slugger from the Pacific Coast League who had been purchased for $25,000. The caption also says that he had hit .291, a figure that left me vastly unimpressed. Tom Yawkey usually bought us a Jimmy Foxx or a Lefty Grove to enliven our winters and infuriate our summers. No skinny .291 hitter from the minor leagues was going to set our pulses to pounding.

But this skinny kid did. Ted was something different right from day one, when he arrived in training camp fashionably late and electrified everyone just by stepping into the batter's box. He was fresh and he was glib and, in those early days, carefree and cocky. He was copy. For despite his compulsion for privacy, Ted Williams—mass of contradictions that he was—always did have an instinct for the front page.

In later years I found myself in the unique position—unique, at any rate, among the kids who had hung out on Boston street corners—of being able to go behind the memories of those early days and find out a little more about what had really been happening.

The first time I met Ted he was buck naked. It was 1954. I was working for a sister publication of *Sport* magazine when Ed Fitzgerald, who had just been elevated to editor-in-chief of *Sport,* called me in to his office. *Sport* wanted to do a long article on Ted (all students of *Sport* magazine will remember the Sport Specials). The problem was that Ted had broken his collarbone in spring training and had remained behind in Florida for therapy and rehabilitation. Since Ted wasn't going to be in Boston where a real sportswriter could get at him, I was being asked whether I wanted to walk around my old hometown and talk to enough people who knew him to get the job done.

As it turned out, Ted had unexpectedly flown up to Boston on the day I showed up in Fenway Park and was, at that very moment, in the trainer's room. The first words I ever heard him speak, therefore, were "Send the sonofabitch in."

It was not going to be that easy. "I'm not going to talk to you," Ted told me. "But I think I owe you an explanation of why." I seemed like a good enough guy, he assured me, but that blankety-blank magazine of mine had a feud against him, going back to the time he had failed to show up for its inauguration luncheon in Boston following the 1948 World Series. Because of that, he said, they had sent some sonofabitch, whose name he assured me he would remember, to write a vicious article about him.

I explained that *Sport* not only had new ownership but that it also had a new editor, a bright young guy who was going to turn the magazine around.

What was his name, Ted asked, looking interested.

"Ed Fitzgerald," I said.

Whereupon Ted slammed his fist against the training table and bellowed, "Ed Fitzgerald! *That's* the sonofabitch!"

So much for that. But at least I could go back and tell Fitzgerald that although I had met with Ted, he had refused to talk to me for reasons that were clearly no fault of mine. Having explained to Ted the difficult position I was in—because, what the hell, the magazine had paid my way from New York to Boston—I said, "Here's what I'd like to do. I'll ask you a question, you'll refuse to answer, and I'll be able to go back and tell them that I tried."

So I asked him a question—and he answered at length. I stayed in Boston for three days interviewing Ted and his teammates. And when one of the teammates would go into the trainer's room and ask Ted if it was really all right for him to talk to a writer from *Sport*, I'd hear the by-now familiar voice boom forth, "Yeah, yeah. Talk to the sonofabitch."

As much as I would have liked to believe that I had won him over by my journalistic enterprise and irresistible charm, I had to admit that the truth was exactly the opposite. Ted could see that he had someone there who had not the slightest idea what he was doing. And Ted has always had a thing about lending a helping hand to the disadvantaged.

The feeling eventually developed—and Ted did little to discourage it—that Boston and Ted Williams had met each other with their fangs instinctively bared for battle. Nothing could have been further from the truth. Ted played right field in his first year, and whenever my friends and I went to a game we would sit in the bleachers behind him and cheer every move he made. He would prowl that huge area nervously between every pitch, and every now and then—this is what we were waiting for—he would pull off his glove and, using it as a bat, take a murderous swing at an imaginary pitch.

During the course of that first interview, I asked Ted whether he'd do anything different if he had his career to live over. "Yes," he said, "the one thing I'd do different, I'd spend more time on my fielding. Not on my hitting. Nobody could spend more time on hitting. I've hurt this team with my fielding at times, and I know it." I commented that when I was a kid I used to watch him play right field on brute strength. "Yeah," he said. "I sure had some tough times out there, and not only with the fans."

Well, I knew better. I reminded him that he had never had any trouble with the fans while he was in right field. I recalled for him how he would run back to his position after hitting a home run and acknowledge their cheers by picking up his cap from the button and raising it as high as those long, skinny arms could take it.

Ted looked genuinely puzzled. "You're wrong," he insisted. "I never tipped my hat. Never."

But I could remember even more than the scenes at the ballpark. I could remember the cartoons of the cap-lifting routine as drawn by Bob Coyne, the estimable *Boston Post* cartoonist. Digging through dusty files at the public library the next day, I found cartoon after cartoon of a young Ted Williams happily lifting his cap to the heavens.

I described that cap-tipping routine in my article, and the next time I interviewed Ted I found him quoting me back to myself almost verbatim. "Hell," he said, "I used to tip my hat. I used to give it the biggest tip in baseball. Right from the button. I was so enthusiastic in those days. But no more. They soured me. I made up my mind a long time ago that I'd never tip my hat. And I won't."

They had soured him so much that he had apparently wiped the memory of that first happy year completely out of his mind.

In the latter years of Ted's career, I suggested to him that his .388 batting average at the age of thirty-nine was really more impressive than his .406 year in 1941, not only because of the changes that had come into the game but because at thirty-nine he had obviously not been able to beat out any infield hits. Ted went along with the general thesis, but when I then asked if he had any idea how many leg hits he had got in 1941, he said, "To tell you the truth, I chipped a bone in my right ankle in spring training, and I played the whole season with that ankle taped up. They forget that now. I had very few infield hits in 1941.''

That ankle injury had bothered him more than he would ever admit. But the adjustments he was forced to make because of it just might have made him a better hitter and, by making him a better hitter, may actually have been a contributing factor to the .406 season.

There are two important discoveries I have made in this long look at Ted Williams. The first is that he would never use an injury as an alibi. He would not even admit to the seriousness of an incapacitating injury. It was almost as if he were saying, ''I'm not going to give them the satisfaction.'' More likely, though, he did not want the opposing pitchers to know he was hurting. When it came to hitting, Ted was always a step ahead of everybody else. He conned pitchers. He stroked them. He praised them to their faces and sang their glories to their hometown sportswriters. When, unaccountably, he became manager of the Washington Senators for a few years he was finally able to give vent to his true feelings. ''Pitchers,'' he would shout at his own pitchers from the dugout, ''are the dumbest people in the world!''

The second thing I learned is that he became an entirely different hitter after suffering an elbow injury in the 1950 All-Star Game that almost ended his career. That's right, almost ended his career. If it hadn't been for that paragon among trainers, Jack Fadden, Ted states flatly, he might never have played again. ''I was never the same hitter, though. I never swung a bat again without feeling some degree of stiffness in that elbow.''

That was the subject that came up constantly: his preoccupation with the sheer craft of hitting. From beginning to end, Ted retained an intense—and innate—curiosity about the world inside the batter's box. In 1958, when he was forty, I asked him if he had finally explored all the facets of the war between the batter and the pitcher, or at least was satisfied that he had developed his own skills to the ultimate of their potentialities. ''You get to know eighty-five percent to ninety percent of it after a while,'' he said. ''But every once in a while something new comes up that you begin to wonder about. I always felt that you had to lift up on a low ball, for instance, but now I'm beginning to wonder whether maybe you shouldn't take the same slice on it. I'm not sure of it now, I'm not sure of it at all; I'm just saying that I'm beginning to wonder. And I'm beginning to wonder whether a pitcher's motion might not be just as important a part of his equipment as his stuff. I think it is." It was the first time I had heard that latter possibility advanced, but, as with so many of Ted's theories, it has now become accepted as gospel.

In that regard, Ted could display a strange combination of arrogance and modesty. If that doesn't make much sense, remember that much of the charm of Ted Williams comes from the contradictions and, even, the perversity of his nature. He wanted to be recognized as the best hitter who ever lived, he kept meticulous account of his accomplishments, and yet he fully understood that, as vital as those accomplishments were to him, they were of no consequence whatsoever in the overall scheme of things.

"Hitting is important to me," he once told me. "Being Ted Williams isn't. Maybe twenty years after I retire. . ." (Asked to bring that statement up to date, his answer is: "I can't believe that becoming Ted Williams is that big a deal. Really and truly. I'll tell you, it does seem like it gets more important with age. I'm probably rated a better hitter now than at any time, because the old guys want to think we were all better then and the young guys don't think I'm going to be around much longer.")

Throughout his life, awards embarrassed him. In conjunction with the honors that were being heaped on him on the fiftieth anniversary of his .406 season, Harvard wanted to award him an honorary doctorate in something or other. Ted turned it down. As much as he appreciated the honor, he explained, he hadn't done anything to deserve it. When he is reminded that public honors had always left him visibly embarrassed, even when they were clearly deserved, he says, "I shouldn't be saying this, because I have great respect for Harvard. But that's really what it was. I'm seventy-three years old. I asked myself whether at my age I wanted to submit myself to something that I knew was going to make me uncomfortable."

He was a mass of contradictions. He was rebellious and he was conservative. He was gregarious and he was a loner. He could be loud, insulting, and profane; he could be unbelievably kind and compassionate.

He was a manager's headache and he was a manager's dream. He didn't drink or smoke. He never missed a train or a plane or a bus. He went to bed early, and he was always one of the first players on the field, carrying a bat and ready to swing. He never argued with or defied a manager. Far from being a clubhouse lawyer, he could be counted on to support any Red Sox manager who was under attack. (It was always the writers' fault, understand. "The manager's pallbearers," he called them.)

The Boston sportswriters once took a vote to pick the players who were most cooperative, least cooperative, least friendly, most temperamental, and most generous. Ted finished first in every category. Clif Keane, the "Che Guevara" of the Boston press corps, puts it this way: "You never knew what it was going to be from the middle of a sentence. No idea what to expect. I spent a lot of time with him. He had a savage mouth. *Unbelievable* dirty mouth. Manufactured new words every day."

Keane came to see the use of language as the safety valve Ted employed to keep his anger from erupting into a physical attack. "He'd get so mad in a conversation he'd scare the hell out of you. He'd go crazy." Ted has always been a great fight fan, and to Keane, who covered all the big fights of the time, he had all the physical tools needed to be a great fighter himself. "He'd go around the locker room throwing left jabs. His hands were so quick. If the temper had ever come out he might have killed somebody. Never threatened anybody, though. Never put his hands on anybody, never hit anybody. Never argued with a teammate."

Bob Holbrook, Keane's colleague on the *Boston Globe,* says, "Something was bugging him. I never knew what it was. Still don't know. He'd take it out on the east wind. He'd take it out on the Irish of New England because they rode him an awful lot in Fenway Park. He'd take it out on anybody who happened to be there."

His best friends would concede that they never ceased to be amazed at the way he could revert from an intelligent adult to a petulant adolescent in a matter of seconds. "He's such a complex guy in so many ways," one old friend says. "He's like the Pied Piper when he turns that charm on, and he can turn it off just as fast. He can get offended just as quickly. I've seen him at functions where he seems to be enjoying himself, and next time you look he's gone. What happened? Oh, someone said something, and he took a walk."

You never knew when an eruption might occur. Lou Boudreau, one of his managers, was standing behind a stanchion in the dugout one day talking to some writers when a bat came flying toward them. "Luckily, the bat ricocheted off the stanchion," Bob Holbrook says. "Otherwise it would have wiped out the manager and half the press corps." Although they never found out what had brought on such a violent explosion, none of them doubted that Ted had done it, on purpose. "It was a spite thing," Holbrook says. "No question about it."

But who knows? When you live in your own little world you are not necessarily aware of the people around you. In the spring of 1948, Ted was stalking through a hotel lobby with his head down, as always, and failed to respond to a cheery greeting from manager Joe McCarthy's wife, Babe. Mrs. McCarthy caught him at the elevator door. "Babe Ruth always said good morning," she told him. "Lou Gehrig always said good morning. And you're going to say good morning." Ted apologized profusely. He hadn't recognized her, he said, because his mind had been off somewhere else.

There is this to be considered, too. A baseball player is performing out there on the field, but he is also living his life. In that regard, there are some players—Reggie Jackson comes irresistibly to mind—who are playing out some private psychodrama in front of the multitudes.

Ted Williams had a childhood that comes right out of Theodore Dreiser. His mother was a Salvation Army zealot. His earliest memories are of standing alongside her on street corners while she harangued hostile and hooting crowds. He had an absent, and perhaps alcoholic, father. There was a younger brother who became a juvenile delinquent, a small-time thief, a jailbird, a bum. Ted found his escape on the ball field. He would leave San Diego at the age of nineteen to become a member of the Boston Red Sox and would seldom return. For the next two decades he played before screaming crowds all summer, idolized and cheered but hearing every boo and hoot. When the season was over he would retreat to the wilds of Minnesota or Florida to fish and hunt. His companions on those trips were his guides and occasionally a carefully selected friend.

Ted Williams was an original, as Babe Ruth was an original. Each was the greatest hitter of his time, and each, in his own way, was a child playing a child's game. Not for nothing was one of them called the Babe and the other the Kid. They dominated their teams and they dominated the game they played, and they did it not only through sheer ability but by the force of their personalities. Each had a personal presence that was striking and arresting; the Babe because he was so grotesque in body and features, the Kid because he was so tall and handsome.

There were differences between them, however, that were just as obvious. The Babe was a raging extrovert who operated on a level of instinct not too far above that of an animal. "Ted is a strange combination," Jack Fadden once said to me. "He is an extrovert with an inferiority complex. Notice the way he always walks, with his head down. Or runs in from the outfield the same way. That's no act. Ted is a shy man. But he is a perfectionist, too. He has to be the best. Whatever he takes up, he has to know everything there is to know about it. When he gets into an argument he has to win. If he can out-yell you, he'll out-yell you. If he can't, he'll get new ammunition. A week after you think a subject has been dropped, he'll come up and say, 'You know when you said such and such? Well, you're wrong.' And then he'll throw a lot of information at you, and you realize that he's been researching the subject all week."

The difference between Williams and Ruth, then, is that the Babe never doubted he was the greatest. Ted had to prove himself constantly—over and over and over. He needed the approval—and the applause—of the crowd so much that he went to abnormal lengths to deny that he needed it. He refused to tip his cap to applause, to acknowledge it in any way at all. Not even after he hit a home run in his final time at bat and the fans gave him a four-minute standing ovation. (Actually, it was the second time he hit a home run on his last time at bat. He had already done it on what he believed to be his farewell to baseball, when he was recalled by the Marines for duty in Korea. He didn't tip his cap that time, either.)

It was Ted's contention that the people who cheered him when he hit a home run were the same people who booed him when he struck out—which was probably not true. More to the point, he always insisted that although he would rather be cheered than booed, he really didn't care what the fans thought of him one way or the other. Obviously, though, if he really didn't care he wouldn't have bothered to make such a show of not caring. He simply would have touched his finger to his cap in that automatic, thoughtless gesture of most players and forgotten about it.

In short, Ted always had it both ways. He got the cheers, and he pretended they meant nothing to him. He was like a rich man's nephew who treats his uncle with disrespect—knowing he is the old man's favorite—to prove he isn't interested in his money, while all the time he is secretly dreaming that the old man is going to reward such probity and independence by leaving him most of his fortune.

Ted had it even better than that. The fans of Boston cheered him more than any other athlete has ever been cheered, and then cheered him all the louder in the hope that he would reward them, at last, with that essentially meaningless tip of the cap.

What Ted refused to recognize was that the jeers were really cheers in disguise. The people who did the jeering had a dream in their hearts, and the dream was that Teddy would come over to them, some sun-filled afternoon, and say, "Don't boo me, fellows. Let's you and me be friends." Meanwhile, they could only let him know they were there by making loud noises. All Ted had to do was ignore them, and the boos would have faded away. Instead, he'd stand in the outfield, hands on hips, and stare at them for minutes on end while the animal cries from the left-field stands grew louder and harsher. Sometimes it almost seemed as if he provoked the booing; sometimes it seemed as if he got some deep-seated confirmation out of it.

Clearly, he got some kind of confirmation out of not tipping his cap.

Without overanalyzing this, *not* tipping his cap became a positive act for Ted, not a negative one. *Not* tipping his cap became as much of an interchange with the cheering fans as Babe Ruth's cap-waving victory trots around the bases. Ted Williams celebrated by *not* tipping his cap. *Not* tipping his cap was what kept Ted Williams firmly in control.

There was something fitting in the circumstance that found Ted Williams leaving the Red Sox in the same year that Casey Stengel left as the manager of the New York Yankees. Beyond any doubt, these were the acknowledged giants of their respective crafts. They were also among the most interesting human beings, the most colorful figures, the best news copy, and the biggest individual box-office attractions.

It was fitting, too, that both men should have remained true to themselves at the end. Stengel refused to go along with the front-office fiction that he and the Yankees were parting company "by mutual agreement." He made it perfectly clear that the Yankees were not renewing his contract because they felt he had become too old, at seventy, to manage effectively.

Ted remained in character by refusing to allow other clubs to honor him on his last road trip around the circuit. When told that Detroit was planning to give him a Day, he said angrily, "To hell they are. I'm not going to let them do any such thing." When he learned that Cleveland had already announced a Day in his honor, he said, "All right, let them do something for the kids."

When Ted talked about the kids, he was talking about the Jimmy Fund and the patients at the Children's Cancer Hospital in Boston, one of the abiding interests of his life. In his capacity as chairman of the fund-raising committee, he had raised almost $4,000,000. Even when you honored Ted Williams, you had to honor him on his own terms.

Even his dominance of the league paralleled Stengel's, because Ted did not stand alone on the pinnacle until Joe DiMaggio retired in 1952, three years after Casey became manager of the Yankees. It has become Ted's fate, however, that he will inevitably be compared with DiMaggio, even though he outlasted DiMag by a full nine years. It is Ted's personal cross that the comparison has rarely been favorable. In DiMag's thirteen years, the Yankees won ten pennants and nine world championships. In Williams's seventeen full seasons, the Red Sox won only one pennant and absolutely no world championships.

There were other factors involved, of course. During the years when Williams's Red Sox were outdistanced by DiMaggio's Yanks, the Yankees always had far superior pitching and—in Bill Dickey and Yogi Berra—far, far superior catching. Joe Cronin, in addressing himself to the comparison, would say: "If we had traded Williams for DiMaggio, do you have any doubt at all that the Yankees still would have won those pennants and we still would have finished second?"

Yet Cronin himself seemed to feel that Ted hadn't been quite the leader he should have been, that something was lacking somewhere. When the *Sporting News* held its Player of the Decade election in 1955, Cronin voted not for Williams, but for Stan Musial.

Ted was always generous in his public statements about other players. When DiMaggio won the Most Valuable Player award in 1941, the year Ted hit .406, Ted was quick to say, "They picked a good man for it." As the years went by, though, and he found himself being consistently rated below DiMaggio, he began to resent it. He resented it so strongly that when DiMaggio retired, at the age of thirty-six, following a .263 season, Ted could not resist saying, with a touch of malice, "When I hit .260, I'll retire, too."

If it was pride that made DiMaggio quit after his bad season, it was pride that kept Ted going after he had suffered his own disastrous .254 season at the age of forty-one. DiMaggio could not bring himself to return as a possibly part-time, second-rate player, even though his front office wanted him back on any terms. Ted could not bring himself to depart with the stigma of a bad year behind him, even though Tom Yawkey had told him straight out that he wanted him to retire.

Ted was determined to go out with a .300 season if it was humanly possible to drag himself onto the field. His .316 batting average may not seem like much against his .344 lifetime average, but in many ways Ted's final season was his most glorious. He hit 29 home runs in 310 times at bat, an average of one home run for every 10.7 times at bat, far better than his lifetime figure of 14.8. He knocked in 72 runs, or one run batted in for every 4.3 times at bat, which compared favorably with his lifetime mark of 4.2. By hitting a home run in his very first time at bat of the season, he tied Lou Gehrig's lifetime record of 493. The next day, in the Fenway Park opener, he hit another homer to break it. He went on to become the fourth man in history to hit 500 home runs, and he raised his total, on his last time at bat, to 521. Only Babe Ruth (714) and Jimmy Foxx (534) had more.

That last home run, a 430-foot drive through the heavy atmosphere of a threatening day at Fenway Park, ranks—along with his two-out, ninth-inning home run that won the 1941 All-Star Game—as one of the most dramatic ever hit.

And yet, even those home runs lent themselves to the perennial charge that Ted Williams's triumphs were always personal rather than team triumphs. The implication being that he was more concerned with personal glory than with winning. The All-Star Game homer in 1941 was a personal triumph, too, his critics said, because the game it won was a mere exhibition. As to the final home run that left a crowd of 10,454 screaming, one Boston columnist wrote: "Outside of the theatrics, what did it all mean? He hadn't won that game. Where the Red Sox had been trailing 4-2, they were now trailing 4-3."

Where was the dramatic home run, the critics asked, when his team needed it? Where was the long drive—or even a clutch single—in the 1946 World Series? Where was it in the last two games of 1949, when the Red Sox, needing one victory at Yankee Stadium to win the pennant, lost both? Where was Ted's big bat in the 1948 play-off game with Cleveland, when Gene Beardon, Lou Boudreau, and Ken Keltner led the Indians to a victory in Fenway Park?

And if Ted's final season was a glorious one for him, it was a year of decay and decline for his team. The Red Sox lost eighty-nine games and plummeted to seventh place, their worst record since Tom Yawkey and his open-wallet policy took over the club in 1933.

It is obviously unfair to hold Ted responsible for the mediocrity of his teammates or the incompetence of the front office, but the fact remains that Ted himself, as the symbol of the Red Sox for more than twenty years, has also become a symbol of their disappointments and failures. This is a side of Ted's record that we will go into later.

There were other charges against him, too. There is no doubt that he poisoned the climate between the Boston press and the other Red Sox players, particularly those who came to the Sox as rookies. Ted treated the writers with such contempt—by having them barred from the locker room, as well as by word, grimace, and attitude—that the young players, who tended to idolize him anyway, became balky and uncooperative, too. For a while there was a sign at the end of the line of lockers facing Ted's that read: NO WRITERS PLEASE.

With it all, those writers who are still around look back on him rather fondly, because they have come to recognize that however difficult the relationship may have been they did have a *relationship* with him. And that covering him was one of the greatest experiences of their lives.

In the fans' attitude toward Ted, there had developed something of the special indulgence and affection that the problem child of the family always seems to get, especially when he has good looks and great charm. And nobody could be more charming than Ted Williams when he set his mind to it.

But that wasn't all of it. In his relationship with the Boston fans, over the years, there was always an element of romance. Ted aroused the passions. He had an electrifying presence, both on the field and off, some special ingredient that lay close to the surface of his complex, troubled nature. When he stepped into the batter's box, jiggled

23

up and down, and gave his bat that quick, nervous wrench, there came the sudden feeling that he was poised for some great deed, that both he and the spectators were at the brink of some great drama. If he failed to provide the anticipated climax—and by the nature of the game every batter must fail most of the time—the drama would begin to build again toward his next turn at bat.

For, say what you want, this was Ted Williams, the greatest hitter of his time. This was the last of the .400 hitters. This was a six-time batting champion and a two-time triple-crown winner. This was a man who overcame injuries and illnesses and two separate hitches in the Marines to win batting titles at the ages of thirty-nine and forty.

This chapter can appropriately be titled "Ted and Me." I always seemed to be there at pivotal moments of his career, first as a fan and then as a sportswriter.

I didn't attend a lot of Sox games after the war—no more than one or two a year—but I was there on that day in 1946 when Elmer Valo made the fence-draping catch that, to my mind, ruined the season for Ted.

I was watching him as he waited for the umpire's call and then kicked the bag in anger. Nothing of great importance in itself, except that I was able to write about it from memory, and whenever I'd see it described in somebody else's piece, I'd feel that I was making some kind of contribution to the growing legend of Ted Williams.

In 1950, my senior year at Boston University, I cut afternoon classes with a friend one day—where have you gone, F. Desales Meyers?—and that allowed me to be there when Ted committed his most notorious indiscretion by giving the fans the elbow.

As a writer, I did an article on him every year after his return from Korea and always seemed to come in on a big day or a turnaround day. In 1956 and 1958, I saw him hit home runs to break out of what were being written of as terminal slumps. In 1957, I picked him up at Yankee Stadium when he came back from an injury and hit the pinch homer off Whitey Ford that started him on one of the greatest concentrated hitting streaks ever. In 1959, when he was assumed to be through,

I was assigned to write an article on "The Last Days of Ted Williams and Stan Musial." Not quite for either of them. For Musial, there would be four more seasons. For Ted, the grand finale lay a year ahead.

I was the only out-of-town writer covering his final game in Boston. Today, there would be so much press and TV equipment on the field that the players would be hard-pressed to take batting practice. I was the only writer in the clubhouse before the game (probably because of the two-hour curfew on the press) and the only writer on the bench when Ted came out (a press conference was being held in Tom Yawkey's office to announce the return of Jackie Jensen). And I was not only the last writer in the clubhouse after the game, but I walked out of the ballpark with him.

One final observation: A great deal of false information becomes engraved in history in the name of research, repetition, and received wisdom. In the course of writing this book, I discovered that there are a few misconceptions about Ted to which I was a major contributor. Item: He hit training camp, in 1938, as a brash and cocky nineteen-year-old, showed little, and was shipped out quickly. He left, still defiant, boasting about what he would do when he returned. What I wrote was: "He was, of course, a frightened kid whistling in the darkness. The one thing he had always been confident of, deep inside himself, was his ability to hit a baseball. When he found he couldn't handle big-league pitching, he panicked."

In his own autobiography, written in 1969, Ted (or his collaborator) put it this way: "Bravado, pure and simple. A kid away from home really for the first time in his life, feeling alone, a little scared, seeking attention."

Baloney. To talk to the people who grew up with him in San Diego is to understand very quickly that the Ted Williams who came to camp was the same Ted Williams they had known on the playground, in high school, and in his year and a half with the San Diego Padres.

But then, almost everything about Ted Williams can be traced back to those early years in San Diego.

III

Growing Up
in San Diego

His mother's maiden name was May Venzer. She was part Mexican-American, part French-American. His father, Sam, was Welsh and English. "Tempestuous Ted," they'd call him when he erupted. With that Mexican and French blood coursing through his veins, why not?

If it had been known during his playing days that Ted Williams was one-fourth Mexican, he might well have become the same kind of icon to the Mexican-American population that Joe DiMaggio was to Italians. On the other hand, there weren't that many Mexicans in the big-league cities of those days. And Ted, with those rabbit ears of his, was spared the crude racial insults that were part of the baseball scene. Not that Ted's lineage was ever any secret in San Diego. May Williams was a well-known local character. Everybody in town knew "Salvation May." How could they miss her? She always wore her Salvation Army uniform and bonnet and carried a tambourine, and she also wore horn-rimmed glasses, a distinctive style for that time. "We kids would see her on the '7' and '11' trolley when we went downtown to see a movie or something," Frank Cushing, one of Ted's old friends, says. "She was hipped on the Salvation Army, no doubt about that. And she neglected her own sons. What I think it was was that she was so sure in her own mind that she meant only the best that she couldn't see what she was doing to them."

Ted's father wasn't any great help. Sam Williams, born in Mount Vernon, New York, had run away to join the cavalry at the age of sixteen and had served in the Philippines with Teddy Roosevelt's old Rough Rider division. He was on his way back to the States to be discharged when he met May Venzer, an eighteen-year-old Salvation Army lieutenant stationed in Honolulu. She lost her commission when she married outside the Salvation Army fold, but as far as her activities were concerned it didn't matter. Her commitment remained all-encompassing.

The couple came to San Diego in 1915 and lived in a succession of apartments until Ted was born, in 1918. A second son, Danny, was born two years later, and when Ted was five the family moved into a small frame house at 4121 Utah Street that had been bought for them by a local benefactor. The story goes that they were supposed to reimburse the benefactor on a monthly basis, but the Williamses never had any money. Every penny May got her hands on went to her work in the Salvation Army. As for Sam Williams, he had a little photography shop above a restaurant, downtown, where he eked out a living of sorts taking passport photos and, presumably, snapshots of sailors and their girlfriends.

The one picture that is always shown of May (cropped from a photo of her with her two baby sons) depicts a sweet-looking, dumpling-faced woman wearing the inevitable Salvation Army uniform. Much of her time was spent hawking the Army's recruiting publication, *War Cry,* playing the cornet in the Army band, or collecting money. On street corners, in bars and nightclubs, from the local business community. Wherever a crowd collected. Her special mission was ministering to the needs of drunks, prostitutes, and unwed mothers. That's a night beat, of course. And in a navy town like San Diego, which had a thriving red-light district, there was never any lack of calls on her services.

Ted's parents were a sorely mismatched pair. The former cavalryman and the religious zealot had almost nothing in common, and Sam spent little time at home. As Ted relates in his autobiography, there were nights that he and his brother sat on the porch long after dark waiting for someone to come home and let them in. One reason Ted was able to spend so many evenings in the backyard swinging his bat was that there was no one at home to call him in.

May Venzer had been formally dedicated to the Salvation Army when she was six years old. Ted was dedicated to the Army at an early age, too, but with him it didn't take. As soon as he was old enough to rebel, he dropped out of Sunday school so that he could play baseball. There was an adult game in nearby North Park every Sunday morning, followed by a kids' game in the afternoon, and by the time Ted was fourteen years old he was starring in both of them.

Still, one of his earliest memories is of standing on a street corner with his mother as she was being harangued by a mocking crowd. His most embarrassing moment, he once confided to Bob Holbrook of the *Boston Globe,* came when he was standing on a corner listening to May tell her audience that "Ted Williams is a bum because he has left the Salvation Army to play baseball," and then hitting anybody else who dared to criticize him over the head with her tambourine.

But there was another side to her, as Del Ballinger, who was a teammate of Ted's in both high school and American Legion ball, is careful to make clear.

Del Ballinger moved to 1226 Nevada Street when he was thirteen years old and Ted was fourteen. His house was on the other side of a narrow alley from Ted's, no more than fifty feet away. Del's family had moved to San Diego from Monterey when his father, an army colonel, retired. The San Francisco Seals of the Pacific Coast League trained in Monterey, and Del had been their batboy. Obviously he and Ted were kindred souls.

The first time he saw Ted, it was not as the kid from across the alley but as a boy swinging a bat on the baseball field at North Park, a block and a half away. Colonel Ballinger had taken Del and his younger brother to take a look at the local playground. As Del remembered it, "I heard a lot of noise and looked through the swings and slides—I'll never forget this—and saw this big, tall stringbean hitting the ball a mile, and all the other kids were chasing after it." A day later, Del and his brother were out there shagging balls for Ted, too.

The same kind of thing happened in high school. Ted would raise his hand and ask to go to the bathroom. "He wouldn't go to the bathroom, though. He'd climb out the window and run out to the field." A few minutes later, Del—who would go on to carve out a good career for himself as a Triple-A catcher—would raise his hand, and in short order he'd be out there shagging for Ted. "This was his life. Ted never shagged for anybody. Nobody wanted him to. Everybody loved to see him hit." (Ted's legs were so skinny then that he was called "Birdlegs" on the playground, a nickname he detested. His arms were so thin that he would beat on his wrists and cry out to them, "Oh, why can't you get bigger and stronger?")

Del Ballinger, probably the only one of Ted's friends who was around enough to get to know May Williams, says, "She wasn't a good mother, because she was never home. She'd be on the corner collecting money, and then she'd sometimes go down across the border to Tijuana and do what she could for the people in jail, and then come back at night and work in the soup kitchen." And then Del, who knew when I interviewed him that he had little time left—he died three weeks later— said: "I'll tell you what it was. Ted didn't like the idea of her being Salvation May and he being Ted Williams. That hurt him pretty good. It shouldn't have. She wasn't hurting people. She was helping them."

Nor did she neglect Ted as completely as everybody seemed to believe, Del said. "Ted was extremely self-conscious about his skinny legs, and when he started to play for Hoover High she sewed two pairs of uniform socks together for him. We had the regular uniform stockings, the white sweat stocking and the red stirrup, and by sewing two pairs together, four stockings in all, they filled out his legs enough so that nobody called him 'Birdlegs' anymore." She also bought him a baseball glove. And, because hunting was his other passion, a rifle. And when he showed an interest in tennis she bought him a tennis racket. The tennis career came to a quick end because he broke so many strings that his mother finally told him she couldn't keep shelling out the 25 cents it cost to get the racket restrung.

There was also the vexing problem of the kid brother. Ted had the playgrounds and the baseball bat to occupy his time. Danny ran with the bad kids. He stole. He packed a gun. He was thrown out of five or six schools. The first car Ted owned was a brand-new 1938 Buick. Del remembered Ted coming home from a road trip during his first season with the minor-league San Diego Padres and finding the car up on cement blocks. Danny had stripped all the tires and sold them. When Ted finally made some money with the Red Sox, after his great season in 1941, he had the house on Utah Street enlarged and completely renovated. Danny promptly backed a truck up to the house, moved out all the new furniture, including a washing machine and a sewing machine, and sold it. May Williams, who had been able to get him out of his previous scrapes, gave up this time and had him arrested. He spent some time in San Quentin—not that it seemed to do any good. Del Ballinger ran into him, in military uniform, in a Minneapolis bar during World War II, while Del was catching for Indianapolis. "You couldn't miss him. Danny had the same voice that Ted had." He was cadging drinks by telling everybody that he was Ted Williams's brother. The next time Del saw Danny he was back in San Diego, in civilian clothes. He had been bounced out of the army too— or, as he told Del, "I was railroaded."

One other thing has to be understood about May Williams. She was a local character, yes, but she was also a personage. It didn't matter that she had lost her Salvation Army commission; she was such a dominating person that she *was* the Salvation Army in San Diego.

She did such yeoman work in raising money to feed and house the families of the navy recruits who were pouring into the city during the war that she was named San Diego's Woman of the Year. She also had an awesome competence. When the Salvation Army sold its downtown building to the *San Diego Union-Tribune*, it was May Williams who negotiated the purchase of the new Army headquarters. In a brilliant series in the *San Diego Union* in 1965, Joe Hamelin wrote: "She was as much a part of the San Diego scene as [any of the leading families], the search for water, Lucky Lindy, the peacetime Navy— and her precious son who so admired baseball." She knew everyone in town, and everyone knew her. She had access to the mayor, the chief of police, newspaper editors, business leaders. Not that they were always overjoyed to see her coming. She would start on the top floor of a building and hit everybody for a donation all the way down, the familiar offices of the *Union-Tribune* included.

One of the writers who covered high-school sports when Ted was playing for Hoover High was Ken Bojens, who had known May Williams for years. Bojens ran with San Diego's legendary police reporter, "Gentleman Joe" Morgan, and May had become accustomed to trading jibes with them during her rounds of the local hot spots. "My Sunshine Boys," she called them. Bojens told Joe Hamelin about the time she ran into them at the College Inn, a downtown nightclub.

"We were flat broke. May said, 'How are my little Sunshine Boys tonight?' and God-blessed the dickens out of us, like she'd always do, and then asked for a donation. I said, 'May, we don't even have the price of a beer,' which in those days was about fifteen cents. And she reached down into her purse and said, 'Well, let the Army buy you one.'"

She was not so understanding where her husband's drinking was concerned. Whether or not Sam Williams was an alcoholic at the time they got married, in the final years of his life he was described as "a semiderelict." One wonders if the youthful, idealistic Salvation Army lassie hadn't seen him originally as a reclamation project.

In 1934, when Ted had just turned sixteen, his father was appointed to a political job by the newly elected governor, Frank Merriam. He was made inspector of prisons for the state of California—a great job during the middle of the Depression, a true political plum. But how smart does anyone have to be to figure out that it was not the quiet Sam Williams who had so strong a claim on the newly elected governor, but May Williams, who knew everybody in San Diego and—in the political jargon of those pretelevision days—"got around the city pretty good."

That marked the end of what little remained of family life in the Williams household. As far as can be determined, Sam Williams worked out of Sacramento, the state capital, and San Quentin Prison, just outside San Francisco. If he came home at all, it was rarely. In 1939, the year Ted went to the Red Sox to stay, Governor Merriam was defeated for reelection. Sam and May Williams formalized their existing relationship by getting a divorce. Sam opened a photography shop in San Francisco and eventually remarried.

However difficult Ted's relationship with his mother may have been, he learned one thing from her that determined everything else. Total commitment. His mother was obsessed with the Salvation Army. Ted was obsessed with hitting a baseball.

How early did the passion for hitting start? It goes back earlier than the twelve-year-old kid swinging his bat in the backyard through the night. Earlier than eleven or ten.

We can go to a small feature story in the *San Diego Tribune* paying tribute to a beloved teacher, Mrs. Leila Bowen, on her retirement after a thirty-one-year career of teaching the fifth grade at Garfield Elementary School. As her most memorable student, Mrs. Bowen has picked out a "skinny, tempestuous ten-year old" who had entered her class in 1928. "My, but he was a nervous boy. Bit his fingernails down to the nub. He was just an average student, but even then he loved his baseball with a passion." It was Teddy Williams. "He had those sharp elbows and he used them. He'd run out to the playground and shout 'first ups.' If he didn't get them, he'd take off his cap and throw it as hard as he could down onto the ground. Then, he'd cry. But that quick, he'd break out in a smile. He was a good boy, never a discipline problem."

We can go back even further than that, back to the first days on Utah Street. For Ted had something special going for him: a succession of surrogate fathers. Living directly across the street was the first of them, a twenty-four-year-old poultry retailer named John Lutz. In an interview in 1983, at a time when Ted was returning to San Diego to take part in the opening of a Sports Museum, Lutz, by now an old man in a wheelchair, related how the five-year-old would drag his little bat across the street and ask Lutz to pitch to him.

John Lutz was an outdoorsman, and it was he who taught the young boy how to hunt and fish. "Mr. Lutz," Ted has always said loyally, "was the best shot I ever saw." Given Ted's eye-to-hand coordination, he was a good shot, too. And even then he was a perfectionist. The one thing Lutz was never able to teach him was patience. "Once he missed," Lutz said, "he would become so disgusted that he would just shoot off the rest of the round wildly." Lutz sometimes took Ted on all-day hunting trips to Mexico. They'd also fish together off the Crystal Pier or spend a day out on San Diego Bay.

A more important surrogate, perhaps, was Rod Luscomb, the playground instructor at North Park. Luscomb would tell the story about how he reported to work at North Park at two o'clock one afternoon and found a scrawny ten-year-old waiting for him. "Where have you been?" the kid demanded. "I want to play baseball." Luscomb packed him off back to school. "When you get out at three o'clock," he said, "come back and we'll play." At three o'clock he looked across the field, and there came the skinny-legged kid, running toward him.

Luscomb was a big blond guy, only a couple of years past college and a failed minor-league career. He would pitch to Ted for a couple of hours, and then Ted would pitch to him. "If there wasn't anyone else on the playground to play with us, Ted would run all the way home, borrow a quarter from his mother, and pay some kid to shag." At least that's what Luscomb thought. What Ted was really doing was tapping into his lunch money. (When the school nurse sent a note home asking Mrs. Williams why her badly underweight son was being sent to school without lunch money, Ted told his mother what he knew would get him off the hook. He had been giving his lunch money, he said, to "the poor kids.")

Another boy from the North Park neighborhood was Roy Engle, who would become the captain of the Hoover High baseball team and the third member of that team, along with Ted and Del Ballinger, to play professional baseball. "Luscomb and Ted worked on hitting five, six, seven hours a day, five, six, seven days a week, for seven years," Engle says. "If he could get someone to throw a ball to him, Ted would hit forever."

North Park was kept lighted at night, and when it got too dark for baseball Luscomb had another game for the kids, which for some reason was called Association. The same game that was played, allowing for the variations of local conditions, all over the country. At North Park it was played on the handball court. "There was a pipe running across the wall of the handball court," Engle says. "If you hit the fence above the pipe, it was a triple. Below the pipe it was a double. And if you hit the pipe, it was a home run." A ball that didn't hit the fence but wasn't caught was a single. If the ball was caught, it was an out, of course. "We'd play until we were so tired we hardly had the strength left to walk home."

At Ted's induction into the Hall of Fame he singled out two people from San Diego for special thanks. One was Rod Luscomb. The other was Wofford (Wos) Caldwell, his coach at Herbert Hoover High School.

Caldwell never forgot the first time he saw Ted Williams, either. An all-sports star at the University of Illinois, he had been hired to coach at Hoover High at the time the school was opened in 1931— not necessarily in anticipation of Hoover's crushing defeat in the presidential race the following year. In January 1934, he was holding tryouts for the baseball team. Not on the ball field, which was still being used by the football team, but in a large open area between buildings. Ted was sitting on the steps, watching, and every once in a while he'd say, "Coach, let me hit." And Caldwell would say, "Too busy now."

But if Caldwell didn't know who the skinny kid on the steps was, he was probably the only one there who didn't. All the best players around the playgrounds knew each other, and Ted had already achieved a considerable reputation. One of the returning lettermen was Les Cassie, Jr., who had played against Ted when the kids from North Park played the kids from Central Park.

"Practice was almost over," Cassie remembers, "and Caldwell had taken over the pitching mound himself before he told Ted to grab a bat. Way out in what would correspond to right field there was a long table with benches on both sides. It was called a lunch arbor in those days, and had a roof across the top as protection against the rain. The first ball Caldwell threw him, he hit it on top of the lunch arbor, and nobody had hit it anywhere near there all day long. I remember Caldwell saying, 'Hey, kid, what's your name?' Ted says, 'My name is Ted Williams. I graduate from Horace Mann Junior High on Friday. I'll be here next Monday.'" So Caldwell threw him a couple more pitches, and Ted hit another one on top of the lunch arbor.

Les and Ted became fast friends. "We used to eat lunch together every day. If I heard him say it once, I heard him say it fifty times, 'God, I wish I had big arms like Jimmy Foxx. I'd roll those sleeves up and I'd dare those pitchers to throw that ball at me.' We used to play pool every night, and then we'd go get a malt at Doc Powelson's drugstore, trying to gain weight." The drugstore was right across the street from Hoover High, and Doc Powelson supported all the athletic teams by awarding malts to any of the players who did well. Ted always had a free malt coming, because he always did well, and because Powelson—like most of the other men in his life—loved him. "Neither of us," says Cassie, "ever gained a pound."

Les Cassie Jr. became almost like a brother to Ted, and his father, Les Cassie, Sr., became the third of Ted's surrogate fathers.

After they left Powelson's Ted would sometimes hop on the back of Les's bicycle and go home with him. "He just knew that he was very welcome at our house. My mother was always ready to lay out another place for dinner, and we'd have a lot of fun horsing around. Unless he was talking about hitting. Any time we talked about hitting it was serious business." The one thing they never talked about was Ted's own parents.

The senior Cassie was foreman of construction for the San Diego city schools, and, like John Lutz, he was a dedicated fisherman. Young Les and his brother weren't interested in fishing. Ted, of course, was. "In those days you'd get a bamboo pole and you'd wrap it between the joints with twine or fishing line, and they'd sit and wrap those poles together by the hour," Les says. "They'd go down to the Strand and cast into the surf all night. They'd go down to Point Loma and fish for albacore."

When Ted signed his first Red Sox contract, in 1939, he went across the street and signed it on John Lutz's table. And then he asked Mr. Cassie to drive down to the training camp with him.

Ted did not return to San Diego after that until he came home from service at the end of World War II. One of the first things he did then was to tell Mr. and Mrs. Cassie that if the Red Sox won the pennant, as he suspected they would, he wanted them to come to the World Series as his guests. On the night the Sox clinched the pennant the phone rang, and young Les heard his dad say, "We'll be there."

"It was," says Les, Jr., "one of the high spots of my dad's life."

Herbert Hoover High was the new school in San Diego. The big school, the established one, was San Diego High. Although Ted lived only two miles from Hoover High, the district lines were drawn so inartfully that his house actually lay just inside the San Diego High district, although the school was considerably farther away. For all his bombast, Ted was apprehensive about his ability to make the team in the larger school—the contradictions were already there. As Del Ballinger heard it, a deal was made between the two schools involving Ted and the other big star on the playground circuit, a hotshot pitcher named Bill Skelly. "The Skellys were even closer to San Diego High than Ted was to Hoover—they only had to walk across a golf course. There was some kind of an agreement between the administrators that Ted would go to Hoover and Bill Skelly would go to San Diego High."

Even for San Diego, the North Park area was at the edge of the earth. There was almost nothing between Hoover High and San Diego State College to the south except miles and miles of undeveloped land. It was not until Ted's junior year that little Hoover High was admitted into the Bay League, which was comprised of high schools ranging up the coast as far as Santa Monica. To their natural rivals at San Diego High, they were not even the Hoover High Cardinals; they were the Hockers from Hockerville, a local term of derision that was synonymous with "rubes." And so the kids from Hockerville, led by Ted Williams, went out and beat San Diego High, beat everybody else, and won the championship. In fifteen league games, Ted hit .588, with seven home runs and twenty-two RBIs. As the number-two pitcher, he won four straight games.

The home-run total is misleading. They were playing on a football field with a track around it, and the right-field fence was probably less than two hundred feet away. No help at all. A pole had been placed in right-center field, and anything leaving the ballpark on the right-field side of the pole was only a double. Bud Maloney, who would grow up to become a sportswriter for the *San Diego Union,* after stints in Baltimore and Denver, was in grammar school while Ted was at Hoover: "I lived three blocks away, and after school I'd come down and watch the games. Ted used to hit some of the most majestic doubles I've ever seen over that short right-field fence. The ball would still be going up when it left the field and would land on a roof a block away. He used to hit a little under the ball even then, and it would go sky-high.''

Del Ballinger never forgot a doubleheader they played in Santa Monica in the spring of 1935. Babe Herman, who was holding out from the Pittsburgh Pirates, was taking batting practice along with a couple of other major-league holdouts, and the high-school boys had to wait until they were finished. ''We were sitting in the dugout while Babe Herman was hitting,'' Del says. ''And Ted is beating on his wrist, and he'd say, 'Oh, I wish I had power like that. I wish I was that big and strong.' And then Ted got up in the game and hit two balls farther than Babe Herman! I mean, seven miles farther. He hit them farther as a high-school boy. I said, Ted, you're a doozy. He never seemed to realize how good he was.''

''I always thought Roy Engle was a better hitter than I was,'' Ted still says. Engle had the kind of compact, muscular build that Ted envied. ''He'd hit bullets down the left-field line. I wished I could hit the ball that hard, but I was too skinny, all arms and legs.''

In his senior year, Ted hit .403. There is no record of the total number of home runs he hit that year in the Hoover *Cardinal,* the school publication, but it does report that he hit two home runs in the same inning against Monrovia and four home runs in a five-game tournament in Pomona.

He was also the star pitcher. He had a good arm, a good curve, and great control. He was undefeated in league play and set a school record of twenty strikeouts in a game against Redondo. He even played shortstop in the semifinal of the San Diego County championship. The regular shortstop had been pressed into service as a pitcher, according to the *Cardinal,* because ''Coach Caldwell is saving Ted's million-dollar pitching arm for the final game against San Diego.''

The statistics were inconclusive, anyway, since they covered only the league games, and there were all kinds of special tournaments taking place during the year. In addition, Wos Caldwell would schedule games against teams from the Navy Yard and the Marine base, and against independents. The boys from Hockerville even played and defeated San Diego State College. "We played about sixty-four games in my senior year," Ted says. And Ted himself probably played in another sixty-four games with various teams in San Diego's fast semi-pro leagues. "There were ten or twelve teams in that Sunday league," he remembers. "We would play in all the major playgrounds and ball-parks that were around, and the rivalry was intense. One of the communities would want to have the best team they could get together, and they'd get a backer for the weekend. Probably cost them about fifty dollars." Does semipro mean that Ted was getting paid? Yup. "I'd get three dollars on a Sunday. Couple of milkshakes, a hamburg or hot dog, and free transportation to the game."

For a really big game, the backer would bring in a pitcher from the Pacific Coast League and pay him as much as $25. The last home run Ted hit before he joined the Padres himself was off a future teammate, Herm Pillette. "A long line drive over the right-center-field fence at Golden Hill." Ted chuckles. "He was just about through, though. Nothing but crappy little curves. Poor guy, he was picking up maybe ten or fifteen bucks for the day."

Through it all, Ted continued to astonish his Hoover teammates not only with the distance of his drives but by his ability to read opposing pitchers. He would watch a pitcher warming up and say, "He's going to throw two fastballs at me and then try to get me with his curve."

In another way, however, he was still the little boy from Mrs. Bowen's fifth-grade class who broke out in tears when he was walked. "He'd sit there on the bench beside me," Del Ballinger said, "and cry like a baby." And they walked him often. At Hoover Field, with its short right-field fence, they would sometimes walk him intentionally with the bases loaded. There was one time when Ted got so mad that he stormed into Caldwell's office after the game and threw his uniform on top of the coach's desk. "I don't want to play anymore," he cried. "All I do is walk. I'm not playing baseball to walk." Roy Engle has never forgotten that day. "Fortunately, Caldwell caught him before he got out of the gym. But the thought has always stayed with

41

me: what would have happened if Ted had gone on with his commitment and walked out for good?''

Engle has one other enduring memory about Ted. The Kiwanis Club of Pomona ran a baseball tournament during the Easter vacation every year for the best high-school teams in southern California. Engle's first recollection of that tournament has to do with Ted's appetite. The Kiwanians always laid out a table full of food for the players, and Ted gobbled down everything he could get his hands on. Then, on the final day of the tournament Governor Merriam made an appearance, accompanied by a claque of officials. ''Ted walked up to the governor and said, 'Hi, Guv,' which seemed to be brazen even for Ted.'' But someone told Engle that the man sitting next to the governor was Ted's father, so Engle assumed—not necessarily correctly—that if Ted's father worked for the governor, Ted must have met the governor before. It was the only time Engle ever saw Sam Williams, and it was not in San Diego but 120 miles away.

The real question was whether Sam was there because the governor had invited him or because Sam had decided to see how good a ballplayer his son really was. Ted was only two months from the end of his high-school career, the scouts had already begun to come around, and, with money being offered, Sam Williams had, for the first time in his life, begun to take an interest in his son's career. He saw Ted pitch a five-hit shutout and hit a mammoth drive out of the park. And it is that drive that Roy Engle remembers most clearly of all.

''There was an orange grove in right field,'' he says, ''and a ground rule that anything hit into the orange grove was a double. Ted hit one so far that the outfielder didn't move. It was so far that nobody bothered to look for the ball. It must have gone 450 feet, and all he got out of it was a double.''

After what he had seen his son do in Pomona, Sam Williams appointed himself Ted's agent and began to contact teams in the Pacific Coast League. Ted loves to tell one story about his father's approach to Truck Hannah, a onetime Yankee catcher who was managing the old Los Angeles Angels.

"When my dad went down to talk to him, Hannah said, 'Where's the kid?' Dad says, 'He's not here.' Hannah said, 'Well, for crying out loud, go get him. He's the one I want to talk to, not you.'"

The conversation never took place. They were not going to have anything more to do with Truck Hannah, a highly insulted Sam Williams told Ted.

All things being equal, Ted would probably have signed with the St. Louis Cardinals and spent most of his career playing alongside Stan Musial. Or he could easily have signed with the Yankees and been a teammate, rather than an opponent, of Joe DiMaggio. And wouldn't the history of baseball have been the poorer for that? He might even have gone to Detroit, played with Hank Greenberg, his favorite player, in Briggs Stadium, his favorite ballpark, and broken all home-run records into smithereens.

Obviously all things weren't equal. The deciding factor was an accident of timing that put a Pacific Coast League team in San Diego in the same year that Ted was finishing his baseball career at Hoover High.

Only the Cardinals, the Dodgers, and the Yankees had "bird dogs" in San Diego. "They followed Ted in high school and in the American Legion," Del Ballinger said, "and he could do no wrong, because he was like a ninety-carat jewel." The Cardinals' bird dog was Herb Benninghaven, an executive with the local gas and electric company. "Benninghaven was the guy who picked Ted out early. You'd look up, and he was always out there in left field, watching." He'd be there when Ted played in a pickup game against servicemen at the Marine base. "Ted would hit them out into the bay, for crying out loud. I couldn't believe it. Not just where they barely got out. It just went out, period, like somebody had shot it out of a mortar."

"The Cardinals had the inside track," Ted agrees. "Benninghaven used to park on the other side of the fence in left field. I knew his car, and I knew he was watching us. And he began to go to the semipro games. Then he'd drive me home, and we'd talk baseball, baseball, baseball."

Early in Ted's senior year, the Cardinals were holding a regional tryout in nearby Fullerton, and Branch Rickey, the "Mahatma" himself, was going to be there. "The tryout was on a Monday, and on Sunday I got hit by a big strong pitcher named Tex Rikard, and, jesus, he hit me solid on the meaty part of the thigh, just above my knee." Benninghaven wanted to show Ted off to Rickey anyway, and to Ted it didn't matter. "I wasn't thinking in terms of a big-league team. I was thinking of playing and continuing gradually from the North Park playground to maybe a better team in that league." The tryout was a fiasco. For one thing, speed was always a prime factor for Rickey. At his best, Ted had never been a speed demon, and by now his leg was black-and-blue. For another thing, those mass tryouts resembled nothing quite so much as cattle calls. "We had big numbers pinned on our back. They had races after races after races. I didn't even attempt to run hard. I don't remember hitting that well, either. Rickey never even wanted to talk with me."

To Benninghaven, it was a setback but not really a tragedy. "I would have signed with Benny, I loved Benny, he was such a nice guy," Ted says. "But some of the people who knew about these things began to warn me that the Cardinals had so many farm teams that it was easy to get lost in the shuffle. But that wasn't it. The big thing was that my mother wanted me to stay home." The real significance of the botched tryout was that if Branch Rickey had seen Ted hit the way Ted could hit, he would have been able to call on his extraordinary powers of persuasion to convince Ted's mother, as one religious person to another, that her boy could not possibly be entrusted to better hands. As it was, Herb Benninghaven managed to come up with an offer of $1,000 on behalf of the Cardinals farm team in Sacramento. He was turned down. In the end, he settled for signing Del Ballinger.

Not that Benninghaven had ever had the field all to himself. Two area scouts had been coming down from Los Angeles to look at Ted, Bill Essick of the Yankees and Marty Krug of Detroit, and both of them were on the scene to make their final decision at Ted's last game for Hoover High.

Essick was one of the three scouts, along with Paul Kitchell and

Joe Devine, who have been credited with building the Yankee dynasty. In other words, he was one of the all-time great scouts.

It is one of the ironies of baseball history that the Red Sox had first crack at Joe DiMaggio and the Yankees had first crack at Ted Williams and that Essick was the Yankee scout at the center of both transactions. The Red Sox had first-refusal rights on DiMaggio, and they could have had him for $75,000, a record sum for a minor-league ballplayer. They turned him down because they had heard that Joe's right knee, which he had fractured the previous season, was not going to heal completely. It was Essick who recommended that the Yankees buy DiMaggio, after he had taken care to have him examined by his own doctor. Even so, Joe was considered such damaged goods that the Yankees were able to get him for $25,000.

Essick had been following Ted for two years. He had first shown up, obviously at the urging of his bird dog, when Ted was a gangling fifteen-year-old pitching for the "Fighting Bob" San Diego American Legion Post No. 6. Ted not only pitched that team into the championship finals; he hit a long home run that went completely out of the playground and through the window of a store across the street. The following day Essick visited Ted's mother, along with the bird dog, a local businessman whom she apparently knew, to express his interest in signing Ted after he graduated from high school.

Essick continued to show up from time to time when Ted was involved in an important game. Marty Krug had shown up a couple of times during Ted's senior year. Ted had always come through big when Essick was there, but he had done little to impress Krug. In his final high-school game, the championship game against Escondido High, Ted was so unimpressive that Krug told May Williams that her son undoubtedly had talent but was far too scrawny to withstand the rigors of professional baseball.

Essick, having seen Ted at his best, came to the house again and renewed his offer of a Yankee contract. "Bill Essick probably liked me as well as anybody," Ted says. "He told me he wouldn't be signing me unless he felt I could make the New York Yankees. I suppose they say that to everybody. But they actually offered me the best deal of anybody.'' Essick wanted to have Ted go to Binghamton, New York, in the Class A Eastern League. The offer was for $250 the first month, which would go up to $500 if Ted made the team. ''Five hundred dollars was a lot of money in those days. But my mother wanted me to stay home. And at that point I was a little afraid to go anyplace myself. I would have had to travel to New York. For a seventeen-year-old boy from southern California, New York seemed like the end of the world.''

Be that as it may, Mrs. Williams also asked Essick for $1,000 for herself. He turned her down, quite probably because he was afraid he was being used to get a bidding war started. And not without reason.

We are back again to that accident of timing that had put a PCL team into San Diego. A year earlier there would have been no chance that Ted could have remained in San Diego. What had happened in the meantime was that Bill Lane, a longtime minor-league operator who then owned the Hollywood Stars, was virtually bankrupt; the Stars were renting Wrigley Field, the home of the Los Angeles Angels, and the rent was killing him. So the business community in San Diego got together to lure him down and the politicians arranged for the WPA, a New Deal agency, to build a ballpark for him. The whole San Diego area still had a population of less than 200,000, and although the other owners in the league had grave doubts that the city would be able to support seventy-five-cent baseball, they had most reluctantly granted permission for the move. Thus the San Diego Padres had been born.

The arrival of a PCL franchise electrified the city. The whole business community had become Padres boosters—the same businessmen May Williams had been hitting up for donations for years. The clincher for Ted was that Wos Caldwell had become a close friend of Bill Lane. ''Wos Caldwell had tremendous influence over Ted,'' says Earl Keller, who covered the Padres for the *Evening Tribune*. ''Bill Lane paid him to get Ted to sign. The sum I heard was five hundred dollars.''

Since Mrs. Williams wanted Ted near her, she was happy enough to sign with Lane. Ted was to be paid only $150 a month, but as an extra inducement, Mrs. Williams would claim later, Lane promised that he would not trade Ted until he was twenty-one. And he also promised her, she would say, that if he sold Ted to a major-league team she would receive 10 percent of the purchase price.

The contract was signed on June 26, 1936, three days after Ted and his teammates had lost the championship game to Escondido High.

IV

The San Diego Kid

When Ted Williams joined the Padres he began an association with another teenager who was also going to move on to Fenway Park in Boston and, eventually, into the Cooperstown Hall of Fame. Bobby Doerr had turned eighteen in April; Ted would celebrate his eighteenth birthday in August.

Bobby Doerr: "It was in the middle of June when I first saw him, and I remember this big, tall, skinny kid standing by the batting cage there, and we didn't know anything about him. Frank Shellenback, our manager, was pitching batting practice, and I remember him saying, 'Let the kid get in and hit a few.' Of course, all the players were around that old batting cage we used to have. They were grumbling because this kid was going to take some of their time in batting practice, and he hit seven or eight balls, and there were a couple-three of them that were hit out of the ballpark. I remember I was standing on the first-base side of the batting cage. Why I was over there I'll never know. Someone over there on the other side, I remember making the statement, 'This kid will be signed before the week's up.' We were a bunch of single hitters. The only hitter we had with any power was Vince DiMaggio."

A couple of days later Ted's name appeared in a Padres box score for the first time. Never mind that he wasn't going to play his final high-school game for another two days and wasn't actually going to sign his contract for another five days. The Padres were playing an exhibition for the Naval Relief Fund against an all-star team of servicemen. After the Padres got off to a big lead, Shellenback sent in five kids who had been working out with the team. One of them got a base hit. His name was Ted Williams.

(There is a connection of sorts here with Joe DiMaggio, if you want to look hard enough. An eighteen-year-old DiMaggio had come to the San Francisco Seals ballpark on the final day of the 1932 season to see his brother Vince. The Seals' shortstop had left the team a few days early to go to Japan; and when Vince told the manager that his kid brother was a shortstop, Joe was pressed instantly into service. Contract? What contract? Money? What money? Joe considered it a privilege just to be allowed to play. If you want another connection, the pitcher Joe faced that day was Herm Pillette. No, Joe didn't hit a home run off him. The best he could manage was a triple.)

The signing of the local high-school star was reported in a two-column story at the bottom of the *Union*'s sports page, alongside a picture of Ted. "Williams, former Hoover star, signed by Padres as Outfielder," the heading said. Under the terms of the contract, the story reported, Williams was to be kept with the Padres for the remainder of the season and all of the next without being farmed out. "By that time he is expected to develop to a point where he will be of first-string caliber." In the meantime, he was going to be given a chance to show what he could do "wherever the opportunity presents itself." The *Evening Tribune* ran only a small picture with a one-paragraph caption announcing that Ted Williams, who had been sought by several major-league scouts, had finally signed a San Diego contract. "The Padres will use Williams in the outfield for his hitting strength," the caption ended. "He will be in uniform tonight against Sacramento."

He was not only in uniform, he was in the box score. Shellenback sent him in to pinch-hit for the not very effective starting pitcher in the second inning. The opposing pitcher was Cotton Pippen, a tall right-hander. Ted stood there with his bat on his shoulder—"too scared to swing," he admitted later—and walked back to the bench.

The date was June 27, 1936. An inauspicious beginning, which dampened Ted's spirits not at all. On Monday, an off day, the club was leaving for San Francisco. "We were at the railroad station that night," Doerr recalls, "and here's Ted parading up and down, all excited to be riding on a train." Already his new teammates were getting a kick out of him. "I look back at that," says Doerr, "and think how fortunate I was that I got to see that, and then going on to play my whole career with Ted and see him go on to be one of the all-time greats."

There was every reason for Ted to be excited. He had never been on a train before. (Fifty years down the line, there was going to be a scene in the film *The Natural* that reproduced Ted's experience so exactly that he kicked himself for having ignored Robert Redford's request to meet with him while he was preparing for the role.) That first train trip remains one of Ted's favorite stories. "My god," he says, "and here I was on the train to San Francisco, the dining car, and, my god, I didn't know how to read the menu. How do you know how to read a menu if all you've ever done is go into some little place where they have the meals and the prices written on a mirror?"

He was a child. His parents had signed the contract for him, and he was dutifully sending most of his salary home until he began to blow so much of it on a fascinating new invention called the pinball machine that his mother told Lane to send the salary directly to her. Which wasn't a complete disaster for Ted, because he had discovered the delight of signing for his meals.

Bobby Doerr never had so much fun, he says, as he had in the last half of that 1936 season. "I remember one time in Oakland, we had just come home from the movies, and we were in the Leamington Hotel there. We were going into the lunchroom, and Lane grabbed Williams and growled, 'You're leading the list, Ted.' Ted says, 'What list?' Lane says, 'The overeaters.' In those days we had a two-dollar-a-day limit, and I can still hear Ted telling him, 'I can't eat on that lousy two dollars a day. Take it out of my paycheck.' "

To Ted, it was more than fun; it was a time of wonder. "It was like a fairyland to me," he says. "Everything was new. The train ride was new. The Pullman. Riding up to Sacramento, riding up to Oakland and to Frisco, and riding up on the train to Portland, all through the Cascades, Mount Shasta, and, jesus, going into Seattle. And seeing all the players and seeing them up close and getting that experience to be a professional ballplayer. Oh jesus, yes, I thought I was in fairyland. It was all like a dream for a year and a half."

The Padres had a nice mix of young players and veterans. There was a third teenager on the club, George McDonald, the first baseman. Doerr had grown up in Los Angeles, near the Watts area, and he and McDonald had made up half the infield for the American Legion team that had won the national championship. Both of them had signed with Lane's Hollywood Stars at the age of sixteen. (The shortstop on that Legion team, Bobby Mattick, signed with Los Angeles and went on to a brief and disappointing career with the Chicago Cubs. Mickey Owen, the third baseman, signed with the Cardinals, was converted into an all-star catcher, and etched a niche for himself in the nether-world of baseball lore as the Brooklyn Dodgers catcher who did not catch the third strike in the 1941 World Series.)

Lane could afford to put such babies in the lineup because the Pacific Coast League clubs were always stocked with a plenitude of former big-leaguers who were more than willing to help the kids learn. Shellenback had Ted room with Cedric Durst, a thirty-six-year-old outfielder who was finishing out his career on the West Coast. "Ced" Durst had been with the 1927 Yankees, generally recognized as the greatest team of all time, as the fourth outfielder behind Babe Ruth, Bob Meusel, and Earle Combs. In the trivia of baseball, he is best known as the throw-in who went to the Red Sox in the Red Ruffing deal.

"Ted was seventeen when he joined the Padres," Durst said later, "but he already knew more about hitting than the veterans on the club." Durst had seen hundreds of young ballplayers break into professional ball. "All of them had one thing in common. They might hit pretty well the first time around the league but then the pitchers learn their weaknesses." With Ted, it was the opposite. "Two of the best pitchers in the Coast League then were Tony Freitas and Jack Salveson. They gave everybody a fit, even the older hitters. But instead of them figuring Ted out, he figured them out." The first time Ted saw Freitas, a perennial twenty-game winner, he turned to Durst, who was sitting alongside him on the bench, and said, "This guy won't give me a fast ball I can hit. I know he won't. He'll waste the fast ball and try to make me hit the curve. He'll get behind on the count, then throw me the curve, and when he does I'll be ready." Exactly what happened. Pitching from behind, it's called. A sophisticated pattern, which only a seasoned pitcher, with absolute confidence in his breaking ball, dares to attempt.

"Nobody had ever taught him this thing," Durst marveled. "It was something he was either born with or had figured out by himself."

Mostly Ted picked the brains of the veteran pitchers on his own team. Always asking questions. Who knew more about pitching than pitchers? Always chattering away. And soon enough his enthusiasm became so infectious that the pitchers were responding to him. "He pumped everybody," Bobby Doerr says. "The pitchers would tell him situations and ask him what he thought he was going to see. They'd explain to him how they set up the hitter for certain pitches. He learned very early about how the smart pitchers worked the count."

"I'd come back to the bench after striking out," Ted has said, "and one of those old pitchers would say, 'Why don't you try waiting on that slow curve ball?' And I'd wait on it and hit a line drive, line drive, line drive. Do you think I wasn't like a sponge soaking all that up?"

Bobby Doerr draws a picture of a kid who was both frenetic and compulsive, while remaining essentially a loner. "He was just excited that he was playing ball, and the older guys kind of enjoyed him. He chewed his fingers all the time. He was so high-strung that he couldn't sit still. I remember—God, it was in Sacramento—Eddie Mulligan, one of our coaches, was sitting next to me at the lunch counter. Ted came in, pounded on the counter to get the attention of the waitress, yelled out his order, and said, 'I want this right away, I got to catch a train.' He'd eat, my gosh, bang-bang-bang, and out he went. You'd wonder, where the heck is he going now?"

George Myatt, the shortstop, was another of Ted's favorites. A tough guy. Myatt, who currently lives in Orlando, Florida, had known exactly who Ted was when he stepped into the batting cage for that first workout at Lang Field. Myatt had not only heard about Ted; he had gone out to Hoover Field to see what all the talk was about. "He was the first one out on the field for practice, and he had three, four bats in his hands, and he was awfully skinny. You looked at him, and his feet were as long as his legs, it looked like. But when he started fooling around with those bats, all you could see was rhythm. It was something to see."

A real brazen kid, Myatt decided after Ted joined the club. "He'd butt in on anybody if they were talking baseball. And we had a couple of guys who had been real good hitters in the majors. He knew everything. All he thought about was hitting.''

One of the things that stands out in Myatt's mind was Ted's first start in left field, after he had been with the club for a couple of weeks. Myatt had the job of positioning the outfielders from his shortstop position. "The first pitch was a ball, and that put the hitter ahead. So I turned around immediately to move Ted closer to the line and all I saw was his back. His back was toward the infield, he had his glove in his hands and was acting like he was swinging a bat. He never even saw the pitch. Well, I gave him hell right there.''

Immediately, they became friends. "He was just an easy guy to talk to. Everything was funny to him, and that made him fun to be around. And eat? My God, he'd put away two T-bone steaks and a platter of rolls for breakfast.''

One of the ways Lane saved money on road trips was by putting his players up in cheap, seedy hotels. "In Sacramento, if I remember right," Myatt says, "it was the Hotel Cluney." The Cluney was the kind of hotel where the doors between rooms had holes drilled in them to allow the person in the next room to spy on his neighbors. "I was rooming with Bobby Doerr, and at six o'clock or so in the morning this darn whistling sound woke me up. I looked through one of the holes, and there was Ted with a newspaper rolled up, standing in front of the mirror and shadow-hitting, with the rolled-up paper serving as the bat.''

Not that it was any bed of roses for Cedric Durst. Durst woke up one morning to find Ted jumping up and down on his bed and beating on his chest. "Christ, Ced," he said to his heavy-lidded roommate, "it's great to be young and full of vinegar.''

"Sure," Durst groaned. "But not at six o'clock in the morning.''

"He'd come out of the clubhouse," Durst said, "and he didn't sit on the bench. The first thing he'd do was to walk through the dugout, grab a bat, and head for the batting cage. Anything that had to do with a bat. If it was a pepper game, he'd be the guy who was hitting. When he talked baseball, all he'd talk about was hitting.''

On the whole, Ted did more talking than hitting in those early days.

Having satisfied the local fans by letting Ted come to bat on his first day in a Padres uniform, Frank Shellenback was content to ease his young kid into the lineup. When he finally did call on Ted again, on that first road trip, it was because the Padres were taking a 12 – 3 walloping in Los Angeles, and with two successive doubleheaders coming up, Shellenback had been wondering aloud whether he could afford to waste any more of his pitchers. "I'm a pitcher, I'm a pitcher," Ted kept yapping, until Shellenback finally told him, "Okay, go out to the bull pen and warm up, and we'll see what you can do."

Almost everything written about Ted's first year with the Padres has achieved a legendary status—which is a nice way of saying that it ain't necessarily so. To get a two-fer out of the situation, Shellenback sent Ted up to pinch-hit for the pitcher. Ted writes in his autobiography that he doubled, and then got up the next inning and doubled again.

That's only one of the mistakes in a book replete with factual errors. Actually, Ted had two singles. By one of those coincidences, we have an eyewitness who comes practically from outer space. Yosh Kawano, who would go on to become the longtime clubhouse man for the Chicago Cubs, had just signed on with the Angels as their 14-year-old batboy. "This tall, skinny kid who was supposed to be a pitcher came up to bat and hit a rocket off the right-field screen." The ball was hit so hard and the right-field fence at Wrigley Field was so short, Yosh explains, that Ted got only a single out of it. "He came up again the next inning and hit another line drive off the fence. By then he was playing in the outfield. I knew right then that we'd be seeing a lot of this kid, and that it wasn't going to be as a pitcher."

Yosh was wrong about one thing. Ted was still the pitcher when he got the second hit. The pinch hit started a five-run rally, which had closed the score to 12 – 8 by the time Ted took the mound. His catcher in a kind of nice touch was Harold Doerr, Bobby's older brother. Harold had come aboard as a fill-in after both the Padres' catchers suffered minor injuries. Facing the bottom of the lineup, pitcher Williams shut out the Angels in their half of the seventh, after putting one man on base with a walk. His second hit came as the leadoff man in the eighth, and he eventually came around to make the score 12 – 9.

In the bottom of the inning, Steve Mesner greeted him with a home run. The second man went out, and then he was facing the cleanup hitter, Wes Schulmerich, a big, bandy-legged guy who'd had a couple of .300 seasons with the Boston Braves and the Pittsburgh Pirates. "I shook Hal Doerr off and threw a high fast ball and, hell, he hit it out of the park. They had two home runs in a row [sic] off me, and we were back in the game by then, and they took me out."

Shellenback had come out and sent him to the outfield. Either Ted was unwilling to show how disappointed he was in his performance or was still on a high from his first two base hits as a professional. Whatever the reason, he remained his own flip self. "You're right, Skip," he told Shellenback. "I think you've got me in the wrong position."

His pitching career was over. It is usually written about as some kind of a joke. But he wasn't a joke as a pitcher any more than he was a joke as a hitter because of his petrified performance in his first time at bat. His old high-school teammate, Roy Engle, has no doubt that Ted would have made it as a pitcher if he hadn't been such a great hitter. "A good Triple A pitcher without doubt, and a decent pitcher in the majors." (Years later, Bobby Doerr asked Schulmerich how Ted had impressed him that day. "I never thought he was ever going to be a good hitter," Schulmerich said. "Because he was too wiggly up at the plate. Funny thing about it, I never got a scouting job, either.")

Yosh Kawano wasn't wrong that the baseball world was going to be seeing a lot more of this kid, but it was not going to be seeing a great deal of him immediately.

On the basis of that first performance, Shellenback put him in the starting lineup, but Ted did no more hitting, and since he wasn't hitting he saw no reason to pay any particular attention to his fielding. When he refused to chase after a ground ball that went skipping through his legs, Shellenback benched him.

The Padres were in the pennant race, they were drawing extremely well in San Diego and there was no pressure on anybody to disrupt the lineup for a crazy seventeen-year-old kid. Except for one key series in Portland—which we will talk about shortly—Ted played only sporadically, mostly as a pinch hitter or a late-inning replacement.

He was batting .229 at the end of August, with no home runs and only three runs batted in, when Chick Shivers, the right-fielder, gave him his chance by leaving the club to accept a job as a football coach. Playing every day over the final month of the season, Ted hit .308, to bring his average up to .271. For the season, he had no home runs, three doubles, two triples, and eleven runs batted in.

His first home run came in the opening game of the play-offs and was hit off lefty Willie Ludoph, the league's top pitcher. But the Padres lost the play-off series, and Ted had only two other hits in the five games. With the season over, he went back to Hoover High and graduated in February 1937.

Despite the fears that San Diego did not have the population to support Pacific Coast League baseball, the Padres were a huge success, both financially and artistically. In their first season, they finished tied for second and were up with the leaders in attendance. In 1937, they played to around 250,000 fans and had the largest paid attendance in the league. Although they slumped in the closing weeks of the race, partly due to injuries, and finished third, behind Sacramento and San Francisco, they went on to ignite the city in the Shaughnessy play-off by sweeping both Sacramento and Portland to win the PCL championship in eight games.

But once again Ted Williams had got off to a very poor start. He was hitting .259 and had only two home runs in mid-June when he suddenly caught fire. In the next eight games he had six home runs and two doubles. In August he went off on another splurge, with six home runs and a double in nine games. Proof—again—that the more he saw of a pitcher, the better he hit him.

And if his final .291 batting average was not overly impressive, his ninety-eight RBIs and twenty-three home runs were. Lane Field was

350 feet to right field and 500 feet in center, and some of those home runs went to areas of the park never before reached by mortal man. But then, even routine home runs tended to be spectacular at Lane Field. The ballpark had been built on the grounds of an old bus terminal situated between San Diego Bay and the railroad yards. A city highway ran between the park and the rail yards, and almost every ball that went over the fence would hit the pavement, bounce high in the air, and rattle off one of the freight cars. Legend has it that one of Ted's home runs bounced into an open boxcar on a train just taking off for Los Angeles, 178 miles away, and was written up in Ripley's "Believe It or Not" as the longest home run ever hit.

In 1937 the Padres had a backup catcher named Bill Starr, who'd "had a cup of coffee" with the Washington Senators. Not much of a hitter, but a great defensive catcher with a reputation for being a brain. He proved how smart he was after his retirement by building the first condominiums in San Diego, along with a string of apartment complexes and shopping centers. He then bought the Padres from Bill Lane's estate, tried to turn the Pacific Coast League into a third major league, and was stopped only by the negative vote of one owner, Seattle's Emil Sick.

With it all, Starr's greatest boast is that he once pinch-hit for Ted Williams. "I was considered a good bunter, and I was sent up to replace Williams with a one-strike count. I wish it was a better story. I bunted foul for the second strike, then flied out." Good story or not, a framed blowup of that box score still hangs on Bill Starr's wall.

To Starr, however, Ted was something of an enigma. "Portland had a big outfielder named Moose Clabaugh, and Ted would oooh and ahhh and say how he wished he had muscles so that he could hit a ball like Clabaugh. And Clabaugh didn't have half the power Ted did." For all Ted's moaning about his lack of muscles, Starr became convinced that he was a great deal stronger than he looked after two other players had jumped him—not necessarily in fun—in the clubhouse. "Ted had them both pinned to the floor in a matter of seconds. Nobody could believe it."

But then, Ted was a man with a bizarre code of honor about what he always referred to as "fair play." In a game against Portland, big Dick Ward, the Padres pitcher, escaped from a rundown between third base and home by barreling into Mike Tresh, the Portland catcher, so hard that Tresh was knocked out cold. While Tresh was being attended to, Ted, who had been standing in the on-deck circle, followed the brawny Ward back to the dugout, screaming, "That's dirty baseball. You ought to have your block knocked off. I won't stand for that kind of dirty play!"

HE wouldn't stand for it? George Detore, the first-string catcher, said, "What are YOU going to do about it?"

"I'll show you what I'm going to do. I'm going up there and strike out."

"If you do that, kid," said Detore, "don't come back to the bench. Just go back and get dressed and go home."

No one will ever know what Ted would have done, because the Portland pitcher threw the first pitch right at his head.

"Why did you do that?" Williams asked, after he had brushed himself off. "I didn't do anything."

"Get in there," yelled the pitcher, as a thousand other pitchers had yelled before him, "and I'll knock you down again."

Down again went Ted Williams. Up again he rose and knocked the next pitch out of the park.

When he got back to the bench he was still bewildered. "Why did he throw at me? I didn't do anything."

Of course he had done something, Detore told him. He had gone up to the plate wearing the San Diego uniform. "Whenever one of us gets in a jam, you're involved, remember that." And whenever it was Ted who got into trouble, they'd be there for him. "The uniform's the thing, kid, you can't get out of it. Always keep that in mind."

It was not a lesson that Ted Williams took to heart. "If you ever hurt anybody again," he told Ward, "I'll never play on the same team with you."

"Nobody could figure him out," George Myatt says. "For myself, I stopped trying."

Indirectly, it was because of George Myatt that Williams eventually got to Boston. Legend has it that Eddie Collins, the Red Sox general manager, discovered both Bobby Doerr and Ted Williams on the only scouting trip he ever made. The story is not completely true. Boston had option rights to both Doerr and Myatt, and when Collins found himself on the West Coast on business in late July of 1936, he decided to pick up the Padres in Portland, where they were playing, and complete the deal. He was not really scouting Doerr, for Bobby was a .342 hitter with the Padres that year and was easily the best prospect in the minors. Collins did want to look at Myatt, though, to confirm the scouting reports that Myatt couldn't field well enough to play shortstop in the big leagues and probably couldn't hit well enough to make it at any other position.

Collins followed the Padres for a week before he exercised the option on Doerr and told Bill Lane that he was no longer interested in Myatt. But Collins had also been watching someone else. He had become fascinated with a gangling part-time outfielder who had the most perfect swing he had ever seen.

And so when Collins drops the option on Myatt, goes the story, he offers to buy an option on Ted Williams. Lane, who doesn't seem to realize what he has, actually refuses to take Tom Yawkey's money. "The boy's only seventeen," Lane tells Collins. "He's green as grass. Frank may still use him as a pitcher. I don't want your option money, but since you're interested in the boy I'll promise you this: Before I sell him to any other big-league team, you'll get a chance to match the bid."

That's the version that has come down to us for more than fifty years. And it is pretty much the version that both Williams and Doerr, having heard and read it for fifty years, will tell you today.

Bobby Doerr: Collins came out in August to decide whether to pick up my option and Myatt's. He was in Seattle-Portland for a week. He came to me and said, "We're going to take your contract but not Myatt." Williams was just taking batting practice then. Collins saw him and liked his swing. Went right to Lane and said, "We'd like to buy his contract." Lane says, "We're not ready to sell him yet." Collins had the foresight to say, "Well, could we have the first chance to buy his contract when you're ready to sell him?" and they shook hands on it, and that's the way that was put together.

Ted Williams: I wasn't playing then. He saw me hitting batting practice. I was just going along for the trip. But I wasn't in the lineup. I was just taking batting practice and throwing batting practice.

What has been lost, misplaced or forgotten over the years, in the repetition of the original story, is that Ted did play in Portland.

When Collins saw Ted in batting practice, his statistics were unimpressive: four singles in twenty times at bat, and he had yet to knock in a run. But the Padres played three straight doubleheaders against the first-place Portland Beavers over the weekend of August 7–9, and Ted was in the starting lineup for the last five of those games.

Now, it's entirely possible that after seeing Ted swing in batting practice Collins had asked to see what he could do against live pitching. But that isn't what seems to have happened. What did happen was that Cedric Durst aggravated a muscle pull in his groin in the first game on Friday and Ted went in to play the final inning because— and here it comes—he was the only outfielder left on the bench.

The reason for that is evident in this background as gleaned from the sports pages of the San Diego newspapers:

(1) Within a week after Ted had been signed by the Padres, Lane had bought Ivy (Chick) Shiver from the American Association to give the Padres another home-run hitter to go with Vince DiMaggio. "Shiver will give Cedric Durst, Vince DiMaggio and Vance Wirthman a chance to get a little relief now and then," the announcement said, "and also help Ted Williams to break into the lineup now and then for the experience he needs."

(2) When the Padres left on their three-week road trip, Bill Lane— always looking to save a buck—had left Wirthman at home. "Shiver,

DiMaggio and Williams will hold down the outfield with no replacement,'' read the report on Durst's injury. "Unless Myatt is put into the picture.'' Myatt, it seemed, had gone to the outfield under similar circumstances earlier in the season "and had covered a lot of ground.'' There wasn't a chance, however, that Myatt would be going to the outfield now. Not when Eddie Collins was in Portland for the specific purpose of watching him play shortstop.

The random chance, again, that governs the lives of us all. Branch Rickey had seen Ted—or failed to see him—amid a mob of kids on a day when Ted was badly hobbled. Eddie Collins had come to look at one player, and because another player had suffered an inconsequential injury he was able to get a good look at Ted Williams.

The best evidence is that Collins arrived on Saturday. At any rate, the first mention of his name comes when the writer of the *Union*'s notes column tries to explain why the sure-handed Bobby Doerr and the steady George Myatt had made six errors between them in the first game of the Saturday doubleheader. They had suffered an attack of the jitters, he wrote, "because of their nervousness at hearing for the first time that Eddie Collins was in the stands.''

If Collins was in the stands for the second game on Friday, he had seen the skinny rookie, batting eighth in the lineup, hit one single in four times at bat, knock in a run, and score a run. On Saturday, while he was watching Doerr and Myatt kick the game away, he was seeing Ted Williams get two hits for three at-bats in the opener and go hitless in the second game. On Sunday Durst was back, but Ted was still in the lineup, too, batting seventh. The Padres won both games by identical 4 – 1 scores. Ted had a single and a double in the first game and knocked in the two key runs. In the second game he had a double in three at-bats.

The box scores tell nothing about how hard the balls were hit or, for that matter, whether any of the outs had been hit with authority. Nor do we know whether Shellenback kept Ted in the lineup and sat Shiver down because Collins had wanted to see as much of Ted as possible.

From Portland, the Padres went to San Francisco to play the Missions. Ted played on Tuesday and Wednesday and did nothing. On Thursday, Earl Keller writes in the *Evening Tribune* that Bill Lane is leaving San Diego for a meeting with Collins on Friday. It would have been in San Francisco, then, that Collins made his handshake deal with Lane on Ted and told Bobby Doerr that he was picking up his option.

However it came about, Collins got himself a good look. He saw Ted go six for seventeen (.353), with two doubles and three runs batted in. It was the only real hitting he did until he broke into the lineup upon Stiver's departure in September.

One final word about those three days in Portland. There was another teenager in that ballpark who would be joining Ted Williams and Bobby Doerr five years later to form the heart of the Boston Red Sox championship team. He wasn't a player then, and he was sitting on the other bench. He was Johnny Pesky, who, at the age of sixteen, had been promoted from batboy to clubhouse boy of the Portland Beavers.

Pesky remembers his first look at Ted very well. "There was a foundry in the street behind the right-field bleachers, and when they started smelting the smoke would come billowing up." Pesky's first memory of Ted is of seeing a tall, thin kid hitting balls against the foundry during batting practice.

He doesn't remember whether the smoke was billowing, but he does remember coming out to the bench to see whether he could do the same thing in the game. "You could see he had a great buggy-whip swing. You could see the quickness. It was all there in Portland on that first day."

The actual purchase of Ted from the Padres came sooner than the Red Sox had anticipated, because Eddie Collins wasn't the only baseball man to fall in love with that swing.

The old baseball hand who got the bidding started was Casey Stengel, who had just been hired as manager of the Boston Braves. While he was being paid not to manage the Brooklyn Dodgers in 1937,

Stengel had spent his time watching Pacific Coast League games and scouting the players. The first thing he did after he was given the Braves portfolio was to put in a bid for Ted Williams.

Another bid came from Lefty O'Doul, the manager of the San Francisco Seals. O'Doul had hit .398 in 1929, to lead the National League, and .368 in 1932. He was still an active player in Ted's first year with the Padres—"my first real look at an all-time great," Ted says—and when Ted had approached him on the field to ask his advice about hitting, O'Doul had told him, "Kid, the best advice I can give you is don't let anybody change your batting style. You have a perfect swing." A year later, at the time when Ted was in the depths of his early-season slump, he had picked up a newspaper in San Francisco and read that O'Doul was calling him the best left-handed hitter to come into the league since Paul Waner, a tribute Ted has never forgotten. "I don't know what he possibly could have seen in me," Ted says. "But it was a tremendous boost. It gave me confidence, for the first time, that I really might be a great hitter."

O'Doul's major-league connections were with the New York Giants, and so when he made a remarkably good offer for Ted, it was clear that he was serving as a stalking horse for the Giants' owner, Charles A. Stoneham.

Tom Yawkey, having failed miserably in his attempts to buy a pennant, had decided to put a second fortune into building a farm system. And so when Lane, true to his promise, informed Collins that it would take $25,000 in cash and another $25,000 in players to match the bids he had received for Ted, Yawkey balked. The only way to stop buying players, he told Collins, was to stop buying them, period.

Collins argued that Williams was something special. Besides, he said, buying a nineteen-year-old minor-leaguer with years of value ahead was not the same as buying an established star; it was, he pointed out, almost like developing him over a period of years. Yawkey was adamant at first, probably because he could not see why everybody was getting so excited over a player who had never hit .300 and admittedly couldn't field. Collins could almost always get Yawkey to see things his way, however. In the end, Yawkey agreed to leave the final decision to Collins and thereby saved himself the embarrassment of being the man who let both Joe DiMaggio and Ted Williams get away.

The deal was effected in December during the major-league meeting in New York, and it came as a complete surprise to Ted. "You're kidding me," he told Earl Keller. "Boy, this is the happiest day of my life. I'll show the Red Sox bosses they didn't make any mistake." He hadn't even known that Collins was interested in him, let alone that he had asked for an option. "The first thing I did, I looked at the map, and it was exactly the farthest point I could go in the United States. I thought, jesus, it's a long ways."

Well, if Ted was surprised he was not any more surprised than his mother was going to be. Not only was Bill Lane denying that he had promised to keep Ted in San Diego until he was twenty-one; Lane was flatly denying that he had promised to give her 10 percent of the receipts from any sale.

Given Lane's reputation, the benefit of all doubt goes to May. She had, after all, turned down better offers because she had wanted to keep Ted close to her. (When you think about it, Lane's original refusal to give Collins the option could well have been because he was observing his promise not to do anything with Ted for another three years.) Nor was it at all unusual for a minor-league operator to give the player a percentage of his sale price.

Given Salvation May's reputation, you could bet the house and tambourine that she was not going to take it lying down. And, here again, there are two versions of what happened. The accepted version is that she simply refused to sign a contract with the Red Sox unless the money that Lane had promised was forthcoming, and that poor Eddie Collins, who was not in the best of health, had to make a wearing three-day train trip to the Coast to find out what was going on. There is no question that Collins came to the house on Utah Street, met with Ted and both his parents, and told them that if it was Mrs. Williams's understanding that she had $2,500 coming, the Red Sox would give her the money themselves.

Ah, but there is the other version, and it makes great sense. The way the second story goes, the New York Giants, who were among the clubs that had wanted to buy him from Lane, had already talked to Sam Williams, and Ted's parents, who would have to sign his contract regardless, were both asserting Ted's right to sign with the Giants or anybody else.

Consider the possible repercussions. The Williams family had a lot more than the claim of a broken oral contract working for them. The legal question could have gone like this: Did the parents of a minor have the right to sign him into what might be called permanent bondage, or did that boy, upon reaching the age of majority (also known as the age of *consent*), have the right to disavow any deal that had been made in his name? More to the situation at hand, did not the parents themselves, in their role as agents for a minor, have the right—indeed, the fiduciary duty—to reconsider, in the light of more favorable circumstances, whether they were still acting in his best interests? This wasn't buying the kid a used Chevy, after all. This was signing away his bargaining rights for his entire professional career.

Organized baseball had always been aware that its Standard Player Contract, with its reserve clause, played fast and loose with the U.S. Constitution. Now, May Williams clearly did not have that dire of a threat in mind. But you can bet that the commissioner of baseball, Kenesaw Mountain Landis, who had been a leading corporation lawyer before he became a federal judge, did. And who wanted to open up that can of worms? It didn't matter what the grounds were. May Williams—and whoever may have been advising her—might have thought she was dealing with the law of contracts, but she was in effect posing a challenge to baseball's reserve clause. Not only would Landis have seen that, but he also would have known that such a dispute was going to inevitably end up on his desk. If—and this is the way the story does go—the Giants had not already asked him unofficially for his advice.

Landis phoned Tom Yawkey and ordered him to send someone to San Diego immediately to sign Ted Williams to a contract, regardless of the cost.

Given those circumstances, Eddie Collins would have been delighted to get by with handing Mrs. Williams a $2,500 check for what was, in effect, a $50,000 deal.

And he would also have been very careful to have her sign a two-year contract, to make sure that the expiration date carried through Ted's twenty-first birthday.

On the surface, it was an idyllic boyhood. Hunting, fishing, playing baseball twelve months of the year in an almost bucolic setting.

He was a star in high school. He was the most important kid in town.

All his boyhood friends have stories about an outsider he befriended. The kid with the harelip. The kid with the crippled leg. When a new boy came to school he'd go up to him, stick out his hand, and say, "How the hell are you? My name is Ted Williams."

But essentially shy. Another of the contradictions. Not only didn't they go out with girls, Del Ballinger says, they, honest to God, didn't even talk about them.

Ted spent as much time with Del as with anyone else. "We'd go fishing overnight," he says. "A lot." They'd hop on the trolley and go down to Crystal Pier. The trolley conductor on the early-morning run knew them well. "As soon as we got on he'd send us to the back of the trolley because we smelled so bad."

They'd go hunting in the large wooded area that lay between their North Park neighborhood and the ocean. "We'd hike into Mission Valley, and Ted would shoot at anything that moved. I want to say that he was one of the finest gentlemen who ever walked, but he was a loner. He was a Huck Finn type who didn't give a damn. He'd throw tomatoes at you if he didn't like you. He'd throw a rock." What Del recalled most vividly about the Ted Williams who didn't give a damn was the way he would take on a whole new character on Halloween. "There was one year we pulled down a garage. And there was one time he scared the hell out of me by shooting a cow." And then Del shook his head and said, "My birthday was on St. Patrick's Day, and he'd always tell me that his birthday was on Halloween."

He hunted and he fished, and he was idolized by his teammates and followed around by smaller kids.

Ray Boone, who would go on to a fine big-league career of his own, grew up in the same neighborhood as Ted, started playing baseball at North Park with Rod Luscomb, and went on to star at Hoover High under Wos Caldwell. Ray was one of the kids who followed Ted around. "I was twelve years old when Ted was in his senior year at Hoover," he says, "and he was already an immortal in San Diego." Ray had an afternoon newspaper route, and he would race through it on the day of a game so that he could get to Hoover Field in time to catch the last couple of innings. "If I missed the game, the first thing I'd ask my friends was how Ted did. They'd tell me, 'Ray, you should have been there. He hit another one into the trees.'"

They'd hang around Del Ballinger's garage in the hope that Ted would drop by. "Del was always such a good-natured guy," Ray remembers. "He loved to paint, and he was always painting everything in the Hoover colors. From time to time some of the other players from the team would come around. Ted wouldn't come by often, and he wouldn't stay long. But it was always a thrill for us when he'd show up."

In Ted's first years after high school, when he was playing for the San Diego Padres and the Minneapolis Millers, he'd come to North Park during the off-season, to see Luscomb and get in some hitting, and Ray was always one of the kids who'd shag for him. "After he'd leave, Luscomb would hand out money to all of us and say, 'Ted left this behind to give to you.'"

When Ray Boone was called up by the Cleveland Indians—and we're jumping ahead eleven years here—he wondered if Ted would remember him. Every inning, as Ray ran out to his shortstop position, Ted would pass him, on his way in from left field, without the slightest sign of recognition. "This is my favorite banquet story," Ray continues. "I came up at the end of 1949, was put right into the lineup against the Red Sox, and left eight men stranded on base to cost us the game. First game I played at Fenway Park, though, I hit my first two major-league home runs. The first one tied the score in the eighth inning. The second was a two-run homer that put Cleveland ahead, 8–6, in the ninth. When I was running out to short at the end of that inning Ted came past me, and without lifting his head he said, 'You can't beat the boys from Hoover High.'" Boone swears he got almost as much of a thrill out of that as out of hitting the home runs.

Al Olsen was a left-handed pitcher who came to Hoover the year after Ted graduated and went on to become a mainstay for the Padres for twelve years. (He was brought up to the Red Sox in the spring of 1943, following an 18–13 season, just in time to receive his draft notice from Uncle Sam.) Olsen went back to college, with 160 wins behind him, earned a Ph.D. in Administration, and became the athletic director at San Diego State (where he had the good fortune to hire Don Coryell and turn the football program big-time).

"Ted was always a topic of conversation among the rest of us kids," Olsen remembers. "We all looked at him with a bit of awe. 'Did you hear what Ted did in the print shop yesterday?' 'Did you see the drive he hit against Monrovia?' He used to take a broomstick, and on the way to school he'd be walking past a line of Eugenia bushes. He'd pick out one particular red berry on each bush to swing at while he was walking along and knock it off clean. And we'd tell each other, 'You ought to see Ted hit those damn Eugenia berries.'"

During Ted's time with the Padres, Olsen got to spend a lot of time around the clubhouse because one of his classmates was the batboy, and since Ted knew Olsen was a left-hander with a good curveball, he would pick up some baseballs as they were leaving the clubhouse and pay Olsen a quarter to pitch to him. "He was obsessive about it. He would hit until his hands would bleed. He'd wear you out." They would go over to the Marine base and keep going until Ted had hit all the balls into the bay. "He was so skinny. It was weird how far the balls would go."

A Huck Finn boyhood. Idolized in his own small world. A celebrity among his peers. He was Teddy Williams whom everybody loved and if his own family life was wanting, he did not lack for other families who were always ready to set a place for him at the dinner table or for men who were more than eager to treat him as if he were their own well-loved son. Ahhhh, but it wasn't his family, and he wasn't their son. When it comes to family, there may be surrogates, but there are no real substitutes. However hospitable the soil may be, you are always a transplant amid the alien corn. Always the little boy looking into the candy store with your nose pressed against the window.

The relationship with his family—the neglectful mother, the absent father, the rotten brother—tormented him through his entire baseball career. Nothing turned him off faster than to bring up the subject of his mother. His hatred of *Sport* magazine arose largely because Ed Fitzgerald had sent a San Francisco writer, Hannibal Coons, down to San Diego to interview her.

And yet he seemed compelled from time to time, especially when he was with someone he trusted, to bring up his troubled childhood himself. Bobby Doerr, who was so close to him in age, probably knew him better than anyone else. Bobby's father would frequently come down from Los Angeles to see him play, and Ted would tell Bobby how much he envied him his family. "Especially my dad," Bobby says. "My dad was always so great about making sure that I had everything I needed to play baseball with. It was hard for Ted, he had to more or less make it on his own. We had a real close family. Ted always enjoyed that. It has a bearing. More than people think."

Better than anybody else, Bobby knew about Ted's problems and how deeply they affected him. When he was in Boston, he'd be getting letters all the time asking for spending money. "Ted knew darn well that his brother would end up spending it," Bobby says. "But he sent the money out to his mother anyway. He never said too much about it. But you'd see him get these letters, you know, and all of a sudden you'd see it crumpled up and go into the wastebasket, and you'd know it was a letter from home just from his looks." After the war, Ted began to get the same kind of letter from his father, asking for money—like say, six thousand dollars—to open a new photography shop, and then asking for more money after he had blown the six grand on something else.

In 1961, the year after Ted retired, he returned to Hoover High to scout their new phenomenon, pitcher Dave Morehead. Bobby Doerr, who had become a roving scout for the Red Sox, was with him along with the farm director, Neil Mahoney. As they were leaving the U.S. Grant Hotel after lunch Ted suddenly said, "I'll show you where my dad's photographer's shop was."

Bobby Doerr: "It was just over a couple of blocks. We walked up those stairs. You could see Ted as a little kid walking up those narrow stairs. He said, 'Right up here. This was where my dad used to have his shop.' Like he was reminiscing. And then when he came back down he took us down to the next corner and said, 'Right here on this corner is where the Salvation Army band used to parade. This is where my mother would make me get in and march.' He said, 'I used to try to get behind the big bass drum so that I could hide.' Gee, right then you thought, my God, this is where the embarrassment all started. You could almost see the six- or seven-year-old kid hiding behind the drum."

It never stopped. In Ted's year and a half with the Padres, she would come to the park with her tambourine. Bill Starr remembers vividly the time one of the players asked Ted if he knew that his mother had been walking around the stands collecting money and telling everybody Ted Williams was her son. "Ted looked down at the floor and didn't say anything for a long time. And then he said, 'I know. She embarrasses me.' The whole clubhouse went absolutely silent. Everybody felt so bad for him."

Al Olsen: "There were a million stories about her. She was a character, and Ted didn't know what to do. The press wasn't kind to him in San Diego. She'd get on the street corner and ring her bell and talk about her son, Ted Williams, and Ted asked her not to and gave her some money, and she took the money and went out anyway to get more money for the Salvation Army. The press guys picked that up and put it in the paper, that's one reason he didn't want to come back to San Diego very often. The press was always trying to find something negative about the guy."

There is a question that presents itself about Ted's birth date. He was born in 1918. When he first came into baseball his birth date was listed as October 30. Later, it turned out—don't ask me how—that it was August 30. He has said that he changed the date because he did not want his birthday to interfere with the baseball season.

His birth certificate says he was born Teddy Samuel Williams on August 20, 1918. On the certificate that he seems to have brought to school (reprinted in the photo section), he made two changes. The name Teddy is changed to Theodore, and the listed birth date of August 20 is changed to August 30. On the face of the certificate, August 20 would seem to be correct, since the attending physician had filed the certificate on August 21.

His mother's maiden name, moreover, is misspelled as Venzor, and her occupation is listed not as a Salvation Army worker but—are you ready for this?—as a housewife. And, according to the birth certificate, Ted was the first of her three children who had been born alive.

In his early days on the playgrounds, according to Del Ballinger, the kids would call him T. Samuel, which would seem to be how he was signing his name on his junior-high-school papers. When he entered Hoover High he gave his name as Ted S. Williams.

In Minneapolis, in 1938, the newspapers referred to him as Theodore Francis, and some of the out-of-town papers were still calling him Theodore Francis in his first year in Boston.

Figure it out. Freudian psychology is a game that anybody can play. When you alter your name and the date of your birth you are doing Freudian things with your parentage. On the other hand, there are times, as Sigmund Freud did not quite say, when a bat is only a bat.

Ted was so obsessed with playing baseball that there is no good reason to doubt that the reason he gave was the correct one. If it sounds a little crazy, so what? Ted has always been a little bit crazy.

As to the dates found on his birth certificate, well, that could easily be accounted for by the well-known incompetence of bureaucrats.

The best evidence is found in a scrapbook his mother kept from the newspaper clippings Ted sent to her during his first year in Boston. Over the box score of the game of August 30, 1939, his mother has written, "Your birthday."

V

The Kid
in Minneapolis

The first time Eddie Collins saw Ted Williams swing the bat in Portland he had known that he was looking at something special. Ted was the player around whom Collins planned to build a dynasty that would take over from the New York Yankees, and he intended to nurture him carefully—as in "tender, loving care"—until it was time to unveil him to the Boston fans.

Having heard that Ted could be a creature of wild impulse, Collins phoned Bobby Doerr in Los Angeles, before Bobby left for spring training, and asked him to pick up Ted in San Diego and deliver him, undamaged, to the spring-training site in Sarasota, Florida.

It was unthinkable, of course, that Ted Williams would make a routine entrance. Just as Doerr was set to leave home, the worst flood of the century hit California, washing out roads, knocking out telephone lines, and leaving Williams and Doerr cut off from the world and from each other. It was Ted, ever innovative, who came up with a solution. He found a ham-radio operator in his neighborhood and asked him to try to make contact with a ham operator in Los Angeles who lived near enough to Doerr to get a message to him. A contact was found, and through the good offices of short-wave communication, they were able to settle on a plan to meet in the train station at El Paso. "We just decided that Ted would go the best way he could, and I'd go the best way I could," Doerr says. Ted was able to catch a train out of San Diego, but he found no one to meet him at the station in El Paso. What had happened was that the solid dependable Doerr had run into two other flood-locked players in Los Angeles, Babe Herman and Max West. They had arrived in El Paso before Ted and had decided to whip across the border to Juárez for a quail dinner. "When we came back, there was Ted parading up and down, wondering whether I was ever going to get there."

The four ballplayers grabbed a train for Florida, and for two days and two nights Ted Williams and Babe Herman boasted about their hitting feats, with Ted taking the opportunity, between tall tales, to pump Herman—who had hit .393 in 1930—for batting tips. The non-stop dialogue didn't bother the quiet, patient Doerr or the even more silent Max West, who was joining the Boston Braves after a great season in the Pacific Coast League. But it did make things rather difficult for the Pullman porter. "Ted was using a pillow for a bat," Doerr recalls, "and in two days he used up all of our pillows. Well, you know that voice of his. There were three old women in a compartment down at the other end of the car, and they kept calling the porter to ask him, 'Can't you keep that guy quiet down there?' "

When Ted and Doerr finally got to Sarasota, ten days late, a fine, almost imperceptible drizzle was falling. Ted, still somewhat water-logged from the California floods, held out his palm, looked skyward, shivered, and said, in that carefully modulated voice that characterizes all his utterings, "So this is Florida, is it? Do they always keep this state under a foot of water?" Under the circumstances, it was funny, as it was meant to be. The rub was that the writers, having prepared themselves for a screwball, arched their eyebrows and passed little nods back and forth as if to say, "And what do we have here, gentlemen?"

Ted promptly suited up for a morning workout of fly shagging, jawed good-naturedly with the fans, as was his wont, and was given an unexpected chance to hit when a newsreel unit showed up to take some batting-cage shots.

Herb Pennock, the great old Yankee left-hander, who was then a Red Sox pitching coach, was pitching batting practice. He threw Ted a couple of big, slow curves, and the rookie, in his eagerness, almost broke his back.

Pennock motioned for Ted to meet him between home plate and the pitching mound and asked, "Kid, can you pull?"

Ted told him that he could.

"I'll throw it right down the pipe for you, then," Pennock said. "But for the love of heaven, don't drill anything back at me. I'm getting too old to duck."

When Ted stepped back into the box, it was the cameraman's turn to ask a question. "Don't you have a cap, kid?" he said. "The people who see this are going to be told they're watching big-leaguers, not sandlotters."

Teddy produced a cap from his back pocket and pulled it down over his head. "Is this all it takes to be a big leaguer?" He grinned. "And I thought it was going to be tough." Not really an unnatural thing for a cocky kid to say.

By the end of the week, however, that routine exchange had been rewritten so that that cameraman had merely requested that Ted put on his cap, which gave Ted's rejoinder an altogether different cast.

The magic of Ted Williams in a batter's box manifested itself that first day in camp. The tall, thin rookie—he was now six feet four and weighed 177 pounds—stepped into the box, set himself in his wide stance, let his bat drop across the far corner of the plate, wiggled his hips and shoulders, and jiggled up and down as if he were trying to tamp himself into the box. He moved his bat back and forth a few times, then brought it back into position and twisted his hands in opposite directions as if he were wringing the neck of a chicken. He was set for the pitch.

And somehow, as if by some common impulse, all sideline activity stopped. Everybody was watching Ted Williams.

When the morning workout was finished he strolled into the clubhouse with the harelipped Jim Bagby, a second-year pitcher. "Okay," he said, "what do I do now?"

"You grab a sandwich and a pint of milk," Bagby told him. "Then in about half an hour we go out to work again."

"Work in these same sweat-stained uniforms?" the rookie asked, insulted.

"Well, what do you expect?" Bagby asked. "Two uniforms a day?"

"Sure," Ted said. "We're here in the big leagues, aren't we?"

Ted hit some solid line drives in the afternoon session. Joe Cronin was so pleased that he wrote the lead for newsmen that evening: "A hush went over the ballpark at the Red Sox training camp this morning. All eyes were focused on one man. Even the veterans stopped and gazed, and the photographers got ready to shoot. For Ted Williams, the Pacific Coast phenom, was about to make his first appearance at the bat in a big-league uniform."

Ted Williams had ended his first day with the Boston Red Sox.

The next day, at a formal news conference, Cronin was asked about his two highly publicized rookies, Ted Williams, from San Diego, and third baseman Jim Tabor, from the University of Alabama, "It's too early to tell about their batting," Cronin said, "but I've seen enough of them already to know that they both are more than all right as fielders. Williams, in fact, is a much better fielder than I had been led to believe. He hasn't had much experience as an outfielder, you know. Less than a year and a half at San Diego. He's sure-handed and he's got a strong arm. He's weak on ground balls still, and he's got a few other things to learn. But he'll be adequate in the field. It's his hitting that's a question."

That made it seem as if nobody had bothered to let Cronin in on the secret, but Joe, who was clearly trying to take the pressure off, went on to say, "He's got good style at the plate—and wonderful wrist action. But you've got to wait and see him at bat against real pitching before you can tell whether he is ready for the big leagues or not. When big-league pitchers really start to operate on him he may have trouble. You can't really tell anything yet."

Cronin had less and less reason to be optimistic as the training season wore on. As the pitching got tougher, the Pacific Coast League phenom made more noise with his mouth than with his bat. "I don't know what I'm fooling around with baseball for, anyway," Ted would say. "I ought to quit fooling around, and go out and get an honest job." When he got tired of knocking Florida he began to knock Boston. From everything he'd heard, he said, the park had been laid out for right-handed hitters. "When I first heard I'd been sold to Boston," he said, "I was going to quit. New York or Detroit, that's where I belong. I could have gone to Southern Cal on a baseball scholarship, too, damnit. Hell, if I'd of known I was going to end up at Fenway Park I'd have taken it."

The less he hit, the more bizarre he became. When a fly ball came his way, he would slap his rump, bellow, "Hi-ho, Silver, away-a-a-ay!" and go galloping after the ball. Every once in a while he caught it. Ground balls went skipping between his legs. Every once in a while he'd chase them.

Jack Wilson, one of the starting pitchers, had the adjoining locker, and he and Ted had a constant bantering exchange going. "I've finally figured out what your problem is," Wilson said finally. "You're nuts."

"Let's get two tickets to the nuthouse, then," Ted said. "When do we leave?"

He needn't have worried, of course. The Red Sox knew very well that he wasn't going to be ready at nineteen. Nor were the Red Sox desperate for outfielders. They had just bought the All-Star left-fielder Joe Vosmik from the St. Louis Browns, where he had hit .325. In center field they had Roger (Doc) Cramer, the only left-hander in the starting lineup; Cramer had hit .305. In right field was the hotheaded Ben Chapman, who had hit .307. In reserve they had Buster Mills, who had hit .295 as the starting left-fielder the previous year, and Fabian Gaffke, who had hit .288.

It was an era where rookies were ridden mercilessly, especially by the players they were trying to replace, and to compound Ted's problem, Ben Chapman and Doc Cramer were two of the most wicked bench jockeys—and clubhouse lawyers—in all of baseball.

"Theodore S. Williams, huh?" one of them would muse. "What does the *S* stand for, 'Screwball'?" No, the other would say, "Saparoo."

But that was nothing. From everything that Johnny Pesky heard when he came up to Boston a few years later, the three of them sometimes got into the kind of personal stuff that was way out of bounds even for those days.

Of course, Ted, in his innocence, made it easy for them by telling one of the sportswriters that he didn't smoke, didn't drink, and was still a virgin. But that was Ted. Ask him a question and you'd get an honest answer. And since there was no lack of writers with a talent for making up both the question and the answer—Hi there, Yogi Berra—it was almost impossible to separate what was real from what had been fabricated.

"Wait until you see Foxx hit," one of the Boston writers was supposed to have said to Ted on his first day in camp. "Wait until Foxx sees me hit," went the rookie's answer, a quote that followed him through his entire career. Well, maybe. Ted always denied that he had said it, and considering Ted's constant refrain about wishing that he had Foxx's muscles, the denial rings true. Not that it matters. Willie Sutton never said, "That's where the money is," but don't try to tell that to anyone, either.

It is on the record, however, that when Lefty Grove, the other Red Sox superstar, was pointed out to Ted in a hotel lobby, from a distance of no more than thirty feet, he did indeed say, "That's Grove? Funny-looking geezer, isn't he?"

And that when he was introduced to Tom Yawkey he said, "Don't look so worried, Tom. Foxx and me will take care of everything." Listen, he could have said "Me and Foxx," couldn't he?

It's also on the record that after all the publicity, Ted was among the first of the rookies to be shipped away. He had hastened his departure by breaking into an impromptu press conference to ask Cronin whether he was making a trip to Tampa with the regulars or staying behind with the substitutes.

"Why don't you go look at the bulletin board like everybody else?" Cronin snapped. "And you'll see whether your name is posted."

"Okay, sport," Ted said, almost condescendingly. "If that's the way you want to be about it."

The next day he was given a bus ticket to Jacksonville and told to report to Donie Bush of the Minneapolis Millers, the top Red Sox farm club.

Johnny Orlando, the Red Sox clubhouse man, accompanied the crestfallen rookie to the bus station. Ted was glum and downhearted, but as he was boarding the bus he showed Orlando that his crest had not fallen completely. Shaking his fist in the direction of the ballpark, Ted cried: "I'll be back. Tell that to all of them. Vosmik, Cramer, and Chapman think I'm just a fresh young punk, don't they? Well, you can tell them I'll be back, and I'll make more money in a single year than the three of them put together!"

The Red Sox management had already passed the word that they expected Williams to be something special, despite his unimpressive performance at Sarasota. Bill Cunningham, the leading Boston sports columnist, wrote: "The Sox seem to think Williams is just cocky enough and gabby enough to make a great and colorful outfielder, possibly the Babe Herman type. Me? I don't like the way he stands at the plate. He bends his front knee inward and moves his foot just before he takes a swing. That's exactly what I do just before I drive a golf ball and knowing what happens to the golf balls I drive, I don't believe this kid will ever hit half a single midget's weight in a bathing suit."

Despite Cunningham's triumph of perception, Ted went to Minneapolis and tore American Association pitching apart as it has never been torn apart since. He led the league in batting with an average of .366, in runs batted in with 142, in runs scored with 130, and in home runs with 43.

He also drove Donie Bush quietly insane.

On March 21, the *Milwaukee Journal* reported: "Theodore Francis *[sic]* Williams became Minneapolis property today. The dope on Williams is that he may be able to hit the ball as far as any modern day batsman if he continues to develop."

Ted reported to the training camp in Jacksonville, and right away he got a break. Rogers Hornsby came in to serve as batting instructor, and Ted, with his eagerness to learn, became his prize student. Hornsby gave Ted what he still considers to be the single best piece of advice he has ever received, the same advice he has been passing on to young ballplayers ever since: "Get a good ball to hit." It sounds so simple and so obvious. But it means "Be patient." It means "Be aware." It means "Do not be a sucker and swing at the pitcher's pitch." It means "Know the strike zone." It means "Know what you can hit and what you cannot hit." It means "In every time at bat there is one pitch that you are looking for, and that is the pitch you had better jump on."

On the field he remained the same cocky kid who was doing almost nothing to back up his talk. His first headline in the *Minneapolis Tribune* sports pages came on the Millers final exhibition game. The story read:

Ted Williams
Goat of Game

Former Bosox Rookie Makes
Two Costly Mistakes

The Millers big chance came in the seventh inning when Ted Williams, former Red Sox rookie, came to bat with two runners on base and hit a grass cutter down the first base line. The young outfielder thought the ball had landed foul and did not attempt to gain first base. The umpire, however, called it fair.

In the Lookouts' half of the inning Williams again was the goat as he booted an easy out of Gill's with two out. Gill then scored on Bloodworth's single to center. Miles then brought him home with a home run for the 4–3 victory.

With the Millers playing their first twelve games of the season on the road, it was going to be two weeks before the Minneapolis fans got a look at him. The team opened in Indianapolis and lost three straight, as Ted went 0 for 12. The catcher for the Millers was Otto Denning: "He was so worried that on the night before we left for Louisville, we went for a long walk, and he kept asking me which of their pitchers I'd ever hit against, and whether they came overhand or sidearm and what was their best pitch. Next thing we knew we saw the city-limits sign. We'd walked clear out of town. And then we got to Louisville, and the first time at bat he hit a five-hundred-and-thirty-foot home run inside the park, and after that you couldn't stop him."

Not quite. In the first game in Louisville, he walked five times and singled. It wasn't until the third game that he hit his first two home runs. Both of them inside the park. Parkway Field in Louisville was 350 feet to right field, 512 feet in center field, and 331 feet in left. The first drive went to the fence in right center and was estimated at approximately 470 feet. The second one went to the farthermost corner of the brick wall in center. "He completed the circuit and was jogging jubilantly to the dugout,'' read the report of the game, ''by the time the ball was relayed to the infield.''

By the time the Millers came home to open against Louisville, Ted's batting average was up to .346.

Nicollet Park, the Millers' home field, was known as a hitter's paradise because the right field wall was only 279 feet away, slanting out to 330 feet in the power alley and 432 feet in center. On the other hand, the right-field wall was 46 feet high. In fact, it looked remarkably like the left-field wall at Fenway Park, which is 37 feet high. Like the ''Green Monster,'' it sported a scoreboard to relay the scores of big-league games. Like the Monster, the scoreboard was low enough to allow Ted to bend over and hold a conversation with the guy inside. And like the Monster, it was topped by a high netting to protect the buildings across the street.

''It didn't matter,'' Otto Denning says. ''When Ted hit a home run, it went over by another hundred feet. The wall was so high that if he'd had a lower wall he would have hit more. He'd get a single where it would have been a home run anywhere else.''

In Ted's introduction to the Minneapolis fans, he singled in his first two times at bat, and then he gave them what they had come to see. ''The slender youngster,'' wrote the *Tribune*'s George Barton, ''boomed a homer a mile high over the right-field wall. The fans almost lost sight of the ball as it sailed through the air and landed on the roof of a building on the far side of Nicollet Avenue.''

Before the season was over, he would hit one that completely cleared the buildings on Nicollet Avenue and landed in an alley halfway down the block.

According to Lefty Lefebvre, a Minneapolis pitcher who joined the Red Sox the following spring, he hit a grand-slam home run off Columbus left-hander Mickey Martynek that cleared the 430-foot fence in center by ten feet. And the fence was eight feet high. (Does Ted remember it? Need you ask? ''Fifth inning, three-and-two count, low fastball.'')

Otto Denning hit fifth in the lineup, right behind Ted. ''I would set on that on-deck circle, and I saw the whole ripple of his body when he swung. He would swing, and that ripple was just like the water in the ocean. You knew it then. He was nineteen years, and he was the best hitter I ever saw.'' (Denning, a right-handed batter, hit .342 himself in eighty-one games.)

Bill Meyer, the manager of the Kansas City Blues, had managed in Oakland of the Pacific Coast League the previous year. ''Nutty but shrewd'' was the way Meyer described Ted. At Oakland, they had been able to get him out by ''going up the ladder'' on him. ''But in 1938 he's at Minneapolis and I'm at Kansas City. Naturally, I tell my players how to pitch Ted, high and then higher. The first time he bats, the first pitch is high, and he fouls it off. The next pitch is a little higher, and Williams starts to swing but stops. He steps out of the box, then looks over at me and calls, 'No, Bill. Not this year.'''

But he was still a little nutty. With his usual indifference to the defensive side of the game, Ted spent much of his time in the field yapping with the fans or practicing his batting form. Once, with the bases loaded and a left-handed hitter up, Donie Bush looked out and saw his right-fielder standing with his back to the plate arguing with a fan. Another time, Ted became so bored with the game that he sat down in the outfield, folded his hands across his knees, and made himself comfortable. Bush didn't have any great success in getting him to snap to, and the umpires finally had to warn him that they were going to throw him out of the game.

Hitting was something else again. Returning to the clubhouse in a rage after going hitless one day, Ted went berserk and tore up everything he could lay his hands on, including towels and uniforms. ''If you have to tear anything,'' said the sorely tried Bush, ''tear into the pitchers. That won't cost you anything. The uniforms and the towels are coming off your pay.''

Donie Bush was a highly respected figure in baseball. He had played sixteen years of shortstop in the big leagues and had managed in the majors for nine. He had managed the Pittsburgh Pirates to a pennant in 1927 and had also been the manager of the Washington Senators, the Chicago White Sox, and the Cincinnati Reds. So why did Bush put up with it? He had no choice. When it seemed to him that he could take no more, he called up Eddie Collins and said: "Look, this kid Williams of yours is leading the league in everything, but I just can't stand him. Move him somewhere else or let me suspend him. Maybe that will wake him up. Nothing else seems to do any good."

Snapped Collins: "The day Williams doesn't put on his uniform, don't you bother to put on your uniform either."

The Minneapolis papers usually referred to the team as the "Kels"— a neat word to squeeze into a headline—after the owner, Mike Kelley. Kelley was an ornament of the minor leagues, as different from Bill Lane as any man could be. During joint major–minor league meetings Kelley would sit in his suite balancing a drink on the arm of his chair while the rest of the baseball world came by to renew acquaintances, pay their respects, or make a deal to help him out by buying one of his players. If the Red Sox, his current benefactor, wanted him to treat their latest phenom with tender, loving care, Mike Kelley was more than willing to accommodate them.

"One of the nicest men I ever met," Ted has said about Kelley. "He was like a father to me. One time I was playing in the sun field there, and it was cloudy, but it cleared up and the sun came out. They asked me if I wanted my sunglasses, and I said never mind, I didn't need them. What happens, a lazy fly ball comes out there, and I can't see it. The thing drops, and Donie Bush, man, he was mad, jumped right off the bench and rushed onto the field, where he began eating me out." According to Ted, he left the field with his head down. That night Mike called him in and said, "Ted, don't you worry about it. Things like that happen, so forget it."

Selective memory. What Ted didn't say was that after Bush had come out to right field, in what was clearly meant to be a public rebuke, Ted had reacted by loafing on everything hit out to him, and then simply lobbing the ball back to the infield while the runners were taking an extra base. Or that he seemed to be completely unaware that a single had been hit past him until his fellow players and the spectators in the right-field grandstand began to yell at him. "Messing up two plays in a single inning was hard enough," George Barton wrote. "But Williams made it worse by starting for the clubhouse after the Red Birds were retired instead of coming in the dugout. Ted kept right on running for the clubhouse as Bush waved him to the bench, and it was necessary for the Miller manager to trot far onto the field and shout at the youngster to come to the dugout."

The Kels were in the process of losing, 21–9, the fans were booing him, and through it all Ted was laughing and joking with the opposing team's bench.

It was no surprise that the boos continued when he came to bat in the ninth inning. What was surprising was that the boos were mixed with a considerable number of cheers.

Charles Johnson of the *Post-Journal* wrote an "open letter" taking Ted to task for his sulking and "apparent indifference" over a period of three days. Halsey Hall, the preeminent sportswriter in the city, wrote: "We trust for his sake (he's a good kid) that he can shovel away these fits of lackadaisical play which seize him now and then. He is too grand a prospect to be crucified by his own foolishness." George Barton, having chastised him for childish behavior, was quick to commend him for a chastened attitude: "So far, he has proved that he can take it. Instead of crawling into his shell and complaining that everyone is picking on him, Ted has turned over a new leaf. As a result, he once again is the hustling enthusiastic young ballplayer that he was before his lapse."

No, it didn't start in Boston. If he wasn't called "the Kid" in Minneapolis, the players did call him "Peter Pan" which amounted to pretty much the same thing, when you come to think about it, danced to a somewhat perkier tune. He earned the name the first day he joined the team, when he borrowed a bicycle from a Western Union messenger and went zipping around the railroad station emitting *yippy-yi-yos* and scattering women and children.

As soon as he hit a slump, he packed his bags and announced that he was sick of baseball and wanted to go home—much to the disgust of Pat Malone, who was trying to make the team after a ten-year career with the Chicago Cubs and the New York Yankees. "You have a chance to be Babe Ruth's successor, you sap," Pat yelled across the locker room. "With your youth and that natural swing, you have a chance to make a million dollars in baseball. And you want to go home? I only wish I was in your shoes." Donie Bush went further. He called Ted into his office and told him the club would happily arrange for his transportation back home and permit him to return whenever he chose to. Whether that was a classical exercise in child psychology on Bush's part or merely wishful thinking, Ted did not take him up on it.

In short order, he was the talk of the league. The Minneapolis fans voted him the most popular player on the Millers, and the sportswriters around the circuit voted him the Screwball King of the American Association. The vote, they said, was unanimous. "He's had arguments with writers in every city," George Barton wrote. He jawed with the fans. In Kansas City, he threatened to fight a fan who was riding his suddenly beloved manager, Donie Bush. He was so outrageous—and yet so loose and likable, Barton admitted—that he was fun to write about. Even Bush liked to tell stories about him. His favorite was the time Williams doubled in a late inning, with two out and the score tied. "I kept yelling at him from the coach's box to be careful, because he was the winning run. Finally Ted yelled back, loud enough for everybody in the park to hear, 'Hey, Donie, I got here by myself, and if you stop bothering me I'll get home by myself, too.'"

Everybody in the league knew that Donie Bush and Ted's teammates were under orders to leave him strictly alone. Late in the season the Red Sox purchased pitcher Joe Heving from Milwaukee. As soon as Heving joined the club, the Boston writers gathered around him to find out what he knew about Ted. "A great hitter," Heving told them. "But he could be a lot greater if somebody would just spank his fanny. He's been spoiled. The Sox are going to regret the way he's been handled." Just before he was called up, Heving went on, he had pitched against Minneapolis. "We were a run behind in the eighth inning. We had runners on first and second with two out. The batter hit to right. Williams should have caught it. He got a slow start. The ball hit his glove on the first bounce; it hurt his hand. So instead of chasing the ball he stood there shaking his fingers while both runners scored.'' Milwaukee won the game, 5–4, and Heving had a win instead of a loss. "If I had been the Minneapolis pitcher, I'd have been swinging punches at Williams as soon as the inning was over. But his manager and his mates can't say anything to him.''

Only once did Bush pull him out of a game.

Otto Denning: "It's the fifth inning, and a fly ball went to right field. I look up and there's Ted with his back to the field. He's looking at the scores of the major league games. I'm yelling. We're all yelling. Stan Spence came running over from center field and made a shoe-string catch right in front of him. Donie Bush called him in and sat him down. He says, 'You big shypoke'—that's what he'd always call him when he was mad.''

Ted finally did get a scare thrown into him toward the end of the season, but it was Fred Haney, the manager of the Toledo Mudhens, who had more to do with it than Donie Bush or the Boston front office. It started after Ted hit his forty-first home run, the mighty wallop that cleared the building on the far side of Nicollet Avenue and landed in an alley between Nicollet and First Avenue. Since he had already knocked in two runs in the first inning, it gave him five RBIs in three innings. To make sure he didn't get any more, Fred Haney ordered his pitchers to walk him whenever he came to bat with a runner in scoring position. The next three times at bat he was walked intentionally. The Mudhens walked him intentionally when they were behind 12–3, and they walked him again with the score 15–3. The next night Haney did the same thing. Six bases on balls in two games, five of them intentional. Then the Columbus Red Birds came in and did it, too. Frustration was not something that Ted had ever shown any great ability to cope with. He had gone a full week without a run batted in by the time he came to the plate in St. Paul with the bases loaded. And when he blew his opportunity by fouling out to the first baseman on a three-

and-one pitch, he heaved his bat high in the air, stormed back to the end of the bench, sat down heavily alongside Fabe Gaffke, and then wheeled around and delivered a karate chop to the water jug alongside him.

Does Gaffke remember it? "Only like it was yesterday. They had those big five-gallon jugs in the corner of the dugout those days, upside down, with the dispenser on the bottom. You'd punch the button and the water would come out. Ted hit that thing and it exploded. Glass flew all over the dugout. His wrist was all cut up and bleeding. He was lucky. If he'd ripped an artery his career was over. Bush threw a fit. I never saw Donie Bush so mad."

But that wasn't the worst scare Ted had in Minneapolis. With all the high jinks, he missed only four games that season, the first three coming in the last week of May, as the result of a stiff neck. He returned to the lineup in the second game of a Memorial Day doubleheader against St. Paul and hit a game-winning home run that landed on top of the Coliseum roof in left center, to launch a twenty-one-game hitting streak that included eleven home runs, two triples, and six doubles.

He was on another hitting tear in August when he was beaned. He had come into Milwaukee with a sixteen-game streak going, and in his first two times at bat he had a single and a double to knock in all four of his team's runs. When he came up again, in the fifth inning, he was hit on the head by Big Bill Zuber, a fastball pitcher, and knocked cold. As he came to, Zuber was bending over him. And that's when Ted started yelling at him.

"I was in the hospital for two days, and all I'm thinking is: This ain't going to stop me. I'm going to hang in there. I'm not going to give way." The question that had always been lurking there in the back of his mind was finally going to have to be confronted. How would he react to a bad beaning? The way he answered that question, he knew, was going to affect the rest of his baseball career.

"I came back in Kansas City three days later. The temperature was 108. Christ, it was hot." And to make it a real walkdown at high noon, he was going up against Kemp Wicker, who had compiled a 7 – 3 record with the world championship New York Yankees the previous season and was probably the best left-hander in the league. "Young left-handed hitters always have a little more trouble with left-handed pitching, and this was a tough little left-hander, and I just kept saying, be quick and hang in there. Which means don't give at the plate. I remember distinctly I hit two grounders, but I hit them on the fist, he got 'em in on me. But that never worried me because I knew I could hit that pitch. The one thing it showed me—and this is important—I was waiting . . . I was waiting. If I'd hit them at the end of the bat to the second baseman, that would have killed me because I would have been committing too soon. I'd have hated that."

In his final two times at bat, he hit a home run and a double to knock in four runs. "That was when I knew that I would never worry about how I was going to react to a beaning. I was proud of myself." And he went on to give himself more and more reasons to be proud. In the first five games after his return, he hit three home runs, including a grand slam, and knocked in twelve runs. Then he kept it going for five more games, to run his consecutive-game streak to twenty-seven.

At the time of the beaning, he was hitting .358. Over the rest of the season he hit .383. But then, Ted always improved as a season wore on. His batting average after the All-Star break was .397.

Unfortunately, the ball club didn't do as well. The trick was to finish in the first division, in order to get into the championship play-offs and pick up some extra money. Minneapolis lost out by two games. To recoup, the players set out to arrange a barnstorming tour through Minnesota and the Dakotas because they knew that Ted Williams would be a great draw. "He was planning to go back to California," Otto Denning says, "but he told us he'd go along with us. He did that for us. We made twenty dollars a game, and in those days twenty bucks was like a thousand now. He was one hell of a wonderful person. Anybody says different, I'll tell them they're full of it."

Also, wittingly or not, one hell of an advance man. When a WCCO sportscaster asked him where they would be playing their first game, Ted said, "Well, we're going down to some jerk town called Worthington."

Otto Denning again: "When we got to Worthington, we had a full house and everybody was booing him. You know how he quieted them? He hit a home run his first time at bat that went out of the park and over some cow barns. It must have gone five hundred feet. For the rest of the game they cheered every move he made."

For Ted, the tour turned out to be a solid loss. For one thing, he blew out the motor of his 1938 Buick, possibly from whipping around the country roads at ninety miles an hour. Notwithstanding that he always had his rifle on the seat alongside him so that he could jump out and pick off a chicken hawk or something along the way.

What Ted remembers most about the barnstorming tour, though, was what he calls "the gambling."

The tour was set up to hit the festival days along what was largely agricultural country. And where there were festivals there were carnivals. Ted couldn't resist. Once a pinball player always a pinball player; once a babe in the woods and still a babe in the woods. "I was taken for two hundred dollars by a sharpie on one of those carnival wheels," he says with a wry chuckle.

The Millers had a veteran pitcher named Walter Tauscher who was keeping an eye on the younger players. When Tauscher found out what had happened, he insisted that they go to the district attorney. "Ted didn't want to go," Denning says. "He was young, he had a strong will, and he thought he'd lost it fair and square. He kept saying he didn't want it back. But a couple of us kept telling him that the guy had been controlling the wheel with his feet, and we dragged Ted with us. The way I understood it, the carnie had taken four hundred dollars off him, and the D.A.—who was also the mayor—got half of it back."

It was Ted's last fling at gambling. He might not have agreed with his mother on many things, but when it came to the evils of gambling he had to admit that she was right.

With it all, and in a foreshadowing of what would happen in the majors, Ted was edged out for the most-valuable-player award. The voting was done by eight writers, one from each city in the league. Whitlow Wyatt of Milwaukee, the league's leading pitcher, had four votes for first place. Ollie Bejma, the second baseman of the pennant-winning St. Paul team, and Ted each had two. In the point totals, Wyatt and Bejma each had 52 points and Ted had 47.

Pee Wee Reese of Louisville, another rookie, had 8 points. The following season the Red Sox bought the Louisville franchise solely to own Reese's contract, but a year later they dealt him to Brooklyn. Otherwise, the Red Sox would have had Reese and Doerr playing side by side for a decade, with Johnny Pesky at third, and would probably have won three or four pennants.

VI

The Kid Comes
to Boston

The team Ted Williams was joining had led the majors in batting in the year 1938 with a *team* average of .299, a full twenty-five points ahead of the pennant-winning Yankees.

Jimmy Foxx had hit 50 home runs and knocked in 175 runs, both all-time Red Sox records, and had an average of .349, to lead the league in hitting. It was an MVP season for Foxx, his third, but not a triple-crown season. Hank Greenberg had hit 58 home runs for Detroit to deprive Foxx of his third triple crown.

The three outfielders Ted had shaken his fist at on his departure the previous spring had been nothing short of spectacular. Ben Chapman had hit .340, Joe Vosmik .324, and Doc Cramer .301. In addition, Vosmik had led the league with 201 hits, and Cramer had finished right behind him with 198. (Jimmy Foxx's 197 hits was third.) But that outfield was no longer a problem. Joe Cronin had traded that notorious trouble-maker Ben Chapman, to make room for Williams—and good riddance.*

Joe Cronin, the manager and shortstop, had hit .324 and knocked in 94 runs.

With it all, the Red Sox had finished with a record of 88–61, the same percentage that had brought them a pennant in 1916. All it got them in 1938 was a second-place finish, nine and a half games behind the Yankees.

There were two glaring weaknesses. They did not have the pitching, and, despite the presence of the looming left-field wall, they did not have the power. Jimmy Foxx had hit fifty home runs, sure. The rest of the team had hit forty-eight. The Yankees, led by Joe DiMaggio, had hit seventy-six more home runs and scored sixty-four more runs. The Red Sox were counting on Ted Williams to supply that extra power.

Once again Ted was a couple of days late in reporting for spring training, only this time the Red Sox management had no idea what

---

* Ted also inherited Chapman's number 9. In his first spring training, he had worn number 5, the same number as Joe DiMaggio. Do you want to take a wild stab at what Joe DiMaggio's number was in his first two years with the Yankees? That's right, it was number 9.

was detaining him. The traveling secretary had sent him a bus ticket from San Diego to Sarasota. That was the way it was done then; if a player preferred some other mode of travel, it was up to him. Which may have been why Ted asked the senior Les Cassie to drive down with him. In Arizona they hit cold weather, and by the time they reached Louisiana Ted had a bad case of the shivers. He insisted on pressing on, and when they got to New Orleans he was so ill that Cassie checked them into a hotel and called a doctor, who found Ted was running a temperature of 102 degrees and ordered him to bed.

The reporters who corralled him when he arrived in Sarasota two days later clearly did not believe his story about what they pointedly referred to as a "mysterious" case of flu. In answer to their questions, Ted said that he was not going down to the field. "I'm too tired to practice today. I think I'd better go to bed and get some more rest. I'll be out there tomorrow, though, and I'll show you guys how it should be done."

Cronin got him out of bed in a hurry. As soon as he learned that Ted had arrived, Joe dispatched a clubhouse boy with instructions for Ted to report to him immediately. Ted, coming down to the field as ordered, flashed his big, boyish smile, tapped Cronin on his bulging middle, and said, "Good to see you, Skip. How's the old boy doing?" Cronin, disarmed, grinned back. Then he sat Ted down for a long talk, not to bawl him out but to assure him that he was going to be in the Boston starting lineup regardless of how he performed in spring training. The days of clowning were over, Cronin said. This was the big leagues. "All I want you to do down here is to pay attention to business, work hard on your fielding, and be in shape to show the fans of Boston that you're as good as you and I think you are."

Ted did hit with power during spring training. In fact, he swung the bat so well that when the Sox broke camp he was leading the club in almost every hitting category.

On the way north, the Sox stopped off in Atlanta to play the local minor-league club. The game was played on April 1—All Fools' Day— a date Ted did his best to honor.

Atlanta had a peculiar park. The fence in right field had been shortened two different times, not by building a bull pen in front of the old fence or running a wire fence around the field but by constructing completely new walls. There were, then, three walls running parallel to each other, like a sort of maze. The day of the game, Johnny Orlando told Ted that Babe Ruth had hit three balls over the original wall during his glory days as a Yankee. The year previously, Max West, as a highly touted Braves' rookie, had also hit three home runs.

Ted Williams, the highly touted Red Sox rookie, was eager to have the same kind of day. Early in the game, he came up with the bases loaded and swept them clean with a triple. The next time, however, he struck out. In the eighth inning, with a chance to knock in two more base runners, he struck out again. This time he hurled his bat away in disgust.

When he took his place in the field for the last of the eighth the fans got on him. Reverting to form, he screamed back at them. With two men on base, a high, wind-blown fly was hit down the right-field foul line. Ted chased it into foul territory, had the ball in his glove, and—just like it had to be—dropped it. As he reached down to pick it up he booted the ball away from himself. Fuming now, his neck a flaming red, he grabbed the ball and heaved it over the top of the grandstand.

Cronin immediately sent Fabe Gaffke out to play right field and let Williams stew on the bench. That night he called Ted to his hotel room. If Ted had expected to be eaten out, Cronin fooled him. "I called you in here," Cronin said, "because I want you to explain something to me. I've had to work hard all my life to make myself a big-leaguer. When I was your age I was a no-hit Class B utility infielder. And here a kid like you comes along with all the natural ability anybody could hope to have, and you behave like you did out there today. I just can't understand what goes on in your mind. See if you can't explain it to me." Ted hung his head in shame, promised almost tearfully that nothing like that would ever happen again, and remained bitterly remorseful until . . . well, until the sun came up the next morning.

The sportswriters viewed this kind of behavior with alarm, with regret, with misgivings, with contempt. In short, they were delighted. The fans of Boston, who had been hearing about Ted and his tantrums for a solid year, could hardly wait to see him.

In those days, the Red Sox and the Braves took turns playing a preseason game against Holy Cross, a top baseball college in Worcester, about thirty-five miles from Boston. The stands were jammed with local buffs and with Boston fans who could not wait for Ted to come to Fenway Park. In the first inning, he came to bat with the bases loaded and hit a tremendous home run. On their way to New York to open the season against the Yankees, the Sox had scheduled a stop in New Haven to play Yale. Ted unaccountably struck out three times against collegiate pitching.

It was not unaccountable at all, Ted says. It had snowed so heavily that they had to clear off the field. Smokey Joe Wood, who had been a great pitcher for the Red Sox in the Babe Ruth era, was the Yale coach. "He was coaching at third base wearing a big sheepskin coat while the rest of us shivered. 'That old sonofabitch is warm over there,' we were saying, 'and we're freezing.' Later I met him. What a nice man. Jeez.''

Ted Williams's major-league debut turned into a cliff-hanger, with rain forcing two postponements. By the time his spikes cut the turf of Yankee Stadium he was as close to a nervous wreck as any twenty-year-old could be.

All spring he had been asking about the ace Yankees pitcher, Red Ruffing. In the middle of an exhibition game he would shout across the field to Cramer, "Ruffing, he's a pretty good pitcher, ain't he?"

"Fair," Cramer would shout back. "He only won twenty last year."

Now, as he sat on the bench watching Ruffing warm up, he turned to Jack Wilson. "That's Ruffing, huh?" he said. "He don't look that tough."

"He don't look tough from here, Bush," Wilson told him. "But when you stand up at the plate with a bat in your hand, then he looks tough."

Ruffing was tough enough to welcome Ted into the big leagues by striking him out. (''He struck me out on a high sliding curveball. A hard curve, more like a slider. They didn't call it a slider then, but it wasn't a big breaking curveball.'')

Ted strode back to the bench, his head down, his bat dragging. ''This is the big leagues, Bush,'' Wilson said, not without sympathy.

Ted, studying Ruffing carefully, barely turned his head. ''That's Ruffing, huh?'' he said. ''He throws me that pitch again, and I'll hit it out of the park.'' The next time up, he lined a long double off the fence in right center, missing the home run he had promised himself by less than a foot. (''High fastball. I didn't hit it that good but it could have been a home run just as easy.'') When he got to second base Joe Gordon, whom he had played against on the Coast, asked him if he was nervous. ''Jesus, am I,'' Ted answered in a high-pitched, quavering voice.

Ruffing struck him out again in his next time at bat. (''I'm not sure whether he struck me out on the same pitch, but certainly both of them were high.'') In the ninth inning, Ruffing got him out on a pop to Gordon.

''Ruffing was one of the sneakiest pitchers I ever saw,'' Ted says, ''because he was a big guy, about six three and two hundred twenty pounds, and he just kind of flipped it at you, and it just—*phfffft*—at the last second came in.''

Ted had little to apologize for, though. With Ruffing pitching an easy 2–0 shutout, Ted had done at least as well as Foxx, Cronin, Vosmik, Cramer, Doerr, and a fellow rookie, Jim Tabor. Besides, it had been a dark, overcast day, and he knew now how Ruffing pitched. High fastballs across the letters were strikes in those days, and Ted had learned to murder them. It was only a matter of adjusting to Ruffing's motion and looking for that last-second swerve. He couldn't wait to face Ruffing again.

The Yankees weren't scheduled to play at Fenway Park until the end of May, which was unusual in those years. More often, the two teams played a home-and-home series in the first week of the season, or at least within the first two weeks. For purely dramatic reasons, it was just as well.

In the opener at Fenway Park, Ted had a single in five attempts as the Red Sox romped over Philadelphia, 9–2. In his third game, he had a double and a single. And if he also misjudged a fly ball that led to one of the A's runs, who cared?

It was on April 23, in the final game of that opening series with Philadelphia, that Ted Williams had his first great day.

In the first inning, with two men on, he belted a Luther Thomas fastball into the right-center-field bleachers. In 1939, the fence running from right to center field measured 400 to 420 feet from home plate, and only Babe Ruth, Lou Gehrig, and Cleveland's Hal Trosky had ever hit balls into that section before.

In the third inning, against Cotton Pippen, the same pitcher who had struck him out on his first time at bat as a pro, he missed another home run by inches when his long drive to straightaway center caromed off the top of the high center-field wall. He singled off Pippen in the fifth, and in the sixth, against lefty Edgar Smith, he lined another single into right.

A big eighth inning put the Athletics ahead, 12–8, so when Ted came to bat in the ninth, against Roy Parmelee, the fans were screaming for him to get another rally started. Ted tried awfully hard. He sliced a long fly ball into deep left center, but Bob Johnson pressed his back against the fence, reached high, and brought it down. "His every move was a signal for an ovation," wrote the *Herald*'s Burt Whitman, who had become Ted's greatest friend among the sportswriters.

A week later, as he was about to play his tenth game in the American League, Ted got his first look at Detroit's Briggs Stadium, the three-tiered stadium that was to become his "Field of Accomplishment." The Briggs Stadium right-field stands were only 325 feet from the plate at the foul line, but because the facade towers 120 feet above ground level, only one ball had ever been hit onto the roof. Nobody had ever hit one over it. Most people seem to believe that Ted reached the roof in the 1941 All-Star Game. He didn't. The All-Star homer bounced off the front facing of the third deck and was referred to in some of the write-ups as Williams's third longest homer in Briggs Stadium. The two longest were hit on successive times at bat on May 4, 1939, in the first game he ever played there.

He had driven out to the park early with Tommy Carey, a utility infielder, because he wanted to watch the two Tigers sluggers, Hank Greenberg and Rudy York, take early batting practice. (The next day, Greenberg came out early to watch Ted.)

On Ted's first time up, Greenberg was guarding first base, and Jim Bagby, Jr., of the harelip, yelled at Greenberg that he'd better move back. "Okay, Hank," Bagby lisped, after Ted had driven a monster of a foul fly. "If you want to look like me, stay right where you are."

"In the second inning," wrote Charles Ward of the *Detroit Times,* "Theodore Francis [*sic* 'em again] hit a high foul into the press box in right field before flying out. Few fouls ever have been hit where that of Theodore Francis dropped."

Up again in the fourth inning, with the Red Sox trailing 4–0, he hit a towering fly ball off Roxie Lawson that landed on the roof of the press box, at a point at least 360 feet from home plate. "I hope that guy is still pitching when I come up again," Ted said to catcher Rudy York as he crossed the plate.

Not quite. In the next inning, Ted came up with the score tied and Jimmy Foxx and Joe Cronin on base. Lawson was removed, and Bob Harris, a rookie who had given Ted lots of trouble a year earlier while pitching for the Detroit farm club in Toledo, was brought in to face him.

The count ran to three balls and no strikes, and Rudy York asked, "You wouldn't be swinging, would you?"

"You bet I am," Ted said.

This time the ball cleared everything—stands, roof, and all—to sail out of the premises near the foul line and slam against a building across the street. It was something nobody had ever done before. The longest ball, it was said, ever hit in Briggs Stadium.

Ted rounded the bases, the same way he would do in the All-Star Game, jumping up and down at first base and clapping his hands. When he reached third base, Billy Rogell said, "What the hell *you* been eating?"

As he crossed the plate, Rudy York said, "You weren't kidding, were you?"

From Detroit the Sox went to St. Louis. The Browns' new manager was Fred Haney, the same Fred Haney who had ordered Ted walked with men in scoring position in Toledo. (To make things even chummier, Haney's pitching coach was Ted's old manager Frank Shellenback.)

Fortunately perhaps for Ted, he came up with nobody on base. He hit another monstrous home run, a 450-foot drive, off a nondescript pitcher named Ed Cole.

On Memorial Day he was back in Fenway Park, to face Red Ruffing and the Yankees again. The crowd came early, filling the little park to its 35,000 capacity, with an estimated 50,000 turned away. And Ted did not disappoint them.

The teams split a doubleheader. Ted had one hit in each game. Both hits were home runs.

The home run off Ruffing landed twenty rows high in those distant stands in right center and was variously estimated at distances of from 460 to 500 feet. The discussion in the press box was about whether Babe Ruth had ever hit one that far in Fenway Park, and it was agreed that nobody except Ruth and Gehrig had ever come close. "The longest drive ever hit in Yawkey Yard," wrote Gerry Moore of the *Post*. Period.

In his first two months in the major leagues, he had hit five of the longest home runs anybody had ever seen. That was the kind of power he brought to Boston in his first year.

From the beginning, the Boston fans cheered his every hit, every catch, every move. He was patrolling the spacious area in right field because he had a strong arm in those days—that's right, a strong arm—

and the right-field bleachers immediately became the most joyous section of the park.

He was not only a baseball idol that first year; he was the city's pet. Kids would mob him outside the park, and he would occasionally round them up and take them on an excursion to Revere Beach. Looking like a big, gangling kid himself, he would ride the roller coaster and visit the fun house with them and fill them up with ice cream and hot dogs. He would, on an impulse, invite the whole clubhouse crew out for a day of fishing. He'd hire a boat and crew, supply the tackle, and order sandwiches, soda, and beer for the entire gang. "And you didn't see him calling up the newspapers to come and take pictures, either," Johnny Orlando, his buddy, said. "All I can say is he gave money away before he was ever in the big money."

He would get into conversations with taxi drivers, busboys, and firemen and bring them back to the clubhouse with him. One of his best friends was Sergeant John Blake of the Massachusetts State Police, whom he had met when Blake stopped him on the road to make a routine check of his car.

Ted lived in Foxboro then, about eighteen miles outside Boston, and he drove into the city every morning the Sox were at home by way of the Providence Turnpike. Blake, a motorcycle trooper patrolling the road, became curious about the bright green Buick with the California license plates. Ted explained the situation, and every day after that he took to waving at him as he drove by. One day he pulled up alongside Blake's motorcycle and asked, "Don't they ever give you a day off?" In the course of their brief conversation, Ted suggested that they have dinner together sometime. Blake said that would be fine, never expecting to hear from him again. Later in the week, Ted phoned Blake at headquarters, asked if he would be free that night, and told him he would pick him up. Blake, who had been a semipro athlete around Boston, began to spend his vacations fishing with Ted in the Florida Everglades, and during the baseball season he would take Ted to the state police pistol range for shooting practice.

It came in handy. Fenway Park had a problem with a cluster of pigeons who had set up housekeeping in the grandstand eaves. Ted would come out to the park early in the morning to pick the pigeons off, a sport that brought protests from the humane societies but delighted the average fan. Once, growing bored with the pigeons, he swung his rifle around to the scoreboard that runs across the bottom of Fenway's famous left-field wall and shot out the "ball," "strike," and "out" lights. The repair bill for that reportedly came to $400. Tom Yawkey got the money up without a murmur of protest, and once again the citizenry of Boston roared.

Everything Ted did in those early days delighted his public. Early in his second year, while he was deep in a batting slump, Ted visited an uncle who was a fireman in Yonkers, New York. They played checkers for three hours, talking baseball and reminiscing. Ted always went into black fits of melancholy when he was in a slump, and so when he reported to the ballpark the next afternoon he told a writer, "That's the life for you, being a fireman. You play checkers all day, and then you get a pension. It sure beats being a ballplayer." The story went over the news wires that Ted wanted to quit baseball and become a fireman, and for the rest of the year he heard the clanging of iron railings from the opposing dugout. Jimmy Dykes, the puckish White Sox manager, once dressed his bull-pen crew in fire helmets and rain slickers and supplied them with sirens and fire bells. Every time Ted came to bat, it sounded as if Chicago was burning to the ground again. Ted just grinned sheepishly through it all, as if to concede that he knew he had it coming. Besides, he was hitting again by then, and when Ted was hitting he was the jolliest guy in town.

The wackiest stunt Ted pulled in those happy early days was ducking out of the park between innings.

In his sophomore year, he had been switched to left field, presumably to protect his eyes from the right-field sun. It didn't take him long to learn that the operator of the scoreboard, directly behind him, had a teletype that brought in all the out-of-town scores, pitching changes, and that by the nature of the service all other baseball news, including home runs, came in too. Ted formed the habit of bending his ear to one of the scoreboard holes, just as he had in Minneapolis, to have the latest news passed on.

In the middle of one game, just as the Cleveland Indians were coming to bat, it suddenly became apparent that the left-field area was empty. The umpires scratched their heads and called to Cronin. Cronin sent someone to check the locker room and then went out to the scoreboard to ask the operator if he had seen any sign of his favorite conversationalist. Just as Cronin got there, Ted stepped out through the little door that leads from the field to the back of the scoreboard.

The papers reported, with amusement, that Ted had ducked out of the sun to pass the time of day with his invisible friend. Soon enough, in the mythology that was developing around his delightful eccentricities, the story became that he had clumped across the street to a hamburger joint to ask for a sandwich on the cuff—which was, in fact, a recycling of an old Rube Waddell story.

So popular was Ted that his onetime critic, Bill Cunningham, conducted a contest to find a suitable nickname for him. In flat defiance of the rules of all contests, however, Ted decided to call himself "the Kid"—the name that Johnny Orlando had hung on him on his first day in training camp—and took to talking about himself in the third person, in such wise as "The Kid sure belted one today, didn't he?" or "Just leave everything to the Kid, Tom, and there'll be nothing to worry about." (Tom, of course, was the Kid's good friend Tom Yawkey.)

Oh, it was great to be young and popular. It was great to be hitting big-league pitching beyond the fondest dreams of that not-so-happy twelve-year-old swinging a bat in his backyard—*whooooosh* . . . *whooooosh* . . . *whooooosh*—under the light of the moon.

Even Joe Cronin treated him with a special fondness and indulgence. Cronin would take a look over his shoulder to check his outfield during a crucial point in a game, and there would be his right-fielder taking private batting practice. Fortunately, Cronin himself had a great sense of showmanship. Once he even stopped a game and, mimicking Ted's swings, shouted, "Hey, Bush. Never mind this." Then, going through the motions of scooping up a ground ball, he yelled, "Practice this!"

Cronin's sense of showmanship was so finely honed that he occasionally liked to pump a little life into the late innings of hopelessly lost games by bringing in one of his hitting stars to pitch. Ted liked to throw a wide-sweeping curve while he was warming up along the sidelines before games, and with a minimum of coaxing he could be induced to hold forth about the loss baseball had suffered when his superior hitting ability had made it necessary for him to give up pitching. Late in Ted's second year—on August 24, 1940—Detroit was trouncing the Red Sox, 11–1, and the fans were beating a path to the exits. "Okay, Kid," Cronin said, during the Red Sox half of the seventh. "Let's see if you're as good as you say. I'm sending you in to pitch."

The umpires, assured that Ted had pitched before, permitted him to take the mound. The first Detroit batter, the weak-hitting shortstop, Frank Croucher, rapped a single off Jim Tabor's glove. Tommy Bridges, the Detroit pitcher, hit a ball back to Ted, though, and he threw to Tommy Carey, forcing Croucher. Pete Fox, a good hitter, grounded down the first-base line to Lou Finney, and Bridges was forced at second. Barney McCoskey, an excellent hitter, flied to Cramer in center. In the ninth inning, it looked as if disaster was about to strike when Mike Higgins singled to center and Hank Greenberg sent him to third with a wrong-way single to right. Ted got Rudy York on a called third strike. Buddy Myer hit a slow grounder to third, and Higgins scored while Myer was being thrown out. But Birdie Tebbetts hit back to Williams for the third out, and the Kid had won himself some bragging rights.

As popular as Ted was in his rookie year, there were a few minor skirmishes, the shadow of things to come.

He got off to a good start, faltered badly, and then came on after a couple of weeks to grab the league lead in runs batted in. Except for one inning, he held the lead—or a piece of it—to the wire. As happens so often when you are talking about Ted Williams, a story goes with it.

After the early barrage of record home runs, Ted went into such a severe slump that after two separate 2-for-21 streaks his batting average was down to .234. Although a 21-for-40 streak brought the average up to .306 by the All-Star break, he had been batting only .268 at the time the All-Star squad was picked. He had been moved all over the batting order. He batted sixth at the beginning of the season, was lifted to third, and then was dropped down to seventh. When he was finally moved into the cleanup spot, between Foxx and Cronin, he was ecstatic.

He was batting fourth when he threw his first big-league tantrum, in the opening game of a doubleheader in Chicago. He struck out, stamped his foot, sent his bat flying into the stratosphere, and slammed his fist into the air. As the Chicago fans booed, he took off his cap and made a derisive, exaggerated curtsy. Only the fast thinking of Cronin kept him in the game. When the plate umpire, Bill Summers, whipped off his mask, Cronin leaped between him and Ted, screaming "Busher!" and then grabbed Ted around the shoulders and walked him toward the bench, giving him hell as they went—and also giving Summers a chance to think things over. It was the closest that Ted came to being thrown out of a game in his entire career. (It didn't hurt any, of course, that Cronin and Summers were close friends.)

Later in the game, Ted kicked his glove as he was walking to his position in the outfield, a minor display of irritation which probably would have gone unnoticed if his toe hadn't caught the glove in such a way that if he had been on a football field he would have had a twenty-five-yard field goal.

After the game, Cronin took him aside in the locker room and tried a new approach. If he got a reputation for being a screwball, Cronin warned, the fans would hoot him for almost anything he did. "Right now everybody is pulling for you," Cronin said. "Keep 'em on your side."

"Aw, Joe," Ted said, "the fans love it. They've been cheering me as much as they cheer Foxx. Haven't you noticed?"

You figure him out.

The inning in which he briefly lost the RBI lead came in a game against the Athletics on August 8, at a time when Ted was in the worst slump of his life. Over a ten-game period he'd had only 3 hits in 29 times at bat. His batting average had fallen from .326 to .309, and his RBI production had suffered accordingly. During those same ten games Jimmy Foxx had gone on an extra-base rampage that had closed the once huge RBI gap between them and was threatening Ted's dream of becoming the first rookie ever to lead either league in that most important of batting categories.

On his first time up against the Athletics, Ted grounded to second and merely jogged down to first. On his next time up, he hit the left-field wall, with nobody on base, and slowed to a walk going into second. "Don't you want to play?" Cronin asked him, back on the bench. Ted hung his head and assured Cronin that he did.

In the fifth inning, Jimmy Foxx hit a two-run homer to pass Ted in the RBI race, 88–87.

In the sixth inning, as luck—or that great dramatist in the sky— would have it, Ted came to bat with the bases loaded and a chance to take the lead back. Instead, he hit a high fly ball to short center field. Hurling his bat away in disgust, he simply stood in the batting box until Cronin, who was in the on-deck circle, screamed at him to run. While Ted was jogging to first base contemplating the baseline, the As' shortstop, second baseman, and center-fielder were contemplating each other. The ball dropped between the three of them, and Ted found himself standing on first base—instead of on second. Cronin immediately yanked him from the base paths and made him sit on the bench to ponder the error of his ways. For the first time in his big-league career, Ted Williams heard the howls of wrath from the Boston fans. Ironically, two runs had scored on the fluke hit, and he had regained the RBI leadership.

The next morning Cronin called Ted into his office for another of their talks. During the course of that conversation, Cronin told him a story about how he, as a rookie, had insisted upon picking up an argument with an old umpire from earlier in the game. "I'm going to give you the best advice you're ever going to get," the umpire had told him. "Forget the last time at bat." If the lesson wasn't clear,

Cronin spelled it out for Ted. If he wanted to be a big-leaguer and a man, he had to learn how to accept the bitter with the sweet. "You can't sulk because things didn't go exactly the way you wanted them to."

Cronin always tended to play it by ear with Ted, to hold him under a very loose rein. "I pulled him out of the lineup to take the busher out of him," he confided a few years later. "But when Ted did things like that, he'd want to crawl into a hole the next minute. The worst possible punishment was to bench him. It killed him to have to sit on the bench."

No more than it killed Cronin to bench him. And so he didn't. Halfway through the first game of the doubleheader, Ted brought laughs and cheers from the stands by sprinting madly to first base after tapping back to the pitcher.

All through that long afternoon Ted and Foxx played out a drama for the RBI lead. In the opening inning of the first game, Foxx tripled in a run, to go back into a tie. He scored as Ted grounded out, putting Ted back out ahead. Foxxie then won the game with a home run in the eighth, and they were tied again.

In the second game, Foxx opened the fourth with a double, and Ted lined a single to right to score him and go back out in front.

In the fifth, Foxx came up with men on second and third and one out and—with a chance to retake the lead—was walked, loading the bases for Ted. His ground ball to second forced Foxx, but it also brought in a run that put Ted two ahead.

It was the same situation in the ninth. Tie game, men on first and third, and Jimmy Foxx coming to bat. Once again Connie Mack opted to walk Foxx and pitch to Williams.

"Just hit it, Kid," Foxx whispered in Ted's ear before he left the box. From the on-deck circle, Cronin was yelling, "You can do it!"

Ted flicked his wrists at the first pitch and sent the ball winging off the left-field wall. All he got out of it, of course, was a single and one run batted in. But he was three ahead in the RBI battle with Foxx, and he was—most certainly—out of Joe Cronin's doghouse and back in the good graces of the Boston fans.

Foxx made one more run at him. He was back to within one RBI of the Kid when he came to bat in the ninth inning of a game in Washington, with the bases loaded, two out, and the Sox losing, 6–4. Once again he walked. They were back in a tie, but now it was Ted up with the bases loaded. And Ted hit a grand-slam home run (the first of seventeen for him), to become the first major-leaguer to reach 100 RBI.

His big burst of power came on the next road trip when he hit a three-run homer against Cleveland to win one game, a second grand-slam the next day to keep his team in contention, and another three-run homer in Detroit the day after that.

A week later, he ran into the right-field wall at Yankee Stadium and bruised his wrist. At first, it was feared that Williams was through for the season. He was back four days later to hit two home runs, two triples, and a single in Philadelphia.

As hot as the Kid was, Joe DiMaggio was hotter. The Williams-DiMaggio competition had begun, and the prize was the RBI title.

Except for one brief period in July, the season itself was not competitive. But in that one brief period of his rookie season, Ted Williams participated in one of the most celebrated series in Red Sox history, the five-game sweep of the Yankees in Yankee Stadium.

The Yankees finished at 106–45 (.702), which placed them alongside the 1927 team as the only American League teams to finish above .700.

The Red Sox came in second again, a distant seventeen games behind, and yet it was the Red Sox who prevented them from going into the record book as the most winning team of all time. And did it in the most dramatic of fashions by winning seven straight games—and nine games out of ten—over the second half of the season. The glory belongs to Joe Cronin. Over the seven-game streak, Cronin knocked in 14 runs. Over the full ten games he drove in 20 runs. But Ted Williams was hardly a passive observer.

By the first of July, the Yankees had not only run off to a 13½-

game lead, but they had managed to do it for the most part without Joe DiMaggio, who had missed five weeks because of a torn ligament.

After a three-game series in Boston and the five-game sweep in New York, the Red Sox had ignited the city of Boston by cutting it down to 6½ games.

The Red Sox took the first two games by beating the Yankee aces, Red Ruffing and Lefty Gomez. "Isn't that Ruffing nice to hit against?" the cocky rookie had been asking incredulous players and sportswriters. This time, Ted belted a long triple and scored two runs.

As well as Ted hit Ruffing, he hit Lefty Gomez even better. Gomez, who wasn't called "Goofy" for nothing, had one of the best curve balls in baseball but insisted on trying to blow his fastball past Ted in the clutch. ("Speed didn't bother me but the delivery and the way the ball acted, that's what made it tough for me. Gomez would give me the big high-kick fastball. Fastball, fastball, fastball, and it always moved the same.")

Ted came up in the eighth inning with two men on, and the score tied. The count ran to 3–1, and Gomez backed off the mound to watch an airplane flying overhead, one of the many eccentricities for which he had become famous. When he stepped back in, he gave Ted the big leg kick and Ted hit a 3-run homer.

Three days later, he was sitting in the stands at Yankee Stadium, on an off day, watching Lou Gehrig deliver his "I'm the luckiest man in the world" speech. The five-game series began the next day. Which does bring up the possibility that the Red Sox were sweeping a team that was in a complete emotional funk.

In the first game, Ted had two more hits off Ruffing, knocked in the run that gave the Sox a 3–2 lead in the fifth, and then scored the winning run in the eighth after opening the inning with a single.

In the second game, he had two singles and a double and knocked in the winning run in a 3–1 victory.

In Game 4, he scored one run after walking in front of Cronin's game-winning home run in a 4–3 victory.

Game 5: With the Red Sox achieving their sweep by means of a 5–3 victory, he singled and scored in the middle of an early two-run rally.

Over the five games, Ted had 6 for 16. DiMaggio had 10 for 20, lifted his average to .435, and knocked in five of the Yankees' 12 runs.

By the time they faced each other again, two months later, in a weekend series in September, the Yankees' lead was back up to 13½ games. Joe DiMaggio was batting .420 and riding a hot streak that had lifted him to within five RBIs of Williams, in 103 fewer times at bat.

Ruffing had come to Boston sporting a 20–4 record and leading the league in everything. Three of his four losses had been handed to him by the Red Sox. On Saturday, they made it four out of five. Once again, Ted laced him for three hits, including a double, scored three runs, and knocked in another.

For Ruffing, it was something close to a career-shattering defeat, as, inexplicably, Joe McCarthy left him in over the full nine innings to take a 12–7 shellacking that cost him both the pitching and ERA titles. Never again was Ruffing going to be the same pitcher. By 1941, McCarthy was no longer using him against the Red Sox.

In the opening game of the Sunday doubleheader, Ted had a double and walked four times in a wild 12–11 victory.

The second game has gone down in Red Sox history as the Forfeit Game, because the game was temporarily forfeited when the unruly Boston crowd showered the field with garbage to protest the Yankees' attempt to beat the Sunday curfew after taking a lead in the top half of the eighth.

After Williams and Cronin had hit back-to-back home runs to put the Red Sox on the road to eight straight, Joe DiMaggio tied it with a two-run homer (his 25th), and Ted put the Sox back ahead with another homer (his 24th). Altogether, Williams knocked in four of the Sox runs in the 5–5 tie.

When DiMaggio left Boston he was batting .410 with only 27 games left in the season but he was now trailing Ted in the RBI race, 124–116. A week later, DiMag suffered a severe infection in his left eye that brought both his chase after the RBI title and his quest for a .400 average to an end.

As for Ted, he had five home runs against the Yankees, all of them in Fenway Park. Yankee Stadium remained the only park where he had not hit a home run.

His last chance came on the final day of the season.

In the final game, he hit his 31st home run to hand Steve Sundra, who had come into the game with an 11−0 record, his first defeat of the season.

Ted Williams had become the first rookie to lead the league in RBI. His figures at the end of the year were .327-31-145. In his final 45 games, less than a third of the season, he hit 14 of his 31 home runs. All in all, an incredible rookie season, possibly the greatest rookie season ever, veteran sportswriters like the *Boston American's* Joe Cashman were arguing.

In the balloting for the Most Valuable Player, he finished fourth behind Joe DiMaggio, Bob Feller, and Jimmy Foxx. Before he was through he was going to win the MVP award twice and finish second four times. If it were not for the souring of his relationship with the Boston press he would have won at least one more time. Of that there is no doubt whatsoever.

VII

The Kid Versus
the Press

I thought I was doing pretty good in 1940, I ended up hitting .344, and I got booed right out of the park because I wasn't breaking Babe Ruth's record. They were pitching differently to me, and I was having a hard time although I finished third in hitting. The press was on me because I wasn't driving in runs. I still drove in one hundred runs, but I still wasn't doing enough, and I got a little burned over that. Then they started writing personal things, and that's all water over the dam, and I shouldn't have taken it quite as seriously, but it affected me. It hurt.

—TED WILLIAMS,
at a press conference on Ted Williams Day
at Fenway Park, May 12, 1991

Tom Yawkey had decided to do something about that distant right-field fence, which was only 302 feet down the foul line but jutted out immediately to 380 feet and then ran on a big curve from 400 feet in right center to 420 feet at the flagpole in center field. He did it by constructing a bull pen that cut all those distances by 20 feet. It was still a mighty blow, of course, and still the least inviting target in the league. But fence moving had not yet become an accepted form for advancing the fortunes of the home team, and for some reason it seemed to offend a lot of people.

As if to accommodate Ted Williams even further, the Red Sox had got rid of Joe Vosmik and moved Ted to left field, presumably to protect his eyes from the sun and give him a minimum amount of territory to cover. Both desirable ends, to be sure, but not the real reason. Dom DiMaggio was joining the club that year, and with Doc Cramer still in center field, it was only common sense to play Dom, with his tremendous range and great arm, in right.

The problem, once the season got under way, was that Ted was not hitting the ball into that newly constructed bullpen. "I was not concerned about the fence in my first season," Ted insists, "because I was concentrating upon trying to figure out the pitchers." Well, over the winter the pitchers had been concentrating on him. "In the second year, they were throwing me slow, breaking stuff on the corners. They were pitching me tougher and tougher, and I had to figure out how to adjust.''

One of the reasons he wasn't getting anything good to hit, he had come to feel, was because Cronin had very quickly shuffled him up to the number-three spot in the batting order and dropped Jimmy Foxx down to fourth. What he was trying to do, Cronin explained, was to protect Ted the way Ted had previously been protecting Foxx. That wasn't the way Ted saw it, though. The way Ted saw it, the RBI potential was being handed over to Foxx and perhaps even more to Cronin himself, who was batting fifth.

When the Red Sox went on their first western trip of the season, in mid-May, Ted was hitting .317. But he had hit only two home runs, had only thirteen runs batted in, and was in such a deep sulk that even Tom Yawkey was letting it be known that he was sick and tired of watching him go through the motions in the field. Unfortunately, the first two games in Detroit, where Ted had always come alive, were rained out, giving him plenty of time to sit around the hotel and brood. In the final two games of the series, he did have four hits in seven times at bat, but they were all singles. In the field, he was no longer even going through the motions.

The scene was set. On May 21, on the train ride from Detroit to Cleveland, Joe Cronin told Harold Kaese of the *Boston Transcript* that Ted was going to be benched. Not because of any failure to hit, Cronin emphasized, but because of his loafing in the field. ''I don't want him to get that kind of a reputation,'' Cronin told Kaese, for attribution. ''Even some of his teammates are fed up with him.''

You bet they were. Lefty Grove was saying that if Ted didn't hustle after the ball when he was pitching, he was going to punch him on the nose. Joe Heving, who had seen it all before, said, ''Instead of killing them with his bat, he's killing us in the field.''

Well, Cronin didn't bench Ted in Cleveland, but Kaese, unwilling to give up an exclusive, ran with the story anyway. After he had quoted Cronin, Kaese accused Ted of being jealous of Foxx, criticized him for complaining that Fenway Park was killing him, and condemned him for his "extreme selfishness, egoism and lack of courage." Tough stuff, to be sure, but well within the limits of fair comment. But then, to give himself a tag line, he wrote: "Whatever it is, it probably traces to his upbringing. Can you imagine a kid, a nice kid with a nimble brain not visiting his father and mother all of last winter."

The column hit Boston like a bombshell, and the other papers moved in swiftly to get a piece of it. It was on that day that the carnivorous Boston sports press was born. Until then, it had been the practice of the sportswriters to hold their stories for a gentlemanly three days in order to protect each other. From then on, they were ordered to hand their stories in immediately. Pool reportage was banned. New writers coming in from other cities were astonished to find that they were not only in competition with the other papers, but were also competing with the writers from their own paper.

And do you know what the real irony of it was? The irony was that Kaese, having second thoughts, had tried to kill that tag line. The *Transcript,* an old-line Brahmin paper that was read mostly for its financial coverage, was in such dire financial straits itself that the writers traveling with the ball clubs had been instructed to airmail their stories, rather than wire them. In order to make his copy appear more timely, Kaese would then wire in a fresh lead the next morning. With the Williams story, Kease had appended a request to omit the reference to Ted and his parents. And the makeup man did pull the offending type out of the story. What happened then was that the sports editor saw the deleted stick of type hanging on the rack, thought it was part of the updated Kaese material, and shoved it back in.

Kaese apologized to the livid Williams the next day. Ted heard out the explanation with a tight smile. He accepted the apology. He never forgot that the offensive passage had been both written and printed.

Another irony was that Harold Kaese was a cerebral and generally responsible writer. He had been a great all-around athlete in high school and college, and at the time he wrote the story he was the national squash champion. He was also a Shakespearean scholar. Like Ted, he was a loner and, like Ted, was devoted to his work. Throughout Ted's career he kept unbelievably detailed statistics on every conceivable aspect of Ted's hitting.* To the end of his days Harold Kaese felt guilty about that long-ago column which he knew had been grossly unfair to Ted.

None of that mattered. When Ted came to Boston, he walked into the middle of a vicious circulation war. Boston had four morning papers, the *Record,* the *Globe,* the *Herald* and the *Post,* and four afternoon papers, the *Transcript,* the *American,* the *Globe,* and the *Traveler.* And that didn't count the *Christian Science Monitor,* a national paper. With subscription sales relatively low, each paper had to hook its customers on the run, which they did by means of the big black headline and the sensational story. Ted Williams was colorful, controversial, spectacular. His name on the front page sold papers. And for twenty years Ted Williams was a front-page rather than a sports-page figure in Boston.

A second front-page story hit in August. With the season two-thirds over, he was batting .336 but had hit only thirteen home runs and knocked in only seventy-one runs, and he was snapping at writers in the locker room and arguing with fans on the field. Sent home from New York with a pulled muscle in his back, he proceeded to pour out his frustrations to Austen (Duke) Lake, the lead columnist for the *American.* Lake caught him, worse luck, sitting alone in the dugout on a dreary, rainy day.

"I've asked Yawkey and Cronin to trade me away from Boston," Ted told Lake. "I don't like the town. I don't like the people, and the newspapermen have been on my back all year. Why? They pay you on your record. The bleachers can boo, the newspapermen can sneer, but right out there in the field is where you get the dough or not, and I'm going to get mine."

---

* See Appendix E. The full compilation of Kaese's statistical breakdowns can be found in the remarkably good coffee-table book *Ted Williams: A Portrait in Words and Pictures* by Dick Johnson and Glenn Stout.

Was he speaking on the record? Lake asked. "That's how I feel about it," Ted said. "You can print the whole rotten mess just as I said it. I want to get out of town, and I'm praying that they trade me."

The blood was in the water again, and the sports editors were screaming for quotes from Ted's teammates. "He's a spoiled child," Jimmy Foxx said, summing it up for all of them.

When Ted rejoined the team in Washington, on the final day of the road trip, Joe Cronin cocked an eye at him and said, "Ted, what the hell did you start all that for?"

"Don't worry, Skip," Ted told him. "I'll hit .400 when we get home, and they'll forget all about it."

He did better than that. Ted always hit when he was coming back from an injury, and he always went on a hitting rampage when he was being hammered by the press. Put them together, and he proceeded to hit a home run in each of three straight games against the Yankees—including yet another massive drive off Ruffing—and ran off a string of fourteen hits in twenty-eight times at bat, including another home run.

On the season, he hit .344, trailing only Joe DiMaggio and Luke Appling. But he had only 23 home runs and knocked in only 113 runs, the lowest he would ever be in both categories. Still, he was third in slugging percentage, behind a couple of guys named Greenberg and DiMaggio, and led the league in runs scored. He was also far ahead in On Base Percentage, a category that was not in use yet and in which he was going to be revealed retroactively to be supreme.

But the relationship with the Boston press had been set. When an AP story came out of San Diego reporting that it had been Ted who had sold the furniture out from under his mother, the Boston papers picked it up and gave it a big play, despite the fact that every sports editor in the city had enough background material to know that it had been his brother. And whether they were punishing him for not being more cooperative, or were just using him to sell newspapers, what difference did that make to Ted?

A year later, when Ted's draft status was changed from 1-A to 3-A, because he was claiming his mother as a dependent, one of the Boston papers sent a private investigator to San Diego to check on May Williams's standard of living, and another sent reporters onto the street to ask casual passersby to pass judgment on Ted's patriotism.

Some years later, reporters were sent onto the streets to conduct a similar poll when Ted was caught fishing in the Everglades while his wife, in Boston, was giving birth to a premature baby daughter. (Ted had met Doris Soule, the daughter of his hunting guide, in Minnesota. She had followed him to Boston, and they were married on May 4, 1944, the day Ted received his wings as a naval lieutenant.) The baby was born on January 28, 1948. According to the Red Sox front office, she arrived two weeks early. The newspapers took the view that Ted should have been there anyway.

He flew back to Boston five days later, and as he got off the plane a reporter asked what had taken him so long. "Look," Ted answered, "this is my baby and my life. But I'll answer your question. The first I heard about it was six o'clock that night. That was ten hours after the baby was born. I tried to get a plane reservation, but couldn't get one until the one I got out of Miami last night." Asked whether he thought the delay would affect public opinion, he took the bait: "To hell with the public. They can't run my life." What, he was asked, were his immediate plans? The answer, to anybody aware of Ted's image of himself as a man indifferent to public opinion, was predictable. He planned to visit briefly with his wife and daughter, he said, and then return to Miami. "This place is too cold for me, and besides the fishing is great."

To this point, the New York press had been relatively silent. But the report of this interview brought forth a blast from Paul Gallico, in the form of one of those open letters that columnists love to write. "You are not a nice fellow, Brother Williams," wrote Gallico. "I do believe that baseball and the sports pages would be better off without you."

Nor was Gallico buying Ted's excuse about the five-day delay. "Oh come, Ted. The great Williams couldn't get a plane out of Miami to return to his wife's bedside? Don't give us that. Any airline would have made room for you or flown you up in the pilot's cockpit if you really wanted to come. . . .

"But, you see, where you are wrong in saying that the public cannot run your life is that we can. For I am a part of that public and I would no longer invest ten cents to see you ply your trade because I have an aversion to finding myself in the same enclosure with a self-confessed mucker, and, particularly, parting with money for the privilege. . . .

"When, oh, when will you thick-headed athletes catch on that the public is your darling, that you may not disillusion us, that you cannot live as other men but dwell in glass houses and that this is the price you pay for wealth and success?"

Gallico was wrong on every count except one. The public was not Ted's darling. On the contrary, Ted was the public's darling. The public continued to woo him, and the more Ted scorned them, the more avidly they pursued him. Gallico was never going to invest another dime to see Williams play? "Oh, come on, Paul," Ted might well have responded. Gallico had never paid his way into a ballpark in his life. The public did pay its way into the park to see Ted Williams. For years, he was about the only player the public would pay to see. Baseball is one of the few pursuits, Gallico notwithstanding, where public opinion and public relations mean absolutely nothing. If you produce, you play. If you produce well enough, long enough, you make yourself a ton of money. If you don't produce, you can make every roll call and you'll still end up back in Peoria.

Where Gallico was correct, however, was in ridiculing Ted's claim that it had taken him five days to book a flight out of Miami. And every Boston sportswriter knew it. Harold Kaese, who had gone to the *Globe* after the *Transcript* folded, had been able to reach Ted in the Everglades and he had in his possession a damning interview. Although Kaese didn't print it—his guilt over the earlier story was evidently still there—he did distribute mimeographed copies around the press box. The first few exchanges went like this:

Reporter: Hello, Ted. This is the *Globe*.

Williams: Yuh.

Reporter: Have you been able to get a reservation to Boston?

Williams: Haven't tried.

Reporter: Aren't you coming up to see the baby?

Williams: For Christ sake! What could I do up there?

Reporter: Were you disappointed that it was a girl?

Williams: Nope.

Reporter: Then you didn't care?

Williams: I didn't give a shit.

Reporter: How's the fishing?

Williams: Pretty good.

Reporter: I didn't get you up, did I?

Williams: Hell, no.

Ted's only support came from a wholly unexpected quarter. Dave Egan, usually his most vituperative critic, wrote: "The hottest controversy of the moment, and I may add, the most despicable controversy of recent years, now revolves around the head of Ted Williams. It seems that his wife has had a wee baby, here in Boston, while he was fishing in Florida. This was sufficient to send one alleged columnist out into the streets, to interview several persons on the subject: Resolved, that Ted Williams should have been pacing the hospital corridors when his firstborn made her world premiere. It was sufficient to induce the city rooms of three newspapers to make needling calls to him, and subsequently inform the public that he did not know the hospital in which his wife was bedded and had no immediate intention of flying there.

"This, dear friend, is what is known as yellow journalism at its very dirtiest. It is an invasion of the domestic life of Ted Williams, his wife, and his child. It is an action which trifles cruelly with the happiness of a family, just for the sake of a headline. It neither achieves nor aims at anything constructive. It is simply an attempt to put Williams in the grease."

Egan had come to Ted's defense one other time when he was being attacked as a private citizen rather than as a ballplayer. That was during one of the worst periods of Ted's life, the weeks and months before he joined the Naval Reserve.

While he was hitting .406 in 1941, Ted earned a salary of $12,500—the same salary he had received the previous year. When he reported to spring-training camp in March 1942, the country was three months into World War II, and the draft had been functioning for well over a year.

Major league ballclubs were soon to learn that all their ballplayers had become targets, because families all over the country were unwilling to accept the drafting of their sons while big-league athletes—the symbol of virile, sweating manhood—remained free to collect their relatively high salaries.

As soon as he began to make decent money as a big-league player, Ted had established a trust fund for his mother, to ensure her future. Because she was financially dependent on him, he had been classified 3-A in the draft. With the attack on Pearl Harbor, however, the entire draft system was overhauled, and Ted was reclassified 1-A, or available for immediate induction. In accordance with the regulations, Ted requested a review of his reclassification by the National Selective Service Board, which agreed that, according to the law, his 3-A deferment should not have been changed.

The ruling came down in early March. Immediately Ted flew to Sarasota, reported to the Boston locker room, and made himself available to the press. "I've got nothing to cover up," he said. "Ask anything you want. Nothing is going to be off the record. I've just made the most important decision of my life. I know that. If I didn't think I was justified in asking for reclassification, I wouldn't have done it. If I hadn't done it, I wouldn't have been doing right by my mother. If I wasn't sure of that, I couldn't steel myself to face all the abuse I'm encouraging." Well aware that such abuse would be forthcoming, he emphasized that nobody in the Red Sox front office had advised him to appeal. "Without saying so, they really advised against it. So don't blame anybody except me. It was my own decision and nobody else's.

"I'll tell you frankly why I need to try to make a few bucks before I go," he continued. "I didn't break even the first year with the Red Sox. I had to spend on my obligations more than I earned. I pulled even at the end of my second year. This year I saved a few bucks, but not enough to take care of my mother. When I get her fixed, I'm going to enlist. Until then, I'm going to do my darnedest to do a good job playing for the Red Sox. And if the fans want to yell at me for what I've done, I've simply got to take it. That's all there is to it."

The abuse came, as anticipated, from the very beginning of the season. In one game, he was being ridden so hard by a group of loud-mouthed fans in the left-field grandstand that he decided, by his own curious form of logic, to get back at them by deliberately striking out. His old buddy Jack Wilson was pitching for Washington, and Ted— barely bothering to swing—missed Wilson's first two pitches. What he was doing was so obvious that umpire Bill McGowan, who always seemed to be behind the plate at crucial moments in Ted's career, warned him that if he took a deliberate third strike he would be thrown out of the game, fined, and probably suspended. With wonderful malice, Ted then decided he would try to stuff the baseball down the throat of one of the fans in the left-field clique. On the first attempt he drove a whistling liner right into the section he had been aiming at. On his next attempt, alas, his aim was off. The ball dropped just inside the foul line, and he had to be content with a base hit. Cronin fined him $250, although it was never made clear whether it was because of those first two feeble swings or because loudmouthed fans were deemed to be out of season. It didn't really matter, because Cronin rescinded the fine a few days later after Ted had won a game with a late-inning home run.

The patriots in the outfield stands continued to blister him. One young kid was so vituperative, during a Sunday doubleheader, that a sportswriter went out and interviewed him. The boy, with tears in his eyes, said that his brother had been killed at Pearl Harbor and that he was bitter at anybody as obviously fit for battle as Ted Williams who ducked the call of his country. The reporter, smelling a good story, checked with the boy's parents to get the full details of the brother's heroic death. There was no such brother, he discovered. The kid who was doing all the screaming was an only child.

Still, abusive mail continued to come in by the bushel basket. In the interests of national security, one guy sent him a daily letter with nothing inside but a piece of yellow paper, blank.

Despite those first defiant words, the abuse got to him so quickly that by the time the Red Sox were ready to leave on their first eastern swing, he had made up his mind to go ahead and enlist in the Navy. When he failed to show up at the railroad station with the rest of the team, general manager Eddie Collins rushed to his room at the Shelton Hotel. He found Ted there, sunk in a big armchair, fly-casting out the hotel window. He had not even packed his bags.

"I'm through with baseball," Ted told Collins. "To hell with everything. I'm going to enlist. I can't take any more of it." Rewinding his rod, he said angrily, "If I could have just paid three more installments on my mother's trust fund, she'd have been all set."

But Collins was able to talk him out of enlisting immediately. "You just get packed and go to the station, and don't worry about anything except playing ball. Forget the trust fund. The Red Sox will take care of it. If you're called tomorrow, the fund will be all paid up. If you let them ride you into the service, they'll be riding every other ballplayer in, too. When the government wants you, they'll let you know, don't worry about that."

Ted's dilemma was ended by Whitey Fuller, a onetime publicity director for Dartmouth College, who had become a recruiting officer for the Naval Air Corps. Fuller approached Ted and Johnny Pesky and suggested that they join the Naval Air Corps Reserve as second-class seamen.

Most of the Boston columnists, their own patriotism aflame, had been castigating Ted for applying for the deferment. Dave Egan, almost alone, had been a voice for the defense. Ted's draft status, he wrote again and again, was a private matter between Ted Williams and his draft board. Instead of trying to drum Ted into the service, he wrote, "the patrioteers should examine their own consciences."

Before Ted and Pesky were able to sign up officially with the reserve, the Sox had to leave on a long western trip. The day they returned, Ted phoned Egan, told him what he was about to do, and invited him to accompany him to the recruiting office. "Because," he said, "I want you to have an exclusive on it." The story, an across-the-board headliner in Boston, was Egan's and Egan's alone.

There is a significance to this that goes beyond Ted's relations with Egan to his relations with the press as a whole. Ted was forever crying that his hatred for the Boston press went to the interference in his private affairs. Yet Egan, who championed Ted through both of his private crises, was the newsman he came to hate above all others.

Egan attacked Williams on his ability in the clutch and on his value to the team, and Ted, despite his disclaimers, could not bear to be attacked on any grounds at all. Egan accused Ted of being completely selfish, jealous of the success of various teammates, more interested in fishing than in baseball, and greedy for money. He went so far as to accuse Ted of contributing to juvenile delinquency because he refused to wear a tie or tip his hat, thereby encouraging the youth of the city to rebel against the established rules of society.

If good writing can cover a multitude of sins, then Dave Egan came equipped with a protective mantle. He was a writer who could draw blood from the hide of a rhinoceros, and he could do it with that most lacerating of weapons, humor. His job was to stir the glands of controversy—some would say the bowels—seven times a week, and he succeeded to the extent that he was Boston's most read, most cursed, most revered, and most discussed sportswriter.

If there had been no Joe DiMaggio on the scene for Ted Williams to be compared with, balanced off, and weighed against, his place in baseball would not have been quite as magnified. And if there had been no Dave Egan around to poke, prod, and beat up on him, his relationship with both the press and the city of Boston would not have been quite the same, either. It was Ted's luck, good or bad, that in both instances he was pitted against a champion of the craft.

Egan was a Harvard graduate with a law degree. He had completed his undergraduate work in three years and had gone through law school in two, working his way by playing the piano in a strip joint in Scollay Square and by writing brilliant baseball columns for the *Globe*.

His first sportswriting career came to an end when he became either a drunk or a drug addict, depending on whom you talk to—an addiction he apparently picked up after the *Globe* switched him to that other sink of corruption, boxing. He was a falling-down drunk when Sam Cohen, the brilliant sports editor of the *Record*, picked him out of the gutter, cleaned him up—he was a scrawny, ratty-looking guy by then—and brought him in to write for the *Record*, under the cognomen of "The Colonel." Between them, Cohen, the great idea man, and Egan, the great writer, were keeping the little Hearst tabloid alive. "What did the Colonel write?" was the query that came to be heard as often around Boston street corners of an evening as "What did Ted do?"

Egan had two prime distinguishing characteristics. He could turn a phrase and he had the integrity of an alley cat. For such a man, the *Record* provided a most congenial setting. Item: Egan was allowed to work as the publicity man for Rockingham Park racetrack at the same time as he was showering its owner with an almost weekly column of shameless praise. Horseracing wasn't the only sports promotion that was paying off, and Egan wasn't the only prominent figure on the sports page, if you get the picture, who was getting paid.

When Egan would show up half crocked and bereft of any idea, Cohen would feed him a subject ("Blast Williams" was the hardy perennial) and Egan would sit at his typewriter and knock it out. When Egan was off on a binge, drying out at Dropkick Murphy's, or had come in too drunk to type, one of the other writers would be called upon to whack out a rough imitation. Among the press contingent, there was a sometimes lively debate over which of the other *Record* writers did the best Egan.

Egan and Cohen dealt in heroes and villains. Ted Williams was both berated and praised. Sam Cohen would say, "Egan will criticize Williams two times and praise him three times. He never forgets the rips, and he never remembers the nosegays." But that wasn't exactly the way Ted saw it. "If he writes nine bad columns and then one good one, I don't see why I'm supposed to forget the nine bad ones."

I once discussed his anti-Williams stance with Egan. For his part, Egan said, he was suitably grateful that Ted had helped him become so controversial and so successful a writer, and he saw no reason why Ted shouldn't be equally grateful in return. Egan was strongly inclined toward the belief that Ted knew perfectly well that the controversy brought money into the box office and thereby added its little weight toward keeping him the game's leading money-winner. It was Egan's belief, therefore, that Ted's show of anger was just an act—his own small contribution toward keeping the controversy alive and prosperous.

Which only showed how little Egan really knew about him. "That goddamn drunk from the *Record!*" Ted exploded after I had passed on Egan's theory to him. "He don't bother me." I had always thought that the expression about somebody being so mad that the vein in his neck was standing out was nothing more than a nice poetic allusion. Which only shows how little I knew about poetic allusions. The big vein in Ted's neck was indeed standing out. The big vein in his neck was throbbing. "I don't know what that goddamn drunk writes about me," he shouted. "I never read him. He don't bother me none."

It is to laugh. Listen to an old Red Sox hand: "Didn't bother him, huh? Ted would cite you chapter and verse, call off the season and the dates of almost everything Egan had written about him. Listen, it's getaway day, and Ted did not have a good game. They get on a train to go to Detroit, the paper comes out in Boston, and somebody gets ahold of Ted. 'Here's what Egan said about your performance yesterday,' and reads it off to him. And now Ted proceeds to have a hell of a series in Detroit. Right away, he's on the phone to Boston. 'What did the sonofabitch write about me today? Did he write I got four hits and knocked in five runs?' Not a word. That's what killed Ted. 'The bastard never gave me credit when I did anything, and he's ready to chop me any time I didn't have a good day.' This is years later that he's telling me this. 'That sonofabitch, the next time he wrote about me was when I did something wrong.'''

But then, Ted was always denying that he read somebody or other. Usually it was somebody or other he had quoted extensively five minutes earlier. The fact was that Ted always read every newspaper in town, plus any New York papers that were on sale in his hotel lobby. Through some sort of sixth sense or through word from friends, he also managed to get hold of and read every magazine article about him.

His ability to smell out any mention of himself was always a source of great amusement to his teammates. Jackie Jensen, in particular. Whenever there was a back-page headline about Ted, Jensen would place the newspaper on the table in the locker room in such a way that the headline would be almost upside down. Ted would come through the door, pass the table, and then stop, as if vibrations from the paper had reached out to him. He would go back, pick up the paper, carry it to his locker at the far corner of the room and sit there, fully dressed, until he had read and reread the story to his satisfaction.

When George Sullivan, who had been a Red Sox batboy in 1949, became a sportswriter, Ted told him, ''Lots of bastards in your trade, and some in mine, too. There's only one guy I hold it in for. If somebody came through that green door over there''—pointing to the entrance—''and said Dave Egan just dropped dead, I'd look at that sonofabitch and I'd say, Good!''

He was not dealing in hyperbole. ''I think he would have lost control of himself if Egan ever showed up,'' Bob Holbrook says. ''There were other writers he didn't like. Egan was the one he truly hated.''

Jim Tabor did lose control of himself after Egan wrote that Tabor's appendectomy was the best thing that had happened to the Red Sox all year. Tried to strangle him or throw him out of the press box, whichever came first.

The day Tabor came out of the hospital, Cronin sent him up to the press box to get him out of the way. The press box at Fenway Park sat high on the roof, looking almost like an elongated diner. As luck would have it, Egan, in one of his rare visits to the ballpark, was standing on the ramp directly in front of the door, talking to an old UPI guy, Jimmy Bagley, as Tabor walked up. "I'd like you to meet a writer who's a great admirer of yours," said the devilish Bagley. "Meet Dave Egan."

"You!!" Tabor screamed, as he made a lunge for him. Grabbing Egan by the throat, Tabor drove him up the steps and through the press box and had him bent over the railing above the batting screen, screaming in terror, before Eddie Collins was able to rush over and pull Tabor away. It was, they say, the last time Egan was seen at the ballpark.

And that was something Ted was always quick to point out too. "The guys that have to come back every day and look me in the eye, I don't have any trouble with them. It's the columnists, like Egan and Austen Lake, who don't come to a game five times a year and don't come to the dugout once a year, they're the bastards who go after me."

His bastard quotient was always subject to the whims of change. At times he'd shake his fist and shout, "The world's worst. No question about it, they're absolutely the world's worst. Not everybody, now. One or two of them are all right. But on the whole, the world's worst." At other times he'd extend five fingers and say, "There's that many bastards." And then, clenching and unclenching his hand some half a dozen times, "And there's that many right guys."

It was not a one-way street, by any means. If the writers had the last word in the public print, Ted was in total control of the day-to-day relationship. "I might walk into the dressing room," Clif Keane says. "He might say, 'Did you see the fight last night, Clif? Hell of a fight.' He might look at me and say, 'What the hell smells around here?'" Ted thought that was hilarious. He'd come into the dugout, sniff at the air, and say, "Something smell here? Did somebody shit in here? Oh, never mind. It's only the sportswriters."

When he was being photographed with a sportswriter, after what had seemed to be a pleasant interview, he might lay his hand in the crack of his elbow in a way that would prevent the picture from ever being printed. Haw! Unless, of course, the gesture wasn't caught by the picture editor. That was even better.

He could be holding an amiable conversation around the batting cage when a glaze would suddenly come over his eyes and he would bray into the empty air, "They ought to keep writers away from the batting cage, we ought to do something about that. What have we got a players' association for anyway?" If the writers got the impression that Ted was really trying to say that they also ought to keep the writers out of the dugout, out of the park, and maybe even out of the country, then that was exactly the impression he wanted them to get.

And yet . . . despite his protestations, Ted was always unhappy when he was being ignored by his blood enemies, the sportswriters. "When things got too quiet," one of them says, "you could always count on Teddy boy to do something to get himself back in the headlines."

In Ted's first year season after his service in Korea, Jimmy Piersall came to town and took the play away from Ted by both his insane antics and his sensational fielding. The fans' eyes were on Piersall. The fans' cheers and jeers were for Piersall. The sports pages were filled with Piersall. For once Ted was just another guy in a baseball uniform, a member of the supporting cast. So what did Ted do? In the final game of the season, he laid a bunt down the third-base line and beat it out—an event guaranteed to push anything short of a world war off the Boston front pages.

When the Red Sox established a curfew for writers, limiting both their pre-game and post-game access, the newspapers could have quashed it within twenty-four hours simply by refusing to print anything about the team except for the box score. The sports editors did meet with the management, and their protests were passed on to the players. The players—meaning Ted Williams—sent back the taunt: "If that's the way you feel, we'll make it thirty minutes after the game instead of fifteen."

"To the top editors, it was all a big joke," Bob Holbrook says.

"They thought we had a cinch, just going to ball games and traveling around the country. When we asked for some support, they took the attitude that the curfew was good for us because it kept us on our toes." The real reason, of course, was that the editors didn't trust each other enough to take a common stand. Anyway, the *Herald-Traveler* owned the radio station that broadcast the Red Sox games, and they were certainly not going to cut down on the publicity given to one of their own properties.

Despite these minor obstacles, the writers were expected to cover Ted Williams thoroughly, since every Williams gurgle was a roaring hurricane in Boston. When the Boston writers lost a story to an out-of-town writer, there was hell to pay. So when Ted sneered at the "gutless sportswriters," he was really looking past them to their gutless bosses. If the editors and publishers did not have enough respect for their writers to demand clubhouse access—in return for the million dollars' worth of free publicity they were giving the club—then why, Ted seemed to be saying, should he?

And yet through it all there was always the sense that it was part real and part playacting. Although he would have denied it indignantly, Ted Williams was a great showman.

He ran the Boston writers ragged, and he did it intentionally (they themselves would say maliciously). When a big Williams story was breaking, Ted would dress hurriedly after a game and disappear. The writers, under pressure from their home offices, would chase him all over town, seldom to any avail. Ted would get back to his hotel at 10:55 P.M., just before the team's curfew, and find the clan gathered in the lobby. "What are you guys doing here?" he would ask, with feigned surprise. "Were you waiting for me?" Patiently, they would tell him they needed some quotes on the story of the moment. "Gee," Ted would say, "I didn't know you guys wanted to talk to me."

On the other hand, Freddie Corcoran, his longtime agent, always believed that the Boston writers would have handled Ted better if they hadn't been afraid of him. "I can remember once when he had come to Boston on one of those signing-of-the-new-contract affairs, and all the writers were gathered in the ballroom of the hotel waiting for him to come in. They stood around in a circle, about a dozen of them, and they took him apart. You never heard such knocking. They hated his guts, everything about him. While they were talking Ted came in, and all of a sudden the place went quiet. If they had just spoken up there, while he was there, you could have had some respect for them. But all anybody said was, 'Well, you've finally got here, huh, Kid?' If Ted overheard anything before they saw him, no wonder he held them in such contempt."

For their part, the writers weren't always happy about what they were called upon to do.

Alone among the players, Ted lived in the Somerset Hotel. You couldn't reach him through the Red Sox office. You had to call the hotel and leave your name and phone number at the switchboard. The switchboard had orders not to call his suite. After a number of messages had been collected, his personal bellboy would deliver them, not by knocking on the door—that was verboten—but by slipping them underneath.

When the Red Sox announced that Ted was being fined $5,000, for making an obscene gesture to the fans, Bob Holbrook of the *Globe* and two of his colleagues found themselves with the unwelcome assignment of going to the Somerset for a quote. The writers knew that the fine was purely for public consumption, and they suspected they were being used just to "keep the ink going." And they had no doubt at all that Ted would have a girl in his suite.

To spell it out, there were always so many gorgeous young women sitting in the Somerset lobby that it looked as if the Ziegfeld Follies had sent out a casting call. Ted would come down and point to one of them, and up to his room they'd go. The others would continue to sit and wait. And there were those of his teammates—we name no names here—who would drop around and try their luck. "I'm not too proud to take Ted's rejects," they would say.

Bob Holbrook was a tough and solid guy. He had once floored a drunken Red Sox pitcher who had threatened him, and he had had to be restrained from cold-cocking Howard Cosell when Cosell tried to elbow past him in the Yankee clubhouse during one of Casey Stengel's World Series press conferences.

Bob Holbrook: "We banged and we banged. Finally, he opened the door. 'What the hell do you guys want? This is the one place where I can have a little privacy, and you bastards still can't leave me alone.' And then, for no reason at all, he lists his Big Five in the Boston sports press. None of us happened to be the Big Five. We're just three not very important guys. He lists Bill Cunningham, Austen Lake, Dave Egan, Harold Kaese, Joe Cashman. Then he said, 'No, take Cashman out of there.' He's bombastic, loud, you can hear him all over the hotel. For fifteen minutes he critiqued the Boston press for us, and all the time he's keeping this woman waiting."

The Big Five had become the Big Four, and the newsmen standing there in the hallway were just three flunkies who could be sent over to someone's hotel room to sniff around. They did not get a quote, but they did get the message. He would be going back to whatever eager beauty was awaiting him, and they would be going back to whatever grubby life they had. And, to make it worse, they couldn't blame him. Chalk up another grand slam for the Kid.

With out-of-town writers, on the other hand, Ted was usually the world's most charming citizen. His favorite gambit, while embroiled in a particularly hot controversy with the Boston writers, was to give a lengthy, sparkling interview to some old-timer from a small weekly newspaper. The old guy would then go back to the Boston writers smiling happily and say: "Gee, what a great guy. What's the matter with you guys, you can't get along with a great guy like that?" And the Boston writers could only groan, lay their heads upon their type-writers and weep.

Ted was still pulling that little trick on them the day he hit his five-hundredth home run, in Cleveland. He left the game in the top of the seventh and did not play in the second game of the day's double-header. The Boston writers, assuming that the fifteen-minute rule held, did not go down to the clubhouse, but Cleveland writers Hal Lebovitz and Ed McCauley did and got great interviews. Lebovitz was not only one of the top sportswriters in the country; he was also one of the toughest, as a long succession of Indians managers could attest. And yet Ted smothered him with so much charm that before Lebovitz had time to sit down and think it over he was writing: "Williams spoke spiritedly and rapidly. His brown eyes sparkled. He was gracious and warm. One wondered how this friendly, charming person ever got the rap that he hates sportswriters. The truth is that Williams gets along well with most writers. Of the many who cover the Boston club, there are only two who spark friction in him." In the past, Ted had blasted the Cleveland writers as second only to Boston's in sheer malevolence and dishonesty.

He paid for it. His bad relations with the Boston press cost him at least one Most Valuable Player award.

In 1941, when Ted Williams hit his sensational .406, the Most Valuable Player award was voted to Joe DiMaggio. The following year, Ted won the triple crown with figures of .356, 36 home runs, and 137 RBIs. The Red Sox finished nine games behind the Yankees, and Joe Gordon, who had hit .322 with 18 home runs and 103 RBIs, won the MVP award.

Okay, the award is supposed to go to the player who has proved most valuable to his team, not to the one who has proved himself the best hitter. Baseball is a game of hitting, but it is also a game of fielding, of base running, of throwing. And, being a competitive sport, it is also a game of leadership and inspiration. As Branch Rickey put it, it is frequently a game of "intangibles."

Ted was not a bad fielder in those years, even if he was—on occasion—a sulky and indifferent one. As the longtime left-fielder at Fenway Park, he played that trick wall to perfection. The trick is to decide immediately whether you can make the catch on a drive near the wall. If you cannot, you turn around and try to catch the rebound on the fly. For if you can get the ball before it hits the turf, you can almost always hold the hitter to a single. Ted, with the good arm he had in those days, very quickly discouraged base runners from trying for two bases, and if they did decide to challenge him he was accurate enough to almost always throw them out.

On the other hand, Joe DiMaggio was one of the great center-fielders of all time. He not only made great plays; he had the ability to make them in the clutch. Before he injured his arm, he could throw as well as almost anybody in the game. (Not to go overboard on this, his brothers Vince and Dominic were at least as good. Willie Mays was a better fielder, and so was Jim Piersall. And nobody was better than the always underpublicized Paul Blair.) Joe Gordon also was a spectacular, if sometimes inconsistent, fielder. And so, in those years, there was disappointment in Boston when Ted failed to win the MVP awards but no feeling that the vote had been prejudiced (although the joke after Gordon edged him out in 1942 was that Ted Williams had led the league in hitting, home runs, runs batted in, total bases, slugging percentage, bases on balls, and runs scored—in short, everything that counted—while Gordon had led in only two categories, errors and strikeouts).

In 1946 the Red Sox won the pennant, and Ted was finally voted the MVP award. He won it again in 1949, when the Red Sox lost the pennant on the last day of the season and Ted lost the triple crown on his last time at bat.

It was in 1947 that Ted's poisonous relations with the sports press did him in.

Although the Red Sox had dropped back to third place that year, fourteen games behind the Yankees, there was a general assumption that Ted would be a repeat MVP winner, and an easy one at that. He had won the triple crown again, with .343 – 32 – 114. Nobody in the American League had ever won two triple crowns before, and only Rogers Hornsby had done it in the National League. Joe DiMaggio, the only possible contender, had followed a .290 with a .315 year, had hit 20 home runs, and knocked in 97 runs.

But the handwriting was on the wall. The MVP voting is done just before the World Series and is supposed to be kept under seal until the official results are announced later in the fall. In Boston, there was suddenly a spate of "suicide" bettors willing to bet that Ted would not win it. There had been a leak. DiMaggio was the winner, 202–201.

The leak in the usually well-guarded balloting eventually revealed something else. To eliminate the factor of hometown prejudice, three leading sportswriters in each of the eight American League cities were appointed to do the voting, with each writer listing the ten players he believed to have been the most valuable, in descending order. One of the Boston writers had not named Ted Williams anywhere on his list! Taken at face value, he did not consider a triple-crown winner to be among the ten most valuable players in the league.

The writer was the ancient Mel Webb of the *Boston Globe,* and the reason his vote became public was because Webb bragged about it. When his fellow writers asked him how he could possibly justify leaving a triple-crown winner completely off his list, he said, "I don't like the sonofabitch, and I'll never vote for him!"

(Ted did have good—and even close—relations with some of the older sportswriters, most notably Burt Whitman, the sports editor of the *Herald,* and Arthur Sampson, also of the *Herald.* When Whitman dropped dead of a heart attack in the press box, Ted broke down and wept. Sampson was a good-natured, completely open guy. He was also an ex–football coach, with close connections in the football and boxing fraternities, and Ted loved football players and fighters. There was also Leo Cloutier of the *Manchester* [New Hampshire] *News,* who didn't actually cover the ball club but who became a surrogate father in the sense that Ted would go out of his way to confide in him when he was having problems with his family back in California.)

Mel Webb went back to the early days of Babe Ruth. He had been one of the two sportswriters who had paced off the 579-foot home run the Babe had hit in Tampa—we're talking dead-ball here—in the spring of 1919.

In his old age, Webb had become a mean and grouchy old bastard. That was the description his colleagues always used to describe him, "A mean and grouchy old bastard."

On the opening day of spring training in 1947, Webb had come strolling over to Ted's locker. "Why don't you drop dead, you old bastard?" Ted snarled, by way of greeting.

"Okay," Webb said evenly. "Thank you. I'll fix you for that." Turning away, he said, "I'll take care of that later."

The vote could not have fallen more perfectly for him. If Webb had decided to punish Ted by listing him tenth, Ted still would have won. The only way he could have deprived Ted of the award was by leaving him completely off the ballot.

VIII

The Wonderful Season
of *1941*

If Ted's second year was his hardest, the third year was his easiest. In 1941 everything went right. He had learned his lessons, and he was coming into his full strength. The wind was with him. The breaks were with him. Hell, the gods were with him. "Everything I hit fell in. Every break that I could get I got."

In the summer of 1941, the twenty-two-year-old Ted Williams and the twenty-six-year-old Joe DiMaggio put together seasons that will last for as long as there are plaques in Cooperstown and new generations to marvel at their deeds.

Joe DiMaggio reeled off his fifty-six-game hitting streak, the best of all time, and Ted became the last man to hit .400.

It was a season that links their names together forever, with each of them magnifying and making more luminous the deeds of the other. And yet they were not really tied that closely together during the season itself.

By its very nature, a consecutive-game streak has no latitude for failure. Any newspaper editor will tell you that there is no story more gripping—or better for circulation—than the Girl in the Hole. Will the rescuers get to her in time to save her life, or won't they? With DiMaggio, it was a life or death story every day.

Ted Williams's quest for a .400 season, by contrast, did not turn into a cliff-hanger until the very last day of the season. And while there is nothing to be gained by glorifying Williams at the expense of DiMaggio, it is fair to say that with the passage of time it is Williams' .406 that has begun to loom larger than DiMaggio's fifty-six games. It was not always thus.

The season with which Ted Williams will be forever identified did not start out too well for him. For the third straight year, he was a no-show on the opening day of spring training. When he finally phoned the long-suffering Eddie Collins a day later, he explained that he had been so busy hunting wolves in the wilds of Minnesota—that must have made Collins feel better—that he had lost all track of the date. To show how contrite he was he promised Collins that he would jump into his car and *drive* right down.

In the second exhibition game, he caught his spikes as he was sliding into second base and chipped a bone in the ankle of his right foot. As a result, he came out of training camp limping and was restricted to little more than pinch-hitting duty over the first twelve games.

And yet the injury just might have helped him. Bobby Doerr thinks it did. "I remember him going into the trainer's room every day to get his ankle taped up. In batting practice you could see him kind of favoring it. I kind of wondered then, and I kind of got to thinking as the season went on, that it was sensitive enough to make him stay back for as long as possible to keep the pressure off his front foot." Ted knows all about Doerr's theory, of course, and he is willing to concede that he was indeed able to hold back a little longer in 1941. "But I never thought it was because of my ankle. I never thought that. From 1941 on, I was getting stronger and stronger and stronger. I was late to mature, and I think I was strongest between the ages of twenty-two and thirty-two. As a result, I was able to hold back and hold back, getting quicker and stronger than at any other time."

Ted's season began for him, to all practical purposes, in his favorite hunting grounds at good old Briggs Stadium in Detroit. He didn't hit two record-breaking home runs this time—he would be saving that for Chicago. The best he was able to do in Detroit was a 440-foot home run and—if you want to talk about hanging back—a long double to deep left field.

In Chicago, he single-handedly wrecked John Rigney, a fast-balling right-hander who liked to challenge hitters up around the letters. (That made him the toughest of pitchers for DiMaggio and the easiest for Williams. The book on Joe was that you could sometimes get him on high fastballs, preferably inside. The book on Ted was that he murdered the high fastball.) Against Rigney, Ted hit two gigantic home runs. The first one was a 500-foot wallop—"one of the longest home runs ever hit in Comiskey Park"—that went into the upper right-field stands. The second came in the eleventh inning, when Rigney tried to cross him up by throwing a slow curve. Ted read what was coming while Rigney was still in his windup, and he hit it over the roof of the second tier in the deepest part of right center. If the first one was 500 feet, that game-winning drive had to be close to 600 feet.

It was, Ted has always said, the longest drive he ever hit. ("You get those long home runs when the conditions are exactly right. When the wind was blowing in, Comiskey Park was a tough, tough park to hit in. When the conditions were right and the wind was blowing out, the ball would just seem to carry and carry.") The *hardest* ball he ever hit was his last base hit in the 1941 season.

When the DiMaggio hitting streak began, on May 15, Ted was hitting .339 against Joe's .304. From there they ran off parallel twenty-three-game streaks, which nobody paid much attention to. In those pre-TV, prestatistician days, streaks weren't looked on as anything to alert the populace about.

Over the course of those twenty-three games, Ted hit .487 (43 for 88) and Joe hit .368 (32 for 87). Head to head, Ted was also the winner. In the eight games DiMaggio played against the Red Sox during those twenty-three games, he had as many as two hits in a game only once, and then not really. The first of his two hits that day came on a scoring decision so outrageous that even the New York writers held their noses. Ted, on the other hand, had some of his biggest days against the Yankees. Over the full season, it came to .453 (29 – 64). Against the rest of the league he hit .398.

Then too—and this shouldn't be any surprise—he fielded better than he ever had. When the Kid was hitting, the Kid could field marvelously well.

All right, then. During the full fifty-six games of the DiMaggio streak, the Yankees and the Red Sox played three series, beginning with a home-and-home series in May and ending with a three-game series, in the first week of July, in which DiMag first tied and then broke Wee Willie Keeler's resurrected record of forty-four straight games.

The two series in May constituted the foundation of Ted's .400 season, coming as they did in the middle of a sixteen-game spurt in which he went 34 for 61, for an average of .557. In the five games against the Yankees, he was 10 for 16 (.625). DiMaggio had one hit in each of those games, and in two of them he was extremely fortunate to keep the fledgling streak alive.

On Saturday, May 24, Joe was hitless when he came to bat in the seventh inning, with runners on second and third, two out, and the Red Sox leading, 6–5. With first base open and the winning runs on base, Joe Cronin ordered Earl Johnson—a left-hander, yet—to pitch to him, and DiMaggio lined the first pitch into left field to win the game. If Cronin had walked him, as all the percentages screamed out for him to do, the streak would have ended, unheralded and unremarked upon, after nine games.

The next day DiMaggio had a hit in his first time at bat. Ted had three singles and a double, behind Lefty Grove, to lift his average to .404 and take over the batting lead for the first time. Over the rest of the season he would drop below .400 only twice, once following hard on his triumph in the All-Star Game and again on the day before his triumphant finish in Philadelphia.

The second May series with the Yankees consisted of a doubleheader at Fenway Park on Memorial Day. Ted's batting average was now up to .421, and Joe's streak was at thirteen. Number fourteen was both the worst game he ever played and his luckiest day of the year.

DiMaggio had come into Boston with a stiff neck and a bad cold. The day was cold and windy, and in the course of the doubleheader he made four errors, including a dropped fly ball. In the first game, his hit again came on his last time at bat, bringing the streak to fourteen. By the second game, he had stiffened up so much that he could barely move his head or his right shoulder. For reasons that are inexplicable, Joe McCarthy not only sent him out to play but kept him in the game even after the Yankees had fallen behind, 10–0, by the fourth inning.

Joe had already made the first of his three errors in the second game by then (to go with the error he had made in the opener) by allowing Williams's first-inning single to skip through his legs. Before the game was over, he made four atrocious throws to third base and home plate.

A less sympathetically inclined scorer could have charged him with five errors. Easily.

Oh yeah. His hit. In the fifth inning, with Mickey Harris pitching a perfect game, DiMaggio hit a creaky little fly to right, an easy out except that Pete Fox, the right-fielder, lost the ball in the sun and the buffeting wind. If he had recovered in time to get a glove on it, Fox would have been charged with an error.

The Yankees got no other hit off Harris until there was one out in the ninth. If DiMaggio's hit had been the only one, might not the Boston scorer have changed his ruling in order to give Harris his no-hitter?

In those two series in May, then, Ted went 7 for 11 in New York and 3 for 5 in Boston. Joe was 5 for 18, with one hit in each game.

Ted's hitting streak came to an end two days after his average reached its high-water mark of .438. It ended on a warm Sunday afternoon in Chicago, when he was shut down, in both ends of a Sunday double-header, by Ted Lyons and Thornton Lee. Lyons walked him three times, once with the bases loaded. Lee walked him once, and that walk became the only run in a 1 − 0 game. The end of the streak meant little to Ted, if indeed he had even been aware of it. The first game had settled into a pitching duel between those two crafty veterans Lefty Grove and Ted Lyons, and Williams spent the better part of his post-game interviews talking about what a pleasure it had been to watch those two old masters at work.

Immediately, he was off on another streak, in which he went 9 for 18. Factor in the 0 for 5 in Chicago, and you have a streak of 44 for 88 over twenty-four games. His average was up to .427. The next day he went 2 for 5, including a game-winning homer, in a doubleheader against Detroit. He also had four walks. In other words, he hit .400 for the day, reached base six times in nine turns at bat, and dropped a point to .426.

On that same day, DiMaggio was hitless against Johnny Rigney in his first three times at bat. His streak was kept alive in the ninth when a routine grounder to short took a bad bounce and ricocheted off Luke Appling's shoulder. The streak was at thirty now, and beginning to attract attention in both the sports world and the nonsports world, partly because he was a New York player, but mostly because he was Joe DiMaggio, the best ballplayer in the game.

Bobby Doerr remembers the sudden surge of publicity well. "We were in New York when he broke Keeler's record. Of course, you were conscious Joe had this streak going. Today, I think it would be in the headlines every day. Then, as I remember, we didn't become conscious of it until it had reached, you know, his twenty-seventh, twenty-eighth game." DiMaggio had tied Keeler's record of 44 in the second game of a three-game series against the Red Sox, and he broke it the following day, with a line drive that went over Ted's head like a cannon shot and into the left-field stands.

Ted did not exactly challenge DiMaggio for the spotlight in that series. On the contrary, he managed only one meaningless single in each of the three games and dropped to .402, his lowest average since he had first reached the .400 level in that same park five weeks earlier. Still, he had batted .412 over the forty-five games to Wee Willie Keeler's record against DiMag's .375.

Five days later Ted had it all. As the best players in both leagues gathered in Detroit for the All-Star Game, both streaks were still alive. Joe's at forty-eight games. Ted's average was up to .405.

Ted had taken the train to Detroit, along with Bobby Doerr, Jimmy Foxx, Joe Cronin, and Dom DiMaggio. Doerr, like Williams, had been selected for the starting lineup: "Ted was all excited about going. In fact, he had a movie camera, an eight-millimeter movie camera, that he let me use and I took a lot of movies; mostly of National and American Leaguers taking batting practice." Many of the pictures shot by Doerr that day were used in the much-praised HBO documentary "When It Was a Game," first shown in 1991. (If you saw the HBO special, you also saw the compact, one-piece Williams swing of those days. *Whhooosh.*)

Ted was keyed up on the field, too, as he always was for big games, and he was up and down all day screaming across the diamond. "In those days," Doerr says with a smile, "you expressed yourself more to the other team."

In his first All-Star Game, in 1940, Ted had gone 0 for 2 before being replaced in left field by Hank Greenberg. Early in the 1941 game he had his first All-Star hit, a double, to drive in a run. But in the eighth inning, in what figured to be his final turn at bat, he was struck out by the Chicago Cubs right-hander, Claude Passeau.

As the last of the ninth got under way, the American League was trailing, 5–3. A few minutes later the bases were loaded, with one out, Joe DiMaggio was at bat, and Ted Williams was kneeling in the batter's circle. DiMaggio's opportunity to be the hero and Ted's chance to come to bat again seemed to disappear together as DiMag ripped what looked to be a perfect double-play ground ball to Eddie Miller at shortstop. Miller slipped the ball nicely to Billy Herman, but Herman's throw to first base pulled Frank McCormick off the base. One run was in. There were men on first and third, and Ted Williams was coming to bat.

Exactly when the story began to circulate that it was DiMaggio who had given Ted his chance by outlegging the throw to first is impossible to pin down. Suffice it to say that the reports of the game at the time gave not the slightest indication that anything of the sort had occurred.

If the double play had been made the inning and the game would have been over. If Frank McCormick hadn't kept the ball from going into the dugout, the tying run would have scored, and—more to the point—the go-ahead run would have been at second base, with first base open. What do you do with first base open and the world's only .400 hitter at bat? Of course. You walk him. Or, at the very least, you bring in a left-handed pitcher. Forget all that. It isn't possible to conceive of the Golden Age of baseball without Ted Williams's home run in the 1941 All-Star Game in Detroit.

Ted fouled away the first pitch and then took two balls. Passeau fired again, Ted swung, and the ball sailed high and deep along the foul line in right. There was no doubt at all that the ball had the distance; the only question was whether it was going to remain fair. Ted took a couple of steps away from the plate and then stopped to watch. When the ball landed fair, high on the top deck, he leaped into the air clapping his hands and went bounding around the bases in sheer juvenile joy. ("That first pitch, I was a little late on, but only because it was bearing in on me. Passeau called it a slider, and I hadn't heard too much about sliders then, and I thought, I've got to quicken up here. And he threw another one, the very same place, and I was just that much ahead of it, and I hit the home run which was so far and away the greatest thrill I ever had in baseball up to that time. Nothing ever hit me quite as hard emotionally. I was twenty-two years old, remember, and these were all great, great players.")

As he crossed home plate, he was mobbed. "There was as much excitement in the All-Star Game as there was in the World Series back then," Doerr recalls. "It was just turmoil in the clubhouse. It was wild." Del Baker, the American League manager, came over and kissed Ted on the side of the head and hugged him.

Bill McKechnie, the opposing manager, came in just long enough to shake his head and say, "Ted, you're just not human." So Ted went out and proved he was human.

The Red Sox were staying on in Detroit for a scheduled four-game series, and before Ted left that oh-so-hospitable ballpark his average had dipped below .400 and his season had almost turned to disaster on its rain-soaked infield.

The first game was rained out. When the teams were finally able to play Ted got collared by Buck Newsom in four times at bat. As if to show how difficult it is to hit .400, those four at-bats dropped his average from .405 to .398. The next day, in the first game of a doubleheader, Ted walked on his first three times at bat. It was after the second walk he twisted his ankle while scrambling back to first base on an attempted pick-off. When he popped out on his last time at bat, his average dipped to .397.

Between games, it became clear that he had aggravated his springtime injury. He spent the next nine days on the bench, recovering.

During those nine days he pinch-hit four times: sacrifice fly, pop out, walk, three-run homer.

The sacrifice fly is worth lingering over because of a change in the scoring rules a year earlier. Under the new rule, a hitter was still credited with an RBI but was also charged with a time at bat. So when Ted limped to the plate in the eighth inning of a scoreless game and sent a long fly to center field to bring in the winning run, all it got him on his batting average was another two-point drop, to .395. The pop fly two days later dropped him to .393.

By the time the Sox headed back to Boston, the three-run homer had put him back up to .396. He was returning well rested and—let us not forget—with that history of coming back to the lineup with a bang after an injury. An argument could even be made that the enforced rest, coming when it did, was the best thing that could have happened to him.

Nor did it hurt that he would be going back into the lineup against John Rigney. Sure enough, he stepped up on his first time at bat and hit a monster shot into the right-center bleachers, to start a twelve-game hitting streak (19 hits in 35 times at bat) that lifted his average to .412. Five of those hits were home runs, including one grand slam.

His average had gone back to .400, on the fourth game of the home stand, as he was contributing a home run, a single, and two walks to Lefty Grove's 300th victory. Ted always murdered the ball when Grove was pitching. (He had gone over .400 three months earlier, remember, when Grove won his 296th game.) It was not a game that he remembers with any pleasure, however, because he is nowhere to be seen in the postgame picture of Grove celebrating his 300th win.

The home run had come in the fifth inning, with one man on base, to give Grove a two-run lead, but Ted quickly gave both runs back by messing up a ball in the outfield. Up again in the eighth, with two men on and a chance to redeem himself, he fouled out weakly behind third base. It was left to Jimmy Foxx, fittingly enough, to win the game for his old Philadelphia A's teammate with a long triple off the center-field wall.

Ted is still wounded by the accusation that he was so upset at not having delivered the winning hit for Lefty—or so jealous of Foxx—that he was sulking in the trainer's room while the pictures were being shot. That wasn't it at all, says Ted. "I drove in two and let in three that day, and that's why I was so mad at myself. And I'm mad now that I'm not in the picture with my arm around Lefty Grove. That's a picture I really wish I had."

While Ted had been recovering from his injury, DiMaggio's bat had been smoking. From the time he broke Keeler's record, he had gone 24 for 44, raising his average over the fifty-six-game streak to .408. He was leading the league in RBIs with 76 and was tied for the home-run lead with 20. And as he told the New York sportswriters, in an unaccustomed burst of candor, he had far from given up on catching Ted for the batting title. Why should he? He had brought his average up to .375 (the highest it was going to be all season), and Ted was then sitting there at .395.

Better he hadn't been so talkative. The next day the streak came to an end on the soggy turf of Cleveland's Municipal Stadium. Although he was off immediately on another 16-game streak, Ted Williams was pulling away. From that point on, it was Joe DiMaggio who receded into the background and Ted Williams who had his eyes set on the Triple Crown.

On August 3, the day Joe's skein of hitting in seventy-two out of seventy-three games unraveled, Ted was extending his own hitting streak to twelve games and was batting .410. (To make the season even more spectacular for him, he had gone fishing on an off day two days earlier and had caught a record-breaking 374-pound tuna.) The streak ended when the Philadelphia A's walked him three times, twice intentionally. One of the intentional walks came with runners on first and third.

Joe's season began to dribble away on August 19, when he went out for three weeks—a little symmetry music here, maestro—with a sprained ankle.

Over the next two days, Ted hit five home runs (and three singles) in a pair of doubleheaders in St. Louis, to bring his home-run total for the year to twenty-eight, moving him ahead of DiMaggio and leaving him only two behind the league leader, Charlie Keller.

By the time DiMag came back, Ted had rapped out eleven homers and knocked in twenty-six runs to take over the home-run lead from Keller and leap onto the leader board in RBIs for the first time all year. Keller, whose own great season was getting wiped out in the media furor over DiMaggio, was leading with 117, DiMag had 107, and Williams had 93.

On Labor Day, just before the team was to leave for New York, Ted hit three titanic home runs in a doubleheader against Washington, to give him thirty-four and take over the major-league lead. He also walked four times. One of the home runs came off Bill Zuber, the pitcher who had beaned him back in the American Association. In the opinion of the Boston writers, it was the longest home run he had hit at Fenway Park all year. In the second game, he hit a foul ball that completely cleared the roof in right field, the first time that had ever been done. The next pitch he hit over the bull-pen and into the right-field bleachers, for the second time that day.

The Red Sox had six games with the Yankees over the last twenty-one games of the season. Two games in Boston, followed immediately by a two-game series in New York, and then back to Boston during the last week of the season for the final two home games. As the series in New York began, it was Keller with 119 RBIs, DiMaggio with 112, and Williams with 106. Ted's batting average was .410.

Not that the Yankees had been doing anything to help Ted while DiMaggio was out. When the Yankees clinched the pennant in Boston on September 4, the earliest ever, they had a lead of seventeen and a half games. Nevertheless, Atley Donald, a control pitcher, walked Ted four straight times, before he managed to single on his final time at bat. They were the only walks Donald issued all day. The same thing had happened three weeks earlier in New York: four straight walks, to the booing of the New York fans, after Ted singled in a run on his first time at bat.

In the first game at Yankee Stadium, Ted had one single and knocked in his 107th run. Keller knocked in his 120th. On Sunday, Ted was facing Lefty Gomez, who almost never got him out. The first time up, his drive hit high off the foul pole and bounced into the stands, foul. Under the ground rules then in force, if a ball hit the inside of the pole and landed in the stands fair, it was a home run. If it hit the outside of the pole and landed in the foul side of the stands—you can imagine how often that happened—it was a double. If it hit flush and landed back on the field, it was in play. Ted had been deprived of both an RBI and a home run, in the only park he didn't hit a home run in all year. Not that he didn't come close one more time. In the third inning, he singled. In the fifth, he lambasted a double off the top of the center-field wall 450 feet away, missing a home run by inches. And so when he came up with the bases loaded in the sixth, Gomez—who was a pal of DiMaggio's—walked Ted on four pitches. It was his only RBI of the game.

Charlie Keller started the day by knocking in two runs, to bring his total to 122. Then he twisted his ankle sliding into home plate and was through for the season.

With it all, Ted came out of the final game at Yankee Stadium with his average up to .413 and only fourteen games left in the season. And, beyond that, with a fighting chance of winning the Triple Crown.

There was one pitcher he hit even better than he hit Gomez—Johnny Rigney. Ted already had five home runs off Rigney, into distant parts of both parks, and before he met the Yankees again he would face Rigney one more time. On September 15, Ted hit yet another monstrous three-run homer off Rigney—his thirty-fifth of the season—giving him 116 RBIs, to tie him with DiMaggio.

And so, when Ted finally found himself on the same field with DiMaggio again, with one week left in the season, he had pretty much locked up two-thirds of the triple crown and was tied with DiMaggio (if you discounted the disabled Keller) for the third leg.

On Saturday, September 20, DiMaggio knocked in two runs, to go ahead of Ted, 118 to 116. On Sunday, Ted pulled even by hitting his thirty-sixth home run, a tremendous wallop into the bleachers, which came on his last swing at bat at Fenway Park in the 1941 season. Both of them were still four RBIs behind Keller.

Understandably enough, considering how late Ted's prospects for winning the Triple Crown had emerged, nobody seemed to be paying any particular attention. Not even in Boston. The paramount concern was that Ted was leaving Fenway Park batting .406, with six games left to play—a single game followed by a doubleheader in both Washington and Philadelphia.

No great bargain. The park in Washington was huge, and the Athletics simply did not pitch to Ted.

In the opening game in Washington, he had one cheap hit off Sid Hudson in three times at bat and dropped a point, to .405. The hit was a gift double on a fly ball to deep center that Doc Cramer, finishing up his career in Washington, failed to hold onto. On the third time up, Ted walked, and on his final time at bat he backed the right-fielder up against the wall.

The doubleheader the next day turned hairy. Dutch Leonard, the best knuckleballer in baseball, shut him out in three times at bat, and one Dick Mulligan, a rookie left-hander who had just been called up from the minors, held him to one single in four times at bat. Against Leonard he had two walks, fouled out, grounded out, and on his last time at bat was retired on a long fly to left center. He was down to .402.

Mulligan turned out to be a skinny left-hander who came at a batter with a variety of motions—sidearm, three-quarters, cross fire. Just the kind of pitcher Ted liked to take a long look at. ("The first time at bat is always the toughest against any pitcher. Seeing what his delivery is, how fast he is, how his ball moves. Awww, he throws a sinker on me. Awww, he's a little faster than I thought he was. And you lose a time at bat.")

His first time up, Mulligan got two strikes on him and then came at him with something new, a big overhand curve that broke right over the plate. Ted was walking out of the batter's box before the strike was even called. It was only the twenty-sixth time he had struck out all year. The next time up, he hit a ground ball to deep second base, and Bill Grieve, umpiring at first, called him safe. It was Ted's fifth infield hit of the year. It was also a gift. The umpires were rooting for him.

On his last time at bat, he drove a patented Williams sinking line drive down the first-base line, but Mickey Vernon, in his rookie year, was there to field it on a short hop behind first base. (When Vernon joined the Red Sox fifteen years later, one of the first things he said was how happy he was that he no longer had to face those sinking line drives that would "hit the ground in front of you and explode in your face.") Ted was down to .401 (actually .4009).

The unforgiving mathematics of .400 were beginning to close in on him. With one fewer time at bat, he would have needed four hits in twelve times at bat in Philadelphia to finish at an even .400. That last time at bat in Washington was making it necessary for him to have a fifth hit in those same twelve times at bat. And he had two days off to think about it.

On Friday, Joe Cronin had coach Tom Daly take Ted out to the A's Shibe Park, along with Frank Shellenback, who had become the Red Sox pitching coach, for some extra batting practice. Cronin not only wanted to give Ted a chance to loosen up and get his timing back; he wanted him to be doing something to keep his mind off the coming games.

And the triple crown was disappearing as well. DiMaggio, who had knocked in four runs in Philadelphia, to catch Keller, knocked in another run on Friday, to take the lead for good. He was going to be topping off his season with a two-run double on Saturday.

That same Saturday, Ted faced a rookie knuckleballer named Roger Wolff, the first of three rookie pitchers Connie Mack was ready to throw at him. Ted walked the first time up, but it was apparent that he was having trouble trying to gauge Wolff's pitches. The second time up, he doubled to deep right center. He was up to .402. But then there was a fly to right (.401) and a foul-out to first, and he was down to .4004.

He was due to be the fifth batter in the ninth. The first two batters went out, but the two hitters in front of him both singled, and he was up again. He slashed a wicked drive that went just foul, then chased a low knuckleball and struck out. His twenty-seventh strikeout of the year had dropped him to .39955.

All to the good, as it developed. All to make what Ted did in that final Sunday doubleheader in Philadelphia a feat to resound in the annals of baseball history.

"After the [Saturday] game, I walked through the streets of Philadelphia with Johnny Orlando. Johnny was my closest confidant on the ball club. He knew all my personal problems. He was my close friend, and he'd always give me something extra. 'Don't worry, everything is going to be all right.' We kept walking and walking, talking about the game and this and this, but underlying it all we were thinking about the next day. I remember I got in about ten-thirty that night." It was not unusual for Ted to walk the streets after a ball game; it was almost a part of his training routine. Usually, however, his companion was Bobby Doerr. The way Orlando always told the story, he ducked into a couple of bars along the way, to beat the Philadelphia curfew, and Ted stopped off in a couple of drugstores to down a malted. For Ted, who was almost always in bed by ten o'clock, it was an unusually late hour. Even then, he found Cronin sitting in the lobby on his return and spent another half hour or so talking to him. ("It was the first time it worried me whether I was going to hit .400 or not, because the papers were writing it up.")

The kid who had run out to the backyard with a bat after reading about Bill Terry's .401 was going to get his chance, eleven years later, to do what he had so clearly visualized doing night after night after night.

Wouldn't it be nice to be able to say that Ted was thinking back on that unhappy twelve-year-old boy who had started it all by swinging a bat under the light of the moon in a cluttered backyard? Wouldn't it warm the cockles of the heart to be able to say that he was promising that little boy to come through for him? Nice, but not very accurate. "No, I didn't think of those nights in the backyard or of being the first one since Terry," Ted says. "I didn't even realize the astronomical height it was. What I was thinking was, I've been there all year, and I want to remain there. Now it's the last day and, jeez, I'm under .400."

Not everybody was rooting for him. Al Simmons, who had hit .390 for Philadelphia in 1930, was finishing up his career as a coach for

Connie Mack. Simmons stopped Ted along the baseline to assure him that he couldn't have hit .400 with a paddle in Simmons's day, and then offered to bet him that he wouldn't hit .400 this year, either.

According to the mythology, Joe Cronin asked Ted if he wanted to sit out the doubleheader to protect what was technically a .400 average. "No," Ted said. "I'm going to play. If I'm going to be a .400 hitter, I'm not going to slip in through the back door, and I'm not going to do it sitting on the bench."

But numbers aren't "technically" anything. Numbers are constants. It is one thing to round off a number during the season, for the sake of convenience, space, or clarity. It's quite another to say that .39955 equals .400. You cannot turn less than .400 into .400 by official fiat. And you certainly cannot do it by journalistic convention.

Mythology aside, nobody tried to. The Associated Press report of the game stated that Ted's average had been "trimmed from .4009 to .3996, with only two games left in which to re-enter the select class." The *Boston Globe* reported that he had fallen below .400 for the first time since he had reached an even .400 on July 25, the day Grove won his three hundredth game. In the daily listing of the leading major-league hitters, Ted was posted at .3996.

Didn't Cronin know that? Of course he did. When you read the journals of the day, you can see that the exchange quite probably took place a day or two earlier, at a time when Ted was hitting .401. "If he's over .400 after two games, I may bench him," Cronin was quoted as saying during the first off day in Philadelphia. "Whether he likes it or not."

In other words, why take a risk in the second game of a double-header, in a ballpark in which the falling shadows of autumn made hitting notoriously difficult? Especially since daylight saving time would be coming to an end that very day, bringing on the shadows an hour earlier.

The umpire that day was Bill McGowan, who was universally regarded as the best umpire of his time. McGowan once told me that when Ted came to the plate for the first time, Frankie Hayes, the A's catcher, said to him, "I wish you all the luck in the world, Ted, but Mr. Mack told us he'd run us all out of baseball if we let up on you. You're going to have to earn it." McGowan then stepped in front of Ted to sweep off the plate and said, "Well, Kid, you got to be loose to hit .400."

What Frankie Hayes really said to him, according to Ted, was, "Mr. Mack says we're not to make it easy for you, Ted. But we're going to pitch to you." That does makes more sense. Connie Mack had adopted the Fred Haney theory of pitching to Ted with men in scoring position. In their eight previous games against the Red Sox, A's pitchers had walked him fourteen times.

The pitcher was Dick Fowler, a rookie right-hander who had been brought up late in the year. On his first time up, Ted hit a wicked drive down the first-base line for a base hit. "I was so nervous when I came to the plate that my hands were shaking. When I got the first hit I felt a little more confident, then I hit a home run over the right-field fence and from there on, *wrrooofff*."

By the sixth inning, Porter Vaughan, another lefty, was pitching, and Ted greeted him with a bullet through the middle for his third straight hit.

The next inning, he came up with a man on first. Instead of having his first baseman, Bob Johnson, hold the runner on base, Connie Mack moved Johnson back on the grass. Since it was almost a rule of life by then that anything old Connie Mack did against Ted was going to backfire, this became the hit Joe Cronin remembered best of all. "Vaughan threw a perfect curve to the outside corner on the three-two count," Cronin said later. "A pitch you'd hardly expect from a rookie. Anxious as Ted was to hit, you'd have expected him to be fooled. At best, he should have been out in front of the ball. He timed the pitch perfectly, though, and pulled it down the right-field line." Right through the spot Johnson had vacated.

Ted was four for four and batting .4048. He could go hitless five straight times and still be at .4004.

On his final time at bat, he hit a ground ball deep in the hole, which was fumbled by the second baseman for an error.

Safely above .400 now, Ted still refused to sit out the second game. As he came to the plate against Fred Caligiuri, another rookie, the Philadelphia fans paid him a roaring tribute. He answered with another base hit, a ground single to right. Up again in the fourth inning, he blasted what Ted—and almost every Boston writer—called the hardest ball he had ever hit in his career, a line drive that streaked into right-center field, rising as it went, and was still on the rise when it rocketed off one of the loudspeaker horns on top of the wall. The ball came back onto the field, and Ted had to settle for a double. Connie Mack had to have the horn replaced over the winter, so badly was it dented.

Ted finally popped up, just before the game was called because of darkness. For his final day, Ted had come through with six hits in eight times at bat, to post a final average of .406.

It was not looked on then as such a monumental achievement. There was no sense that his was the last face that would be carved upon Mount Rushmore, or even that a .400 batting average was going to qualify as the Mount Rushmore of baseball royalty.

Ted was twenty-three years old when the season ended. He was just beginning to come into his full strength. He knew the pitchers. Ty Cobb and Rogers Hornsby had hit .400 three times. George Sisler had done it twice. Joe DiMaggio had come close only two years earlier.

In 1942, Ted won the triple crown. A year later he was in the navy. When he came back from service he led the Red Sox to their first pennant in twenty-eight years. Over the next three years he won the batting championship two more times and lost out the third time on his final at-bat of the season.

Then, in 1950, he ran into a fence during the All-Star Game, in Chicago, and suffered an injury that put his career in jeopardy—far more than he allowed anybody, including and especially the Red Sox front office, to realize.

IX

Ted and Joe

It wasn't the Red Sox and the Yankees. It was Ted Williams and Joe DiMaggio. They were the knights of the joust. They had both been smiled upon by the forces of nature. They were beings from a higher realm.

The only thing they had in common was that private/shared dimension. In every other way, they were such complete opposites that it was possible to define each of them in terms of the other.

Joe was a statue at the plate, legs spraddled, bat held high. A sculpted piece of work. Ted was all bounce and twist and fidget.

Ted swung at strikes. Joe swung at anything that looked good to him.

They were appealing to their hometown fans in entirely different ways. Joe DiMaggio was treated as a prince of the city, and he looked and dressed the part. There was an elegant, seignorial look about him. Ted dressed casually and refused to wear a tie. He was looked upon as the mischievous kid down the street who wasn't really a bad boy once you got to know him.

They were aware of each other. They eyed each other from afar. Neither of them would make the concession of going to the other's dugout for a joint photograph. Photographers would have to approach them individually and arrange for them to meet behind the backstop.

Joe was multidimensional as a player and one-dimensional as a person. Ted was one-dimensional as a player and multidimensional as a person.

Joe was a denizen of nightclubs. Ted was an aficionado of the great outdoors.

Joe had ulcers. Ted gave them. Joe DiMaggio, the greatest ballplayer of his time, did not really enjoy. The pressure he put on himself to lead the Yankees to yet another pennant was so unceasing that he was always ducking into the runway to grab a smoke.

Joe never showed emotion. Ted never let an emotion go unexpressed. Ted would break his bat against the dugout steps and curse himself out. ("You goddamn fool, you gave away a time at bat.") When Joe was upset, he would go back to the bench mumbling to himself. ("Mumblemumblemumble.")

For the record, each was careful to praise the other. The only known harsh words spoken by either of them about the other came wafting through the thin wall that separated the home and visitors' locker rooms at Fenway Park while Ted was complaining bitterly about being booed for loafing into second base on what the fans clearly believed should have been a triple.

"Ted," came the unmistakable voice of Joe DiMaggio, "you're a crybaby!"

Ted would argue with the fans and castigate them in print. Joe was so solicitous of the good opinion of his fans that he would apologize to the bleacherites for having to turn his back on them in order to speak into a microphone while accepting an award at home plate.

Ted was a chatterbox. Joe was pathologically silent. Dom Di-Maggio would come into Yankee Stadium and ask Joe's pal Lefty Gomez, "Is Joe talking?"

"He said a complete sentence a couple of days ago," Lefty would say.

"I guess I'll leave him alone," Dom would say.

And yet—there is something wistful about this—Joe's closest companion on the Yankees was always the wild man of the team, starting with Pat Malone and going on to Lefty Gomez, Joe Page, and Billy Martin.

Ted's closest friends on the Red Sox were the three other West Coasters who had come up from the minors at roughly the same time and formed the core of the ball club. Bobby Doerr was quiet, Johnny Pesky was self-effacing, and Dom DiMaggio was shy to the point of bashfulness.

Joe knew exactly who he was and what he represented. His uniform always had a tailored look. His cap was set on his head just so, his hair was neatly cut and slicked down, his jacket carefully buttoned. He never stuffed his glove in his back pocket. He never chewed tobacco. He had a way of putting on his glove and pounding it, as he was running out to center field, that amounted to a kind of public announcement that he knew how good he was. "He never dove for a ball or rolled in the dirt like the common people,'' Clif Keane says. ''But he got to every ball he should have got to. You couldn't get a hit in front of him. Other players had good games. He had a good game, it seemed like, every time.''

Ted had his great games. And, as we know, he also had his share of sulking, go-to-hell games.

Joe's appeal went far beyond the drumbeating of the New York press. This silent athlete was an integral part of the folklore. Silence was synonymous with modesty and decency and good citizenship, for much the same reason that it was an accepted rule of baseball that you always caught the ball with two hands. ''Twoooo haaaands for beginners!'' was the cry that never failed to go up in a sandlot or a major-league park when anybody showboated. Sound technical reasons were put forth to explain why one-handed catches were risky, but it was somehow understood that catching the ball with two hands had more to do with character than with technique. It was an offer of proof that you were a team player, sensitive to the good opinion of all mankind, as represented by the management, the other players, and the customers. And a good example for all those dirty-faced kids on the sandlots.

Ted was fun to watch. There was the anticipation of something more than just his next time at bat. There was an underlying tension. You never knew what might happen. You were always hoping that something would.

Joe was not the speed demon he had been before he fractured his knee in the Pacific Coast League. Nobody got out of the batter's box faster, though, because nobody could accelerate quicker. Going from first to third, he had all the sleekness of a cutter prowing through still water.

Ted came out of the batter's box with everything flapping—arms, legs, and head.

Question: If Ted had been able to accelerate out of the left-hand side of the box as fast as DiMaggio did from the right, might not he have added a minimum of twenty points to his batting average every year?

"That's one of the most erroneous beliefs in baseball," Ted says. "A real full-swinging left-handed hitter falls toward third base, and a full-swinging right-handed hitter falls toward first. Absolutely a fact. You can see it yourself. It's the left-handed singles hitter who is halfway down to first when he hits the ball. The full-swinging left-handed hitter never gets out of the box fast."

Ted was never as slow, however, as he sometimes likes to say he was. Or, even, as his loose, loping stride made him look. Press him and he'll admit that he could go from first to third, or from second to the plate, with anybody. ("I led the league in scoring runs seven times, and I was playing in a park where it wasn't always easy to score from second. I must have been able to run pretty well to do that.")

Joe, who had left high school in his second year, felt keenly his lack of education. During the long train trips that were an important part of a player's life in that era, he would listen in eagerly whenever the sportswriters and his teammates began to talk about books or plays or music.

Joe was a clotheshorse, and his friends, never numerous, were upper-echelon Broadway types who wrapped him in the protective cocoon he desired.

Ted was loud and profane, but he was also intellectually adventurous. He had a keen mind and a wide range of interests. His friendships covered a broad spectrum. To the public at large, he was remarkably open and completely accessible.

To the Yankee players Ted was The Thumper. To the Red Sox players Joe was The Jolter.

The way the public saw them, Joe DiMaggio was grace, and Ted Williams was spirit.

In 1941, the Most Valuable Player award went to Joe DiMaggio. The vote was 291 to 254. Ted said that DiMaggio deserved it. And you could make a strong case that he did.

In the course of the 56-game streak and the subsequent 16-game mini-streak, the Yankees won 44 out of 52 games, a record that has never been equaled. And, in the process, ran away with the pennant.

On the other hand, the Yankees were heavily favored to win. The Red Sox were supposed to finish exactly where they had finished the previous season. Fourth.

Dave Egan, working the other side of the street on this one, had given his personal Award to the Kid. "Certainly DiMaggio sparked the Yankees to the pennant," he wrote, "but he was sparking a smart and nimble and intelligent and ambitious team. It did not require very much to set them off. . . .

"On the other hand, Master Williams was carrying, on his slim, young shoulders, a lot of tired veterans and pleasant yes-men and family retainers. The Red Sox are not a baseball team; they are a country club."

Each of them had help. Joe's hitting streak was kept alive, more than once, by the tender, loving care accorded to him by the dean of New York sportswriters, Dan Daniel. Ted was helped, at the very end, not by any member of the Boston press corps but by an official scorer in Washington and a sympathetic first-base umpire.

Granting that DiMaggio deserved the MVP, which of them had the greater season? Clearly, it was Ted Williams.

Any streak is a statistical freak. Baseball is the game of the long season. What is so important, after all, about hitting in 56 straight games, instead of 55 out of 56. Or 54 of 56. There are statistics that define accomplishment and there are statistics that exist only because there are writers with columns to fill and statisticians with mouths to feed.

Before DiMaggio's 56-game streak nobody had paid any attention to such things. George Sisler's 37-game streak, which was the real record, had merited nothing more than a bottom-of-the-notes mention in 1922. Willie Keeler's 44 games was a kind of fake record which had been compiled in 1897, under entirely different rules, and dug up long after the fact to keep the DiMaggio cliffhanger going.

It was a statistician's record, a publicity man's delight, a merchandiser's dream.

But there were also other factors involved. In addition to the massive publicity that had fallen to him during the 56-game streak, all the presuppositions went his way. In his five seasons in New York the Yankees had won five pennants. During Williams's previous two seasons in the major leagues, DiMaggio had outhit him .381 to .327 and .352 to .344 and won the batting title both years. In the minds of baseball fans everywhere, Joe DiMaggio reigned supreme.

Joe himself doesn't look back on 1941 as one of his two greatest seasons. Bobby Doerr had played against Joe in the Pacific Coast League when Joe hit .398—and got beaten out by a guy named Oscar (Ox) Eckhardt, who led the league with .399. Bobby had always told everybody that the twenty-year-old DiMaggio of that season was the greatest ballplayer he'd ever seen. Years later, when the three of them—Doerr, DiMaggio, and Williams—were together at Cooperstown, Bobby asked Joe whether that wasn't really his greatest season. No, said Joe. To Joe, that season in the Pacific League was only his second-best. His greatest season, he thought, had come in 1939 when he had been hitting well over .400 with less than two weeks left in the season. And then he'd come down with an eye inflammation and had to stand with his head turned to the pitcher in order to see the ball. "We'd already clinched the pennant by then," he told them. "Why Joe McCarthy insisted on playing me, I'll never know."

If you want to know something, his greatest year may well have been 1937, when he hit .346, and had his highest power figures with 46 home runs and 167 RBIs.

In 1941, Ted Williams led the league in batting average, home runs, runs, bases on balls, slugging percentage, and on-base percentage. Joe DiMaggio led in runs batted in and total bases. Their comparative figures were as follows:

	G	ab	runs	hits	2b	3b	HR	rbi	bb	so	pct	OBA	Slg
Williams	143	456	**135**	181	33	3	**37**	120	**145**	27	**.406**	**.551**	**.735**
DiMaggio	139	541	122	193	43	11	30	**125**	76	13	.357	.440	.643

For a couple of power hitters, the strikeout totals are—well—striking. Ted struck out only 27 times; DiMaggio an almost unbelievably minuscule 13 times.

Don't dismiss DiMaggio's .357 too quickly, either. It is the second-highest average of his entire career. Perhaps even more significant, no right-handed hitter has had a higher average since, although Pittsburgh's Roberto Clemente did match it in winning the National League title in 1967.

His On-Base average of .440 was also the second-highest of his career, and yet it was more than 100 points behind Ted's. And it is right here, in this generally overlooked statistic, that the best case for Ted's value to his team can be shown.

In a game where it is customary to say that even the best hitters fail two times out of three (saying it doesn't make it so), Ted Williams reached base more often than he didn't. Every 100 times he came to the plate, he reached base 55 times and made out 45 times. With DiMaggio it was the other way around. DiMaggio was reaching base 44 times and going out 56 times.

The job of any manager is to have more runs up there on the scoreboard by the time he has got the other team to make 27 outs. Break it down and we see that Williams came to bat 601 times and went out 275 times. DiMaggio came to bat 617 times and went out 348 times. The opposition got 73 more outs of him than out of Williams.

There is a very good reason for such a huge differential during one of Joe DiMaggio's greatest seasons. Ted Williams's .551 on-base percentage in 1941 is, purely and simply, the best of all time.

But what influenced the coverage more than anything else was that a .400 batting average was not such a showstopping achievement in 1941. Bill Terry had hit .401 in 1930, and there had been a couple of good runs at it since. Any middle-aged writer or baseball fan had a handful of .400 seasons in his memory bank.

Let's take a look at it:

The modern era begins in 1909. Until then (hi there, Willie Keeler) foul balls were not counted as strikes and the batter could attempt to bunt forever on the third strike without having to worry about being called out if he fouled it off.

Since then, there had been eleven .400 seasons (divided among six players) in the previous three decades. Seven in the previous two decades. What follows here are those eleven .400 seasons.

Note: In order to expand the coverage, the second column lists their On Base averages and slugging percentages during their immortal seasons.

And since it is only fair to compare them to their own times as well as to each other, Column Three shows how much they had hit above the league average. PRO we will get to later.

			OBA	Slg	LgAv	above	PRO
1924	Rogers Hornsby	.424	.507	.696	.283	141	1.203
1922	George Sisler	.420	.467	.594	.285	135	1.061
1911	Ty Cobb	.420	.467	.621	.273	147	1.088
1912	Ty Cobb	.410	.458	.586	.265	145	1.044
1911	Joe Jackson	.408	.468	.590	.273	135	1.058
1920	George Sisler	.407	.449	.632	.283	124	1.081
1941	**Ted Williams**	**.406**	**.551**	**.735**	**.266**	**140**	1.286
1925	Rogers Hornsby	.403	.489	.756	.292	111	1.245
1923	Harry Heilmann	.403	.481	.632	.282	121	1.113
1922	Ty Cobb	.401	.462	.565	.285	116	1.027
1922	Rogers Hornsby	.401	.459	.728	.292	109	1.187
1930	Bill Terry	.401	.452	.619	.303	98	1.071

Breaking it down, then, we find that Ted had the only .400 average, except for Terry's, in 16 years, and if it is possible to hit a weak .401, then Terry's .401 is weak.

In 1930, the ball had been hopped up so much that the batting average for *the entire National League* was .303. In addition to Terry's .401, there was Babe Herman, .393; Chuck Klein, .386; Lefty O'Doul, .383; Freddie Lindstrom, .379. In the power departments, Hack Wilson hit 56 home runs, still the National League record, and knocked in 190 runs, which is still the Major League record.

There is still another factor that has to be considered. Bill Terry operated under a more generous sacrifice fly rule than any of the others.

The rule kept changing:

1908	Sac fly, no time at bat
1926	Sac Fly *if any runner advances*
1931	No Sac fly
1939	Sac fly *if runner scores*
1940	RBI if runner scores *but charged with time at bat*
1954	Sac Fly reinstated

· Bill Terry was the only .400 hitter who had the benefit of not being charged with a time at bat on a fly ball which advanced a runner from one base to another, regardless.

· Ted Williams was the only .400 hitter who did not benefit from the sacrifice fly rule at all.

In 1941, Ted had six sacrifice flies. Under the old rules his average would have been .412, which would have given him the fourth-highest of all time.

There was also at least one occasion when his long fly ball advanced a runner from second to third. Under the rules extant for Bill Terry in 1930, that one wouldn't have counted as a time at bat either.

More important by far, when we consider the variables, was the improved fielding. Not necessarily because the players had become significantly more skillful but because the gloves had been so greatly improved. All you have to do is look at the pictures of the gloves that were being used in the twenties, and you can see that they were not much bigger than mittens. By 1941, they had become large enough so that it was the glove, not the fielder, that was making a certain number of plays.

Compare his season to those of the other .400 hitters, and it can be seen that only Rogers Hornsby comes close to him in combining both power and average.

· He is far ahead in on-base percentage—which is a function of both base hits and walks—and second only to Hornsby in slugging percentage.

· He was 140 points above the league average, which ranks him third to Ty Cobb's 147 in 1911 and Hornsby's 141 in 1924.

Is it the best season ever? How do you compare eras? And how can you compare anybody to Babe Ruth? Well, you do your best to take all the variables into consideration, and you find out what respected baseball men who have seen them all have to say. When Del Baker was retiring in 1960, after fifty-six years in the game, he said, "Ted Williams in 1941 was the best hitter I ever saw, and that includes Ty Cobb and Babe Ruth." Keep in mind that Del Baker, as the manager of the Detroit Tigers—and the All-Star Game—had seen Ted at his very best.

It is fair to say that Ted's 1941 season has grown ever larger and more luminous through the years. And not only because nobody has hit .400 since.

Sabermatics is one reason. The influx of the New Statistics. Why wasn't Ted's record-shattering .551 On Base Percentage given more weight, you may ask. The answer is simple. There was no such statistic in 1941. And, as the story of Rumpelstiltskin told us back in grammar school, you can't handle it unless you can give it a name.

On Base Percentage is simple enough to figure. You take the number of At Bats and add to it the number of times the batter reached base on a base on balls or by being hit by the pitch. Then you take his base hit total and do the same thing.

The statistic was invented by Allan Roth, the grand wizard of statistics, for Branch Rickey and the Brooklyn Dodgers back in the 1950s. In 1974, Pete Palmer, who was then the statistician for the American League, tried to introduce it to a wider audience by writing an article for the *Research Journal*. But despite Palmer's best efforts, it was not accepted as an official stat until 1984.

By then, Ted had been preaching the value of getting on base for forty years. "I first heard there was such a statistic sometime back in the middle forties." Not as a statistic used by baseball people but by those most pragmatic of men, the gamblers.

There was, Ted says, a little pocket of gamblers who used to sit high up in the right-field bleachers at Fenway Park. The kind of action gamblers who would bet on every pitch. "One of the guys that I knew had either been in the group or had seen it or heard it and he said, 'You know, you're an even money bet to get on base any time you come to the plate.'

"That always stuck with me. I started to relate it to other players, to Ruth, Foxx, and Gehrig and those other guys who got all the walks and the base hits, and of course they fared the best." He went back twenty years, and the pattern was the same. There were great sluggers, he could see, who were more than sluggers. "And I realized they didn't get the credit they should have gotten for getting on base all the time."

Joe Cronin didn't have to be convinced. Joe Cronin was always trying to tell the writers that Ted was as much of a table-setter for the Red Sox as Dom DiMaggio and Johnny Pesky were, because he was able to advance the runner from first to second on his ground balls, and walk so often with men on base to give the guy behind him a chance to drive them in. "The first time I ever heard the expression 'table-setter,'" Ted remembers. "Joe Cronin was applying it to me."

It works both ways. The slugger becomes more valuable when he is also reaching base with consistency, and the hitter who is always on base has a limited value if he is not also hitting with power. To combine the two, Pete Palmer and John Thorn combined the On Base Percentage and the Slugging Average—that is, added them together—for their massive tome, *Total Baseball*. To find a word that would fit atop the column on the statistical charts, the publisher settled upon PRO (for PRODUCTION). A lamentably colorless appellation for what has become, by general agreement, the most valuable of all statistics.

The OBA and the PRO stats have put an added glow on Ted's 1941 season and, for that matter, upon his whole career. Ted's OBA is .483 lifetime. The best ever. The Babe is second with .474.

On PRODUCTION, the Babe leads Ted 1.163 to 1.116.

When Ted is told that he and Babe Ruth run neck and neck in those categories and that nobody else is even close, he says, "What about

Lou Gehrig? God almighty, how could anybody be better than *Gehrig!* Look up *Gehrig* again!''

OK. Gehrig runs third in OBA with .447 and in PRO with 1.080. Not a distant third. A very respectable third. But, nevertheless, third. See Appendix F.

From 1941 through 1949, Ted Williams had an OBA of .5026. That's six seasons, inclusive, in which he reached base more than half the time.

Stretch it out between 1941 and 1957 (his two greatest seasons) and he was .498, which is reaching base almost half the time over twelve seasons.

Ahh, but what about Fenway Park? The gamblers out in right field weren't basing their odds on Ted's overall percentages. They were wheeling and dealing in his home park, and wasn't Fenway Park supposed to be a tough park for him to hit in? *Au contraire.* Ted Williams's lifetime OBA at Fenway Park was .497. And doesn't that suggest that over the prime years of his career anybody placing an even-money bet on him was getting all the best of it?

You bet they were. From 1941 through 1957, his OBA average at Fenway Park was an almost unbelievable .515.

In the year we are charting here—the wondrous year of 1941—his on-base percentage at home was **.574**

If you take Ted Williams's entire career with the Red Sox against Babe Ruth's entire career with the Yankees (which means eliminating Ruth's early years with the Red Sox and the final unhappy snippet of a season with the Boston Braves), the Babe goes ahead .484 to .483. With one demurrer. The pesky Sacrifice fly rule again. To be perfectly logical about this, the Sacrifice fly *should* count as an out in this context. As it did for Ted in eight of those seasons. But the fact remains that the Babe's Sacrifice flies were not charged against his batting average at any time during his career, and so if you want to keep the playing field even—and since it's our playing field we can make the rules—Ted would finish a good five points ahead of the Babe when they are matched, head to head, as the greatest of all Red Sox sluggers vs. the greatest of all Yankee sluggers.

With the added luster provided by the New Statistics you could make an excellent case that Ted Williams's 1941 season was indeed the best that anybody has ever had.

· The best On Base Percentage in the history of baseball. Ever.

· The best PRO figure of any of the .400 hitters.

· The fourth-best PRODUCTION figure—ever—behind Babe Ruth's overwhelming seasons of 1920, 1921, and 1923.

· The seventh-highest batting average of all time.

· The tenth-highest slugging average.

· The second-best base on balls percentage, ever. One walk in every 4.14 times at bat.

· His 145 bases on balls were the fourth-highest total of all time behind Ruth in 1923 (170) and 1920 (148) and one Jimmy Scheckard, who walked 147 times in 1911.*

Too bad they didn't think it was deserving of the MVP award.

---

* Ted's 1941 total now leaves him tied with himself for twelfth on the all-time list, with Ted himself ranking second, third, and fourth.)

X

The Hitter at Work

*Whenever I swung at a bad ball a little bit high or even inside I didn't
like it, but when I swung at a ball that was in the dirt or outside,
Jesus, I just wanted to puke because I knew that if I hit it I wouldn't
have done anything with it anyway.*

—TED WILLIAMS

In the springtime of 1938 Rogers Hornsby had imparted the words
of advice that Ted would repeat for the rest of his career: "Get a
good ball to hit."

Why, one cannot help but wonder, did that advice leave such a
lasting impression? There was hardly anything revolutionary about it.
Hornsby was really only confirming what Ted had been doing all his
life.

When Ted was visualizing pitches for himself in his backyard, was
he not, almost by definition, swinging at nothing but strikes? Yes, he
would sometimes burst into tears when he was walked in high school,
but did that not reveal better than anything that he was refusing to
swing at a bad pitch? Even his mother, who never did learn anything
about baseball, would ask spectators while she was touring the park
with her tambourine, "Why do they keep walking Teddy? He wants
to hit the ball."

The contradiction here is mind-boggling. Who would have dreamed
that the kid who cried when he was walked would be able to discipline
himself so completely that his base-on-balls percentage would be the
highest of anybody who has ever played the game? Let alone that he
would be criticized through the greater part of his career for being
"willing to take a walk in the clutch instead of swinging at a ball just
a little off the plate."

Ted himself can't explain why Hornsby's words hit him so forcefully. "It wasn't anything I hadn't thought of before," he concedes.
"It wasn't anything new. I'd walked an awful lot in high school and
in San Diego. Hornsby just put it in a way that clicked for me."

Do you know what it was? Do you know what the answer has to
be? Hornsby had put it to him in such a way as to turn a negative into

a positive. *They* weren't doing it to *him* by not giving him a pitch he could swing at. *He* was doing it to *them* by refusing to swing at a bad pitch.

In San Diego, he'd had roughly similar discussions with that wise old head, Bill Starr. Starr didn't go along with the conventional belief that home-run hitters had to expect to strike out more than anybody else because they swung harder than anybody else. The reason home-run hitters struck out so much, Starr would tell Ted, was because they went after more bad pitches than anybody else. And nobody, Starr would emphasize, hit home runs off bad pitches.

"There was a lot of truth to Starr's theories," Ted says, "and it may have been in my mind, subconsciously." But essentially he had come to feel that Starr was simply not a good enough hitter to understand how a home-run hitter functioned.

It's not only what home-run hitters swing at, Ted decided, but (1) when they swing, (2) how they swing, and (3) what they are trying to accomplish. Take a hitting lesson from Ted Williams:

(1) "You're really starting to commit yourself when the pitcher lets the ball go, but you really go through with that commitment when the ball's fifteen or sixteen feet from the plate. That's the area where you decide whether you're going to swing or that you're not ready for that pitch. So you've got a little time. But some guys never program themselves into that finer tuning. Johnny Mize never swung at the bad pitch. Joe DiMaggio didn't, either. I was with Joe one time, and we were talking about it. He said, 'Oh, jesus, I swung at a lot of bad balls.' I said, 'Goddamn, that's news to me. I never saw you swing at very many bad pitches.' "

(2) The home-run hitter swings harder because he swings faster. And he swings faster because he waits longer. "For me, the long-ball hitters, the fly-ball hitters, generally do strike out the most. The reason they do is that they probably are hitting it just a little bit later than most guys. They're laying back, and they're always striving to get out in front, and when they do they've made that all-out-effort swing to get to the ball out there, and as a result it's generally a more powerful swing."

Ted's secret was that he had perfected the swing, the eye, and the discipline that allowed him to do all that while still swinging well within himself. "The average hitter tries to hit the ball too hard. The secret of hitting is to get your power one hundred percent from your forearms, wrists, and hands."

The finer tuning on the timing determines everything, he says. And that is divided between whether the batter swings a microsecond early or late, or hits the ball a millifraction too high or too low. "If you hit the ball a little early it's a ground ball. A little late, it's a pop fly. That isn't ironclad, but it's pretty much of a cardinal rule."

(3) An even finer element of timing comes into play to constitute the difference between a towering home run and a sinking line drive. "Home runs come from striking the ball in the right place with a slight uppercut, if you can call a four-to-five-degree upswing an uppercut. The sinking liner comes when you were just above center of that slight uppercut on the ball, which is enough to get it in the air but still get top spin to it. But occasionally you'll get under it and get the under spin with all the power you needed, and it just keeps going, and then if you get a little wind behind it, it goes a ton."

That's what it's all about as far as Ted Williams is concerned. To get the ball up in the air, with power. "To hit a bullet line drive is one thing; to hit it hard in the air is another thing. I've criticized some hitters who had extreme power and they'd hit line drives and blue darters through the infield—as hard as anybody could hit it—and they're singles or potential double-play balls. That never meant much to me, a hard-hit ball through the infield. Nice. Felt great off the bat. But I'd go to first base and say, 'Boy, I wish I'd have got that in the air.'"

One other thing: with two strikes he'd choke up and go through the middle, something no other power hitter had ever done. "You give something away when you pull," he explains. "Up the middle, you can wait a little longer, and you're hitting the ball at right angles to the direction of the pitch. When you pull you're striking the ball at an angle of forty-five degrees and losing thirty percent of the sweet spot on the hitting surface."

Ted talks like that when he's talking about hitting—philosophy and discipline combined with geometry and physics. As Bob Lemon, who came to the big leagues as an outfielder and went on to become a Hall of Fame pitcher, can attest. "Williams was the only hitter I ever knew that it was like somebody looking at your hole card," Lemon says. "You'd look down at him, and you knew that he knew. We talked about it one day, and that's when I realized why I had become a pitcher. You had to be an MIT graduate to know what the hell he was talking about."

Ted's original exposure to the physics of a thrown or batted baseballs came when he studied aerodynamics in the service. "There was a little professor there, Doc Ewen, who was really great because he could answer all my questions about why a ball curved and why one bat could hit a ball farther than the other, and he could make it all so simple and basic."

It all started, it seems, not with Abner Doubleday but with Daniel Bernoulli, an eighteenth-century Swiss mathematician, whose seminal work on the theory of gases and fluids provided the basic theory for aerodynamics. The Bernoulli effect states that an increase in the velocity of air reduces the static pressure. Ted can give a fifteen-minute lecture on how the formula can be applied to the movement of a curveball, which is almost self-evident, and how it can also be applied—if you happen to be Ted Williams—to air and velocity and weight and force as they affect the movement of a bat into a ball.

"Bernoulli had three rules of physics. One was that the faster the speed, the less the pressure. In a hose, the faster the water goes out, the less the pressure is on the side of the hose. When you apply that to the wing of an airplane, the wind goes over the cambered top and under the flat surface at the bottom, and they both reach the back at the same time. Because of the camber of the wing—it's got a little curve to it—more air has to move over the top than under the bottom, but it wants to go over and meet the associated wind at the same time, and that means it's had to go faster. Bernoulli found that out—he made the principle of physics that was applied later on—and that's the reason the airplane gets lifted. The resultant air, which means the air it's going toward, is going fifty miles an hour with no wind. So the difference between the speed of the air going over the wing, and of the wind going under the lower surface, creates a differential of pressure—it's lighter on top—and that's the reason the plane wants to go up.

"It's also the reason a curve ball curves. If you rotate a curveball, and it's thrown into the resultant wind, it's spinning toward the resultant wind, right? Same principle. The wind that hits the ball in the middle and goes under is going with the spin of the ball, and the wind that's going to the center of the ball and goes to the top edge of the ball meets the spin of what the baseball is doing, and that has a *buffering* effect, and because of that, that wind becomes a little bit slower. So it's faster under the ball than it is on top of the ball, so it wants to drop down, doesn't it?''

Okay, but how did that help him as a hitter?

"It doesn't. Not at all. But here's where it helped me with hitting. You can take a twenty-ounce bat and move it at fifty miles an hour, say, and you've got a one thousand factor there, and you can take a thirty-five-ounce bat and move it at twenty miles an hour, and you've only got seven hundred at the end result of the swing. So there's more power in a light bat going faster than a heavy bat going slower.

"Now, power or force or whatever you want to call it at the end of that stroke, at whatever weight you have plus the speed you've generated, is your power and your total force at the point of impact. That's the reason you can take a big steam shovel and move it two feet and it ain't going to hurt anybody. Take eight ounces and flick it at him, and it jars him because there's more total force and energy in the little eight-ounce zinger. Pushed to the ultimate, you can take a tiny particle and speed it up enough so that it will go right through you.

"So what's the advantage of the lighter bat? You can wait longer. Understand that? The lighter bat goes faster. Even if you don't hit the ball any farther, you're going to be able to wait longer and be fooled less.''

It was not until the Red Sox lost some key games at the end of 1948 and 1949 that the Boston press—and not the Boston press alone—

began to taunt Ted for his refusal to go after a pitch a little out of the strike zone when a game was on the line.

"Suppose I started swinging at off-center pitching," Ted would say. "Say, an inch or two off the plate, either side. Right away I'm working for the pitcher instead of myself. I'm making the plate twenty-one inches wide instead of the regulation seventeen. So then I'm going to be swinging at pitches below my knees and above my armpits. Don't think the pitchers aren't quick to notice. So they feed me more teasers, a bit farther away—sucker stuff which I foul off, dribble in the dirt, or pop up."

Once you had established yourself as a good hitter, as Ted discovered in his second season, the pitchers were going to pitch you tougher and tougher, and that made it more essential than ever to understand what you were doing. "A good hitter has that one instinctive thing about him, that he knows a ball that's tough and he doesn't go after it. Otherwise, he's going to have a thirty percent bigger strike zone, and he's never really going to get a helluva lot better. The good pitchers make him hit at bad balls, he can't lay off of them, and that's where the pitchers make a heyday out of it."

And, oh yeah, one other thing. "The umpires make the strike zone," Ted says. And so he studied the umpires almost as closely as he studied the pitchers. On his first time at bat he was looking not only for what the pitcher was throwing but also for where the umpire's strike zone was going to be.

"If he called one, and I thought, jeez, this guy is going to call a high strike, instinctively I'd gear up for that a little more. I knew the umpire that called low strikes and the umpire that called high strikes, and a lot of them were built for that very thing. For instance, a shorter, dumpier umpire might be more low ball, and a big tall guy would be a high ball. Big Cal Hubbard was a high-ball umpire. Anything titty high was a strike. And you knew that. You accommodated yourself to the pitcher, to the umpire, to everything as you go along. That's the reason it's easier to play in the big leagues. You know the pitcher and umpire."

He not only adjusted himself to the umpire and to the pitcher, he was—despite everything that has been written—not at all unwilling to go outside the strike zone for a pitch he knew he could handle. Ted murdered high-fast-ball pitchers like Red Ruffing and Johnny Rigney. Just because he had an umpire who wasn't going to call a "titty high" strike didn't make his eyes light up any the less when he saw one coming. "Boy," he says, those expressive features of his lighting up, "a ball above the waist is a helluva ball to hit. The guys who had the best luck with me never gave me anything except quick breaking stuff, down in the dirt. They'd show me the fast ball, but it was never one I could hit."

Purely as a spectator, he laments the lowering of the strike zone over the past ten or fifteen years. "The most exciting swing in baseball is the guy who takes a big swing at the high, hard pitch and you can hear it pop in the catcher's glove." Instead, the hitter today has to protect himself against the low strike. "You see the ball down in the dirt, low, skidding. The guy swings at it and looks lousy doing it." Why? "Because the hitter isn't disciplined enough so that he lays off it."

As for Ted, he not only adjusted to the umpires; he played them like a virtuoso. Don't kid yourself, the umpires deal in strikes and balls, but they also deal in reward and punishment. Give them a hard time—known as "showing me up"—and they'll get you. Make it easy for them, especially if you were a superstar like Williams or DiMaggio, and they'd give you the benefit of every doubt—sometimes, even, when the doubt wasn't visible to the naked eye. Even as a rookie, Ted would almost congratulate an umpire for calling him out on strikes. "What a dope I was to take it," he would say as he was walking away.

As his career progressed, he cultivated an ongoing relationship with umpires. "He treated them like gods," Don Fitzpatrick, the Red Sox clubhouse man, remembers. "For two reasons. He figured they might help him, plus he got a lot of information from them." During rain delays Ted could always be found down in the tunnel swapping stories with them. "He'd let them tell their stories. Then he'd say, 'Hey, how did so-and-so look in Cleveland?' They'd say, 'You know, Teddy, he got so-and-so out with this.' They'd tell him everything he wanted to know. Oh, genius."

Absolutely true, Ted laughs. "Who knew better than the umpires who was sharp and who was losing his fast ball and all the rest of it? Especially when a new pitcher had come in the league. They'd tell me, 'This kid is a real good pitcher and can thread a needle on that outside.' On somebody else, 'You won't have any trouble with him, Ted. He's nothing.'"

It was to his friends the umpires that he went for information when he became the manager of the Washington Senators in 1969. "I didn't know the personnel around the league. I'd been gone for nine years. Who could fill me in better? I can remember Hank Soar telling me about John Tudor, the little lefty with the Red Sox. How he'd paint the corner and then keep going out a little farther, a little farther. 'The way he flips it in there,' Soar said. 'I don't see how they ever hit him.'" (For whatever reason, Tudor couldn't win with the Red Sox, but then he went over to the other league and became every bit the unhittable pitcher Soar had described.)

It wasn't only the pitchers he asked about. And he didn't always wait for it to rain. Ed Runge came to the American League in 1954, the year Ted returned from Korea. He is now in retirement in San Diego: "I remember real well he would come into the umpires' room in Washington. He'd say he wanted to get away from the press. He didn't talk too much about the pitchers with us. He always talked about trades. Who would you trade for who, that kind of stuff." And yeah, Runge says, he can see where Ted was getting a complete scouting report on the players' strengths and weaknesses from them.

More important to Ted than the umpires were the pitchers themselves, and over a period of twenty-one years he never stopped stroking them. Never said an unkind word about them. Never showed them up. He could have hit two home runs and two doubles off someone, and he would say, "He really has good stuff. I was just lucky off him today."

He'd go out of his way to tell a pitcher who had given him trouble how tough he was. "My number-one nemesis," he'd call him. If all his number-one nemeses had been laid end to end, they'd have reached about five rows up into the center-field bleachers.

The best proof of how well the stroking succeeded was that he was almost never knocked down. All pitchers loved to say, "Nobody digs in against me." Nobody dug in more firmly than Williams, and yet Clif Keane can remember seeing him knocked down, deliberately, only once. "One day in Washington, Camilo Pascual knocked him on his ass. Threw it right at his head, and his cap came off and his bat went flying through the air. This was in the middle of his career. He got up and a pitch later hit it off the wall in right field."

Well, he did show up a pitcher once. And that was in Washington, too. Mel Parnell still laughs about it: "During Pedro Ramos's rookie season, he struck out Ted and was so elated that he came into the clubhouse after the game to have Ted sign the ball for him. Williams says, 'I don't sign any balls I struck out on,' and Pedro, who didn't realize that Ted was teasing him, was so disappointed you could almost see tears rolling out of his eyes. Well, as soon as Williams saw that, he said, 'Sure, give me the ball. I'll sign it for you.' And Pedro goes out of our clubhouse happy as a lark. The next game Pedro pitches against us, Williams hits one about halfway up the right-field bleachers, and as he was running around the bases he yelled out to Pedro, 'If you find that sonofabitch, I'll sign it, too!' "

If there was anything that angered Ted more than to be accused of hurting his team by taking too many walks, it was to be characterized as a born hitter. Very early in his career, it became a rule of the lodge to call him "the greatest natural hitter since Shoeless Joe Jackson," or, to those who wanted to burn all their bridges, "the greatest natural hitter of all time."

Ted did not take that as a compliment. What about all the practice?

he would ask. What about the years of dedication? Sure, his eyes tested out at a remarkable 20/10 at the time he joined the Naval Reserve, but by the latter half of his career, as he liked to point out, his eyesight was down to 20/15. "Half the major-leaguers have eyes as good as that," he would say. "It isn't eyesight that makes a hitter. It's practice. Con-sci-en-tious practice. I say that Williams has hit more balls than any guy living, except maybe Ty Cobb. I don't say it to brag; I just state it as a fact. From the time I was eleven years old, I've taken every possible opportunity to swing at a ball. I've swung and I've swung and I've swung."

Without departing from the obvious advantages of Ted's superior eyesight and reflexes, it is well to point out that there was nothing all that shoeless about his .285 overall average at San Diego.

Del Baker, who ended his career in baseball as a coach for the Red Sox, would tell you that Williams was the smartest hitter he ever saw. "When Joe Jackson was asked the secret of his hitting, he said, 'It's no secret. I just wait until the ball gets right *here* and then I hit it.' Ted Williams can tell you *why* he hit it. Ted Williams can get out of a slump because he knows what is happening."

Del Baker was managing in Detroit, of course, when Ted came up. "All young hitters have trouble defining the strike zone," Del said. "The book on Ted when he first came up was that he would chase high balls." Halfway through Ted's third season, Jimmy Dykes, the manager of the White Sox, was saying, "If he has any weakness at all, it's his anxiety to hit the ball. That's why we sometimes get him out by giving him bad balls on the first couple of pitches. If he lets them go, we just about have to walk him. If he happens to slash at one of those bad ones and doesn't hit it safely, then he's done us a favor."

Ted had what baseball men call "great bat control"—meaning that he could wait until the ball was right on the plate and still swing easily and smoothly. But he had great willpower at bat, too, and that was something he had to develop.

To Bobby Doerr, he was the most disciplined hitter he ever saw. "I look back now," Doerr says, "and it seems that seventy-five to eighty percent of hitters in the major leagues give about seventy-five times at bat away in five hundred times at bat. One way or another. Either not being ready for the pitch or going out of the strike zone. With Ted, if he gave ten times at bat away in the season it was a rarity. That's where he was so great.''

He was also, in Doerr's opinion, the most innovative. He was, for instance, the first hitter to use rosin to keep his hands dry. ''And then he got the idea of mixing the rosin with olive oil to concoct a sticky substance to apply to the bat. He mixed up a batch for all of us.'' That, says Doerr, was years before players began to use pine tar. ''The olive oil and rosin would make the bat dark, the way it does now when they're using the pine tar, and, God, he had that little spot about that big on the fat part of the bat that was white where he hit every ball. Not a mark anywhere else on the bat. It was amazing.''

In addition to being the first power hitter to shorten up with two strikes on him, Ted was the first home-run hitter to go to a light bat. He was swinging a thirty-two- or thirty-three-ounce bat at a time when thirty-four or thirty-five ounces was the norm.

He was also one of the first to bring weights into the clubhouse, at a time when it was an article of faith that weight lifting would leave a player muscle-bound. He had come into baseball as a skinny 146-pounder and had built himself up through a carefully devised regime of weights, pulleys, and calisthenics.

Even back in San Diego, he would tighten up his left fist and ask Doerr to feel his arm. ''On the outside of his elbow, there'd be a big knot about as big as an egg.'' But when he somehow came to the conclusion that a hitter got most of his power from his lead hand, he put in hours of extra time strengthening his right wrist. When he narrowed the hitting area to the forearms, wrists, and hands, he rigged up a pulley arrangement by which he rotated a thirteen-pound weight (attached to a six-foot cord) around a wooden spool. By turning the spool over and over and over, he exercised only the muscles he felt he needed for hitting.

''It wasn't a matter that I could do so much more than anyone else,'' Ted says, ''because I couldn't. But I would try to do chin-ups both ways. Push-ups, fingertips, and otherwise.'' To make it harder, he would do the push-ups with his feet up on a trunk. ''Those were the main ones. And I swung a bat, my God, I used to take a heavy bat and swing it until I couldn't swing it anymore. Again hitting at an imaginary pitch and visualizing what I would do with it.''

Visualizing what he would do with it, he did that all his life. What nobody seemed to realize was that when he was swinging his glove in the outfield it was because he had either just seen a new pitcher and was putting him into his computer, or had been fooled by a veteran pitcher who had gone to something new.

''As you got older and got more familiar with the pitchers, they were getting more familiar with you and when, surprisingly, somebody would do something a little different, especially in a tough spot, and, jesus, they'd get you out going the other way, you know, I'd want to deal with that immediately.''

And so when you saw Ted out in the field the next inning, shadow swinging, he wasn't feeling especially exuberant as was generally supposed, he was doing some instant visualization on how he was going to handle this new way of pitching to him. ''The same way I was doing it in the backyard when I was a kid,'' he says. ''Absolutely. I did that all my life.''

Summer and winter, he would squeeze a hard little sponge ball. ''I did everything to try to get my hands stronger, and apparently all those little things helped a little bit, because I was strong in my arms. And I still believe that hitting is the rotation of the body with a push with the arms rather than wrist action. I think your wrists certainly play a part in it, at the tail end, where you make that little adjustment as you're hitting the ball. But the main work is the rotation of your body and your pulling through with your arms.''

To keep his legs in shape, he did a tremendous amount of walking. In most cities, he made it a habit to walk from his hotel to the ballpark, even in Kansas City, where it was a long, long haul. He would run backward for fifteen minutes at a time. The secret of Ted's baseball longevity was quite probably that he was never out of shape.

It was the mental dedication that marked him, though. The obsession with finding out everything he could about every pitcher he was going to face. From his first day at Sarasota as a rookie, he began to pester the veterans for information about the big-league pitchers. On Joe Cronin's advice, he wrote it all down in a little black book. And he never stopped asking. As soon as a new pitcher came into the league, Ted would run around to find anybody who had played against him. "When you're trying to find out about a new pitcher, you try to get the man who knows something about him to compare him with pitchers already in the league. They'll say, 'His curve is like so-and-so's. His fastball takes off like so-and-so's.' They might say, 'He reminds me of Spud Chandler. Good curve, good slider, sinking fastball. Nothing too good to hit, but always around the plate.' Well, when you faced him yourself, he might be nothing like Spud Chandler. With a young pitcher, you can be pretty sure that if he misses with his fastball and misses with his curve, he's going to try to come in with his fastball. That's about the only thing you can be sure of."

He had the perfectionist's eye for detail. He made a private study of the prevailing winds in all the ballparks. He knew the height of every pitcher's mound (it varies from park to park). He could tell you which batter's boxes sloped upward and which sloped downward, which were packed firmly and which loosely. At his first batting practice in Fenway Park after his return from Korea, he told Joe Cronin that home plate was a little out of line. To humor him, Cronin had the plate surveyed with a transit, and, sure enough, the report came back that it was indeed a fraction of an inch off.

The first thing Ted would do when he came out to the park, according to Johnny Pesky, was to see which way the flag was flying. "He always said to me, 'A little bit of wind affects a one-hundred-thousand-pound aircraft. What do you think it does to a baseball?' And he's right. In a football game, you'll hear the announcer talking about whether they're kicking into the wind or with the wind to their back. It's the same thing with a baseball." Ted would adjust his swing to the conditions. If the wind was blowing against him, he'd swing for base hits, not distance. On a really hot day, when he could see that the ball was carrying, he'd let out all the stops.

Joe Cronin probably put it as accurately as anyone when, very early in Ted's career, he said that if Ted had been playing in Ty Cobb's day he would have been battling Cobb for the batting average title every year, and if he had played in the Babe Ruth era he would have been battling Ruth every year in home runs.

He always remained on the bench before a game to study the opposing pitcher as he warmed up. Ted felt it was very important to study every little movement a pitcher made. It was his theory that we are all creatures of habit, himself included. "Everybody," he liked to say, "gets out of bed the same way every morning and gets dressed in the same order and pattern."

A pitcher at work, he believed, tended to fall into observable patterns. A certain succession of movements was a tip-off that a certain pitch was coming. Given a particular situation and a particular count, he would go to a particular pitch. Most pitchers, he discovered, would go to their "out" pitch, the pitch they wanted the batter to swing at, on a two-two count. He discovered that if a run-of-the-mound pitcher struck him out, he would never come back with the same pitch, in a key situation, during the same game. A good pitcher, on the other hand, would almost always come back with it on Ted's very next time at bat—possibly because the pitcher had more confidence in throwing his best pitch against Ted and possibly because he figured Ted would not be looking for it again. As a result, time after time, Ted was able to go back to the bench after striking out and predict a home run on his next time at bat.

The most spectacular call came the first time he faced Hal Newhouser after Ted's return from World War II. Newhouser had won twenty-nine and twenty-five games against wartime competition, and, indeed, he went on to win twenty-six games in 1946 and run a close second to Ted himself in the MVP voting. Newhouser had great speed and a great big curveball, and he had them both in good working order that day. He dusted Ted off with his first pitch and then struck him out on three straight pitches. As Ted came back to the bench, he heard his teammates *ooohing* and *aaahing* about Newhouser's stuff. "I'll bet anyone here anything they want to bet," he said evenly, "that I hit one out of here next time up." Rip Russell, a utility infielder, took him on for $5, and Ted hit one into the upper right-field deck at Briggs Stadium his next time at bat.

He did the same thing against Herb Score in the first game he faced him. Score struck Ted out with a blinding fastball his first time at bat. Ted told his teammates, "If he throws me the pitch I struck out on again, I'll hit one today." Herb did, and Ted did.

He studied box scores, too, for he realized that pitchers have slumps, just as hitters do. If he saw that a pitcher was going badly, he would assume that the pitcher was having trouble with his best pitch, and Ted would spend the early innings watching to see what pitch he was switching to when he had the batter in a hole.

And so, Ted would frequently ask a teammate, "What was the pitch he struck you out on?" or "What did he throw you on the two-two pitch?" If a young player confessed that he didn't know what the pitch had been, Ted would become incredulous. "You don't know the pitch he struck you out on? I'm not talking about last week or last month. I'm not even talking about yesterday. Today! Just now! I'm talking about the pitch he struck you out on just now." Returning to his place on the bench, he'd slump back in disgust and mutter, "What a rockhead. The guy's taking the bread and butter out of his mouth, and he doesn't even care how."

In a very short time, the player in question would have an answer ready. For Ted always was able to get young hitters thinking about their craft. Not only was he ready to instruct them; he would go out of his way to build up their confidence. "When you want to know who the best hitter in the league is," he'd tell the rookies, "just look into the mirror."

To the end, Ted said, "A bad day should bother a ballplayer. I still can't sleep when I'm not hitting. All your life you've got to adjust. The pitchers are constantly trying different things on you, so you have to constantly adjust to new conditions and new problems."

He was at war with the pitchers, and he missed nothing.

Item: In the late summer of Johnny Pesky's rookie year, Johnny, who was leading the league in base hits, was told that he was nothing for fourteen against Spud Chandler, the tough Yankee right-hander he'd be facing that afternoon: "Ted hears this, and here he comes. 'For crissake, you're trying to pull him, and you're hitting ground balls to second base.' And I've got to bite my tongue, because I hadn't seen where he'd done all that much against Chandler's hard sinker, either.

"Saturday afternoon game, big crowd, 1–1 game in bottom of eighth inning, runners on second and third, two out. I'm ready to step into the batting box. Ted says, 'Johnny, he's going to throw that hard sinker, away from you. When you pull it you're just going to hit a ground ball to second base. Goddamnit, listen to me. You've got to go up the middle or to left field.'

"So now I'm getting ready to step back into the box, he says, 'You know goddamn well they're not going to walk you to get to me.' Ball one, strike one, ball two, here comes that hard sinker. I go to left field, both runners score, and we're leading 3–1. I'm standing on first base, and Ted's looking at me with his big shit-eating grin. Chandler, in the meantime, is stomping around the mound. I hung up his jock-strap when he was pitching in the Coast League, and that was only three years earlier.

"Chandler finally gets ready to pitch to Ted, then he steps off, he looks over to me and says, 'You little shit!' I say, 'Go fuck yourself. You were a horseshit pitcher when you were in the Coast League. I could have hit you then.' He fires the first pitch to Ted, and it's a fastball right there, and Ted hits it thirty rows in the bleachers. I'm in the dugout by the time he gets to third base. When Ted hit the ball, everybody in the dugout got up to see where it was going. He really crushed it. A crack. We never got up and give it this high-five crap, just shaking his hand and saying, 'Jeez, you got all of that, Ted.' He's looking around, he says, 'Yeah, where's that horn-nosed little short-stop of ours?' I'm sitting next to Bobby in the dugout. I'm thinking, Jesus Christ, I got the big hit this inning and nobody even said nice going to me. Ted sits down. 'Goddamnit, Johnny, didn't I tell you how to hit Chandler?' I said, 'Let me tell you something, Ted, he was so goddamn mad at me that he forgot you were the next hitter.' He winks at me and he says, 'I know, I know. And I was ready, wasn't I?' "

Baseball changed in the period immediately after World War II. Ted himself was convinced that the ball was not as lively as the one that was used in his first four seasons. Add the checkerboard schedule of day and night games, which broke the routine of the players' eating and sleeping habits, add the big improvement in fielding (due in some part to better equipment), and add the great improvement in pitching, and it became easy for Ted to account for the diminished batting averages of the postwar years.

With Ted, there was one other consideration. As he played on into his late thirties and early forties, he got almost no "leg" hits. Yet he was always still able to adjust to changing conditions.

The best example of that came with the arrival of the slider. When Ted broke in, there were fastball pitchers and curveball pitchers. The fastball pitcher mixed his specialty with a curveball, and the curveball pitcher mixed his with a fastball. The batter had only to settle into a groove in which he was ready for either. Any pitcher so creative as to throw a pitch that dropped earned himself the title of "sinker-ball specialist" and was looked upon as a romantic and maybe even an eccentric. Sinker-ball specialists usually drank.

After the war, all the pitchers began to develop three or four different deliveries and three or four different speeds. Every rookie pitcher was told that he needed a third pitch or even a fourth pitch. That third pitch usually was the slider, which is thrown like a fastball and swerves at the last second like a curve.

"If you had two walnuts," Ted says, in explaining the problem the slider posed to the hitter, "you'd be able to pick out the right one half the time. If you had three walnuts, your chances would drop proportionately. Pitchers were able to pick up the slider so easily that it gave them that third walnut."

It was the slider that forced hitters to go to lighter, thinner bats, so that they could wait on the pitch until the last possible moment. The slider was made for the hitter who was quick with the bat, and Ted, who was already both the lightest and the quickest bat in town, made himself even quicker by going to a buggy-whip thirty-one-ouncer.

Still, right to the end, he never lost an opportunity to tell a writer with an opposing team what a tough time he was having with one of that team's slider-ball pitchers. A complete con job. He got to love the slider. He murdered the slider. "If that's what they're throwing the most," he admits today, with some delight, "that's what you want to learn to hit, isn't it?"

As a result, he was the only hitter who was able to hold his batting percentage while he went for the long ball. A comparison with Joe DiMaggio, in this respect, demonstrates how well Ted was able to adjust. For DiMaggio—as every pitcher in the American League knew— was always bothered by the slider. He was never the hitter after the war that he was before.

In seven seasons before he went into the army, DiMaggio had a lifetime average of .339. In his six seasons afterward, his average was .304. Take away his final disastrous year, when he fell to .263, and his postwar average would still be only .311.

Ted went into service with a four-year average of .356. His postwar average, over what amounted to thirteen seasons, was .340. Take away his last three seasons, when he began to show signs of decline, and it was .348 over ten seasons. He closed out the 1957 season, at the age of thirty-nine, with a lifetime average of .350. Those final three seasons knocked it down to .344.

Yet even at the end Ted Williams was as good a hitter as could be found anywhere in the league. His "poor" 1958 season (a twenty-two-point drop off his lifetime average) was good enough to win the batting championship. And in his final season, in 1960, his average of .316 was only four points below the league-leading average of Pete Runnels.

XI

1946 and
the World Series

With all their stars, the Red Sox of Ted Williams's youth had the reputation of being a team that never had it in the clutch. In 1939, his first year, they finished in second place, seventeen games behind the Yankees. The following year the Yankees finished third, but the best the Sox could do was a fourth-place tie with the straggling White Sox. In 1941, the year Ted hit .406, the Sox were second to the Yankees again, but again a distant seventeen games behind. In 1942, Ted's final year before he went off to war, they had their best season under Tom Yawkey and Joe Cronin, up to that point, winning ninety-three games. All it got them was another second-place finish, ten full games behind the Yankees.

In 1946, with Ted Williams and countless other veterans returning to big-league baseball, the Red Sox finally made it. They did it by getting off to a running start and pulling so far out in front that it was obvious they were going to win the American League pennant no more than two months into the season. After the halfway mark they were never fewer than ten games ahead. By early September the lead was sixteen games, and the Sox seemed on their way to break the 1927 Yankees record of 110 wins. As it was, a bad September slump—including six straight losses before they won the game that clinched the pennant—held their record to 104–50, twelve games ahead of Detroit and seventeen games ahead of the staggering New York Yankees.

Ted Williams has always said, "I hate front-runners." One of the reasons he refused to tip his cap, he would say, was because the same fans who cheered him when he was going well booed him when he was going badly. But the Red Sox turned out to be front-runners themselves. The *only* pennant they won came when they had no competition, no challenge. In the World Series, the St. Louis Cardinals, the pronounced underdog, stayed with the Red Sox, tied the Series three times, and in the showdown seventh game they beat them. This was the indictment that Ted—fairly or unfairly—had to live with from then on. The charge that he didn't have it when the pressure was on.

The prize exhibit for that indictment was his complete collapse in the World Series. In his defense, it must be said that he had not been hitting at the end of the regular season. Worse, he was playing with a sore elbow. And in all probability he had let the "Boudreau shift" get under his skin.

The first half of the season was pure joy for Ted. From his first time at bat, when he stepped up the plate in Washington's Griffith Stadium, in front of President Harry S. Truman and General Dwight D. Eisenhower, and hit the first pitch thrown to him into the left-center-field bleachers, a dozen rows above the 418-foot sign. According to the Washington writers, it not only was the first ball hit into that section by a left-hander since Lou Gehrig had done it fifteen years earlier but was the longest drive ever hit into that section by anybody.

The granddaddy of them all—the longest home run Ted ever hit at Fenway Park—came on June 9, against the Tigers' Fred Hutchinson. The exact spot where the ball landed was easily identifiable because it came down on the head of a construction worker sitting in the thirty-third row of the bleachers, putting a hole in his straw hat. The seat is still easy enough to identify, should you happen to find yourself in Fenway Park, because when Bill Crowley became the Red Sox publicity man he had it painted a commemorative red.

By one of those coincidences, the Red Sox were playing host to the All-Star Game that year, and as Ted went into the game he was leading the league in almost everything. On his first time up, against Kirby Higbe, he gave the fans what they had come for by smashing a line-drive home run into the center-field bleachers. In the following inning, he knocked in another run with a single. When he came to bat in the seventh, Ewell Blackwell, a mean, side-wheeling right-hander, was on the mound. Ted whistled a drive past first base to set off another rally.

The score had run up to 9–0 as Ted stepped to the plate in the eighth inning with two men on base. Pitching for the National League was Rip Sewell, and despite the lopsided score this was the confrontation everybody had been waiting for. Because Sewell had developed the most celebrated pitch in baseball, the "eephus" ball. What made the eephus such a spectacular pitch was that it was thrown off Sewell's normal motion but was held in such a way that it came floating up to the plate like a pop fly. More amazingly, Sewell had developed such control of it that he was using it as his "out" pitch. Stan Musial had once hit the eephus to the wall for a triple, but there was general agreement that it was impossible for a batter to generate enough power to hit it out of the park.

Nobody doubted that Sewell was going to give Ted his chance to try. The first pitch came floating up, and Ted, giving it the big riffle, fouled it back. An excited roar followed by nervous laughter went through the park. The second pitch was a fast ball, in for a strike. Ahead on the count, no balls and two strikes, Sewell served up another eephus. After taking a look at the first eephus, Ted had decided that the only way he could generate enough power to hit it for distance was to run up on the ball and get the momentum of his body behind it. Now, as the ball floated down, Ted took two full steps forward and swung. Away went the eephus . . . up, up, and away . . . and into the right-field bull pen. Pandemonium.

If you wanted to get technical, the whole thing was probably illegal, since Ted had stepped out of the box as he moved into the ball. But who wanted to get technical? For Ted, it was four hits and five runs batted in for the day. And, most important of all, he had hit Sewell's freakish pitch farther than anybody had thought humanly possible.

Ted's late-season problems may well have started on July 14—a day that the French, with uncanny foresight, had long ago designated as Bastille Day, and a day that, in the record books, appears to be the greatest in Ted's career. As Williams reported to Fenway Park that day, the Sox were romping to the pennant, and Ted looked like a living cinch to win his second Triple Crown.

In the first game of a doubleheader against Cleveland, the Sox quickly fell behind, 5–0. Ted, coming up in the third inning with the bases loaded, belted the ball into the stands. Later in the game, he pulled the Red Sox into a tie by hitting a three-run homer off Don Black.

And in the ninth inning, with the score tied 10 – 10, he hit a long drive off Joe Berry that just curved foul and then—as he did at least half a dozen times in his career—hit the next pitch into the stands fair, for his third home run, his eighth RBI, and an 11 – 10 Red Sox victory.

Lou Boudreau, the Cleveland player-manager (who had his own greatest day at bat in that same game, with four doubles and a home run), had been toying with the idea of throwing a packed defense against Ted. Obviously there is no defense against a drive into the bleachers, but just as obviously, Boudreau, with a sixth-place club, had little to lose.

Many misconceptions have developed about the "Boudreau shift." In his autobiography in the *Saturday Evening Post,* Ted—or his ghost— wrote: "Boudreau moved the second baseman into short right field, played the shortstop behind second base and the third baseman at the regular shortstop position. He moved the right-fielder to the foul line, put the center-fielder in right center and the left-fielder over almost to dead center."

That is how most people remember the Boudreau shift, but it is not the shift that Boudreau first threw at Ted at all. Boudreau, in describing it in his own autobiography, wrote: "It consisted of assigning virtually all our defensive strength around to the right side of the diamond. I stationed the first baseman and the right fielder virtually on the right-field foul line, moved the second baseman over much closer to first and back on the grass, placed myself to the right of second base, and ordered the third baseman to operate directly behind second. The center-fielder moved far to the right, taking care of the area normally patrolled by the right-fielder, and only the left-fielder remained to cover the vast expanse of open territory in left field."

Actually, the left-fielder, George Case, was pulled into short left center, only about thirty feet beyond the edge of the infield. The third baseman, you will notice, did not play in the shortstop position, he played directly behind second base. The shortstop did not play directly behind second base; he played the normal second-base position. The second baseman, who was really the key to it all, was a good twenty-five feet out on the grass and no more than fifteen feet inside the foul line. Since the shift was as much psychological as anything else, and also was something of a publicity stunt, Boudreau was not hedging his bets. It was only when Ted declined the invitation to amuse the spectators further by either bunting or hitting to left that the shift became something serious. And once the shift became serious, adjustments had to be made. In the original shift, there was nobody at all on the left side of the infield. Ted could have pushed a bunt down there and been assured of a hit. If he had wanted to push a swinging bunt into left, he could quite probably have hit it into the corner for at least two bases.

There is another misconception about the shift, even as it was later modified. The shift could not be set up under all circumstances. With a man on second, for instance, the third baseman had to remain close enough to the bag to prevent the runner from stealing third. And so, in its later refinements, the shift did have the shortstop playing behind second, and the third baseman played not at shortstop but a little toward the hole and somewhat drawn in.

The shift always depended on the situation, though. And that brings us to yet another misconception that has arisen over the years. Boudreau did not pull the shift on Ted the first time he came to bat in the second game of that Bastille Day doubleheader. Ted came up in the first inning with the bases loaded and nobody out, and Boudreau was not about to give him the whole of left field. It is even possible that if Ted had gone out routinely on that first trip to the plate, the shift would not have been thrown at him at all. But Ted doubled into right center, clearing the bases and giving himself eleven runs batted in for the day. It was on Ted's second time at bat, with nobody on base, that Boudreau signaled for the shift. Ted looked at the lineup against him, stepped out of the box, and laughed. He stepped back in shaking his head. Then he tried to hit through it.

And that brings up the final misconception. Boudreau was not the first manager to throw so radical a shift against Ted. Far from it. An earlier Cleveland manager, Roger Peckinpaugh, had deployed a reasonable approximation of the shift in 1941, while Ted was on that hot streak following his return to the lineup. To set the time precisely, it had come on the day after Lefty Grove won his three-hundredth game. Ted had walked the first time up that day, too, but he had then made the shift look good by lining to the second baseman on the outfield grass. On his final two times at bat, though, Ted had singled and doubled. And that was the end of that. Jimmy Dykes had set up a similar defense in Chicago—one time. He abandoned it fast when Ted doubled down the third-base line.

If Ted had done something like that on Bastille Day, Boudreau probably would have laid the shift to rest. And if it had not been thrown at Ted when he was so hot, he might well have been willing to accept a bunt single. As it was, he hit a hard ground ball down to what would normally have been the second baseman's position. Boudreau fielded the ball and threw him out. In Ted's next two times at bat, he walked. "With seven men on the right side of the diamond," Hy Hurwitz of the *Globe* wrote the next day, "you would expect the Cleveland pitchers to try to make Williams hit to right. Instead, they pitched him with great care, nibbling, as usual, at the outside corner." In his final time at bat, there were men on base again, and so Boudreau stationed his players in their normal positions.

So what did you have? The Boudreau shift was used against Ted three times, and the only difference it made, in the one time the Indians got him out, was that his ground ball was handled by the shortstop instead of the second baseman. It was the publicity that came out of the shift that day, not the success Boudreau had with it, that inspired other managers to devise some version of their own. And the publicity came not because it was the first time such a radical shift was used but because it was a good way of dramatizing the stories about Ted Williams's greatest day.

As the final irony, it was because of all the publicity that Ted, by the nature of his personality, was unable to resist the challenge. There is no doubt that he could have hit to left if he had wanted to. He was, above everything else, the master batsman, the scientific batsman, the grand pooh-bah of batsmanship. Somewhere in his mind, however, Ted accepted the proposition that to evade the shift would be the equivalent of being defeated by the shift.

Ted hit to left many times during his career. An outstanding instance came the very next year, in fact, after he had been to a hospital to visit an eleven-year-old boy who had just had both legs amputated after being severely burned. Ted, who is profoundly moved by this kind of tragedy, talked with the boy, gave him an autographed bat, then took out a ball and wrote on it, "To my pal, Glenny, from Ted Williams." And then he told the boy, "I'm not sure I can promise you a home run, but you listen to the game, and if I do hit one you'll know it was for you." He hit not one but two home runs, both of them over the left-field wall.

Ted hit that neighborly left-field wall at Fenway often, as a matter of fact. "I didn't hit to left field," is the way he puts it. "But I hit to left center more than most people thought. The defense, even though they moved it radically around, they still covered left center a little bit. But the big area for me was from second to first. The second baseman out in the grass, he was the culprit." Not just because he was there to grab those sinking line drives, but because he was also able to throw Ted out, on occasion, from right field. "I think Boudreau figured I hit eighty percent of my balls out there. He had it pretty good."

Ted continued to buck the various shifts thrown against him, and, according to the conventional wisdom, his stubbornness hurt him. There were other reasons why his hitting began to slacken off, though. Ted, as we have indicated, seemed to be headed for the triple crown. He was well ahead in home runs and runs batted in, and although he was trailing the Washington Senators' Mickey Vernon for the batting title, nobody doubted how that was going to come out. Vernon, who had never hit .300 before, was obviously over his head at .360, and when the inevitable law of averages caught up with him—so everybody said—his average would begin to plummet. "I stand by the batting cage just to watch Ted Williams swing,'' Vernon said. ''It embarrasses me to think that I'm ahead of him. I'm not really in the same class with him.''

The only trouble was that Vernon continued to pick up a couple of hits almost every day. All at once the suspicion arose that, over his head or not, Vernon had reached a point at which he was traveling on his momentum. This, it suddenly became apparent, was going to be Mickey Vernon's year.

Ted began to show the strain. In previous years, he had usually been philosophical about being robbed, even when Boston's strong east wind blew one of his long drives out of the bleachers and back to the waiting glove of an outfielder. The fielders were out there to catch the ball, Ted knew, and by the nature of things the good hitters were going to be robbed more often than the banjo hitters. His temper tantrums and brief bursts of anger had always come when he was furious at himself for failing to hit the ball as well as he knew he should have.

Into the duel between Williams and Vernon came the Philadelphia right-fielder, Elmer Valo. Philadelphia came to Fenway Park for a four-game series, and in each of the games Valo took a home run away from Ted. At least, that's the way the newspapers put it. Actually, the catches were not quite that good. In each case, the ball would have gone into the stands if no right-fielder had been there, but that was only because the balls were hit to the low right-field barrier. Only once did Valo actually have to jump. In every case, it was obvious that any right-fielder would have made the catch.

Then, by one of those freaks of fate, the same thing happened again the next time the Athletics came to Boston.

In the first game, Valo made a good one-handed catch, running with his back to the ball to pluck a wicked line drive out of the air just as it was about to fall into the bleachers. The next day, he backed against the barrier and, timing his jump perfectly, took another homer away from Ted. Later in the same game, with the Sox well ahead, Ted hit a vicious blow out toward the corner where the wall begins to curve toward center field. Valo raced back as far as he could go and hurled himself into the air, twisting his body in mid-flight to keep from hurtling into the bleachers. He came down horizontally, the small of his back hitting the top of the barrier with a thud. For what seemed like seconds he hung there with the upper half of his body bending into the bleachers and his feet dangling toward the field. And he had the ball.

If Valo had fallen into the bleachers, Williams still would have had a home run. Instead, Valo slid very slowly down the low wall and crumpled in a heap on the grass. He had to be carried off the field. Ted had been robbed—and this time really robbed—of another home run.

In the thrill of seeing the catch and then paying tribute to Valo as he was carried off the field, the crowd had not paid much attention to the man who hit the ball. Ted had waited at first base, staring out toward Valo's body like everybody else and waiting for the umpire's sign. When the umpire's hand shot into the air, Ted kicked the bag savagely and headed out to left field.

Two innings later, he came slouching into the batter's box with his bat resting limply on his shoulder. When the pitch was delivered he swung weakly, almost with one hand, and pushed a little ground ball to the second baseman. Making the merest show at running out the hit, he took a couple of desultory steps toward first and then turned into the dugout.

The fans, utterly astonished, began to boo. When Ted took his post in the outfield at the end of the inning they really gave it to him. As luck would have it, the inning ended with a routine fly to left. Ted made the catch, and as he was running in toward the infield he tossed first the ball and then his glove high into the air.

"What can I do with him?" Cronin said with a shrug, when he was asked whether Ted would be fined. The Sox were virtually assured of winning the pennant. Nothing was involved except Ted's batting average. And when it became evident that he wasn't going to catch Vernon, his attitude seemed to become, "If I can't win the triple crown, I'm not going to win anything."

There were no further outbursts, no nasty exchanges with the crowds.

His play simply turned listless. A spark seemed to have gone out of him. He had seemed too far ahead of the field in both home runs and runs batted in for anyone to catch him, but then Hank Greenberg, always a late-season hitter, began to come on strong. Hank's burst of home runs over the final month carried the Tigers into second place and put him ahead of Ted, 44–38. The RBIs added up, too. Greenberg, old and sore-footed, had gone back to playing first base, but he had one last burst of glory in him. He caught Ted right at the wire and beat him out in that category, too, 127–123. (The next season, Greenberg was limping around in Pittsburgh, obviously washed up.)

Right behind Greenberg and Williams in the RBI column was Rudy York, who had been Greenberg's old slugging partner in Detroit. York, who had come to Boston that year in a trade, hit only .276, had only 17 home runs, and his slugging average was only .437. Ted's slugging average was .667 and Greenberg's .604. But York knocked in 119 runs, and he knocked them in when they were needed.

"The biggest surprise I ever had," Joe Cronin once said, "was Rudy York. He gave us the clutch hits, and he gave them to us in Yankee Stadium." For years the Red Sox had managed to find ways to lose at Yankee Stadium. "We lost because balls got lost in the sun, because they rolled up tarpaulins, because runners forgot to leave third on base hits. And we lost them year after year because we could never seem to get the base hit we needed to win the big game. York gave it to us." Not Williams, York.

Let's not underestimate Ted here, though. Half the time it was Ted Williams whom York was knocking in. Ted led the league not only in slugging percentage but also in bases on balls, with 156—an average of a walk a game—and in a closely related category, runs scored. Ted scored 142 times, for in the early part of the season he was always on base.

And Ted did hit the home run that clinched the pennant. Yet even there he managed to leave a bad taste in everybody's mouth.

The Red Sox lead went to sixteen and a half games on September 5—only two days after Labor Day—and their "magic number" dropped to two. They were playing in Washington, where they figured to win, and since a Boston victory and a Detroit loss would clinch the pennant, a victory party was looming on the horizon. Tom Yawkey sent word that as soon as the pennant was mathematically clinched he would fly down to Washington with an adequate supply of champagne. Washington upset the timetable by beating the Sox, and Detroit, refusing to cooperate, won its game, too. The Red Sox moved on to Philadelphia for a weekend series against the last-place Athletics, and Yawkey had his plane warming up at the airport. The Athletics walloped the Sox on Saturday and walloped them again on Sunday. Detroit kept winning.

The Sox were headed for Detroit next. Since a victory over the Tigers would automatically bring the agony to an end, Yawkey ordered his road secretary, Tom Dowd, to purchase the champagne on the scene. Yawkey himself flew to Detroit and got ready to party. Instead, he saw the Red Sox take yet another beating.

He also saw both Hank Greenberg and Ted Williams hit monster home runs into the teeth of a biting wind. Greenberg's drive, his thirty-second, landed in the upper left-field stand and was called one of the hardest drives hit in Detroit all season. Ted came right back with his thirty-sixth, a long, high fly ball that rattled off the press-box extension atop the roof in right center field. "The longest drive hit in Briggs Stadium all season," according to the *Detroit Press*. The report also said it was the first time a home run had hit the press-box extension that far out toward center field. How quickly they forgot. Ted had hit one *over* the press box in that same spot in the first game he had ever played at Briggs Stadium.

The Sox lost again the next day, 7–3, and the champagne had to be taken off the ice and placed aboard a plane to Cleveland. Yawkey, still determined to have his party, accompanied the team to Cleveland and watched Bob Feller pin the Sox's ears back, 4–1. Meanwhile, Detroit won its sixth straight game.

On Friday, September 13, Yawkey's agony finally ended. Red Embree was on the mound for Cleveland, and Tex Hughson was trying to clinch it for the Sox. In the first inning, Ted came to bat with two men out and nobody on. This was the situation in which Boudreau used his most extreme shift, with left-fielder Pat Seerey drawn in close to protect the vacated infield area. Ted hit a routine fly ball over Seerey's head. The ball rolled clear to the 400-foot mark. Ted raced around the bases and slid into the plate under the throw, the first inside-the-park home run of his major-league career. It turned out to be the only one he ever did hit, and it also turned out to be the run that clinched the pennant. The Sox got only one other hit off Embree, but Hughson, a twenty-game winner that year, shut the Indians out with three hits.

Ted was ghosting a column for the *Boston Globe* at the time, and he insisted on having the writer come down to the clubhouse after every game to clear the column with him. "Now look," Ted told him, "I want you to make it very clear that all the credit goes to Hughson. He pitched a helluva game. My home run didn't mean a thing when I hit it."

But Detroit still had to lose before the Sox were officially in. The Tigers were playing a twilight game against the Yankees, and so it was several hours before the final score came in. The champagne was finally taken off the ice, and the party was on.

Ted Williams wasn't there.

Tom Dowd tried to make the excuse that in the interval between the end of the Sox game and the end of the Tigers game the players had scattered. "I couldn't find Pesky until seven o'clock," he said, "and I wasn't able to get Williams at all. He was visiting some old fishing friends, and I didn't locate him until he returned to the hotel that night to go to bed."

That was Dowd's story. But there were other stories—too many of them not to leave the distinct impression that Ted was in need of a cover story. It was reported, "reliably," that he was visiting a hospital. Can't knock that. It was also reported, just as reliably, that he was in his room at the Hotel Statler, very much aware of the situation. The fact is that everybody knew there was going to be a party if Detroit lost; the story of the stale champagne had been played up heavily in all the papers for five days. One magazine writer, who questioned everybody involved in the affair, wrote: "It was no secret to Williams that a big bust was scheduled for the hour the pennant was won. The casual observer cannot help but feel he didn't try very hard to get there. In fact, it's hard to disagree with the people who insist he tried very hard not to be there."

If Ted Williams didn't want to join his teammates in the victory celebration, that was between him and them. The matter is of interest only as it casts light on his frame of mind. Not even Dave Egan, Ted Williams knocker deluxe, could accuse him of being jealous of anybody. Hadn't he hit the home run that would be putting the Red Sox in their first World Series since Babe Ruth left town?

Egan spent most of his sober hours dreaming up ways to send Ted on his way, too. Rarely a spring turned into summer without Egan trading the Kid away for the good of the team, the well-being of the city, and the best interests of all mankind. While the Sox were on the train en route to St. Louis for the opening game of the World Series, "the Colonel" pulled off one of his most spectacular deals. Ted Williams, according to Egan, was going to be traded, either to the Yankees for Joe DiMaggio and a catcher or to the Tigers for Hal Newhouser and a third baseman. Ted's teammates, wrote Egan—by way of solidifying the Red Sox for the coming battle—would be happy to see him go. "He does not associate with them," Egan wrote. "He would not even attend the victory party with them. He is utterly lacking in anything that bears even a remote resemblance to team spirit or team pride. First and last and at all times in between he is for Ted Williams and Ted Williams alone."

Then, as the same rumors began to come in from other sources, it became evident that this time Egan might be on to something. Any doubts were dispelled by the inexplicable reaction of the Red Sox officials. Tom Yawkey responded by saying that the trade stories had been designed to hurt the Red Sox. But he didn't deny them. Neither did Joe Cronin. Eddie Collins said it was all news to him. He also said he didn't want to be quoted.

Before we enter upon the painful duty of setting down Ted Williams's World Series performance in all its horrible detail, let us provide a little background music. While the Red Sox were running off with the American League pennant, the National League race had settled into a grueling struggle between Leo Durocher's Brooklyn Dodgers and Eddie Dyer's St. Louis Cardinals. When the season ended in a flat-footed tie, a three-game play-off series, the first in baseball history, was set up.

The Red Sox, who had been sputtering along in low gear after clinching the pennant, now had to sit back and wait for the Dodgers and the Cards to battle it out. Concerned that the team might go stale, the Boston management came up with the rotten idea of rounding up an all-star team from around the league to face the Red Sox in what was supposed to be a three-game exhibition series. The players, one of whom was Joe DiMaggio, were to be paid from the receipts of the games.

Financially, the first game was a flop. A crowd of 1,996 not necessarily immortal souls huddled together on a cold raw day. For Ted Williams—and therefore for the Red Sox—it was pure disaster. Mickey Haefner, a clever little left-hander from Washington who always had given the Sox trouble, was the starting pitcher. In Ted's third time at bat, Haefner hit him on the right elbow with his first pitch. ("I laid back waiting for it to curve," Ted said. "But as it came on me, I saw it was just spinning and wasn't going to curve. I tried pulling away from it, but it hit me in the elbow.")

The rest of the Series was called off.

Ted had been in that sulking slump anyway, and, added to that, he had to enter the World Series with a badly swollen elbow. He maintained before, during, and after the Series that the elbow did not bother him a bit, although there is little doubt that it did.

Williams, you will remember, had invited the Les Cassies to the Series, and on the night of their arrival Mr. Cassie called home and told Les, Jr., "His elbow is three times as big as it's supposed to be. He's all stuffed up with antibiotics. I don't see how he can play."

Ted with his mother, May, and his younger brother, Danny. He hated that Buster Brown haircut—who wouldn't?

(Courtesy *Sporting News*)

Ted's birth certificate. Early on, his first name was changed from Teddy to Theodore. The birth date is a puzzlement. The listed date is August 20—altered to August 30—and the certificate of the attending physician is dated August 21.

(Courtesy Brian Interland)

BOSTON AMERICAN LEAGUE BASEBALL COMPANY

FENWAY PARK
BOSTON, MASS.

THOMAS A. YAWKEY, PRESIDENT
EDWARD T. COLLINS, VICE PRES. & GEN. MGR.

JOSEPH E. CRONIN, MANAGER
"BILLY" EVANS, DIRECTOR MINOR LEAGUE CLUBS

February 15th, 1939.

Mr. Ted Williams
San Diego, Cal.

Dear Ted:

This is to notify you that you are to report to the Sarasota
Terrace Hotel, Sarasota, Fla. for Spring training on March 6th.

A railroad representative will call on you and furnish you
with transportation to Sarasota. Upon arrival in Sarasota I will reimburse you for your meals en route.

Kindly acknowledge receipt of this letter so that we may know
that you have received your reporting notice.

Very truly yours,

Secretary.

BOSTON AMERICAN LEAGUE
BASEBALL COMPANY
FENWAY PARK
BOSTON, MASS.

Mr. Theodore Williams,
3659 36th Street
San Diego, California

This letter from traveling secretary Phil Troy marks the first correspondence between
Ted Williams and the Red Sox. For the next twenty-one years the Red Sox and Ted
Williams would become virtually synonymous. (Courtesy of Les Cassie, Jr.)

(Courtesy George Sullivan)

(a)

(Courtesy Boston Public Library, Print Department)

(b)

Ted with Johnny Pesky (a), with Bobby Doerr (b), and Eddie Collins (c). All four were in the ballpark in Portland on August 7, 1936, when Collins first saw Ted Williams swing a bat. In the picture with Collins, the twitch in Ted's neck may be due to the unaccustomed necktie, or possibly to his discomfort at appearing as the honored guest at an annual dinner of the Boston Baseball Writers. As for Eddie Collins's ears, they defy any glib explanation.

(Courtesy Sporting News)

(c)

In the early Red Sox years, Ted Williams and Jimmy Foxx provided a one-two punch that struck terror in the hearts of opposing pitchers.

(Courtesy National Baseball Library, Cooperstown, NY)

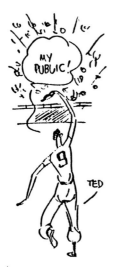

Never tipped his hat, huh? Nobody ever acknowledged the cheers of the fans with a greater flourish than did Ted Williams during his rookie year, as illustrated in this Bob Coyne cartoon of a doubleheader against the Yankees at Fenway Park on September 3, 1939.

(Courtesy of Les Cassie, Jr.)

In Ted's final years he battled another teammate, Pete Runnels, for the league batting title.
(Courtesy Richard Darcey)

Ted working out in the morning while recovering from an injury. In this case, he was getting back into shape after breaking his elbow.
(Courtesy Boston Public Library, Print Department)

That's Joe DiMaggio (number 5) waiting to clasp Ted's hand after the dramatic 3-run home run that won the 1941 All-Star Game. (Courtesy Sports Museum)

(Courtesy George Sullivan)

Two moments of high drama:
The inside-the-park homer that
won the pennant in 1946 . . .

. . . Yes, that's the
home-run swing of
Ted's dramatic last
time at bat.

(Courtesy George Sullivan)

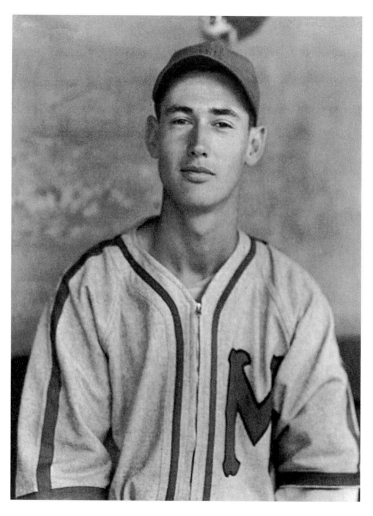

This is Ted's favorite picture. "I saw it for the first time the other day. My God, what a picture. I was a young nineteen-year-old kid, straight and skinny, with a little baseball cap on and a smile, and I'm looking right into the camera, so innocent. Oh, what a picture." (Courtesy Brian Interland)

Who says photos don't lie? In this one, often used to "show" Ted screaming at the press, he is actually demonstrating the limited movement of his arm caused by a broken collarbone. (Courtesy Brian Interland)

This one, taken with Joe Cronin in the dugout before Ted's last game, supposedly shows Ted waving a kind of sad farewell. What he is really doing is waving the photographers away. (Courtesy Wide World)

But some photographs are exactly what they seem. An angry Ted flinging his bat away after being walked with the bases loaded, against the Yankees on September 23, 1958—never mind that the walk brought in the winning run.

(Courtesy National Baseball Library, Cooperstown, NY)

Jack Fadden, the nonpareil trainer, working on Ted's collarbone in the spring of 1954. Ted says that without Fadden's ministrations on his broken elbow two years earlier, his career would have been over.

(Courtesy Boston Public Library, Print Department)

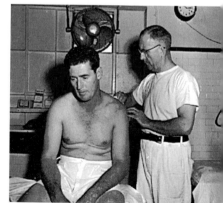

Ted spitting toward the press box as he crosses the plate after hitting his 400th home run on July 18, 1956. That'll show 'em.

(Courtesy *Sporting News*)

Two of Ted's passions are fishing and jazz. Here he is, fishing reel in hand, talking with his good friend the jazz pianist Errol Garner.

(Courtesy Sports Museum)

The fighter pilot in Korea. (Courtesy San Diego Hall of Champions)

Ted with some of his Jimmy Fund colleagues: Dr. Sidney Farber, the father of chemotherapy, is at the far right; Cardinal Richard Cushing, a strong supporter of the fund, is next to Ted; at far left is Tom Yawkey, the Red Sox owner.
(Courtesy Dana-Farber Cancer Institute and the Jimmy Fund, Boston, MA)

The weathered veteran with his fishing pal Bud Leavitt. Ted looks like an old Indian fighter here, doesn't he?
(Courtesy Bud Leavitt)

The Kid's kid. John Henry Williams, an eager thirteen-year-old, receives some tips from the batting instructor at the Red Sox training camp in Winter Haven, Florida.

(Courtesy George Sullivan)

Senator John Glenn appears at "A Tribute to #9" to talk about Ted's exploits as Glenn's wingman in Korea

(Courtesy Dana-Farber Cancer Institute and the Jimmy Fund, Boston, MA)

Farewell, good-bye, and hello. Leaving for Korea, April 30, 1952. (Courtesy Sports Museum)

The "last good-bye" before his real last good-bye on September 28, 1960.
(Courtesy George Sullivan)

Tipping his cap to the fans on Ted Williams Day, May 12, 1991. (Courtesy Dick Johnson)

The opening game was played in St. Louis, with Hughson (20-11) going against left-hander Howie Pollett (21-10). To show exactly how Williams performed, we are going to present, in full, every Series inning in which he came to bat.

Ted's first appearance came as leadoff man in the second inning, and Eddie Dyer immediately threw a shift against him. The Dyer shift was almost as radical as Boudreau's original shift, and it was far more radical than anything that had been used against Ted during the final months of the American League race. Marty Marion remained pretty much in his regular shortstop position, in this version, but the third baseman, Whitey Kurowski, ran across the diamond and stationed himself in the second baseman's normal position. The first baseman played along the line, and the second baseman played out on the grass, well over toward the baseline. The left-fielder played in dead center, and the other two outfielders were staggered in the right-field area.

It is quite likely that Dyer was testing Ted's reaction in this opening stage of the Series. As the leadoff man, Ted should have been trying to get on base. If, instead, he swung away, Dyer would be sure that he could set up his defenses with impunity. Ted swung away. He sent a hard grounder right at second baseman Red Schoendienst that probably would have been a hit against a conventional defense.

In the third inning, the Red Sox were leading, 1-0. Tom McBride grounded to Kurowski. Johnny Pesky flied to Enos Slaughter. Dom DiMaggio singled into left center. WILLIAMS walked. York fouled to Harry Walker.

The score was still 1-0 in the sixth. Dom DiMaggio lined to Musial. WILLIAMS slapped a vicious line single to right center. York flied to Terry Moore. Doerr fouled out to Kurowski.

The Cards tied the game in the last of the sixth when Stan Musial doubled off the right-field wall to score Schoendienst.

In the eighth inning, the score was 1-1. Pesky flied to Slaughter. DiMaggio singled into center but was thrown out at second as he tried to advance when Moore momentarily fumbled. WILLIAMS walked. York fouled out to Joe Garagiola.

The Cardinals went ahead, 2-1, in the last of the eighth when

DiMaggio lost Garagiola's fly in the sun. The Sox tied it with a lucky run of their own in the ninth. Pinky Higgins got a single when his ground ball took a weird hop and skidded through Marion's legs. He scored, after two were out, when Tom McBride, a surprise starter, squeezed a ground ball through the hole.

Tenth inning: Red Sox 2, Cardinals 2. DiMaggio grounded to Marion. WILLIAMS fouled to Musial. York hit a 2–0 pitch into the left-field bleachers. Doerr singled to center. Relief pitcher Earl Johnson forced Doerr at second.

The Red Sox won the opener, 3–2. Ted Williams had one meaningless single. The only time he came up with a man on base, he walked.

Second game: October 7, at St. Louis; Mickey Harris (17–9) vs. Harry Brecheen (15–15).

Second inning: no score. WILLIAMS grounded to Musial. York walked. Doerr was thrown out by Schoendienst, York going to second. Higgins was purposely passed. Roy Partee grounded to Schoendienst.

Fourth inning: Cardinals 1, Red Sox 0. DiMaggio flied to Moore. WILLIAMS struck out swinging. York walked. Doerr singled to right. Higgins forced Doerr, Marion to Schoendienst.

Sixth inning: Cardinals 3, Red Sox 0. DiMaggio grounded to Marion. WILLIAMS lined to Schoendienst out on the grass (a base hit without the shift). York was thrown out by Kurowski.

Ninth inning: Cardinals 3, Red Sox 0. DiMaggio singled. WILLIAMS fouled to Marion. York flied to Slaughter. Doerr flied to Walker to end the game.

In his first look at Harry Brecheen, who was going to win three games, Ted went hitless. Without the shift he would have had at least one hit and possibly two. The only time he came to bat with a man on base—in the ninth inning—he tried to hit to left and sent an awkward little pop fly down the left-field line. Despite Brecheen's not-too-impressive record, he was known to be the Cards' best pitcher. His ERA during the season had been 2.49. Over ten seasons with the Cards, his ERA was 2.91. He was, then, one of the best pitchers of his era.

Third game: October 9, at Boston; Dave Ferriss (25−6) vs. Murry Dickson (15−6).

First inning: no score. Wally Moses flied to Walker. Pesky singled down the third-base line. DiMaggio grounded to Musial, Pesky taking second. WILLIAMS was purposely passed. York hit a 3−2 pitch over the left-field wall, bringing in three runs. Doerr struck out.

Third inning: Red Sox 3, Cardinals 0. Pesky lined to Slaughter. DiMaggio grounded to Marion. WILLIAMS bunted the first pitch down the third-base line and into left field for a single. York grounded to Marion and Williams was forced at second.

Fifth inning: Red Sox 3, Cardinals 0. Moses struck out. Pesky hit back to Dickson. DiMaggio doubled off the left-field wall. WILLIAMS struck out swinging.

Eighth inning: Red Sox 3, Cardinals 0; Wilks now pitching for St. Louis. WILLIAMS lined to Slaughter down the right-field line. York singled to center. Doerr doubled off the wall, sending York to third. Higgins hit back to Wilks, both men holding. York scored when Schoendienst kicked Hal Wagner's ground ball. Ferris grounded to Schoendienst.

Once again, Rudy York had delivered the clutch home run. It is worth noting that Ted bunted against the shift in the worst possible situation, two men out and nobody on. On the other hand, the wind was blowing in, and Dyer had challenged him by playing nobody at all on the left side of second base.

The first time Ted was pitched to with a man in scoring position, he struck out.

Fourth game: October 10, at Boston; Tex Hughson vs. Red Munger (2−2).

Second inning: Cardinals 3, Red Sox 0. WILLIAMS walked. York flied to Moore. Doerr flied to Slaughter. Higgins flied to Slaughter.

Fourth inning: Cardinals 6, Red Sox 0. DiMaggio was thrown out by Schoendienst. WILLIAMS singled to right. York doubled to deep center, scoring Williams. Doerr walked. Higgins flied to Walker. Wagner flied to Slaughter.

Sixth inning: Cardinals 7, Red Sox 1. WILLIAMS grounded to Schoendienst. York walked. Doerr singled to left. Higgins singled off Kurowski's glove, filling the bases. Wagner flied to Slaughter, who threw out York at the plate.

Eighth inning: Cardinals 8, Red Sox 1. DiMaggio reached base on Marion's error. WILLIAMS fouled to Kurowski. York struck out. Doerr homered over the left-field wall, scoring behind DiMaggio. Higgins fouled to Garagiola.

The final score was 12–4. Ted led off an inning twice and did not come up with anybody on base. The single in the fourth inning was a sinking line drive, which went over the head of Kurowski, playing in the second baseman's position.

Fifth game: October 11, at Boston; Joe Dobson (13–7) vs. Howie Pollet.

First inning: no score. Don Gutteridge singled off Musial's glove on Pollet's first pitch. Pesky singled to right, sending Gutteridge to second. DiMaggio grounded to Kurowski, who stepped on third to force Gutteridge. WILLIAMS singled to right, scoring Pesky and sending DiMaggio to third, and went to second on the throw to third. Alpha Brazle replaced Pollet. York was purposely passed, filling the bases. Higgins grounded to Kurowski, who forced DiMaggio at the plate. Leon Culberson forced Higgins, Marion to Schoendienst.

Third inning: Red Sox 2, Cardinals 1. WILLIAMS grounded to Marion. York popped to Marion. Higgins lined to Walker.

Fifth inning: Red Sox 2, Cardinals 1. Pesky singled to center. Pesky stole second. DiMaggio walked. WILLIAMS struck out. Pesky was thrown out attempting to steal third. York was purposely passed. Higgins grounded to Marion.

Seventh inning: Red Sox 3, Cardinals 1. DiMaggio doubled to left. WILLIAMS was called out on strikes. York was purposely passed for the third time in the game. Higgins doubled to left center, scoring DiMaggio. Culberson was purposely passed, filling the bases. Partee hit to Marion, who threw wildly to second, York and Higgins scoring. Gutteridge flied to Moore.

Eighth inning: Red Sox 6, Cardinals 1; John Beazley now pitching for St. Louis. Pesky beat out a hit to short. DiMaggio sacrificed. WILLIAMS fouled to Garagiola. York fanned.

The final score was 6 – 3. For the first time in five games, Ted came up with more than one man on base, and he came through with a run-scoring single. Two other times he came up with men in scoring position, and he struck out both times. A change in Cardinals tactics was evident in the seventh inning, after DiMaggio led off with a double. Dyer had Brazle pitch to Williams and walk York. There is no denying that, all things being equal, this is percentage baseball. For one thing, Fenway Park is built for right-handers, not left-handers. For another, Brazle was a left-hander. With Ted Williams at bat, however, all things were not supposed to be equal. St. Louis had decided that Rudy York, not Ted Williams, was the man they had to fear.

Despite Ted's dismal Series so far, the Red Sox held a 3 – 2 lead in games as they headed back to St. Louis.

Sixth game: October 13, at St. Louis; Mickey Harris vs. Harry Brecheen.

First inning: Culberson struck out. Pesky singled to right. DiMaggio singled to left, sending Pesky to second. WILLIAMS walked, filling the bases. York grounded into a double play, Kurowski to Schoendienst to Musial.

Fourth inning: Cardinals 3, Red Sox 0. WILLIAMS popped to Musial. York flied to Schoendienst. Doerr popped to Musial.

Sixth inning: Cardinals 3, Red Sox 0. Pesky walked. DiMaggio grounded to Kurowski, who started a double play. WILLIAMS struck out swinging.

Ninth inning: Cardinals 4, Red Sox 1. DiMaggio lined to Moore. WILLIAMS singled through the tiny hole between Marion and Schoendienst. York ended the game when his shot through the middle was deflected off Brecheen's glove and converted into a double play by Schoendienst.

The only time Ted came up with anybody on base he walked. He got on base, which was what he was expected to do, in the ninth.

Seventh game: October 15, at St. Louis; Dave Ferriss vs. Murry Dickson.

First inning: Moses singled to center. Pesky singled through the middle, sending Moses to third. DiMaggio flied to Slaughter, Moses scoring after the catch. WILLIAMS hit a long, 400-foot drive into the open space in dead center, but Terry Moore, racing over from where he had been stationed in right, made a beautiful catch. York popped to Schoendienst.

Fourth inning Red Sox 1, Cardinals 1. WILLIAMS hit another 400-foot drive to deep center field, and this time Harry Walker, the left-fielder, raced over to make a fine catch. York struck out. Doerr flied to Slaughter.

Sixth inning: Cardinals 3, Red Sox 1. Moses grounded to Musial. Pesky lined to Kurowski. DiMaggio walked. WILLIAMS skied to Slaughter.

Eighth inning: Cardinals 3, Red Sox 1. Rip Russell, batting for Wagner, singled to center. George Metkovich, batting for Dobson, doubled to left, sending Russell to third. Brecheen replaced Dickson for St. Louis. Pesky lined to Slaughter. DiMaggio doubled off the fence in right center, scoring Russell and Metkovich with the tying runs. DiMaggio pulled a muscle in his thigh rounding first base and barely made it to second; Culberson replaced him. WILLIAMS hit a foul tip that split a finger on Garagiola's throwing hand, and the game was held up while Del Rice replaced him. WILLIAMS popped to Schoendienst.

St. Louis scored what proved to be the winning run in the eighth, when Enos Slaughter scored from first as Pesky hesitated for a split second after taking Culberson's throw on Harry Walker's double.

Ted hit the ball well on his first two times at bat. With luck, he could have broken the game open in the first inning. The wheel really turned to him in the eighth, though, when he came to bat with the score tied, a man on second and the momentum of the game moving with the Red Sox. This is the kind of spot in which the big hitter on the team is supposed to deliver. This was the spot where Ted Williams popped up.

Breaking down Ted's statistics, what do we find? In twenty-five times at bat, he had five singles, one of them a bunt. He scored only two runs and knocked in only one. Just once in the entire seven-game Series did he get a base hit with anybody on base.

But let's look at it from another angle. Winning overcomes everything. Stan Musial, who had hit .365 during the season to lead the major leagues, had six for twenty-seven and four RBIs in the same Series, and nobody was saying that he choked. Marty Marion, "Mr. Shortstop" himself, had a dreadful Series in the field, and nobody even commented.

In addition to his hits, Ted had five bases on balls, which means that in thirty at-bats he reached base ten times. On the other hand, he walked only once in the last three games, which shows more than anything else that the Cardinals had practically discounted him.

There are other indicators as one looks over that play-by-play. Ted came to bat as the leadoff man seven times, and that is precisely where the opposition wants the big hitter. In his first seventeen times at bat there was a grand total of five Red Sox base runners and never more than one man on base at the same time. Two of those times Ted walked. In other words, he left only three men on base in the first four games, even though he failed to drive in a single run.

Through the entire Series, he came up with fifteen men on base and left nine men stranded. The three times he came up with two men on base, he walked, singled, and struck out. He never came up with the bases loaded.

After the Series, Tom Yawkey came into the clubhouse to try to cheer up the devastated Johnny Pesky and, while he was about it, to tell Ted Williams that he'd be wearing a Red Sox uniform the next season.

In Bobby Doerr's opinion, Ted got a bad rap. "Every year Ted would come up with a cold virus. He had kind of a half flu going into that Series, and he was stuffed with antibiotics. His elbow was swelled up quite a bit at first, everybody knows that, but I think the big thing was the flu. He wouldn't tell anybody about it, and he wouldn't let any of us say anything about it. I always admired him for that."

Even now, when the Les Cassie and Doerr quotes are put to him, Ted's normally booming voice trails away into a kind of mumbled embarrassment. "I never did make an excuse for my poor performance. For sure, I was taking antibiotics, and I also had been hit on the elbow, and I, gee, did nothing. I couldn't even think straight on the damn thing. I don't know what the hell happened."

The mystery virus that would hit him at the onset of cold weather every autumn was something he had to deal with all his life. Thinking back, he could remember that he'd had a hacking cough even as a kid in San Diego. He had been hit hard with the virus for the first time on that motor trip with Les Cassie to training camp, when he had been forced to bed for two days in New Orleans. After that, it had been a rare year when he didn't suffer some kind of a recurrence in late August or early September. And no matter what combination of antibiotics was pumped into him, he would be left in such a weakened condition that he would be spending every hour away from the ballpark in bed. "They never could find out what the hell that was, and they tested me for everything. When I get the little bug, I can't shake it off until I go through the whole goddamn cycle." Even today he takes a flu shot every year and a pneumonia shot every other year. And they still don't seem to help.

The Series failure in 1946 followed Ted ever afterward as the prize exhibit to support the charge that he was never there in the clutch. Dave Egan never tired of writing, "In the ten most important games of his life, the great man batted .205 and knocked in one run." The other three games on Egan's failure list were the play-off game against Cleveland in 1948 and the final two games of 1949, when the Red Sox, needing only one victory over the Yankees to clinch the pennant, lost both games. Against Cleveland, Ted had one single in four times at bat. Against the Yankees, he had a single in three tries in the first game and went nothing for two in the second.

Out of those ten games came a perennial debate as to whether Ted Williams helped the Red Sox or hurt them. Those who insisted that Ted hurt the team not only cited this alleged inability to hit in the clutch, but also maintained that his Red Sox teammates disliked and resented him. The best set of statistics in support of this argument came out of the 1950 season. At the All-Star break, the Red Sox had a record of 42–35 and were sputtering along eight games out of first place. When Ted came back from his elbow injury they were 87–52 and only one and a half games off the pace. They finished at 94–60, four games out.

No matter how you slice it, the Sox had a 49–43 (.533) record with Williams and a 45–17 (.726) record without him.

Two can play at that game, however. Before the 1955 season Ted announced his retirement, but he came back to the lineup as soon as his divorce was settled. When he returned the Red Sox were 20–30 and eleven games off the lead. Over the next sixty games they compiled a 44–16 record and shot to within a game and a half of the lead.

While Joe Cronin was the general manager, he would answer the attacks on Ted by saying, "How can a man who hits .350 with thirty-five home runs and a hundred and forty to a hundred and fifty runs batted in be anything but a help to you? Even if he didn't want to help you, how could he be anything but a help to you?"

The flat statement that Ted hurt the team was silly, of course, but it was silly only because the criticism was never couched in the appropriate terms. Ted's critics didn't really mean that he hurt the team. What they did mean was that he did not help the team as much as a man with his record should have. As Dave Egan once wrote: "The trouble with Williams is that he has looked too good in the record book and too bad in the clutch."

This was written in 1950, after Joe McCarthy, who was supposed to have done for the Red Sox what he had done for the Yankees, had given it all up and shuffled back to Buffalo. Egan, a great admirer of

McCarthy, wrote: "The cruelest part of it, where McCarthy is concerned, is that he was beaten not by the Yankees and not by the Tigers and not by rivals against whom he could prepare himself; he was struck down from behind, in the last hours of his professional lifetime, by members of his own forces and, to be very explicit on the subject, Ted Williams, Mel Parnell, Ellis Kinder and Maurice McDermott."

The Red Sox record during McCarthy's reign (1948–1950) is worth looking at. An unfailing pattern developed during those years. The Sox would start miserably, come storming back to push into the lead, and then blow it. In 1948, the first year of McCarthy's reign, the Sox were eleven and a half games behind before the end of May, yet with twenty-one games still to play they had shot up to first place, four and a half games ahead of Cleveland, the eventual winner. In 1949, they were twelve games behind on July 4 but went a game ahead with five games to play and carried that lead into Yankee Stadium for those final two games. In 1950, they were eight and a half off when McCarthy quit in June, but under Steve O'Neill they got to within a half game of the leader with twelve games left.

Without ignoring Ted's quiescence in the play-off game of 1948 and the crucial two games in 1949, it is certainly relevant to look at his contributions over the last few days of those pressure-packed seasons. In 1948, the Red Sox won their last three games and moved into a tie with Cleveland when Hal Newhouser and the Tigers beat the Indians on the final day of the season. In those three games, Ted was two for two against Washington; two for two, including a home run and a double, two RBIs and two runs scored against the Yankees; and two for four, both doubles, in the final game against the Yankees. That adds up to six for eight in pretty rough going.

In 1949, the Sox went a game ahead in the last week of the season by knocking off the Yankees three straight, to top off a nine-game winning streak. In that streak Ted had one of the best stretch runs a hitter could have. He beat Newhouser, 1–0, with a homer, he beat Steve Gromek with a homer, he beat Eddie Lopat with a homer, and he beat Allie Reynolds with a homer. All this work was washed out to sea when the Red Sox lost those final two games in Yankee Stadium, but that doesn't mean it never happened.

The loss of the pennant in 1949 on the last day of the season was probably an even more crushing blow than the disaster that befell him in the World Series. On his last time at bat, Ted Williams lost the batting championship that would have made him the only hitter except for Ty Cobb to win five batting championships and the only three-time triple crown winner in history. He lost it—what's that about he who lives by the sword?—by walking. What made it particularly hard to take was that the batting title was the only triple-crown category in which he had seemed to be the unquestioned leader through the greater part of the season.

On September 18, with ten games left, Ted hit two home runs (his thirty-ninth and fortieth) and a single and batted in six runs to take the lead in all categories of the triple crown. He was leading George Kell, .351 to .341.

Five days earlier, Kell had jammed his thumb on a play at third base at Fenway Park and was out of the lineup. He would play only four more games, and that was only because Detroit was battling Cleveland for third place. On September 23, one week before the end of the season, he went back into the lineup with his left thumb bandaged. For many years George Kell has been a member of the team announcing the Detroit games. "I knew I was going to have to swing easy and just try to hit the ball to right field," he says. "And I did." He had two ringing line singles to right field off Early Wynn, but had to be removed for a pinch hitter in the seventh. Still and all, he had gone two for three and raised his batting average to .342. And that one point was going to make all the difference.

On that same weekend, the Red Sox were defeating the Yankees two straight at Fenway Park to tie them for the league lead. Williams had a home run in each game, to run his home-run total to forty-three. The next day, in a rescheduled game in New York, he went one for three. The one hit came in the eighth inning and was part of a four-run rally that pulled out a 7–6 victory and put the Red Sox into first place.

For the Red Sox, there were two games in Washington before they returned to New York. In those four games, Ted had only two hits (along with the usual assortment of walks) in twelve times at bat. Looking back, it was the Washington games that did him in. He had one hit in four at-bats in the first game and then was held hitless in three at-bats by Rae Scarborough, who was, to put it mildly, always tough for him.

Through a freak in the schedule, Detroit had four straight off days leading into the final weekend of the season. In Friday's game against Cleveland, Bob Feller shut Ted out in three at-bats, and so as he went into those two decisive games against the Yankees he was ahead of Kell, .346 to .340.

In the opener in New York, the Red Sox blew a 4–0 lead. In the first inning, Ted hit a rocket down the first-base line that hit umpire Cal Hubbard and turned what should have been a double into a single. It was the only hit he had in three times at bat, and it cost him two points.

In Detroit, Kell was one for two against Mike Garcia and picked up a point. Going into the final game, then, it was .344 to .341.

Ted walked in the first inning. Then popped out twice. In the top of the ninth he was up again, with one out and nobody on base. Having just scored four runs, following the removal of starting pitcher Ellis Kinder for a pinch hitter, the Yankees were leading 5–0.

And Ted walked. That's all he had to do. In those circumstances, a walk was as good as a home run. The Red Sox did go on to rally. Stephens followed with a single. Bobby Doerr hit a long drive to right center that Joe DiMaggio, playing on a gimpy leg, couldn't run down, and two runs scored. With two out, Billy Goodman singled Doerr in. The score was 5–3. But Birdie Tebbetts, representing the tying run, fouled out to first base, and the season was over for Boston.

The season still wasn't over in Detroit. "When I came to the park that day," Kell says, "Pat Mullin, who dressed in the locker next to me, told me that if I got two hits I'd win the batting title. That was the first I thought about it." After he had singled and doubled off Bob Lemon on his first two times at bat, he thought about it some more. Bob Feller came in to relieve Lemon in the sixth and walked him. In the seventh he flied out. Not that Kell had any more of an idea about how Williams was doing than Williams had about Kell. But Red Rolfe, the Detroit manager, did. Lyall Smith, who was covering the game for the *Detroit Free Press,* had been on the phone with the reporter his paper had sent to New York to cover the showdown between the Yanks and the Red Sox. With Kell scheduled to be the fourth batter to come to bat in the ninth, Smith phoned down to the Detroit dugout to tell Rolfe that Kell had won the batting title by a very narrow amount "if he doesn't bat again."

After the first batter went out, Dick Wakefield pinch-hit a single, and as Kell went to the on-deck circle Rolfe turned to Joe Ginsberg, a reserve catcher who had just been brought up from the minors. "Grab a bat," he told him. "I'm not going to let Kell hit."

Ginsberg never had a chance to leave the dugout. Eddie Lake, the Tigers' leadoff man, hit the first pitch toward the second-base side of the shortstop, and Ray Boone (there he is again) had only to field the ball on one hop, step on second, and throw to first for an easy double play.

"When we got back into the clubhouse," says Kell, "Rolfe told me I had won the batting title, and that was the first I heard about it."

The final figures were .3429 to .34275. Here's how close it was: one fewer time at bat and Ted would have hit .34336 and won. One more time at bat and Kell would have hit .34226 and lost. If Kell had sat out the final weekend, he'd have finished with .3424. And lost.

Give Kell credit. He had been facing the toughest pitching staff in baseball. In those final three games, he went three for eight. In the four games he played with a sore thumb, he was five for eleven.

"I've always felt bad about beating Ted out," Kell says. "Because when it's that close, it's just a matter of luck. I felt even worse later when I learned that it had cost Ted the triple crown." After the game, he had gone right home to Arkansas, and it was some time before he heard that Rolfe was not going to let him come to bat. "I didn't know whether to believe it. Years later, I bumped into Joe Ginsberg at Cooperstown and told him I hadn't seen him with a bat, and he said, 'You didn't have time to. Eddie hit the first pitch.'"

Something else. The sacrifice fly rule wasn't in effect in 1949. If it had been, and Ted had picked up one more sacrifice fly than Kell, he would now be the only man in history to have won three triple crowns. When you compare the type of hitters they were, and consider that Ted didn't miss a game all season, it is almost impossible to believe that the spread between them wasn't larger than that. Nobody was thinking in those terms, of course. The rule, as it existed, had been in effect for ten years.

Ted finds the information more interesting than conclusive. "I wouldn't be so sure about it," he says. "I didn't have many sacrifice flies ever, because they never gave me anything to hit with a man on third and less than two outs."

In his six seasons between 1941 and 1949, he had won four batting titles and finished second twice. There were other triple crowns out there waiting for him. And then in the All-Star Game of 1950 he injured his elbow, and that changed everything.

XII

1950:
The Broken Elbow

From literally the day he first reported to Sarasota, Ted was saying that he would never risk his career by running into a fence. How could anybody argue with him? "I'm in the survival business," he would say. To take the risk of removing his bat from the lineup in order to, just possibly, make a catch made no sense at all. Besides, he would add, he wasn't being paid to field; he was being paid to hit. "Yes," Doc Cramer would say dryly. "I can see that."

There are the things you say and there are things you do. There are also the things you surprise yourself by doing. In his first season, Ted ran into the right-field fence at Yankee Stadium and had to be sent home with what was thought to be a season-ending wrist injury. It was not the only time he ran into a fence at Yankee Stadium. He always got himself pumped up for big games, and any game against the Yankees was a big game by definition. And, for reasons that undoubtedly came from deep within his psyche, no game was bigger for him than the All-Star Game.

The first major crisis of his career had been resolved when he proved to himself in the heat of one Kansas City afternoon that he was not going to be stopped by a beaning. The second came when he ran into a wall during the 1950 All-Star Game and suffered an injury that was going to affect the rest of his career.

The 1950 season was pivotal for Ted in the sense that it encapsulated his career in so many ways.

On May 17, with the season four weeks old, he achieved a pinnacle of boorish behavior, even for him, by responding to the braying of the fans with a time-honored hand gesture of contempt and insult followed by a sudden squall of expert expectorating.

The booing had begun in the first game of a doubleheader against Detroit when he dropped a short fly and was rewarded with the usual animal cries from his private zoo in the left-field stands. He answered in kind by putting his hands to his ears and waggling them like a donkey's in an obvious commentary on their mentality. In the eighth inning of that game, with the Sox trailing 13–0, he came up with the bases loaded, hit a long fly ball to right field, and ended up with a grand-slam home run when the ball bounced off the outstretched glove of Vic Wertz and dropped into the bull pen. Some of the fans seemed to view those four meaningless RBIs as a personal affront, and the abuse came raining down anew.

The Sox were leading, 3–1, in the eighth inning of a relatively uneventful second game when the Tigers loaded the bases off Tommy Fine, a young right-hander who had seemed to be on the way to his first big-league victory. Vic Wertz thereupon sliced a sharp single to left, and as Williams came dashing in to try to cut off the tying run the ball skidded to one side and rolled past him to the foot of the wall. The error was excusable; what happened next was not. Reverting to his sulky minor-league ways, the Kid jogged out to the wall, took his own sweet time picking the ball up, and lobbed it lazily back to the infield. All three runners scored, and Vic Wertz became perhaps the first batter in history to reach third base on a ball hit straightaway to the short left-field fence in Fenway Park. It is part of Williams's personality that he seethes and smolders before he erupts, and he had been seething and smoldering all day. The left-field stands gave it to him good after that disgraceful display, and when he came sprinting back to the dugout at the end of the inning the grandstand customers rose up and gave it to him even better. In the full stride of his six-four frame, Ted leaped forward, as if he were clearing an invisible hurdle, and with bent elbow and open palm delivered the obscene gesture. To make sure the message was fully understood, he then turned to his left and his right—like a thespian giving a curtain call—and repeated the performance two more times. The Boston papers had pictures of Williams in the full flowering of his performance, but none of them was ever printed.

As the third batter of the Sox half of the inning, Ted came into the batter's circle after the first man had gone out. Once again the full scorn of the spectators descended on him. His response this time was to turn around and spit toward them, slowly and contemptuously.

The next day, the following announcement was issued on Red Sox stationery: "After a talk with Mr. Yawkey, Ted Williams has requested that this announcement be made to the fans: Ted is sorry for his impulsive actions on the field yesterday and wishes to apologize to any and all whom he may have offended.''

In other words, the club said Williams was sorry, or anyway he should be. Ted went along to the extent of conceding that he was sorry he had embarrassed Big Daddy Yawkey.

That was by far Williams's worst offense on the field. The kindest thing that can be said is that it was a childish display of vulgarity by a presumably grown man. But, not to be hypocritical about it, whom did he hurt? The people in the stands? Awww, come on. They all rushed home to tell their friends and families about it, with the blissful feeling of self-importance that always accompanies the bearing of an eyewitness report to great and meaningful events.

The next day Fenway Park was crammed with people who should have been at work. They had come ostensibly to convey their shock and anger, but actually to make sure they would be on hand in the event of a repeat performance.

The incident upset Ted more than he was willing to admit, and when Ted was in that kind of a mood—as well we know—he always "showed them" by dogging it in the field or at the plate.

Jack Orr, reporting on Ted's performance in the Memorial Day doubleheader at Yankee Stadium two weeks later, wrote: "Anybody who saw him would say the Boston fans are justified in anything up to throwing him into the Charles River. Tuesday he loafed shamelessly in one of the big days of the season. He failed to deliver when his remarkable bat was needed. He sulked like an adolescent when he popped up. On one occasion he threw leisurely to second as a runner scored from third on a medium fly ball. His one long hit of the day was well belted, but he gave up and settled for a double when he probably could have made three bases.

"What made that performance look so bad," Orr continued, "was that earlier, Tommy Henrich, a guy they call Hopalong in the dugout because he's playing on a wobbly knee, hit a similar drive which was good for a triple. Despite the dragging leg, Henrich kept going at second and slid boisterously into third. The whole Yankee bench winced as Henrich hit the dirt, for he's been told not to slide."

A story had already been planted with the *New York Post*'s Jimmy Cannon that Ted was going to be asked to be traded to Detroit at the end of the year "because of Boston's hostile and abusive baseball fanatics." The story was promptly denied, by Williams and by everybody else, although there was undoubtedly some basis of truth in it. Ted had made it abundantly clear to the newpapermen that the "apology" for the obscene gesture had not come from him and that the gesture expressed, accurately and graphically, his opinion of Boston, of New England, and of the indigenous sportswriters and fans.

It all became academic when Ted was injured in the All-Star Game. Ted had been in a terrible slump throughout that tempestuous month of May, closing it out with an average of .283. As always, however, he had come back strong. In the month of June he hit 13 home runs, a personal record, homering once in every 8.38 times at bat. At the halfway mark he was hitting .321. In the power departments, he was tied with his teammate Walt Dropo for the RBI lead with 83, and tied with Cleveland's Al Rosen at 25 home runs.

The 25th home run had been hit two days before the All Star break, and was the longest he had ever hit at Yankee Stadium. "A mighty, soaring drive that vanished down the runway at the extreme right wing of the top deck," wrote John Drebinger of the *New York Times*.

"I was hitting better in the month before the All-Star Game," Ted says, "than I had ever hit in my life."

Ted had always hit in All-Star Games, but that was no great surprise since everybody had always known he could hit. In the 1950 All-Star Game he challenged two of the harshest criticisms that had been leveled against him. One was that he was a poor fielder and the other was that he was not a team player.

The temperature was up to 91 degrees as a sweltering crowd of 46,127 settled down in Comiskey Park to watch Robin Roberts open against Vic Raschi. Those who had come early enough to watch batting practice had seen Ted Williams drive four balls out of the park.

The second batter for the National League was Ralph Kiner, and Kiner, acting like the cleanup hitter he was, sent a long drive into left-center field. Williams got a good jump on the ball, made a nice over-the-shoulder catch as he ran toward the wall, and then stuck out both hands to fend off the fence as he was slowing down. The only suggestion that he had suffered any injury came when he shook his arm, as if he were in pain, after he threw the ball back to the infield. Casey Stengel, the American League manager, came to the top of the dugout to see whether he was hurt. Ted just resumed his outfield position, though, and everybody put the matter out of mind—Ted Williams included. ("I didn't think I'd run into the fence that hard. I thought I'd warded it off. But apparently my arm just happened to be at the wrong angle.")

At the close of the inning, Ted admitted to Stengel that the elbow was beginning to hurt, but he insisted on remaining in the game. From the way he played no one would have thought he was in any difficulty at all. In the last of the first, he came to bat with two out and Phil Rizzuto on second base and drove a hard ground ball toward right field. Normally it would have gone into right field for a base hit, but Jackie Robinson was out on the grass, in the National League's version of the Boudreau shift, and threw him out.

The National League was leading, 2–0, in the third inning, when Kiner came up again, and for the second straight time he found himself robbed by a fine Williams catch. Kiner got his revenge in the last half of the inning by leaping against the fence to haul in Ted's long drive.

In the fifth, with the score tied at 2–2, Ted put his side ahead with a line single to right. He struck out in his final turn at bat in the eighth, and Dom DiMaggio was sent out to replace him.

Williams, in real pain by now, went into the locker room and asked the White Sox trainer, Packy Schwartz, to examine the arm. Schwartz worked on it for thirty minutes and then told the collected sportswriters, "He'll be okay." Ted, who had been wincing and grimacing throughout the massage, looked at the writers and shook his head in obvious disagreement. He flew back to Boston that evening to have the elbow examined by the Red Sox's new trainer, Jack Fadden. By then, the elbow had swelled to twice its normal size.

"Jack Fadden stood alone in diagnosing an injury," Ted says. "He was the most professional trainer I ever knew. He diagnosed exactly what it was, told me it was bad, and sent me to the hospital. I was operated on the next day." Fifteen bone chips were taken out of the elbow. "I had two top orthopedic surgeons there. One of them wanted to take the whole head of the radius out. That's the way it was always done when you had that much damage. 'It's going to be kinky in there, and it's going to hurt him, and there's not enough left to give him the support he'd need anyway.' The other fellow said, 'Well, he's an athlete, he's a ballplayer. And he's still young. We've got to leave as much strength as we can in there and see what happens.' Fortunately, it worked out." Otherwise, Ted would have had to go back for a second operation.

The damage was there, though, and it was irreversible. "If you really want to get technical about it," says Ted, "my left arm bent about fifteen to twenty degrees after the operation, and I never had quite the extension on an outside pitch that I had before." Ninety percent of his extension eventually came back, Ted estimates. On his good days. But never the whole thing. "And I lost a little power. I lost a little of the *whooooosh*. My arm always hurt me a little bit after that, there was always a kind of stiffness. I really was surprised that I hit as well as I did for five years."

As soon as possible, he began a rehabilitation program under Jack Fadden. But he had not the slightest thought of trying to play again that year.

The Red Sox, led by the slugging of Junior Stephens and Walt Dropo and the steady hitting of Billy Goodman (who was on his way to winning the batting title), ran off a streak of twenty-three out of twenty-six from mid-August to mid-September, to pull to within a game and a half of New York and Detroit with sixteen games left to play. The first ten of those sixteen games, however, were going to be played on the road, where the Red Sox, with their predominantly right-handed power, were having difficulty breaking even. When they were beaten by the last-place St. Louis Browns, Steve O'Neill, who had replaced Joe McCarthy two weeks before the All-Star Game, urged Ted to give it a try. O'Neill's argument was that it would be better for Ted to find out now how well he could play, rather than to spend the whole winter wondering. Even more persuasive to Ted, perhaps, was the chance of reaching one hundred RBIs for the ninth straight year.

Typically, Ted got himself three line singles and a tremendous home run against the Browns to lead the Red Sox to a 12–9 win. He also made a jumping one-handed catch in the eighth inning to cut off a Browns rally.

But if the first day astounded him, it didn't really fool him. ("It was one of those hot, hot afternoons in St. Louis. I had a long workout and was loosened up. After that, I did nothing.") The only hitting he did after that came against the Yankees. After beating Detroit two straight, the Sox were only half a game behind the Yankees with twelve games left to play. Four of them were against the Yankees on the last two weekends of the season, two in New York and two in Boston. And in those final ten days of the 1950 season a phantom competition between Ted Williams and Joe DiMaggio was also going to be playing itself out.

If Ted's career was hanging in the balance, Joe DiMaggio's career seemed to be slipping away. His old knee injury was catching up to him, his reflexes were beginning to rust, and to make his discontent complete he hated his manager, Casey Stengel, almost as much as Stengel hated him.

In July of 1950, the coldness between them had turned frigid when Joe looked at the lineup card posted in the Fenway Park dugout and saw that he was listed to play first base. Now, first base is historically where old outfielders went—not ungratefully—to finish out their careers. But you did not do that to the great DiMaggio. Joe DiMaggio was incensed at the suggestion that he was no longer the premier center-fielder in the league and furious with Stengel for lying to the New

York writers by telling them that he had talked to Joe ahead of time and that Joe had agreed to make the move for the good of the team.

"There are two ways to play first," Joe told those same writers pointedly. "The old man's way, and the right way. I'll try to play it the right way."

While Joe was practicing at his new position before the game, Birdie Tebbetts, the Red Sox catcher, managed to coax a smile out of him by shouting out that he was going to be eating corn on the cob with false teeth. But when Ted Williams then shouted, "Hey, Jolter, those grounders come a lot faster there than in the outfield," Joe froze Ted with his famous glare.

Jerry Coleman, the Yankees second baseman, will take it from there: "Joe was hitting about .250 and having a terrible time, and in early August Stengel sat him down for a week to give him a rest." It was, in all probability, exactly what he needed. But once again the great DiMaggio was incensed. When he got back into the lineup he was determined to vindicate himself. During the month of September he had nine home runs and thirty RBIs and a rapidly rising batting average. "He was a guy at war with himself to get that .300 average so he could live with himself," Coleman says, in a voice still full of wonder. "That was the greatest war in history, and nobody outside our clubhouse knew that it ever happened."

So, in a way, we have the final chapter in the Williams-DiMaggio competition, even though they were traveling on separate tracks toward personal goals that the other was not necessarily aware of. Joe Di-Maggio was on a personal mission to bat .300. Ted Williams was after his hundred RBIs.

By the time the Red Sox arrived in New York for the first of the four games with the Yankees, DiMaggio had brought his average to .297, and Ted's RBI total stood at ninety-two. There were ten games left in the season. The Sox had dropped to two games off the lead. A sweep of this series would bring them into a tie, and a double loss would pretty much eliminate them.

In the opener, Joe had a single and a slicing little fly ball that dropped into the corner of the right-field stands for a home run and brought his average up to .299. All Ted managed was a single. The next day their roles were reversed. Joe had one single in five attempts and dropped back to .298. Ted hit two home runs, his first ones since the comeback game in St. Louis, but he got only two RBIs out of them. Even worse, the Red Sox lost both games and fell out of the race.

On the return to Boston for those final six games, the Boston fans turned out to greet Ted with another of their tremendous receptions. Unhappily, both Ted and the Red Sox got shut out by the Washington Senators.

Jerry Coleman picks up the story again: "We were playing Philadelphia the final week, before going to Boston, and Joe was like .299. He hit a shot to Eddie Joost, and Joost jumped way up and caught it. It was a hell of a play. So now I'm out there at second base waiting as DiMaggio comes by, mumbling to himself like he'd always do, as he was going to center field. Berra unloads one of those Hail-Mary shots over my head, and it hits DiMaggio right in the heel, and Joe goes down. He looks up and he sees me looking at him, and he figures I'm the guy who let the ball go through. He picked it up and he one-hops me and hits me on the knee, he knew what he was doing. *You fancy Dan sonofabitch, catch the goddamn ball.* He's hobbling around, I'm on the ground holding my knee, Berra's standing at home plate with his hands down, looking innocent. That was the tension of DiMag going for that .300 batting average."

On the last day of the season, DiMaggio, having succeeded in bringing his average up to .301, decided to sit out the game. Ted still had only ninety-four RBIs; on the front burner, Vern Stephens and Walt Dropo were tied for the RBI lead with 144 apiece. With the Yankees having clinched the pennant over Detroit on the same day they came to Boston, it marked the first time in three years that the pennant race was not going down to the final game.

Everybody was so relaxed before the game that Ted was shooting the breeze with Eddie Lopat alongside the Red Sox dugout, something that would have got them both fined during a pennant race.

We are now going to turn the podium over to Eddie Lopat: "I'm going to pitch a couple of innings the next day, getting ready for the World Series. I'm bullshitting with him. 'You want one hundred RBIs, right? What do you want me to throw you?' He said, 'Throw me your chickenshit slider.'

"I said, 'Hey, fastball, three-quarter speed down the pike.' He said, 'No, throw me the chickenshit slider.'

"I call Stephens over. 'Steve, what do you want to hit?'

"He said, 'Just bust it right in.' Dropo tells me the same thing.

"I said, 'If I come into the game and I got a chance to lose, the deal's off. I don't take a loss. A few runs, I don't mind.'

"In the fifth inning, man on first and Ted's the hitter. I said, okay, gang, get ready. I throw the first slider right down the pike, and he takes it. I said, 'What's wrong with that?'

"He said, 'I'm *gauging* it.'

"The second one I throw, it slipped out of my hand, and I mean I thought I hit him. It's right there, and he went down on all fours. I went halfway down to the plate, he's looking at me as if to say, *What's that?* I said, 'I told you, Ted, to try a fastball.'

"He said, 'Throw me the chickenshit slider.'

"Next pitch, he hits one on the screws, and it goes over the infield with that sinking overspin for a single.

"Next guy up is Stephens. Runners on first and second. I said, okay, Stevie. Three-quarter fastball right down the pike. He hits it four hundred feet straight up at home plate, and he slams home plate with his bat and broke it in forty pieces. Next guy is Dropo. With Di-Maggio out, Gene Woodling is in center. Woodling is standing about eight feet from the wall by the flag, down in the corner where the two walls meet. I laid one in there for Dropo, and he hit a screamer. I mean a shot. Woodling never had to move. I was laughing for a month. Three guys. I tell them what's coming, and they get one lousy single out of it."

Sometimes it doesn't pay to oververify a good story. In this instance, though, Ted tells the story the same way, almost word for word. "Lopat said, 'I want to see how far you can hit one. What do you want to hit?' I don't know whether he's trying to find out what I *like* to hit or what I *wanted* to hit. I said, 'Just throw me a slider.' I took the first one like I would in batting practice if I had been taking five swings and wanted to see how many good ones I could hit out of the five. And this was right down the middle. I thought, *Oh boy, this is it . . .* and the next one, Christ, it's behind my ear, and down I went, and he said it just got away from him, that's all.''

For the day, Ted had three singles and a double and knocked in three runs, to bring his final batting average to .317 and his RBI total to ninety-seven in eighty-nine games. But he wasn't kidding himself. The other hits had come off a rookie, Ernie Nevel, starting his first game, and another rookie, Lou Burdette, who would be heard from again. Nobody had to tell Ted that he hadn't been able to hit the good pitchers when it meant something.

He had played those final games against his better judgment, because he had been asked to. It was a mistake. By the end of the year the elbow hurt so much that he didn't think he could come back. But Tom Yawkey asked Jack Fadden to go down to Ted's new home, in Islamorada, Florida, to work out with him, and Ted was never able to turn Yawkey down.

Over the winter, he worked at it. He'd get up before dawn and drive out to the Flats, a long narrow stretch of water on the Key that extended for something over a mile. The Flats were known to have the best bonefishing in Florida, and bonefish live in shallow water. Ted would sit in his low-slung bonefishing boat with one huge oar and push himself back and forth through that shallow water from one end to the other, back and forth, back and forth, to build up the strength in his elbow.

Then he'd go back to the house and go through Fadden's rehabilitation program. Forty years later, Jack Fadden, ninety years old and quite ill, was relating how Ted had always thanked him for saving his career. "He was ready to quit, you know. He didn't believe that he was ever going to be able to hit again."

Fadden also remembered how impressed he was watching Ted's nimble fingers tying his fishing flies. But, most of all, he remembered how unbearable Ted could be when he had you on his own grounds, how he'd order you around and find fault with everything you'd do.

"The last day I was there," Fadden said, "I started out the door, and he screamed at me. 'That's the *wrong* door. You've been going out the *wrong* door ever since you got here.' Wrong door? There was nothing out there. If you didn't go fishing, there was nothing to do."

XIII

Korea

Ted Williams is not the only ballplayer to have hit a home run in his last time at bat, but he is certainly the only one to do it once and then come back to do it again as an encore, more than eight years later.

As the 1952 season began, Ted was called back into the Marine Corps, with whom he had served for three years in World War II. He was thirty-three years old, he was married, and he had a daughter, but he was being called back for combat duty in the Korean War. On April 30, two days before he was to report, 25,000 Bostonians gathered in Fenway Park to say good-bye.

"It seems disgraceful to me that a person such as Williams is to be given the keys to the city," wrote Dave Egan, by way of wishing him Godspeed. "We talk about juvenile delinquency, and fight against it, and then officially honor a man whom we should officially horsewhip. If this is leadership I'll have strychnine." Thus spake the drunk from the *Record*.

Ted himself hadn't exactly turned handsprings about the send-off. He had withdrawn his objections only after being told that too many people had done too many things for it to be called off. Under normal circumstances, he wouldn't even have been playing. Having injured his leg in spring training, he had appeared almost exclusively as a pinch hitter and had only two hits to show for seven times at bat.

The *Boston Herald-Traveler* had been hard at work compiling a memory book signed by four hundred thousand fans from every section of the country. The governor and the mayor were there to sing his praises in the pregame festivities. He was showered with gifts. At home plate, in a wheelchair, sat a decorated Korean veteran crippled in both arms and legs. Ted held the soldier's hand in his right hand and Dom DiMaggio's in his left as the entire Red Sox squad and the entire Detroit squad lined up on their respective sides of the field and joined hands while the band played "Auld Lang Syne."

Williams, obviously moved, told the crowd, "I never thought this could happen to me. I wish to thank you from the bottom of my heart." As he finished he pulled off his cap and waved it to the crowd, the first time he had weakened since he had adopted his policy of diplomatic nonrecognition.

In the first inning, Ted singled through what would normally be thought of as the shortstop position. The fans assumed that he really had reformed and was deliberately hitting to left, but the truth was that he had played so little that his timing was off. He struck out his next time up, after hitting a towering foul drive into the right-field bleachers, and on his third time at bat he walked.

When he came up in the seventh, the score was tied, 3–3. Dom DiMaggio was on first, and two men were out. Pitching for Detroit was Ted's old fishing buddy, Dizzy Trout. Ted took the first pitch for a strike. The second pitch was quite probably a strike, too. Ted timed it perfectly and sent a long drive into the bull pen in right field as the fans screamed themselves hoarse.

He did not tip his cap as he rounded the bases. It was one thing to wave it as a good-bye to those who were honoring him. It was quite another to tip it after hitting a home run—a distinction that was perfectly clear to Ted but kind of murky to everyone else.

But it did give him four hits in ten at-bats for the season and put an impressive-looking .400 onto his record block.

Ted had been called back into service, along with about 1,100 other senior lieutenants and captains, because the Marine Corps had bitten off a big chunk of the Korean conflict and didn't have either the pilots that were needed or the time to train them.

Ted had missed combat in World War II, when he was young and full of pizzazz and vinegar, not because he wasn't good enough for combat but because he was too good. As Johnny Pesky, who went into the V-5 program with him then, is happy to attest, "We were assigned to Amherst for training. I was terrible. Ted was brilliant."

At Amherst College, in Massachusetts, they went through crash courses in such subjects as algebra, trigonometry, and navigation, and the kid who had been content with passing grades at Hoover High in San Diego came through with an overall grade of 3.85 out of a possible 4.0. "He mastered intricate problems in fifteen minutes which took the average cadet an hour," Pesky says. "And half of the other cadets there were college grads." After six months at Amherst, they were sent to Chapel Hill, North Carolina, for preflight training and then on to Peru, Indiana, for primary flying. "They really ran us through the wringer there," Pesky says. "Up by the light of the moon, double time all day, classes until your brain spun. Drill until your tongue hung out. Hikes, inspections, every sport you could think of. The object was to find out who was going to crack." Given his reputation as "the great Ted Williams"—to say nothing of his reputation as a pop-off— Ted was ridden extra hard. "But he never lost his temper or got a single bad-behavior demerit."

It was Pesky, who had been hanging on by his fingertips all along, who was finally washed out, while Ted was sent on to Pensacola, Florida, for advance training. But Pesky kept in touch. "I heard he literally tore the 'sleeve target' to shreds with his angle dives. He'd shoot from wingovers, zooms, and barrel rolls, and after a few passes the sleeve was ribbons. At any rate, I know he broke the all-time record for hits." From Pensacola Ted went to Jacksonville for a course in air gunnery, the combat pilot's payoff test, and broke all the records in reflexes, coordination, and visual-reaction time. "From what I heard, Ted could make a plane and its six 'pianos' [machine guns] play like a symphony orchestra," Pesky says. "From what they said, his reflexes, coordination, and visual reaction made him a built-in part of the machine."

In other words, he was too good. The top graduates in every class were made instructors, and Ted was one of the best they had ever seen. He was sent to Bronson Field to put the Marine cadets there through their final qualifying stages. It was as an instructor that he finally got into trouble with the authorities. Not on his own behalf, though, but on behalf of his students. With a sudden surfeit of pilots, the instructors were ordered to pass only the top third of a class. Anybody who so much as dipped a wing or made a false landing pass was to be washed out. Ted wouldn't do it. That Boy Scout code of his again; his sense of fair play. When he was hauled before the brass, he held his ground. "If I think a kid is going to make a competent flier," he told them, "I won't wash him."

"I never met a Marine pilot who trained under Ted," says Pesky, "who didn't think he was a right Joe."

In August 1945 Ted finally got his wish to be transferred to a combat wing. He was in Pearl Harbor awaiting orders to join the China fleet when he bumped into Pesky again. "He was itching to get into combat," Pesky says. "A few days later the war ended, and we both got discharged in December."

During the early training at Chapel Hill and Peru, Ted had turned away all offers to sit out the war in comfort as a member of a service baseball team. "If it takes me ten years," he had vowed to Pesky, "I'm going to earn my wings." It was because of his pride in what those wings represented that he had held onto his commission as a captain in the Reserves.

Jerry Coleman was called back at the same time. The two met at El Toro, California, in December 1952, for their physical examinations, and despite Ted's injured elbow he passed the physical. He was thirty-three years old, he hadn't flown in eight years, and he had little doubt that his baseball career was over. In fact, as he wrote to several friends, he had a strong premonition that he was not going to come back alive. But, then, maybe that was the same thing to him.

In Korea, he flew thirty-nine missions in a squadron whose operations commander was John Glenn. Yes, *that* John Glenn. In the last half of those missions, he was serving as Glenn's wingman.

It tells something about Williams that almost nobody knew about their relationship until Glenn appeared as one of the guests on a program that Ted had agreed to do for the Jimmy Fund, on the occasion of his seventieth birthday. "An Evening with Number 9," it was called.

Johnny Pesky, for one, learned about it for the first time that evening. It didn't surprise him, though. "He rarely talked about his service. Once he told me about the time he nearly cracked up after blacking out at seventeen thousand feet without oxygen. He fell fifteen thousand feet before regaining consciousness and pulled out at treetop level. Scared the hell out of him, he said.'' Bobby Doerr did know, but he had heard about it only in a specific context. "Any time he'd be in a group of people,'' Doerr says, "Ted would seek out some person who was extra sharp about something. The story I heard from Ted was that when he went over there, and he knew he would be going into combat, he was going to pick someone who was the sharpest and best person to fly with.'' Ted had met Glenn in the reception center before shipping cut and had been told that Glenn was one of the best test pilots in the world. "He stayed pretty close to John Glenn, he told me. He thought a lot of Glenn.''

Glenn obviously came to think a lot of Ted, too. In tapping him to serve as his wingman, he was saying that Ted was the best and sharpest pilot he had.

Nevertheless, Ted's premonition of disaster almost came true on his very first taste of combat. "It was on a strike at a troop encampment near Kyomipo,'' Ted says. "The funny thing was I didn't feel anything. I knew I was hit when the stick started shaking like mad in my hands. Then everything went out, my radio, landing gear, everything. The red warning lights were on all over the plane.''

He was flying an F-9 jet, an apt designation for the man who was known throughout the world of baseball as "Number 9.''

"The F-9 had a centrifugal flow engine,'' Glenn told the audience at the Wang Center in Boston that night. "And when it got hit and caught on fire the tail would blow off almost every time. So the standard orders were that if you had a fire in the back of the plane you were to eject immediately. Ted was trailing smoke and fire. People were yelling at him over the radio, 'Get out!' But his radio was out, and he couldn't see all this going on behind him.'' With all his instruments gone, Ted was following another of the standard orders, which was to eject over the ocean. "I looked down and saw that the water was half frozen over, and I could see myself breaking through and not being able to get out. I said to myself, 'Not for this boy,' and I headed for dry land. I heard later they were telling me to eject. It might not have been the worst thing that the radio was out.''

His radio had continued to function just long enough for him to call out his Mayday and pick up a couple of exchanges. A plane came up alongside to lead him to the nearest airport. "Larry Hawkins," Ted says. "A young lieutenant from Pennsylvania. He saved my life." But if Ted couldn't hear what was being said to him, he was possibly the only pilot in the air wing who couldn't. Jerry Coleman, for one: "The entire Marine Air was over North Korea that day, and we were all tuned in to the emergency frequency coming back, and we heard this conversation between two planes. One was hit, he was on fire, and the other was talking him in and telling him where he was and that the wheels wouldn't come down and the flaps wouldn't work. He was vectoring him to one of the fields. We learned later that it was Ted Williams, and that somewhere in there he had lost radio contact.''

When they reached the airstrip Hawkins pulled alongside and signaled to Ted that his wheels were jammed. "But I decided to ride my plane in," Ted explained. "If I knew then that my ship was on fire, I damn well would have shot the canopy and jumped." That, it seemed, was exactly what Hawkins had been trying to tell him.

Ted was too busy trying to hold his plane together to be frightened. "I let down over the strip and saw formations of planes right in front of me, all on landing approaches. Every one of those planes just broke and scattered. I came barreling in at a little more than two hundred miles an hour and fighting the stick all the way. Nothing worked. No dive brakes, flaps, nothing to slow up the plane. Then I heard a hollow *whoomph* behind me." The whole plane was now enveloped by fire, and smoke and flames were pouring out of the wheel housing, and still he didn't know it. "I thought I'd never stop. When I did, I released the canopy and almost fell out.''

According to Del Ballinger, Ted's boyhood friend from San Diego, there exists a film in something called "the Red Navy files" that shows Ted running away from the plane and diving—"as if he were diving headfirst into second base"—while the plane is exploding behind him.

Ted has never heard of such a film, though, which puts its existence very much in question. Nor can Ted remember whether he was running or diving when the plane exploded. "The main concern at that time is to get the pilot out of there. The canopy was open, and as soon as it stopped I can see fire coming up around me. I just tumbled out and ran. I was scared stiff that the tanks might blow."

Ted has estimated that he could not have had much more than twenty or thirty seconds' worth of fuel left. "If I had a minute I'd have been lucky." There was a margin of error in that regard, which, unbeknownst to Ted, he had just barely managed to squeeze through. On one side of the equation, he'd had just enough gas left to get him down. On the other side, it was only because he was out of fuel that the plane didn't blow up as soon as he hit the runway.

Jerry Coleman never heard of another case like it. "He was coming in at two hundred miles per hour. He skidded about two or three thousand feet in a burning plane on one of those old Marsden mattings that looked like a waffle. He didn't blow, and he got out of it. It was a miracle thing." *

The next day Ted was in the air again. He flew thirty-nine missions in all before an ear ailment, not unconnected with that chronic virus of his, cut short his tour of duty. The condition, aggravated by the cold and damp Korean weather and the flying altitudes, hung on so persistently that he was logging almost as much time in the infirmary as in the air. Officially, he was discharged because of "lack of ventilation in the ear and nose."

---

* Great trivia question: Name the player who as a Marine pilot served in World War II, was called back into the service for Korea, and finished off his career by hitting a home run in Fenway Park in his last time at bat in the final game of the season. The answer is Jerry Coleman. Ted's final home run was *his* final game and also the final game of the season at Fenway Park in 1960. But the team went on to New York for three more games. Coleman, pressed into the game at shortstop for the final game of the 1957 season, hit a home run in the seventh inning—just after Ted Williams had been removed from the lineup after going two for two to bring his average up to .388.

"The difference between us," Coleman says, "is that Ted knew it was his last time at bat and I didn't. When we got back to New York, George Weiss called me in and offered me a job in the front office. I had nine and a half years and I wanted to go for ten. I said, 'What happens if I don't take it?' He said, 'You'll be traded.' So I took it."

He was discharged on July 10, 1953 from Moffett Field in San Francisco. As soon as word of his arrival spread through the sprawling installation, several hundred sailors found excuses to pull duty near the ramp. The same thing had occurred when he left Honolulu.

Which brings up that other question. When John Glenn burst on the scene as the ultimate celebrity, how was Ted able to resist the temptation to tell his friends about being Glenn's wingman in Korea? Well, there's that Code again. To boast about such a thing would be calling his own military career to their attention, and that was the kind of thing one did not do. The other explanation, of course, is that Ted was always so absorbed in himself that nobody else really mattered.

Ted sums up his feelings about Glenn this way: "I was back in the States when he flew across the country in world-record time, two hours and something. And I was thrilled about that." The next time he heard anything about Glenn was in 1959, when Ted was in the hospital with a neck condition so painful that he couldn't move his head. "I get a letter from John Glenn, and he tells me he is in the space program of weight lifting and pressure chambers and centrifuges and all the rest of it. It was quite a lengthy letter, I wish to hell I'd kept it, but I don't keep letters. Mrs. Yawkey was in the hospital at the same time, and I showed it to her. He said when you get to Washington, why don't you come down and see what we're doing."

Ted never got the chance. By the time he had rejoined the Sox and was playing in Washington, the astronauts had been shipped across the country for cold-weather training. "When things started happening with John Glenn, I was so happy and proud of the fact that I knew him. John Glenn is an extraordinary talented, brave hero. He's a hell of a man."

That is exactly what Ted Williams, the passionate Republican, said to Senator John Glenn (D-Ohio) at the Wang Center on the evening when he reappeared in his life. With one reservation. "It's just too bad," Ted told him, "that you're a Democrat."

Looking back, Ted compares the Korean experience with the experience of managing the Washington Senators fifteen years later. Both episodes clearly fall into the category of things he's glad he did but would never want to do again. "Managing gives me another view and aspect of baseball I would never have gotten any other way. No other way. It's the same thing with going back into the Marines. Okay, you didn't see combat the first time, and when you go back in and you do see combat, it's an altogether different ball game, and you have a different feeling altogether for the Marine Corps."

Ted had followed baseball while he was in Korea. The *Sporting News* was sent to him by airmail, and he had received enough mail from former teammates to know what was going on in the Boston clubhouse.

Ted returned to the States just in time to throw out the first ball in the 1953 All-Star Game. He was dubious about playing ball at all, and he had not the slightest intention of trying to get into shape for the current season. Yawkey and Cronin both told him they thought he should get right back into uniform, but Ted was looking forward to some relaxed fishing. Then Fred Corcoran, his longtime business manager, told him, "You're not a fisherman. You're a ballplayer."

"All right," Ted said. "But wouldn't it be better if I started fresh next year?"

"That's just what you don't want to do," Corcoran said. "There are still more than two months left of the season. This is the time for you to work yourself slowly into shape, get into as many games as you can, swing that bat again, and prove to everybody, and particularly to yourself, that you're just as good as you ever were."

So Ted worked hard, running, shagging fly balls, and hitting, hitting, hitting until his hands were blistered—and then hitting some more. No, he didn't hit a home run on his first time at bat, that had to wait for his second.

The first time at bat, as a pinch hitter in Baltimore, he popped up against Marlin Stuart, a pitcher who had always been tough for him. He came up for the second time, before a Sunday crowd of 27,000, against another pitcher who had always been tough for him,

Cleveland's Mike Garcia. It was the seventh inning, the Sox were trailing, 5 – 2, and no one was on base. Garcia got behind Ted, three and one, and then made the mistake of trying to blow his good fastball past him. Ted belted it well up into the right-field stands.

Joe Cashman of the *Boston American* described the ensuing scene this way: "We were present when Detroit fandom went mad as the Tigers won the '35 championship. We thrilled at countless mass cheering incidents inspired by the immortal Babe Ruth. We witnessed the dramatic Fenway Park tribute to Joe DiMaggio in the final game of the '48 regular season. None of them came close to matching the ovation Williams was accorded yesterday."

Ted appeared in thirty-seven games over the rest of the season. In ninety-one times at bat he had thirty-seven base hits, which included thirteen home runs and six doubles. His batting average was .407; his slugging average—are you ready for this?—was .901.

The Kid was back.

With it all, he was inclined to be either unduly skeptical or unduly modest. The pitchers, he would say, had been worn out and weary from the long season, while he had swung into action, following the battle to get into shape, fresh and eager. The real test, he felt, would come the following season, when he and the pitchers would face each other from scratch.

Ted reported to Sarasota early, determined to work himself into top shape. His training season lasted barely ten minutes.

He had just suited up and gone to the outfield when Hoot Evers hit a sinking liner into left field. Ted started in after it, stumbled as he tried to pull up, and felt himself falling. He tried to break the force of the fall by rolling over, but at thirty-five he was apparently too old for that kind of tumbling act. He landed hard on his left shoulder and felt something give. Jim Piersall, coming over from center field, heard him cry out in disgust, "I broke it."

There is this about Ted. Healthy or sick, he has always worked hard at his job. "There are a lot of things I cannot do," he said grimly, "so that means I'll have to work harder than ever on the things I can do." He continued to work out in order to keep his legs in shape, but it seemed as if fate was against him. Just before the Sox broke camp, it became apparent that the break—a fairly routine one, as those things go—was not healing properly. The bones would have to be nailed into place, a technique that had been developed by the army during World War II. Holes were drilled in the two segments of the broken collarbone, tiny steel pins were inserted into the holes, and a wire was coiled between the pins to hold the collarbone in place. Ted still has those steel pins in his shoulder, and he still has a scar to mark the incision.

And so once again Ted had to start working himself into shape after the season opened. Once again he had to take his private batting practice, complete with blistered hands and aching bones. Back to the morning workouts with the clubhouse kids. Back to calling the pitches, as if he were still the little kid in the backyard. "Okay, I'm in Detroit. Runners on first and third. One out. The score is tied. The count is two and two. Curveball on the inside corner. I want to hit a long fly." The only difference was that he was facing a real pitcher and hitting a real ball.

He did not get into the starting lineup until May 14, when he played both games of a doubleheader in Detroit. With all his spectacular returns, this was the best one of all. All he did was go eight for nine, including two home runs, a double, and five RBIs.

His first start, yes. But not his first game. A day earlier, manager Lou Boudreau had sent him up as a pinch hitter in the seventh inning of a cold damp day against Baltimore's Joe Coleman. On his first swing of the bat, he lifted a soft fly to left. Boudreau then sent him out to left field and, batting against Marlin Stuart, he made the final out of the game by grounding to shortstop.

Clearly, he had not been able to get his bat around. The shoulder pained him so much when he swung that he was talking about returning to Boston for further treatment.

The thought of Briggs Field was irresistible, though, and when it turned out to be a warm sunny afternoon, he went into the starting lineup. "He was nervous as a rookie," wrote Hal Middlesworth of the

Detroit Free Press. "Fidgeting in the field, waving his arms in wind-mill fashion to keep the shoulder loose and walking around in short circles."

In the first game, he hit singles to left, right, and center. After the third hit, Boudreau took him out for a pinch runner and left it up to Ted to decide whether he wanted to start the second game.

He made the right decision. In the first inning he singled, and in the third he blasted a long home run off the right-field upper deck that was exceeded in distance only by that monster of a drive he had hit on the roof back in his freshman season. His third hit was a double, his fourth a single. In the eighth inning he finished off his day with a two-run homer off the front of the right-field roof, to put the Red Sox ahead, and went circling around the bases in his head-down, head-flopping fashion.

"I'm going to have all my players put pins in their shoulders," said Casey Stengel.

His batting average for the year, .345, was actually higher than Bobby Avila's official winning mark of .341. Ted lost out because he came to bat only 386 times, 14 fewer than the rules required.

The same thing happened again the following year, in what was becoming an annual thriller in which Ted, after being out of the lineup early in the season, would miss another week or two in early autumn because of the virus, and then try to drive to the finish with enough times at bat to qualify for the batting championship. With all the bases on balls he received, it was not easy. One of those who protested that Ted should have been given more consideration in this purely legalistic business about times at bat was Casey Stengel. "That rule is in the books to keep some humpty-dumpty from stealing a title with half a season," Casey said. "It ain't never going to be a disgrace to have Williams win it."

In 1955 Ted "retired." A purely strategic retirement, necessitated by the divorce proceedings his wife had brought against him. If Ted were drawing his huge baseball salary ($60,000 in cash, another $60,000 spread out over the next five years), the alimony demands would have been correspondingly high, and, more to the point, so would the actual alimony figure set by the court. Ted unretired himself in mid-May, after the divorce papers had been duly signed, and was back in uniform at Fenway Park getting himself in shape once more. And once more he found himself, at season's end, with a .356 average, as against Al Kaline's league-leading .340. In 1955, however, Ted had only come to bat 320 times.

A year later, Mickey Mantle replaced Avila and Kaline in the duel down the stretch, and the statistical thriller was more dramatic than ever. This time, to show that life can be beautiful, Ted hit his 400 at-bats right on the nose. Unfortunately for him, Mantle came on strong in the last week to finish at .353—and take the triple crown—while Ted was withering away to .345.

When you consider that Ted won the batting titles in 1957 and 1958, you find that in the first five years following his return from Korea, Williams led the league four times—officially or unofficially—and finished the second the fifth.

And with all that, he was saving the best for the last.

XIV

Post-Korea

I didn't want to make an issue of the elbow. Partly because I didn't want anybody to know I wasn't quite as good a hitter as I had been, and partly because I didn't want the Red Sox to think that maybe I couldn't do it any more.

—TED WILLIAMS

The elbow injury is the dividing line of Ted Williams's career. Or, for the sake of convenience, it can be divided into pre-Korea and post-Korea, with the 1951 season sitting in between as a kind of island.

He still had that beautiful swing. Teammates who had seen him before the injury saw no difference. What they were seeing, however, was the second best swing in their memory. To see the best swing, they'd have had to go back to films of the Kid in 1941.

He had always preached the necessity of making adjustments. "The pitcher is adjusting all the time," he would say, "and you have to adjust, too." He had ten years experience behind him now. "I was a smarter hitter. I knew pitchers very well. I knew what I had to do to compensate for different things probably better than the previous ten years. And now I had to make some real adjustments." He had always conceded with two strikes on him. "There were other circumstances now where I was ready to concede a little bit. I was not quite the pull hitter that I had been when they put the shift on. I accommodated that fact with the fact that I couldn't quite rip it the way I used to. And it all kind of fell in."

And here is the delicious irony of it. He was able to use the Boudreau shift to his advantage. The old Ted Williams "tell 'em nothing." He continued to argue that he was right in not changing his stroke, even while he was changing it. He continued to complain about that "radical, exaggerated shift" that was taking hits away from him, even while he was getting a lot of hits through the holes the shift created. In a way it was funny. Where before he had refused to keep the defenses honest by challenging the shift, he was now keeping the shift honest by pulling whenever he was able to. "When everything

261

was warm and I was loose and I had the right type of pitcher, I could still pull it with anybody."

But, still, he couldn't believe that they were not catching on to what he was doing. "It took five years for them to finally wake up and see that, gee, he's not trying to pull the ball as much; or he can't pull the ball as much."

The writers would ask him whether he was hitting differently because of the elbow, and he'd deny it. If he seemed to be hitting to left more than he used to, he'd tell them, it was only because he didn't start off the year as strong or as sharp as when he was younger. "But," he'd say, "you'll notice that as the season goes along I pull the ball more and more. Over the last half of the year you'll hardly ever see me hit to left."

When the question of any lingering effect from the injury was put to him directly, he would say that (a) the elbow had begun to loosen up during the last half of 1951, and (b) the one good thing about being called back to the Marines was that it had given the elbow a chance to heal completely.

In many ways, his return in 1951, the year after the injury, was remarkably successful. When you run your eyes down his record block, the .318 batting average doesn't look very impressive. In fact he was adapting to his new swing in much the same way he had been forced to adapt to the new way he was being pitched to in 1940. It was the last time he played a full season, the last time he faced the pressure of a pennant race into September, and when it was over he was convinced that he had been able to make the necessary adjustments. ("I was very worried going into the 1951 season. I was not worried after Korea because I had proved to myself in 1951 that I could do it.")

His batting average may have been only .318, but he played in 148 games, hit 30 home runs, knocked in 124 runs, and scored 109. When he is judged against the league rather than against himself, those figures loom larger. All right, his slugging average was only .556, the lowest it would ever be except for the injury-ridden season of 1959. Still and all, it was good enough to win the slugging title for the seventh straight time (if you want to count the "unofficial" title in 1950). He also led the league with 144 walks. Keep that in mind. We're going to be coming back to it.

For that matter, the .318 average was the fourth best in the league. His 30 home runs placed him second to Gus Zernial's 33, and his 126 RBIs were second to Zernial's 129. Even the 109 runs, as severe a drop as it was from his usual production, were good enough to place him third. (Dom DiMaggio led with 113.)

What does it all show? Well, it shows that the sluggers of the Golden Era were gone. Joe DiMaggio's "private war" at the end of 1950 had been his last hurrah. Foxx and Greenberg were long gone. Ted's teammates Vern Stephens and Walt Dropo had collapsed completely. Bobby Doerr, who had been playing for years with a bad back, announced his retirement before the season was over. (Characteristically, Bobby asked that there be no announcement, let alone any fuss, and when the club sneaked in a "day" for him anyway he donated all the gifts to charity.)

And for Ted . . . no longer an overpowering hitter, perhaps, but in an environment that had run out of dominating hitters he had been able, at the age of thirty-three, to more than hold his own.

There was one statistic, however, in which he was still dominant. Those 144 walks put him in an eleventh-place tie for the most walks in a single season, ever.* In his first year back from Korea the bases on balls were going to be even more spectacular.

After recovering from the broken collarbone, Ted was able to play in 117 games. And although he was deprived of the batting title because he was shy those 14 times at bat, he did lead the league in his two virtual monopolies, slugging percentage and walks. It would have been foolish to deny him the slugging title when his .635 average was a full hundred points ahead of anybody else, and it would have been a logical absurdity—even for baseball—to say that he didn't have the most bases on balls when, regardless of how few times he batted, he still had more bases on balls than anybody else. Speaking of catch-22,

---

* It is still the fifteenth highest total of all time.

it was only because he had walked 136 times that he just barely fell short of the required 400 times at bat.*

Focus down upon those walks. Dolly in on them, shoot them in Technicolor. Give them their own star on Hollywood Boulevard. Better yet, call Mr. Ripley.

The reason Ted wasn't able to come to bat 400 times was that he walked once in every 3.8 times at bat. In the long and infinitely charted history of baseball, nobody else has ever gone less than 1 in 4.00. Babe Ruth's best was 1 in 4.07, and that was in the year he walked a record 170 times. The only other figure that comes close is Ted Williams's own 4.14 in 1941.

Focus now on his on-base percentage, which is a function of batting average and walks. The comparison of Ted's on-base percentage and his slugging average all but defines the way he was being pitched to.

Here are the six highest on-base averages in the history of the game:

	on-base pct		slugging av.
Ted Williams	.551	1941	.735
Babe Ruth	.545	1923	.764
Babe Ruth	.530	1920	.847
Ted Williams	.528	1957	.731
*Ted Williams	.516	1954	.635
Babe Ruth	.516	1926	.737

---

* The rule requiring 400 times at bat went back only to 1945. Before that, a player simply had to appear in 100 games, a standard by which Ted would have qualified. In 1950, the rule was changed so that a player had to appear in at least two-thirds of his team's scheduled games, to all practical purposes turning the clock back to the 100-game standard. Again, Ted would have won the batting title. In 1951, it was changed back to 400 times at bat, with the added proviso that if the leading hitter was still ahead after being charged with the required bat total he would win. This was the guideline in effect in 1954. Bringing Ted's total up to 400, he would have hit .332, nine points behind Avila's .341. In 1955, the reaction to widespread criticism of the 1951 rule was to go back to the 1945 rule of a flat 400 times at bat, which would have made things easier for the figure filberts a year earlier but would have taken the slugging-percentage title away from Williams.

Two years later, in 1957, the rule was changed again so that a player had to have a total of at least 3.1 plate *appearances* for every scheduled game to qualify as league leader. That's the rule still extant. If it had been in effect in 1954, when Ted had at least 512 appearances, he would now own seven batting titles. As a result, many of the encyclopedias and compendiums that are being printed these days—those big, unwieldy books that tell you everything about everything—have begun to list him as the 1954 batting champion. Poetic justice, since the rule was passed because of Ted's down-to-the-wire battle with Mickey Mantle in 1956. Who needed an embarrassing controversy surrounding Ted Williams's times at bat every year?

On his first year back from Korea, Ted's on-base percentage was his own second best and the fourth best (tied) of all time.* And while he also led again in slugging percentage, as he had every year since 1941, the slugging percentage was only the sixty-fourth best. (It's now eighty-fourth.) Ted's explanation for the discrepancy sums it up quite succinctly. "They were still scared of me," he says, "and I wasn't near the hitter I'd been." It also shows that he was taking more pitches than ever, especially in the early innings when he was still trying to loosen up the elbow. It also shows that with nothing behind him in the Red Sox lineup except singles hitters, the opposition was more than willing to pitch around him.

Yet there is an oddity here that demonstrates either how much he did adjust or how greatly, perfectionist that he is, he overestimated the difficulty the elbow was causing him. The oddity is that the percentage of home runs was even higher after Korea (see Appendix D). The difference, as anybody who followed him knows, was that the home runs were leaving the park as high line drives, rather than the majestic, up-up-in-the-sky fly balls of the past.

"I never had the same power," Ted says with an air of finality. "I'd say if I hit twenty tremendous home runs, fifteen of them came before 1950. The conditions had to be just right. Got to hit one just right, got to be the pitch, got to be the pitcher, got to be the wind factors and all that." And the temperature, too. On a good hot day he was as loose as ever, and when he was loose he could still, as he says, pull the ball with anybody. "The ball is going to travel farther in hot weather, anyway," he says. "If the day was hot I couldn't wait to grab hold of a bat."

It was one thing to hide his difficulties, such as they were, from the opposition. It would seem to be quite another to hide them from the management of the Red Sox.

There were only six years (1951–56) in which Ted wouldn't have been deemed to have come to bat enough times to win the title. During those six years, he lost one title and almost lost another.

* For reasons having everything to do with Ted's miracle season of 1957, it's now tied for fifth best.

He had good reason. It had taken him a couple of years—and a fishing trip with the operating surgeon—to figure out that when Steve O'Neill had suggested he return to the lineup at the end of 1950, it was not Ted's frame of mind the management was concerned about, but their own. The Red Sox, after all, had the full medical report on the injury. They knew better than Ted did how chancy the operation had been and how dubious the prognosis. Given everything they knew, the Red Sox couldn't afford to spend all winter wondering whether they were going to have to replace him.

Whatever doubts Ted might have had were confirmed when he asked Joe Cronin for a two-year contract, going into the 1954 season, and was turned down. Whenever anybody would congratulate Ted on having a great day during the season, he would say, "Don't tell me. Tell Cronin."

XV

The Jimmy Fund

Ted Williams left two monuments behind in Boston. One of them can be found in any baseball record book. The other can be found in the hospital rooms and laboratories of the Jimmy Fund Hospital for Children's Cancer, the foremost cancer research center in the world.

It was in his work for the Jimmy Fund that Ted not only achieved a lasting connection with the people of New England but also forged a tie between his boyhood in San Diego and his life in Boston.

The temptation to bring everything back to that Salvation Army up-bringing is impossible to resist. Most of his high-school teammates have a story about some handicapped kid whom Ted befriended. The kid with the harelip, the kid with the bad leg, the kid who stuttered. One of the things George Myatt had found most attractive about the wisecracking seventeen-year-old just out of high school was his un-failing instinct for the underdog. "Even then, he was doing things for old people and kids." And during Ted's year in Minneapolis one can find any number of newspaper pictures of him visiting a sick child in the hospital.

The Jimmy Fund has been a forty-year commitment for Ted. When he signed on, he signed on for life.

The Variety Club of New England is a charitable and social asso-ciation that was set up by the people of show business. In 1947, the directors decided to channel their funds into a single charity, and the Children's Hospital of Boston sounded like a natural. Touring one of the smaller wards one day, a member of the committee commented, "These are a bunch of nice-looking kids. When will they be going home?" They would all be leaving soon, he was told, "but none of them will ever be going home." That was how the group discovered, almost by accident, that cancer, far from being exclusively an adult disease, as most people believed, was a killer of children ranking sec-ond only to accidents. Every child in the ward, the group was told, would be dead within two months.

The Variety Club immediately raised $47,000, through a raffle, and set about to establish the Children's Cancer Research Foundation. Within the first year, Dr. Sidney Farber, its director of research, developed an antibiotic that not only kept many of the children alive for as long as a year but also allowed them to spend most of that time at home. When word of Dr. Farber's discovery got around, the little one-ward infirmary was deluged with calls from all over the country and, indeed, from around the world.

Faced with the need to raise a considerable amount of money in the shortest possible time, the Variety Club—which, after all, was a show-business organization—went to Ralph Edwards, the host of the leading radio program of the day, "Truth or Consequences." Not the most tasteful of shows, but a natural enough choice, since Edwards had already raised $41 million for the Heart Foundation through a promotion that challenged his three million listeners to identify a celebrity known as "The Walking Man." (It turned out to be Jack Benny.)

The most dramatic way to inform the public about the plight of the children, the club decided, was to take advantage of the well-known connection between little boys and baseball. The Boston Braves were tapped for the occasion, because it was they rather than the Red Sox who happened to be playing at home. One of the stricken little boys was picked out and given the name of Jimmy, to symbolize everybody's little boy. His real name was never disclosed.

The program was planned for May 22, 1948. In the middle of his broadcast, Ralph Edwards switched to Boston, and after briefly outlining the facts he began to talk to Jimmy. What, he asked, was Jimmy's favorite sport?

"Baseball," said Jimmy.

And who was his favorite player?

"Johnny Sain."

"Have you ever met him?" Edwards asked.

"No."

"Well," Edwards said, "you're going to meet him right now."

At that, Johnny Sain, the Braves' star pitcher, came into Jimmy's hospital room with an autographed ball and a few words of encouragement. One by one, the other members of the Braves followed. At the end of the program Billy Southworth, the Braves manager, promised Jimmy that he would be taken out to the ballpark for a doubleheader the following day. "And while I've never before predicted the outcome of a ball game," he said, "I promise you now that we'll win at least one of those games for you."

It turned out to be a winning promotion for everybody involved. The next day, with Jimmy in a box seat, the Braves came from far behind to win both games of the doubleheader. Lou Perini, the Braves owner, forever after maintained that it was the impetus of those two emotional victories that carried the Braves to their first pennant in thirty-four years. As for Ralph Edwards, the reaction was so overwhelming that it led him to create an entirely new show that is a part of the American culture. That's right. "This Is Your Life."

Most important of all, money began to roll in to the Jimmy Fund the very next day.

The Jimmy Fund became an all–New England project, with the governors of the various states proclaiming an annual Jimmy Day, at which both children and adults, at a neighborhood level, raised money by the most ingenious methods they could devise.

Baseball, having been in on the opening pitch, remained a participant, with the players of both teams offering their services in fundraising. In 1953, when the Braves moved from Boston, Tom Yawkey and the Red Sox took over, and in short order Ted Williams became both the symbol and the standard bearer. So much so that by working for or simply contributing to the Jimmy Fund it was possible to identify oneself with Ted Williams. An asset of such importance that when he went up to Bangor, Maine, on a fund-raiser he outdrew a personal appearance by President Dwight D. Eisenhower.

He went everywhere. He went to the banquets of the American-Italian associations and the Spanish-American clubs. He went to Civil Liberties Union meetings, to temples and churches, to Little League games. To department stores, where he autographed various items of clothing, and to cookouts on Boston Common. Mark Cummings, who is in charge of fund-raising today, says, "I have a picture of him standing on a trailer in a drive-in movie. The spotlight is down, Ted has a microphone in front of him, and he's talking to the people in the cars. He'd go *anywhere*.''

Mort Lederman, the chief of security, is the only surviving official from the earliest days. Lederman, a onetime national amateur tennis champion, would usually accompany Ted to the larger gatherings. ''Unlike most celebrities,'' he says, ''Williams never had a demand. He doesn't care about getting into front door, back door, special car, special food, special spot. He never saw himself as a celebrity. He was a back-door guy, and I admired him for that.''

It was not in fund-raising that Ted made his most significant contributions, though. He made himself available for that most wracking of all experiences, visiting the kids in their hospital beds. Whenever one of the children asked to see him, whatever the hour of day or night, he would come. His only stipulation was that there must be no publicity, no reporters, no cameramen.

What Williams took upon himself was the agonizing task of trying to bring some cheer into the lives of dying children and, perhaps more difficult, comforting their parents. Over the years he permitted himself to become attached to thousands of these kids, knowing full well that he was going to lose them, one by one. He became so attached to some of them that he chartered special planes to fly to their deathbeds.

Obviously they were not token visits. He knew most of the patients' birthdays and as much about their backgrounds as possible. When he was about to meet a new patient, he would rummage through the child's mail, while the child was in the examining room, in order to find some personal way of reaching out to him.

The most difficult thing in the world, as any adult knows, is to communicate with children at their own level without being patronizing. Ted had no trouble at all. He would come into a ward like a warm, friendly puppy and remain exactly that way until he left, a big child among little children.

When Ted returned from Korea, the Variety Club asked if it could put on a $100-a-plate welcome-home dinner for him. Now, if there is one thing Ted loathes more than a formal banquet, it is a formal banquet at which he is the guest of honor. But when he learned that an anonymous benefactor had agreed to underwrite the affair, leaving all the proceeds to go directly into the Jimmy Fund, Ted took a hundred dollars out of his wallet and said, "All right, here's my money. Just make sure that everybody else at the head table pays, too."

In the course of his two-minute speech, Ted said, "The way I look at it, there is always something we can do for some youngster somewhere. Here, we don't have to look any further than the Jimmy Fund. Somehow, it strikes me that a dollar tossed into this drive is the whole American way of life in a nutshell. All the bullets and all the bombs that explode all over the world won't leave the impact, when all is said and done, of a dollar bill dropped in the Jimmy Fund pot by a warm heart and a willing hand."

Ted worked so hard for the fund—getting out of a sickbed on occasion to make a scheduled appearance—that it is obvious he must have been getting something very fundamental in return. When the question is put to him directly, however, Ted, who is normally loud and articulate, becomes vague and uncomfortable. "Look," he says, "it embarrasses me to be praised for anything like this. The embarrassing thing is that I don't feel I've done anything compared to the people at the hospital who are really doing the important work. It makes me happy to think I've done a little good. I suppose that's what I get out of it. Anyway, it's only a freak of fate, isn't it, that one of those kids isn't going to grow up to be an athlete and I wasn't the one who had the cancer?"

Not that he wasn't taken advantage of. There was the time he traveled to Connecticut to visit a dying child who, he was told, had asked for him. The boy didn't have the slightest idea who he was. It was the father who wanted to meet him.

There were promotions that were almost amateurish. John Wayne, who was promoting a well-forgotten movie called *Hatari,* came to Boston with his costars, Bruce Cabot and Red Buttons, and somebody decided it would be a wonderful idea to get Ted Williams together with John

Wayne, with whom he was frequently compared, for a publicity shot. After all, they were both war heroes—Ted in Korea and Wayne on film.

When Ted reported dutifully to the hospital for the photo, he found that Joe Cronin, who was on the hospital's Board of Directors, was closeted with Dr. Farber, and so Ted was waiting outside the office door, in that lowered-head, gangling, neck-rolling way of his, when John Wayne came out of the elevator, accompanied by Buttons and Cabot. Now, Ted may be six-four, but according to Mort Lederman, who was shepherding the actors, "John Wayne must have been fifteen feet tall. Everything about him was big. Even his nose looked huge."

Ted looked up, stuck out his hand and said, "I'm Ted Williams."

John Wayne placed his hand on Ted's shoulder, looked down at him and boomed, "Heard about you, boy!"

The driving force behind the Jimmy Fund was the executive director, Bill Koster. "Ted liked Bill Koster," Lederman says, "because he could see that Bill Koster was a sincere guy. He had a wife and kid, and he didn't run around. He didn't drive a fancy car. He was an ordinary guy who was dedicated to this hospital with kids who were dying. This meant something to Ted Williams." Ted says it himself. "I admired Bill Koster because I knew he was heart and soul committed to the Jimmy Fund and Dr. Farber. As a result of being close to him over quite a lengthy period of time I came to respect him so much that I was unable to say no to him. Anything he wanted me to do, boom, I did it."

Oh, Ted would complain from time to time, as was his wont, that Koster was getting to be a real pain in the ass, but he always had a weakness for people who were totally committed. Also he was being given a chance to do something worthwhile, because Ted Williams was hardly living the kind of spare and spartan life that Bill Koster led. "He saw these kids and it did a job on him," Lederman says. "Koster had a lot to do it. Dr. Farber had a lot to do with it. This hospital had a lot to do with it. Everybody who works here feels they're lucky because they're doing something for society. This was Ted Williams's way of making a contribution.'' And with it all, Ted was authenticating himself as an American icon. He cared about the kids, but that doesn't mean he wasn't very cognizant of the part that Babe Ruth's visits to sick kids played in his legend.

He became close to Dr. Farber. The great man took him into his confidence. Became his mentor in the fight against cancer; became his teacher. For Dr. Farber to have a friend like Ted Williams was not an inconsiderable thing for him, but for Ted Williams to have a friend like Dr. Farber was even bigger. Dr. Farber was a world-renowned cancer specialist, the father of chemotherapy. He had been working on cancer in infants and children for at least a decade before Ted met him. He was one of those rare men from whose eyes, truly, there shone an inner light. Nobody could understand why he hadn't won the Nobel Prize.

For twenty years Dr. Sidney Farber battled in the halls of the U.S. Senate for his plan to construct a network of regional treatment and research hospitals throughout the country, and it was this plan that became the model for President Richard M. Nixon's War on Cancer.

Dr. Farber lived just long enough to see his dream become a reality.* In February 1973 he died of cancer. Do you want to hear something eerie? Bill Koster died of cancer five years later. And so did three other members of the Jimmy Fund's board of directors, Joe Cronin,

---

* Don't overlook the possibility that Ted might have played a role in it. Ted and Nixon had been introduced during a stopover at the Miami airport, by a mutual friend who knew how much Ted admired him, and they were great friends.

When Nixon was vice-president, he would come to the Statler almost every time the Sox were in town and have lunch with Ted in one of the hotel's private dining rooms. "Next thing I know I'm in Washington, and the next year he's president of the United States. He was a pretty good baseball fan. He was only five minutes from the ballpark, and he'd come down for the last five or six innings with Julie and David Eisenhower, then come to the clubhouse to see me after the game."

Did Ted lobby his friend the president for his dying friend, Dr. Farber?

"I can't recollect, to be honest, that I sat down and talked to Nixon that way, but certainly it was always brought up somewhere around my conversation. Every place I went in those years I talked about it. You'd work all year, and you might raise a million and a half bucks, and you'd need three or four million. It was very, very important that we get those donations in New England because the federal government was giving us matching funds."

Tom Yawkey, and the Red Sox attorney, Jack Hayes. Everybody on the board except general manager Dick O'Connell.

By the time Ted retired, the Jimmy Fund Hospital was the largest clinic in the world treating children with cancer and had the largest group of scientists working to produce a cure. And, at the bottom line, it could boast the first real breakthrough in the field, a "cure" rate of almost 50 percent in the two most common strains of leukemia. (In the vocabulary of cancer treatment, a "cure" is defined as a five-year period of uninterrupted remission.)

On the final Saturday that Ted Williams would be playing in a Red Sox uniform, a ceremony was scheduled at Fenway Park for what was hoped to be the burning of the original $1-million mortgage on the hospital. The way the promotion was planned, the names of all the contributors to the 1960 Jimmy Fund drive would be piled at home plate, and, in a sort of raffle, Ted would pick out the winning envelope. The prize was a replica of the bat and ball with which Ted had hit his five hundredth home run. After the presentation, Ted was to be joined by Richard Cardinal Cushing, another patron of the Jimmy Fund, for the mortgage-burning ceremony.

The mortgage was not for burning that day, alas. Although 80,000 letters came in over the final weeks—all of them begging Ted not to retire—the total contributions fell $50,000 short. And that wasn't the only thing that went wrong. The field microphone failed to operate, forcing Ted and Cardinal Cushing to make the long climb up to the rooftop press box to use the public-address system.

"We didn't make it," Williams told the 30,761 spectators. "But the drive isn't over yet, and we've come a long way toward burning the mortgage. I've realized for a long time that you're the country's greatest baseball fans, and now I know that you're also the country's most charitable. I want to thank you personally for all you've given."

But Ted's day wasn't over yet. Following the ceremony, he was scheduled to travel to Rhode Island for four separate Jimmy Fund appearances. When Koster came to pick him up, though, Ted appeared agitated. He insisted on stopping off at the hospital even though they were already behind schedule, to visit a little fellow who had begun to fail. The kid was delighted. He had just put the finishing touches on a belt he had been making for him, and he buckled it around Ted's waist. If Ted had not stopped in, he might not have seen him again because the boy died a couple of days later.

When Ted retired from baseball, he did not retire from the Jimmy Fund. Once he had signed on, he was committed for life.

With the infusion of government money, the research budget began to soar. The Dana-Farber Institute (as it is now called) is such an acknowledged leader in the field—the "cure" rate in the two strains of leukemia is up to 77 percent—that it is usually at the top of the list for federal grants. As a result, the Jimmy Fund, which once subsidized the whole budget, now provides only about 15 percent (roughly $9 million, against $135 million). Nevertheless, the fund still provides all the money for pure research, since federal grants have to be targeted in approved directions. "We're able to use the Jimmy Fund money to let these brilliant scientists go in any direction they choose," Cummings says. "And that's why we're always leading the way." Of equal importance, the institute is able to use those funds to recruit the best and the brightest of young researchers coming out of Harvard Medical School before they have established enough of a reputation to be considered for a government grant.

The executive director of the Jimmy Fund since 1978 has been Mike Andrews, a former Red Sox second baseman. "Ted *is* the Jimmy Fund," Andrews says. "From the beginning, the first words I'd hear would be, 'The Jimmy Fund? Oh yeah, that's Ted Williams's charity.'"

A few years ago, a market survey was conducted to find out how many people knew what the Jimmy Fund was. The recognition factor through all of New England was well over 90 percent, a figure that put the fund up there with the likes of Coca-Cola and Pepsi. As a regional charity, it ranks alone in every conceivable category. So much so that other regional charities constantly come to Boston to find out how they do it. They go away with a new understanding of what it means to have Ted Williams on your team.

"He wants us to use his name in any way we can to raise money," Mike Andrews says. "He has come in and made several appearances for us since I've been here, as much as he doesn't like appearances. There are events where we auction off things and raise a lot of money. We will periodically send him down baseballs to sign, and he'll mail them back, dozens of them. We stockpile them, and we use them mostly for golf tournament auctions where we get five hundred bucks for an autographed ball.

"Ted has been so good to us. Even today, he will go out and do a card show, and all of sudden here comes a check for the Jimmy Fund." The checks come in, unexpectedly, from all over the country. "Only last week, a check came in from Detroit. It turned out that Ted had agreed to speak at some banquet there but only if they'd send his fee to the Jimmy Fund. He still thinks of us all the time. He gives personally, he gives of his time and of his name. Just as much as he did at the beginning."

XVI

The Miracle of 1957

As he looks back over his career, Ted Williams has pretty much decided that the 1957 season was the best year he ever had. For some reason—perhaps having to do with sunspots—it was a great year for the grape that had been ripening on the vine. The batting leaders were Ted Williams (age 39) and Stan Musial (36). The leading pitcher was Warren Spahn (36). The only no-hitter was thrown by Bob Keegan (36).

The most imposing accomplishment was that of Ted Williams, whose .388 batting average was the highest in the majors since Ted himself hit .406 in 1941.

A comparison of the eras bears him out. In the five years before he hit his .406, the league-leading averages were .388, .371, .349, .381, and .352, for an *average* average of .368. From 1952 to 1956, the figures were .327, .337, .341, .340, and .353, for an overall average of .342.

In 1941, then, Ted was 38 points above the preceding five years; in 1957, he was 46 points above. (In the National League, the leaders from 1936 to 1940 averaged .359; between 1952 and 1956, it was .338.)

In many ways, it was a season which recapitulated his entire career. Not the least of which was that ability of his to perform at the top of his game when there was controversy swirling all around him.

The old antagonism with the press had reasserted itself in spring training a year earlier, and had quickened all through the season. The occasion was the drafting of Johnny Podres, the young lefthander who had pitched the Brooklyn Dodgers to their first World Championship. When Williams leveled a blast at the "gutless" draft boards, politicians, and sportswriters who were permitting Podres to be shanghaied, he sounded off not to the Boston press but to a couple of writers from the San Francisco Seals who had dropped in on the Red Sox training camp to see what big-leaguers looked like. It was anybody's guess whether Ted found something humorous in giving what was clearly going to be a front-page story to a couple of minor-league writers or whether he just popped off to whoever happened to be standing in front of him. At various times, Ted put it both ways. When the Boston writers, stung by their own editors, accused Ted of deliberately hosing them, he shot back, "Good, I wish I could do it more often." Later he claimed that he had become so angry at reading about the change in Podres's draft status that he had decided to sound off to the first reporter who brought the subject up.

On the morning of Tuesday, March 13, Ted was sitting in front of his locker, in full game uniform, when Charlie Wagner, the assistant director of the Red Sox farm system and a onetime Williams roommate, came over with five San Francisco writers in tow. The conversation started off quietly enough, with Williams and the writers making small talk about the Pacific Coast League. One of them had been present when Williams hit his last home run for San Diego, in the final game of the 1937 season, and a fruitless discussion followed about the identity of the pitcher. Then someone brought up the drafting of Johnny Podres, and in less than three minutes Williams got a lot of things that had been eating him off his chest. "Podres is paying the penalty for being a star," he said. "If Podres had lost those World Series games, he would probably still be with the Dodgers. But when Podres became a hero in the Series some politician said, 'Why isn't a big strong kid like that in the army?' The draft boards didn't have the guts to oppose the politicians, and the sportswriters are equally to blame because they didn't take up for him."

Having handed the startled San Francisco writers the story of their lives, Ted grabbed his glove and announced that he was going out to the field. Either out of sheer innocence or sardonic humor, he wished the writers good luck as he left.

If Ted were indeed spitting in the face of the Boston press by giving his Blue-Plate special to a couple of writers he had never seen before, he spat at them more literally during the season. To put it directly, he embarked on what can only be called a public spitting jag, a form of artistic expression directed primarily toward the tenants of the press box, although the spray was apparently perfectly free to moisten the people in the stands.

He was at the time, a mere stripling of thirty-seven.

Since Ted was a man who was always known to pick his spots, the two most notable episodes came on the occasion of his four hundredth home run and at the celebration of Joe Cronin Day in Boston. Both times, the score was 1 − 0, and both times, the saliva came flying forth at the moment Ted was accounting for the winning run. To set the scene, Ted had come into June slumping so badly as to provoke speculation that he could no longer get around on the fastball. But by the end of June he was hitting like Ted Williams, and when he finally got the long-awaited four hundredth home run, on July 17, his reaction was to look up to the press box and spit, as if he had done it all just to spite them. He spat again as he hit each base and as he was crossing the plate he reared back and went for the Olympic record.

Manager Mike Higgins spoke to Ted after the game with some degree of firmness. The only result was a repeat performance a couple of days later, after Ted hit a home run against Detroit.

Upon his return to Boston after the next western swing, Ted turned his moist attentions to the Boston fans. Unhappily, he picked the day when the Red Sox, along with most of baseball's top brass, were honoring Joe Cronin on his election to the Hall of Fame.

The trouble started in the eleventh inning of a scoreless game against the Yankees, when Mickey Mantle hit a towering fly into left field. Now, the outfielders on both teams had been having trouble all day due to a tricky wind, sporadic showers, and a high, bright sky. Nobody had actually dropped a ball, though. . . . until now. The ball popped out of Ted's glove, Mantle ended up on second base, and the howl of the banshees assaulted Ted's acutely sensitive ears. Yogi Berra followed with a long line drive into left center. Ted, breaking nicely, made a fine running catch, and the boos turned to cheers.

As Ted started to run in, he turned to the stands and spat. *Front-running bastards,* you could almost hear him say. A few more strides, and he rocked his head back and forth and spat again. Just to make sure everybody got the message, he turned around as he was running down the steps of the dugout and spat one more time.

In the last of the eleventh, the Sox loaded the bases off Don Larsen with nobody out, on an error, a late throw to second on a sacrifice, and a walk. Up to the plate came Ted Williams. In from the bull pen came Tommy Byrne, who had started out as a wild left-hander with a blazing fastball but had come back to the Yankees, in the twilight of his career, as a wily left-hander with excellent control.

Ted always tried to get as close to the plate as he could while a pitcher was warming up, the better to get a good look at his stuff. What he would do, in fact, would be to move just alongside the batter's box and time the pitcher's speed by swinging as the ball reached the plate. Sal Maglie, upon coming into the league with the Cleveland Indians, had issued public notice that the first time Ted tried that with him he was going to throw the ball at his head. Tommy Byrne had apparently been reading the papers, because he warned Ted to back off. When Ted refused to budge, Byrne threw at him, the first time— in all probability—that a hitter had even been brushed back before he even came to bat. The second time came a few seconds later when Byrne threw at him again.

Ted fouled off Byrne's first two pitches to fall into a nothing-and-two hole. The next four pitches were balls. At that stage of the game, a base on balls was as good as a home run, since the game was over either way. But it was not as good as a home run as far as Ted Williams was concerned. Flipping his bat high in the air, in a final gesture of defiance and disgust, he began to stalk off the field.

Ed Runge was the umpire behind the plate. Runge, who is now in retirement in San Diego, says he had no thought whatsoever of putting Ted on report. "He wasn't criticizing me. He was teed off because the fans were on him and he wanted to drive the run in. He threw the bat about fifty yards in the air and stormed to the dugout. I was watching him very closely, though. All he had to do was step onto the top step of the dugout and he'd have been out, and the run wouldn't have counted. He stopped before he stepped into the dugout and stepped on first and that ended the game."

The reports of the game talked about the swirling winds and about grass "slick from the intermittent rains." Nothing was written about the brief, narrowly funneled showers that fell throughout the game. What actually happened, Ted says, was that a sudden shower of huge, quarter-sized raindrops descended upon him along with Mantle's fly ball. So why didn't he say, "For crissake, didn't you guys see the raindrops that were plopping on my head? Couldn't you see me staggering all over the place?" Of course he couldn't. "I never like to make excuses on anything I did wrong. I never wanted to alibi." Just as Ted Williams got some kind of confirmation out of *not* tipping his cap, Ted Williams got some kind of confirmation out of *not* alibiing. Why give them the satisfaction?

At first he refused to talk to the press about his conduct at all. When he finally did, he said, "Even after I made the catch on Berra, I came in burning, and then when I heard those bastards booing me all I wanted to do was to show my contempt for them." Was he sorry he'd done it? "Not a damned bit," Ted roared. "You writers are responsible for this—the whole thing. I'm no rockhead, you know. If it didn't bother me I wouldn't be fired up as I am now."

Soon enough, he had reason to be sorry. Tom Yawkey, furious at the way Ted had spoiled Joe Cronin's day, ordered Cronin to fine him $5,000.

Upon being informed of the fine, Ted took an attitude that could best be described as sorry but not penitent. "I'd spit again at the same people who booed me today," he snapped. Then he added, more prudently, "If I could stand a fine of $5,000 a day, I wouldn't be playing ball."

Few events in his career had a more lasting effect on him. The next night, the Red Sox were holding their first Family Night, and the Boston writers were having a field day, along the lines of "Bring your kids to Fenway Park so that Ted Williams can spit at them."

"The way they were writing," Ted says, "I thought they had a chance to drive me right the hell out of the city. I didn't know what to expect. The New York writers stayed over, some of them, to see what was going to happen, the Baltimore writers were there because their club was coming in, and there were writers and cameras and everything from all around the league. But I want to tell you, I got the greatest single ovation I ever got in my life going to home plate after a day and a half of solid derogatory writing toward me. And that was when I realized that no matter what anybody said the Boston fans were behind me.''

He responded, not untypically, by hitting a home run and, in one of his rare displays of humor, clamped his hand over his mouth as he crossed the plate.

It was one thing to admit to himself, finally, that he knew the fans of Boston loved him. It was something else entirely to say it publicly or to allow it to change his behavior. ''I realized in the years following the World Series loss that they were always with me. I had a love affair with them, and they had a love affair with me, and I couldn't show it. I couldn't have acted any different but I felt that way.''

If anything, his feelings about the fans only served to exacerbate his grievance against the writers. ''They'd print their lies about me, and the fans would believe what they read and come out to the park the next day and boo me. That's what got me so mad.''

Through the years the shifting emotions of those two days in 1956 stayed with him. When he began to have a belated relationship with his son, John Henry, he would tell him about the dropped Mantle fly ball as a way of explaining the terrible things that had been done to him by the Boston press. Thirty-five years afterward, during a brief summer rainstorm, he excitedly called John Henry out of the house. Huge raindrops were falling out of a bright sky. ''Look up at the sky,'' Ted ordered. ''Look up and tell me what you can see.'' John Henry couldn't see anything. ''That's the kind of raindrops were falling,'' said Ted triumphantly, ''on the day I dropped Mantle's fly.''

The first controversy of 1957 also arose early in spring training, when Mike Higgins allowed Ted to sit out the first few exhibition games. He did not play when the Yankees came to Sarasota, nor did he accompany the squad to St. Petersburg the next day. The Yankees were peeved. "We sent Mantle and Berra to Sarasota, but Williams doesn't come here. It's not right. Not when we're charging $2.50 for our best seats."

Another mild controversy came during a Red Sox trip to the West Coast to give Los Angeles and San Francisco a look at major-league baseball, in anticipation of the imminent arrival of the Dodgers and the Giants. In Los Angeles, the players were invited to a luncheon at Paramount Studios in honor of Jim Piersall, whose mental breakdown the studio had dramatized a year earlier in the film *Fear Strikes Out*. The real attraction, of course, was Ted Williams. Such disparate types as Cecil B. DeMille, Jerry Lewis, and Zsa Zsa showed up to meet him, only to be left wandering around asking, "Where's Ted Williams?" If the Red Sox were to be believed, Ted was "visiting a friend with cancer."

On the way back to Sarasota, the team had a plane change in New Orleans. New Orleans in the springtime had never been particularly lucky for Ted. In his freshman year, he had been laid low by the flu bug on his way to camp. In the spring of 1948 he had been hit by what was diagnosed as an attack of appendicitis, bringing on fears that he might miss the opening month of Joe McCarthy's first season as manager. Ted still shakes his head over that one. "They said, This is serious, send him to Boston as fast as you can. I was on the train for two days, for crissake. It turned out to be stomachache. Johnny Orlando and I had gone to Antoine's and eaten everything. Oysters, crab, catfish, everything."

In the late spring of 1957, New Orleans hit the fan.

The sports editor of the *New Orleans States,* Crozet Duplantier, an ex-Marine, wanted to get Ted to do something for the Marine reserves, so he had asked *Boston Globe* writer Hy Hurwitz, also an ex-Marine, to set up a meeting at the airport.

Ted had always resented being called back to fight in Korea. For public consumption, he had stated that he was no different from anybody else the Marines had felt it necessary to recall. In point of fact, he had little doubt that he and Jerry Coleman had been called up solely for their publicity value. He had resented the interruption of his career. In the following years, as the divorce settlement stripped him of most of his savings, he had become increasingly angry about the loss of his salary over those two years. And so, in what he thought was a private, off-the-record conversation among three former Marines, he passed his gripes on to Duplantier. "If they had called back everyone in the same category as me, I'd have no beef," he said. "But they didn't. They picked on me because I was well known."

A few minutes later, Duplantier turned up again to let Ted know that he had been a Korean War retread himself. This time, Ted launched himself into a bitter attack on politicians. "I used to respect Senator Taft," he said. "I thought he was a wonderful man. But he was just a gutless politician. A friend of mine was recalled for Korea. He knew Taft. He asked him to help him get deferred. Do you know what Senator Taft told my friend? He said, 'I can't touch you. You're pretty well known where you live. If you were just another guy, I'd be able to help you.' Now do you know why I think politicians are gutless?"

Having gutted Senator Robert Taft, the symbol of the Republican party, he went on to blast Harry Truman, the symbol of the Democratic party, as another "gutless politician," sprinkling his comments all the while with a little bipartisan spitting.

He could have met Eisenhower and Truman many times, Ted continued, but he wasn't interested in meeting any "phony politicians," from the President on down.

To Ted's astonishment, the griping session among the ex-Marines turned out to be a newspaper interview. Duplantier printed it all. Ted stormed back that the writer had been too drunk to quote him accurately—a charge Duplantier did nothing to dispel by getting himself picked up for drunken driving a couple of weeks later.

While his blast at the Marines, Truman, Taft, and Eisenhower was still reverberating on sports and editorial pages around the nation, Ted proceeded to take a swing at the Internal Revenue Service. "It's a shame the way Joe Louis is being hounded for payment of back income taxes," he said. "Here's a guy who has been a credit to his race and his country, and look at the treatment he's getting. If some big-shot, phony politician was in the same predicament, they'd allow him to settle it by paying two cents on the dollar.''

For the next few weeks, Ted found himself in the eye of the hurricane. But if editorial writers and sports columnists looked on his remarks with horror, the fans in the stands were all for him. In a very real way, he seemed to be expressing their own distaste for "phony politicians," and, needless to say, nobody has ever got himself ridden out of town on a rail for lambasting the tax collector. When Ted came to the plate for the first time that season, the Boston fans gave him a tremendous ovation—which Ted quite naturally disdained to acknowledge.

Once the furor had quieted down, Ted did feel it wise to resume diplomatic relations with his old alma mater, the U.S. Marines, and while he was at it he extended his apology to include any and all who might have been offended by his remarks. "I have too many friends and have spent too much time in the Marine Corps not to know that that organization is tops," he said. It was a knowledge that had apparently come to him overnight, for he had flatly refused to pose for Marine Corps photographers only a few days earlier.

It was also typical of Ted that he blamed the incident not on his own big mouth but on Hy Hurwitz, who was little more than a bystander—and, by extension, on the whole Boston press corps, which he always suspected of setting such booby traps for him. The next time Hurwitz, who was only about five-feet-five, came over to Ted's locker in the clubhouse, Ted exploded. "If you were five inches bigger," he screamed, "I'd whack you right on the nose."

"If you were five inches smaller," the feisty Hurwitz snapped back, "I'd whack *you* right on the nose." The shouting match ended with Hurwitz vowing not to speak to Ted again until he apologized and Ted vowing that he was going to hold Hurwitz to that promise.

He did better than that. Since Ted was always up there with the greats when it came to nursing a grievance, he went through the entire season without speaking to *any* of the writers regularly assigned to the club save for one old friend, Ed Rumill of the *Christian Science Monitor*. Rumill had been a batting-practice pitcher for the Sox the year Ted joined the club, and so Ted was usually willing to forgive him the company he kept. Whenever a Boston writer approached him during the early part of the season, Ted would say, somewhat haughtily, "You know I'm not talking to you guys." Later on he might deign to answer a simple question if he was in an expansive mood, but when a sportswriter was assigned to get a Williams interview he had to go to the one writer Williams would talk to and funnel the questions through him. When Ted really wanted to have some fun, he would plant a story on Rumill and then sit back and watch the others scurry around trying to verify it.

Under these conditions of total warfare, Ted had the best opening month in his career. After twenty-one games, he was hitting .443 and had nine home runs. By the end of May he was hitting .413.

Austen Lake wrote that never had "this child-of-turmoil" gone to such extremes of vituperation, hostility, and malice with Boston sportswriters or been so charming and cooperative with the out-of-town press. "The curly-haired feudist is magnificent! Hate seems to activate his reflexes like adrenaline stimulates the heart. Animosity is his fuel! He has to be agitated before his network is triggered to explode. C'mon Ted, hate us for a dozen home runs during the current homestay! Loathe us for a flock of RBIs! We the ball authors get the bricks from which columns are built, and Boston's fans get a round-the-clock topic for lunch-bar and table talk. Everybody gains!"

There was, of course, more to it than that. The "curly-haired feudist" was nurturing another of his little secrets. He was using a heavier bat—a good four ounces heavier than he ordinarily used—and choking up from the first pitch. "It was a piece of iron," Ted says. "A real piece of wood. I'd had it the year before, and I thought, well, I'm just going to use it in spring training. Not trying to hit home runs, just trying to hit the ball hard, hit it through the middle, right center. They had that terrible drastic shift on me. Still had it. They had been taking that extra base hit away from me in the eighth and ninth inning, because that was my natural way to go, and I'd be trying to pull and hit a good hard ball, and it would be right at somebody. Looked like a poop ground ball in the box score, but it was right at somebody. So I'm not going to try to pull the ball, I'm just going to hit it hard. Before I know it I'm hitting the ball great, hitting it all over the place.

"Here comes the start of the season. It's cold. I said what the hell, I'm just going to keep using this bat. Little heavier bat isn't going to hurt anything at this point. Damn, I started hitting the ball through the hole in short. Line drive to center and right center. Line shot off the fence in left. I've always said the best hitters could wait until the last second to meet the ball. Well, I was swinging late. And all of a sudden after two or three series of doing this . . . God, the infield started moving over, opening up. Like they're saying, God, this guy is getting old now; he can't pull the ball. Now it's coming into late May and early June. And then the hot weather came, and when it was real hot I could pull the ball pretty near as well as I ever could. And, by God, they have scattered out. Now I got my other bat again, and I began to pull the ball to right field, and I've got holes I never had for eight years. And that's what happened in 1957. That's why I hit so well that year."

Not only was everything falling in for him, but he was hitting with such power that by the middle of June he had become the first American Leaguer to hit three home runs in a game twice in the same season.

It wasn't going to last forever, though. He came into the All-Star Game in a one for sixteen slump and was so worn out that he even thought about begging off. "Not seriously," he said afterward, "but I will admit that it went through my mind." After going hitless in the All-Star Game, he flew to Detroit, checked into a hotel, and remained in bed for almost two days. "When I went out to the park," he said, "I felt good. Just great. I'd never felt better."

He broke out of the slump with two doubles, and over the last half of the season he hit a rousing .453.

On the last day of August, when Ted's average was up to .373 and he was battling Mickey Mantle, head to head, for the batting championship, that mystery virus knocked him flat on his back. While he was recuperating, Hy Hurwitz came into possession of a medical report that allowed Hurwitz to reveal, for the first time, that Williams's troubles stemmed from a "chronic lung condition." According to the medical report, Hurwitz wrote, Williams was not only through for the year but was probably finished forever.

Characteristically, Ted reacted as if Hurwitz's story was a reflection of wishful thinking rather than objective reporting. "I'll get back now," he swore, "even if they have to carry me out there on a stretcher. I'll get back there just to show that little so-and-so up."

Seventeen days after the bug hit, Ted was back in the lineup as a pinch hitter against Kansas City. The Red Sox, having blown a 6–2 lead, were trailing by a run. And—you guessed it—Ted tied the score quickly by driving a four-hundred-foot blow down the throat of the wind. The next day, he pinch hit in Washington and walked.

When the Sox got to Yankee Stadium Ted still wasn't ready to start. Whitey Ford had a shutout when Ted came in as a pinch hitter in the ninth; he had it no longer after Ted's long drive landed in the upper deck. It was the first home run Ted had ever hit off Ford, and he closed out his career without hitting another.

Since nothing uncongests a lung faster than a couple of long home runs, Ted was in the starting lineup the following afternoon. In the first inning, he came to the plate with a man on second and one out. With first base open, he walked on four straight pitches—one of the hundreds of intentionally unintentional walks he received in the course of his career. The next time he came up, there were no bases open. With the count at two and nothing, he got the pitch he wanted off Bob Turley and hit a high, towering fly that dropped into the right-field stands for the fifteenth grand slam of his career. It was the only ball thrown to him inside the strike zone all afternoon; the next two times up, he was walked on four straight balls.

In the final game of the series, he walked, lined a homer into the seats, singled, and walked again. The home run was his fourth in four official times at bat, a performance that tied one of those miscellaneous records that keep statisticians happy. Before his on-base streak ended, Ted ran the figure up to sixteen, an all-time record. From the time he returned to the lineup to the end of the season, he had twelve hits in eighteen times at bat, for an average of .667. In his final thirty-one trips to the plate, he reached base twenty-five times.

The only segment of the populace that remained unmoved was the very one that should have been most impressed, the sportswriters. They voted to give the Most Valuable Player award not to Ted but to Mickey Mantle—much to Mantle's surprise. The New York writers did show their appreciation for Ted's artistry by voting him the Sid Mercer award as "Player of the Year." Ted showed his appreciation for being accorded that honor by declining to appear at the banquet at which the award was to be presented.

But it was not any Boston writer who had dropped Williams down the MVP list this time, for Ted had become so popular in the city because of his comeback that all criticism of him had to be muffled. When a three-week newspaper strike hit the city, the editorial offices were flooded with calls each day asking what Ted had done. Whether the Red Sox had won or lost seemed of minor importance.

During that same period, a crowd of 30,000 turned out for a night game between the Red Sox and the Tigers to watch Ted make his run at another .400 season. At the time, he was hitting .392. When he came up to bat, the Tigers went into their routine shift, with the shortstop moving over to the first-base side of second and the second baseman moving out onto the grass. Ted hit a line drive toward the right-field side of center, and shortstop Harvey Kuenn, leaping too soon, had the ball carom off his glove. The official scorer flashed the "error" sign, and Fenway Park took on the appearance of the mob storming the Bastille. One writer, describing the scene, said: "Never before had Boston come so close to a baseball riot. Fans glared at the press box. They shouted insults and made threatening gestures. It was an unprecedented display of anger, and it seemed to refuse to subside. The earmarks of a mob riot were all there. An hour after the game ended, people were still lingering around the exit from the press box, jeering at the writers as they came out.'' The ruling was later changed to give Ted a base hit.

The city rallied so ferociously behind the thirty-nine-year-old Williams that Tim Horgan of the *Boston Traveler* felt it necessary to write: "It's getting so a citizen can't voice the minority, or dim view of Teddy without getting shot on the spot. . . . Teddy may be 100 percent strong, clean and pure. He may also be a bum. He may be terribly misunderstood, maligned and everything else, except underpaid. He may also court his knocks. It's a cinch he is, was and always will be surrounded by controversy. That's wholesome enough if nobody comes in armed. Teddy can incite any emotion from anger and anguish to zeal and zounds!

"The trouble seems to be that one vital piece has gone out of the affair, and that's what's turning it into a peril. It's been forgotten that Teddy is still only human. Please, girls, when the old gorge rises, just pause, ponder and laugh a little bit, too."

When Ted appeared in Boston to sign his 1958 contract, he was in an especially jolly mood. "Let's have peace in our time," he told the assembled writers and cameramen. "This is going to be my last year."

For a good ten years, Ted had been insisting that he would have hung up his spikes by sundown if he hadn't needed the money. The suspicion existed that he played on not because he needed the money but because he needed to be standing there at the plate challenging a hostile world on his own battleground. It was always suspected that every batting championship was not only a professional accomplishment but another act of confirmation and defiance in that enduring battle.

In the spring of 1958, however, Ted did leave the impression that he had definitely decided to make it his last season. During the training season, he made himself readily available to the press, asking only that the reporters get together so that he could answer all their questions at the same time and then be free to take his workouts without interruption. His one fight came when Jimmy Cannon arrived just after

Ted had finished an extensive forty-five-minute interview with a sizable group of other out-of-town writers. Joe McKenney, the Red Sox publicity director, asked Cannon to wait until Ted came back in, but Cannon insisted on going out to left field to see Ted immediately. Predictably, Ted blew his stack.

Even though Ted's league-leading average fell off sixty points, the 1958 season was in certain respects a greater accomplishment than the season of 1957. Not only was he beset by injury or illness throughout the year, but his physical problems were complicated, during the first half of the season, by that unseemly truce with his old enemies in the press box. If the human race has learned anything from history, it is that peace treaties do not do a thing for either world peace or for Ted Williams's batting average.

He had reported to camp with a tender ankle, the result of an accident suffered on a fishing trip in Labrador. On the second day he pulled a muscle in his side. He didn't even get into the lineup until after the Sox broke camp, and then he went in only as a pinch hitter against minor-league opposition. In his five appearances, he was sharp enough to get two home runs, a single, and two walks.

Then, on the night before the opening-day game against Washington, he ate some tainted oysters and came down with a case of food poisoning. When he returned to the lineup, his timing was a little off, and just when it was coming back into focus, he banged his wrist against the fence while catching a long fly ball. The wrist remained sore almost all year; Ted reinjured it again and again while sliding into base. The last time came, most uncharacteristically, while he was trying to go from second to third on a short fly ball to right field. On top of all that, he ran into a terrible streak of bad luck where by actual count, outfielders reached into the distant right-field bull pen at Fenway Park to take home runs away from him seven separate times in less than two months. There was also the annual arrival of the lung ailment, which put him out of action for thirteen days in September.

The result of it all was that Ted got off to such a terrible start that for the first time since his freshman season he did not make the starting All-Star lineup. The Boston writers, having studied him for twenty years, shook their heads and let you know that Ted was not getting around with those wrists anymore. They were reluctant, however, to put their opinion into print. They had eaten those words too many times. And, anyway, peace had descended comfortably between them.

During that early low point, Ted told me, "I know what's wrong. The little injuries that have kept me from getting my timing down real sharp. Little things bother you in this game. It's not like hockey or football, where they can strap you up and send you out almost as good as new. That's not an alibi, now, it's just a way of saying that as long as I know why I'm not hitting, I'm not worried. When the time comes when I'm not hitting and I don't know why I'm not hitting, that will be the time to quit. When they're throwing the fastball by me, when I find myself striking out two or three times a game, that will be the time I'll know my reactions are going. And nobody will have to tell me. I'll know it first of all."

He was down to .225 when a Kansas City writer finally broke security silence and wrote that Ted was obviously washed up. The next day, as was to be expected, Ted hit a grand-slam home run, the sixteenth grand slammer of his career, to give the Sox an 8–5 victory. The day after that he slashed out three hits.

It was not until July, though, that he brought his average up to .300, and it was not until a Boston writer accused him of choking in the clutch that he really begin to move. The day after the magazine carrying that article hit the stands, Ted hit two home runs and a single, to knock in seven runs in an 11–8 victory. One of the home runs was his seventeenth grand slammer, tying him with Babe Ruth for second place in that category, behind Lou Gehrig's twenty-third.

By that time, the uneasy peace had already been shattered. One week earlier, in point of fact, Ted had brought the newspapers down on him again by spitting at a Kansas City crowd that was booing him for not running out a ball hit back at the pitcher. "I'm really sorry I did it," Ted said, after Cronin fined him $250. "I was so mad that I lost my temper, and afterward I was so sorry. I'm principally sorry about losing the $250."

Once the feud with both the press and the public was on again, Ted's average began to move up in the charts like a bullet. On August 8, he pushed into a tie with his teammate, Pete Runnels, for the batting lead. Then, with the season running out, he began to slip back. Desperate measures were called for. With a week remaining, Ted landed on the front pages again, brought the wrath of the civilized world down upon him, and, needless to say, embarked immediately on a hitting streak that carried him to another batting championship.

Ted entered the game in question, on September 22, trailing Runnels by six points. He had gone hitless in seven straight times at bat. In the first inning, Runnels singled, and Ted, hitting right behind him, grounded into a double play. Two innings later, Runnels singled again, and Ted took a third strike. Completely disgusted with himself for taking the pitch, Ted turned toward the dugout and angrily flung his bat away. Unfortunately, the bat caught for a moment on the sticky substance he used on it to give himself a firmer grip. Instead of skidding across the dirt, the bat spiraled into the air, sailed into the box seats seventy-five feet away, and hit a sixty-year-old woman. The woman, Mrs. Gladys Heffernan, turned out to be Joe Cronin's housekeeper and a longtime admirer of Ted Williams. Otherwise, the Sox would have had a healthy lawsuit on their hands.

Ted, appalled, rushed to the railing, where the motherly Mrs. Heffernan paused to reassure him before being taken off to the first-aid room. Ted went back to the dugout with tears streaming down his face and emerged only after the umpire-in-chief, Bill Summers, had assured him that everybody knew he had not meant to throw the bat. Ted took his outfield position to the familiar strains of unrestrained booing. On his next turn at bat, he answered the boos by doubling home a run.

Cronin, who was almost as upset as Ted was, told the press, "It was an impetuous act, but no one is sorrier than Ted is. He feels awful. We will take no disciplinary action. It was unfortunate, but we certainly know Williams didn't do it intentionally." Mrs. Heffernan, interviewed from her hospital bed, said, "I don't see why they had to boo him. It was not the dear boy's fault. I felt awfully sorry for him after it happened. I should have ducked.'' Williams said, ''I just almost died.''

From the time of the bat-throwing incident to the end of the season, he had nine hits in thirteen times at bat. The Red Sox were ending their season in Washington, and with two games remaining Ted and Runnels were tied down to the ninth decimal point, .322857643. Frank Malzone was Runnels's roommate: ''Pete and I were talking before the game. He said, 'What do you think?' I said, 'Just go out and get some hits. You can still win it.''' Runnels started off with a triple. Ted followed with a walk. Runnels then singled, and Ted singled behind him. On his third time at bat, Runnels hit a home run, only to have Ted hit one right behind him.

''He comes over to me,'' Malzone says, ''and he said, 'He's not going to let me win this thing, is he?' ''

''I said, 'Naw, I guess not, Pete.' I said, 'Got to get another one. If you get another one, he can't catch you.'''

On his fourth try, Runnels finally made out. Ted singled, to take over the batting lead for the first time that season. At the end of the day, Runnels was three for six, but Ted was three for four. On the season, Runnels was .324. Ted was .326.

In the final game, Ted clenched the batting title with a double and a seventh-inning, game-winning home run, that lifted the Red Sox into third place.

''I don't think anyone else in this league but Ted could have beaten me in a race like this,'' Runnels said. ''It's no disgrace to finish runner-up to Williams in a batting championship.''

An equally gracious Williams was saying that Runnels had hit the ball just as hard as he had over that final week, and maybe harder. ''I was lucky,'' he said, ''because my balls had distance and some of his were hit right at the fielders.''

At the age of forty, Ted Williams had won another American League batting title. He was going to have two more years—the dreadful, injury-ridden season of 1959 and a year of injuries and personal anguish capped off in triumph.

XVII

Tom Yawkey and the Country Club

I realized what a great guy Tom Yawkey was, and I will always sing his praises as a terrific guy and a man. I knew he would have liked to have a stronger relationship with me, but I never did want to pursue that aspect of it.

—TED WILLIAMS

One of the standard flights of fantasy when baseball fans get together centers on the stupendous feats of hitting that would have been achieved if Ted Williams had been able to play half his games in Yankee Stadium and Joe DiMaggio had been able to take dead aim at the left-field wall at Fenway Park.

Ted Williams, for one, isn't so sure. "The thing of it is, when you get in them short ballparks, like DiMag in Fenway and Williams at New York, they pitch a little different to you. All you got to do is look at the statistics. Doggone it, you don't get anything to hit."

It was Joe Cronin who first gave Ted reason to think about it, and Cronin wasn't talking so much about the ballpark as about the recognition and acclaim. "It was my first or second year in the big leagues," Ted says, "and Joe took me to a restaurant with his wife and somebody else. He said 'You know, Ted, some day when you're looking back, you may be sorry you didn't play in New York.' I was just a young kid. I didn't have an opinion really. He said, 'No, there are two things you are going to wish you could have done in your career. First, that you didn't play in New York, and also that you weren't a faster runner.' For damn sure, he was right on that last one."

It could have happened. There were at least two times during Ted's career when there were serious conversations between Tom Yawkey and Dan Topping, the Yankees owner, about a Williams-for-DiMaggio trade. And that's not counting a most intriguing proposition that came to Ted within a week after he retired.

A more fruitful area for speculation, however, would go like this: Forget the fences and look to the ownership. What would have happened, in other words, if Ted Williams had grown up under the hard-eyed businessmen who ran the Yankees organization and Joe DiMaggio had fallen under Tom Yawkey's beneficent gaze?

With the Yankees ownership you either toed the line or you were gone. It didn't matter how much the players hated Casey Stengel. George Weiss, the general manager, had impressed on them that nobody was indispensable, and so when Stengel barked at them they jumped. For that matter, the players themselves were known to haul a fresh rookie out into the back alley and show him their knuckles. "You're fooling with our money" was the way that tune went.

On the other hand, it's entirely possible that the Red Sox's permissive attitude was exactly what Ted needed. Birdie Tebbetts, the old psychologist (he has a B.S. in philosophy from Providence College), seems to think so. "Joe Cronin has never got the credit he deserves in the way he treated Williams," Tebbetts says. "He knew he had a troubled kid, and he held him under a loose rein. He disciplined him only when he had to and then went back to allowing Ted Williams to be Ted Williams."

On that assessment, Ted agrees completely. "I know how lucky I was—I *know* how lucky I was—that I played for a manager like Joe Cronin. Joe Cronin came closer to treating me like a father, with good advice, friendly advice, intimate advice, than any other single man in my life. He had a beautiful family, and he was a tremendous father. Lovely kids. Lovely wife. He was a handsome Irish guy, and I envied him how he could bullshit the press. He could get a guy he didn't like and have him going out of the office thinking Joe Cronin was a helluva guy. Joe Cronin would have been as good a politician as a ballplayer."

With the passage of time and the clouding of memory, Ted has wondered why Cronin didn't use his diplomatic skills more often in the early years ("I was just a young kid") to smooth the relationship between Ted and the sportswriters. "But maybe I don't know how protective he was of me. And maybe I didn't always listen to him. I'm not making excuses for myself. I just want to say he was so great with me. I loved him."

The trade talks are of interest for the light they shed on the relationship between Ted and Tom Yawkey.

In the spring of 1946, Larry MacPhail, having pulled off the baseball deal of the century in taking over the ownership of the Yankees, along with Dan Topping and Del Webb, proposed to Yawkey that they get the brave new postwar world off to a glorious flag-waving start by pulling off the dream trade that would put Joe DiMaggio in Fenway Park and Ted Williams in Yankee Stadium. In later years, MacPhail would maintain that the deal was all set until Ed Barrow, with malice aforethought, pulled the rug out from under it.

The way the story goes, Ed Barrow was a guest of Yawkey at his island estate in South Carolina, and although Barrow was still nominally the Yankees general manager, MacPhail, who was a little crazy in a genius kind of a way, had stripped him of all his authority. Hating MacPhail as he did, Barrow—who just might have invited himself down to the island for that purpose—told Yawkey he'd have to be crazy to trade the twenty-seven-year-old Williams for the thirty-year-old, ulcer-ridden DiMaggio.

In the winter of 1948, Yawkey and Dan Topping shook hands on a Williams-for-DiMaggio trade during a drinking session in New York. The next morning, Yawkey was supposed to have told him, "I think I ought to get another player. If you throw in that little left-fielder of yours, it's a deal." The little left-fielder was Yogi Berra.

"I'm sure that story was true," Ted says. "No question about it. The way I heard the story, it was a matter of these guys getting together one night, half looped. Players were like prize possessions to them, I guess, and they made this deal, and supposedly they agreed on it, and the next day Yawkey called Topping and told him, 'You know I'm a man of my word, but I just can't go through with it.' " Ted has heard the Yogi Berra version, too, and he doesn't completely discount it. "DiMaggio wasn't at the height of his career and I was. But of course the great DiMaggio was such a great player. He would have hit better at Fenway Park, and I might have hit better at Yankee Stadium."

Ted is also sure—no question whatsoever about this—that he came very close to signing with the Yankees a few days after he played his final game for the Red Sox. When Ted left the ballpark that day, he was unemployed, not terribly solvent, and in view of all the responsibilities he had taken on, terribly worried. Because if the truth be known, he had retired only because Tom Yawkey had been after him to retire for at least two years.

The season had ended for Ted on a Wednesday. Thursday was an off day. "I didn't go to New York with the team, and Saturday morning I got a telegram from George Struthers, the merchandising vice president of Sears, telling me they had something they wanted to talk to me about. I knew exactly what it was going to be." They wanted Ted to come in and upgrade their entire sporting goods line. "Everything involved with sporting goods. Hunting, fishing, camping, skiing." They were offering him far more money than he had ever made in baseball. And they were offering him a ten-year contract.

The American League season ended on Sunday, and on Monday the Yankees asked Ted—through his manager, Fred Corcoran—for permission to talk to the Red Sox about signing him for one year, exclusively as a pinch hitter, at the same salary he had been getting with the Red Sox.

Ted has little doubt that if the talks with Sears hadn't been progressing so rapidly he would have given it very serious consideration. "It had got to the point, though, where I was just tired of what had been going on. And I thought, Hell, I'm going to do this with Sears. So I told Fred Corcoran I wasn't interested. And that was the end of it."

The tantalizing question is whether Yawkey would have given his permission for Ted Williams to end his career in Yankee pinstripes or whether he would have heaved up a sigh and told Ted that if he really wanted to stick around for another year he would match the Yankees' offer.

What does Ted think?

"Yawkey's relations with me were always to do what I wanted to do, more or less. I think that—" Suddenly, his voice took on a tone of certainty. "I don't know how he would have reacted. I think he was pretty sure, like I was, that I didn't want to play anymore."

Like everybody else in Boston, Ted Williams genuflected toward

Tom Yawkey in public. There was nothing Yawkey could ask of him, for as long as Yawkey was alive, that Ted wouldn't do. There was also a kind of pretense to a closer relationship than actually existed. Yawkey's island in South Carolina was a hunting preserve, and everybody assumed that Ted spent a great deal of time down there with him. Everybody was wrong. Ted went down to the hunting preserve in South Carolina exactly once.

"It was not a father-and-son relationship," Ted says flatly. "I felt Yawkey liked me, but I never pursued trying to get extra close to him." Then, so there would be no misunderstanding: "He was there. He was a simple man. He knew how lucky he had been in his life and he tried to do everything he could to be a good guy. He had an open heart for charity, an open heart for a sad story. He was just a nice easy man, really and truly."

But, when you think about it, why should Ted have wanted to get close to him? Yawkey wasn't really bright. There was nothing Ted could learn from him. Yawkey did two things: he drank and he played bridge. Ted did not drink, and he did not play cards.

True enough, they were involved in the Jimmy Fund together, but that association was also more apparent than real. As important as Yawkey was in placing the imprimatur of the Red Sox on the Jimmy Fund, Tom Yawkey was a figurehead and Ted Williams was the blood of its heart.

Ted's relationship with Yawkey was not nearly as crucial to Ted's career as was Yawkey's personality and character as the owner of the ballclub.

Yawkey was a frustrated ballplayer who loved all his players and positively worshiped Ted. As a result, the Red Sox became a soft and pampered ball club. The general managers were Yawkey's drinking buddies. The managers were without authority. The discipline was fake discipline, the fines were fake fines.

Yawkey was a rich man's son who had been around baseball all his life. On the death of his father he was adopted by his uncle, William

H. Yawkey, a lumber and mining magnate, who had helped Ban Johnson launch the American League and had maintained a financial interest in the Detroit Tigers all his life. Tom led such a privileged childhood that ballplayers from Ty Cobb on down were invited to the Yawkey estate to play catch with him. He was twelve years old when Bill Yawkey was killed in an automobile accident. As the sole heir of his foster father—and the prospective heir of his even wealthier mother—young Tom was written up in Sunday feature articles as "the richest boy in the world," a characterization that owed as much to the richness of the journalists' imagination as to Tom's true place in the hierarchy of wealth. On the other hand, if you're rich enough to be looked on as a contender for the title, what difference does it make?

Yawkey was thirty years old when he bought the Red Sox, a hopelessly bankrupt team that had won only forty-three games the previous season and averaged only 2,365 paying customers. The ball club became his toy. Because he loved his players, he spoiled them rotten. And because he spoiled them rotten, they praised him to the skies. Yet there was always the sense that the praise was so unreserved ("the greatest owner in baseball" was practically engraved on his forehead) that it was being overdone. There was always the whiff of something obligatory about it.

Joe Cronin had little power to discipline his big-name players. As if being a playing manager wasn't tough enough on him, Cronin knew that his biggest stars could always walk the back stairs and cry on Tom's shoulder. When Yawkey purchased Robert Moses (Lefty) Grove, his first superstar, Grove was thirty-five years old and Yawkey thirty-one. To Yawkey, Grove became Mose, his idol and his dinner companion. Mose was a cranky old geezer. He would scream at Cronin for making an error behind him, and there was nothing much that Cronin could do about it. Not when Old Mose could rip him apart to the boss a couple of hours later over the drinks.

Unlike Grove, Jimmy Foxx was a man of enormous good nature and generosity. So convivial a fellow, in fact, that he took a rather cavalier attitude toward curfews.

Johnny Pesky: "Cronin sat in the lobby until two in the morning waiting to grab him. Sure enough, the door of the hotel opened, and Foxx comes in, half stiff. Cronin gets up ready to blast him. Then the door opened again, and in comes Yawkey. They had been out together. What do you say when the owner of the team is taking your players out?"

That was the team that Ted Williams joined in Boston.

There is a well-publicized exchange in which Bobby Doerr asks Tommy Henrich why the Red Sox weren't able to beat the Yankees in big games. "Weren't we good enough?" Doerr asks. It wasn't that they weren't good enough, Henrich answers. "Your owner was too good to you. The Red Sox didn't have to get into the World Series to drive Cadillacs. The Yankees did."

Oversimplified, to be sure. But essentially true. And that's where the soft, permissive environment established by Yawkey did hurt Ted. The accusation that has always haunted him is that he was a great hitter but not a winning player. A more generous assessment might be that he was a great hitter on a team that was too undisciplined to become a winner.

Worse yet, it was an amateur operation—not so much a business as a hobby—pitted against the toughest, most professional operation of all time.

Bobby Doerr's answer to Henrich is to point out that immediately after winning the pennant in 1946, the Red Sox lost their three top starting pitchers to injuries. "Does anybody doubt that if Hughson, Ferriss, and Harris had remained healthy we wouldn't have won two or three more pennants?" But that's just the point. When the history of the Yawkey Era is written it could be titled "Always One Pitcher Short." The Red Sox could always put a powerful, highly salaried starting lineup on the field. The Yankees had a powerful, not-so-well-paid twenty-five-man squad.

Ted always was paid more than Joe DiMaggio, you know. Not because Ted wanted it that way, but because Tom Yawkey did. In 1948, immediately after the Yankees had made DiMaggio the first $100,000 player, a pack of writers caught Yawkey on the way up to his office. He had just sent Williams his contract, Yawkey told them, and it was going to be for more than DiMaggio's. "It may be only $1,000 more," he said, in answer to their prodding. "But Ted Williams will always get more money than anybody else." It was $115,000, and a year later it was $125,000.

Yawkey had a blind spot toward the value of the supporting cast, however. During the 1949 season, the thirty-six-year-old Johnny Mize was offered to Yawkey by his good friend Horace Stoneham, the owner of the New York Giants. In the previous two seasons, Mize—a lifetime .320 hitter—had hit forty and fifty-one home runs. "What would we do with him?" Yawkey asked. The Red Sox already had a first baseman in Billy Goodman, didn't they? The Yankees jumped at the chance, and Mize became one of eight first basemen Casey Stengel used that year. He also won game after game as a pinch hitter. The Red Sox number-one pinch hitter, Billy Hitchcock, did not get a base hit all year.

It wasn't simply that the Red Sox regulars were overpaid and the Red Sox bench understaffed. There was no firm hand in the front office, no guiding philosophy, because the front office, in a perfect reflection of their employer, was always awash in booze.

To put this within its proper context, drinking was so much the occupational disease of baseball in that era that it wasn't even recognized as a disease. Or even as a vice. It proved that you were a real man, or, at least, one of the guys. The Red Sox weren't the only team that did a lot of drinking; they may not even have been the worst. But no other team offered quite the same combination of paternalism and permissiveness, because no other team was being operated as a rich man's hobby. Yawkey not only drank with the troops; he would send the heavy drinkers a bottle of his favorite brand of scotch, Old Forester, as a reward for an especially good performance.

And—just in case—the traveling secretary was always given a wad of money at the beginning of a road trip to bail out anybody who might get into trouble.

In 1948 Joe McCarthy had been hired to bring some order and discipline—to say nothing of a team concept—to the Red Sox. Tom Yawkey, making his final attempt to buy a pennant, gave him what was easily the strongest ball club the Red Sox ever had. The new players were Vern (Junior) Stephens, a hard-hitting shortstop, two right-handed pitchers, Jack Kramer and Ellis Kinder, and a great rookie, Billy Goodman.

As soon as McCarthy was hired, the Boston papers tried to whip up a controversy over whether he would be able to get along with Ted Williams, with particular emphasis on whether he would try to impose his rigid dress code on Ted. McCarthy's answer was to show up at Sarasota wearing a Hawaiian sports shirt open at the neck. "If I can't get along with a .400 hitter," he said, "then there's something wrong with me." Ted liked McCarthy as a manager. "He was all business. His coaches were all business. Just coming into the clubhouse was business." But then Ted adds, without exactly saying that Joe McCarthy was not the manager he had once been, "I don't know what would have happened if he had been the same man the Yankees players talked about."

When it came to managing a ball club, McCarthy was impressive. When it came to managing himself, he was a disaster. Always solitary and aloof, he would sit at the far end of the bench. Ted was the only player who would sit near him. The usual explanation was that Ted was the only member of the team who wasn't a little afraid of him. A perhaps more persuasive explanation might be that he was the only player who could stand his breath.

Joe McCarthy was an alcoholic. Not just someone who drank a lot, but an alcoholic in the truest sense of the word. Even in his great days with the Yankees, he would disappear for days on end and be found in some seedy hotel lying in his own bodily wastes. To explain his absence, the Yankees would announce that he had gone to his farm near Buffalo to recover from an attack of bursitis.

He drank when he was under stress, and Boston was the stress capital of the baseball world. Instead of running away with the pennant as they should have in 1948 the Red Sox lost their play-off game to the

Cleveland Indians when McCarthy locked himself in his hotel room with a bottle and received a message from God telling him to pitch Denny Galehouse (8 – 7) instead of Mel Parnell (15 – 8).

His wife, Babe, took care of him when the Red Sox were playing at home. Tom Dowd, the traveling secretary, took care of him on the road. During the game, Eddie Froelich, the trainer he had brought over from New York, would keep an eye on him, and Del Baker, who had been hired for precisely this purpose, would take charge when it became apparent that McCarthy was out of it.

Two stories, both classics, tell it all. The datelines read: St, Louis, September 17, 1948, and Boston, June 5, 1950. The first story involves Sam Mele, the second Ellis Kinder.

McCarthy hated Sam Mele, for reasons directly connected with Ted Williams. Ted and Mele were good friends, and Ted, ever the fight fan, had a habit of throwing light feints at his friends, almost as a gesture of affection. In this particular incident, they met in the aisle of a train, coming from opposite directions, and as they squeezed past each other Ted threw a feint and proceeded on his way. When Ted woke up the next morning he couldn't breathe. He had separated a cartilage from the ribs and was out for three weeks. Sam Mele, who had been Rookie of the Year the previous season, immediately became a part-time player.

In what turned out to be a roller coaster of a season, the Red Sox came back from an eleven-and-a-half-game deficit to go four and a half games ahead in mid-September—and then began to dribble their lead away. After losing the opening game of what had been expected to be an easy series in St. Louis, the lead was down to one game, with fifteen games to go. By the next morning, McCarthy was so drunk that when it came time to take the team bus to the ballpark, Tom Dowd locked him in his room. The bus arrived at the park, the players filed into the clubhouse, and there was McCarthy sitting on a stool. ("How he beat us to the park," Dowd would say, "I will never know.")

Del Baker wrote Mele's name into the lineup, and in the first inning he came up with the bases loaded and two out and cleared the bases with a double. Two batters later, he was thrown out at third base on an attempted double steal and lay there writhing in agony with a twisted ankle. Eddie Froelich went running out to treat him. Del Baker followed. McCarthy, left unattended, staggered out of the dugout and went wandering up the first-base line and into right field. It was one of those sweltering summer afternoons in St. Louis, with 1,500 fans scattered around the stands. In that sparsely inhabited, hollow arena, the voice of one leather-lunged fan came ringing forth: *"When are you going to switch to wine, Joe?"*

When McCarthy finally found his bearings and joined the crowd at third base, he bent over the fallen Mele and screamed, "Get up, you fucken dago!" Then he turned to Baker and demanded to know why he had called for a double steal. "You called for it," said Baker.

Ellis Kinder was one of those drinkers who usually pitched better after a long night on the town. Cronin once offered him fifty dollars to go to bed early the night before he pitched, but after Kinder was knocked out of the box three straight times Cronin handed him a hundred and told him to go out and get drunk. He didn't always pitch better, though. McCarthy's downfall came when Joe got so drunk that he couldn't see how drunk Kinder was. The love affair between Yawkey and McCarthy was over by then, anyway. Yawkey's pets were climbing the stairs to complain about how cruelly their manager was treating them, and Yawkey was ordering McCarthy to lay off.

On the game in question, Kinder got so drunk that it slipped his mind he was supposed to be pitching until Clif Keane, who knew both his habits and his habitats, hurried down to the Kenmore Hotel, interrupted his liaison with a young lady, and broke the not necessarily welcome news to him. Then Keane helped him get dressed and lugged him to the ballpark. In those days, starting pitchers still warmed up in front of their respective dugouts. Drunk as he was, Kinder was throwing the ball all over the place, something everybody in the ballpark except Joe McCarthy could see, possibly because Joe McCarthy was kind of sleeping it off himself.

Kinder, well aware that he needed a stiffener, cut his warm-up short and went into the clubhouse for "a cup of coffee." Or something. Slick-haired Jack Kramer, who had the locker next to his, was always complaining that Kinder was drinking his hair tonic.

Clif Keane: "Nellie Fox was the first hitter. The first pitch went up on the backstop. The second one came in on a couple of bounces. Dave Philley was the second batter. The first pitch came bouncing up to the plate, and the second one went up against the backstop." Birdie Tebbetts, his catcher, was yelling, "Get him out of here. He's drunk." Eight straight pitches Kinder threw without coming anywhere near the plate, and somewhere along the way Joe McCarthy woke up enough to sense that something was amiss. "I'll never forget this scene," says Keane. "Here comes McCarthy. Kinder sees McCarthy coming and, thinking quickly, he begins to work his left arm. He's a right-handed pitcher. McCarthy says, '*That* costs you five hundred dollars.' He brings in Maurie McDermott. McDermott pitches a four-hit shutout, and McCarthy never takes the money from Kinder."

The way the story went out over the news wires, it read: "After issuing passes to the first two batters, the right-hander left the game with a kink in his left shoulder." A not-so-cryptic message to the rest of the baseball world.

McCarthy was indisposed again in Chicago two weeks later, at a time when the Red Sox were losing steadily. It was said that he resigned because of his health. If so, Tom Yawkey was suitably grateful.

McCarthy was replaced by Steve O'Neill, who was Joe Cronin's drinking buddy.

By the time Ted returned from Korea, the manager was Lou Boudreau, who got the job by playing pepper with Yawkey at Fenway Park every morning. The "country club," otherwise known as the Yawkey follies, was in full flower over the rest of Ted's career.

It all came to a climax, during Ted's last two years, with the hiring and firing of Billy Jurges. Or, if you prefer, the firing and hiring of Mike Higgins.

It began in the spring of 1959 when Joe Cronin was named president of the American League. He was hired because (1) he had always wanted the job, and (2) Yawkey had confided to his fellow owners that he wanted to get rid of him and (3) it was a job with such limited responsibilities that it didn't matter who held it. What followed with the Red Sox was not so much musical comedy as pure slapstick.

To replace Cronin as general manager, Yawkey hired Bucky Harris—the man Cronin had replaced as manager twenty-three years earlier. A neat symmetry there. Yawkey had always felt guilty about letting Bucky go.

He was, alas, doing Bucky no favor. Bucky had a gorgeous young wife, and until Yawkey felt the need to go rummaging around in his conscience he had been living a perfectly happy life. Bucky wasn't an administrator. Bucky wasn't an executive. Bucky was a falling-down drunk. By 1959, he was so far gone that the office help had to guide his hand through his signature on official papers. Dick O'Connell, the business manager, was running the club. "Dick," Bucky would tell him, "I don't want this job. I don't want it."

Mike Higgins was in his fifth year as the field manager. He was another of Yawkey's drinking buddies, but he was also a very strong and solid man, with a lot of personal problems which he drowned, as he liked to say, with "cherry bombs." To say he was a player's manager was to understate it. "I love playing for Higgins," one of the players was quoted as saying. "He never gets mad at us when we lose." By June of 1959, the Red Sox had fallen into last place, the anti-Higgins faction of the press was howling for his head, and Yawkey dispatched Bucky Harris to Washington with orders to fire him.

Already the geography was unfortunate. Washington was Bucky Harris's home ground, and instead of going to the team's hotel, to make the announcement to the hastily gathered press, he went roaming off to his old haunts and disappeared for two days—although "Bucky sightings" were posted periodically in the press box. From Washington, the Red Sox traveled up to Baltimore by bus. When they arrived at the Lord Baltimore Hotel they found their missing general manager sitting in the lobby.

Within thirty seconds, Harris and Higgins were headed out the door and across the street to the Gaiety Bar. Right behind them were three members of the Boston press corps, plus Bill Crowley, then a member of the broadcasting team. Harris and Higgins were at one end of the huge oval bar, arguing. The media guys settled down at the other end. Otherwise the place was empty.

Three scenes are going to be taking place in separate venues. One at the Gaiety Bar, another in Ed Rumill's hotel room, in the hotel, and the third at the rooftop press room at Fenway Park.

Bill Crowley: "The Gaiety had this fat, ugly bar girl, Audrey, who looked like Tugboat Annie. Jake Liston of the *Traveler* hands her a sawbuck and says, 'Go down and wash some glasses, and come back and tell us what they're talking about.' She comes back in a couple of minutes. 'The little guy keeps telling the big guy he should resign. The big guy keeps telling the little guy to go fuck himself.'"

Off that promising beginning, Lyn Raymond of the *Quincy Ledger* slipped her another ten spot and sent her back to wipe around the bar. Back she came with her new report. "The little one says to the big one he's fired. The big one tells him he's a little shit, he can't fire him. The little one says, 'I can fire you, and I have to fire you, because Yawkey wants me to fire you.'"

Meanwhile, back at the hotel, Ed Rumill of the *Christian Science Monitor* had been taking a phone call from one of his numerous ex-wives. The former Mrs. Rumill had been in Duke Zeibert's restaurant in Washington the previous night and had overheard a conversation between George Preston Marshall, the owner of the Washington Redskins, and Bucky Harris in which Marshall, the football man, had been holding forth on the merits of the Senators' third-base coach, Billy Jurges. "I think you're right," she had heard Bucky say. "He might be just the right man for us at this time."

Okay, the Boston writers now had it all. Which was more than could be said for Tom Yawkey, back in Boston. Yawkey had called a press conference to announce the dismissal of Higgins. Unfortunately, nobody at Fenway Park had been able to locate Bucky Harris during those two days, either. With nothing to tell the press, Yawkey was at the bar, drinking heavily. He was also doing something he almost never did, he was taking questions. Unaccustomed as he was to being cross-examined, he turned hostile. "There are people here who are trying to tell me how to run a seven-million-dollar operation," he said, "and there's not one of you who could even run a streetcar." To show how bad things were going for him, one of the writers delivered a stiff protest. He had worked his way through college driving a streetcar, he wanted Yawkey to know. Through Harvard University yet.

Soon enough, Yawkey retreated to the position that he hadn't called the press conference to announce the name of a new manager but only to inform them that there was going to be a club meeting over the All-Star break to decide what direction the Red Sox were going to take.

Right on cue, the phone rang. The call wasn't for Yawkey, though. It was for Hy Hurwitz. As soon as he put down the phone, Hurwitz said, "You haven't decided who your new manager is going to be?"

"I haven't decided whether there's going to *be* a new manager."

Hurwitz said, "Down in Baltimore they're announcing that Bucky Harris is saying that Billy Jurges is going to be the new manager."

"Who? Who?"

"Mr. Yawkey, the *Globe* is printing that you hired Billy Jurges today. Two hours ago."

"We did?" said Thomas Austin Yawkey, the sole owner of the Boston Red Sox Baseball Club.

Billy Jurges had been a great shortstop for the Chicago Cubs and the New York Giants. He had played for the Cubs, as a young buckaroo, in the Chicago of Al Capone. In the spirit of the times, he had once taken a bullet through the hand while trying to convince teammate Kiki Cuyler's gun-toting girlfriend that Kiki wasn't being unfaithful to her. Obviously he was the perfect manager for the Boston Red Sox.

Wrong. It wasn't Capone's Chicago, and Billy wasn't twenty-three years old. Billy Jurges tried to instill some discipline into the ball club, some rules even. A curfew, for crissake. The players hated him. They also ignored him. Let him fine away to his heart's content; they knew nothing would ever be taken out of their paychecks. Frank Sullivan, the ringleader of the not-so-jolly band of hell-raisers, summed it up perfectly at the end of one road trip. "If a bomb had hit the hotel in Detroit at two in the morning," he said, "we'd have still been able to put a team on the field."

In the spring of 1960, as Ted was getting ready for his final year, the former Higgins supporters in the press corps began to print that there was dissension in the Red Sox clubhouse over the way Jurges was running the club. Ted Williams jumped to Jurges's defense and was quoted by Joe Reichler of the AP as saying, "It's all a bunch of horsefeathers. It's those damn Boston writers again. They're always starting trouble."

But that was almost a reflex action. "I was for every manager I ever played for," he says, "every one of them." What he really means is that all he ever wanted from the manager was to be left alone. "My game was right there to play, to hit the best I could, and I tried to do that every time I got to the plate. The manager wasn't going to affect me. I think if I had hated a manager, I'd have hit better because I'd have been mad at him when I got to the plate. You can get too damn happy with it all, and too self-satisfied, and bam, you go down the tubes."

In June the Red Sox were back in last place, and on their way to Minneapolis to play an exhibition game against their farm club (which had a new kid, just out of Notre Dame, named Carl Yastrzemski). A mediocre sore-armed minor-league pitcher who hadn't won a game all year pitched a no-hitter against them, and by the time they boarded the plane for Kansas City there was a story on the wire quoting an unidentified player as saying that Jurges had lost control of the team.

Everybody knew that the source was Tom Brewer, the team's best pitcher. As they arrived in the hotel lobby in Kansas City, Jurges announced that there would be a clubhouse meeting and he wanted all the players and all the newspapermen to be there.

The newspapermen at a clubhouse meeting? Already disaster was in the air. The players were sitting or standing at their lockers. The writers were scattered around the walls.

Ted Williams, still being protective of Jurges, was glowering at any writer who dared to come near him. Pumpsie Green, who had just been called up from the minors to become the Red Sox's first black player, had just sat down at the end of the table in the middle of the room and been handed an ice-cream bar when Jurges came clomping out of his office.

Bill Crowley was there again: "The great lesson I learned that day was that if you want to make a dramatic entrance do not wear shower clogs."

Standing there in his shower clogs, Jurges demanded that the player quoted in the wire story step forward and identify himself.

Nobody moved. (Talking about it later, the Boston writers decided that if Brewer had stepped forward, Jurges would have had a heart attack. And that if, God forbid, Ted Williams had stepped forward, he'd have gone into cardiac arrest.)

The identity of the culprit having gone undisclosed, the press now discovered why they were there. "We're all in this together," Jurges informed them, "We're all working for the city of Boston and the Boston Red Sox."

Not one of the writers who had been hammering at him so mercilessly said a word. It was left to Roger Birtwell of the *Globe,* an aging and shall we say over-genteel member of the press corps, to arise from his crouch, and in his broad prissy Harvard accent deliver a lecture to Mr. Jurges on the duties and responsibilities of the press.

The ballplayers were chortling, Ted Williams was still glowering, and Pumpsie Green was so astonished at this introduction to the major leagues that he just sat there while the ice-cream bar melted and dripped down his hand. You could almost hear him thinking, *"This* is the big leagues . . . ?"

And then it got worse. After the meeting was over, the distraught Jurges gave an exclusive interview to Larry Claflin of the *American* to the effect that he felt he wasn't being supported by the front office. He was so far gone that he even criticized Mr. Yawkey for not backing him properly, an all-time first in Boston. By the time the team reached Washington, the word had come back from Fenway Park so forcefully that he called another press conference to mend his fences. Nobody came. "We don't have any story to clarify" was the message that was sent back to him. "Give it to your private correspondent, Claflin, and let him do your apologizing for you."

With the club continuing to lose, the Red Sox sent the club physician down to give Jurges what was called a "physical examination." The next day he was told to go to his home in nearby Silver Spring, Maryland, for a rest, and not to worry, because when he was ready to come back the job would still be his.

Tom Yawkey, who never held press conferences, held his second press conference in two years. This one ended with him threatening to take the Red Sox out of Boston because the Boston press had exceeded the bounds of decency. The purpose of the press conference was to issue a statement, over the signatures of Tom Yawkey and Bucky Harris, saying that Jurges was the manager and no changes were contemplated. Ted Williams had already issued a statement reiterating his support of Jurges through *his* personal columnist, Joe Reichler.

While Jurges was resting in his home in Silver Spring, he received a registered letter from Yawkey and Harris granting him his unconditional release.

When the Red Sox arrived back in Boston, they found that Mike Higgins was their manager again. Yawkey had located Higgins at a convention of postmasters in New Orleans and had told him to fly to Cleveland. He had then sent Dick O'Connell to Cleveland with instructions to bring Higgins to Boston, sober.

"Rehiring Higgins raises a question," wrote Jerry Nason, the sports editor of the *Boston Globe*. "Do the Red Sox know what they are doing?"

That was the Red Sox in 1960, as the career of Ted Williams was coming to an end.

XVIII

The Kid's Last Game

Forever, and forever, farewell, Cassius!
if we do meet again, why, we shall smile;
if not, why then, this parting was well made.

—SHAKESPEARE

Harold Kaese's lead in
the *Boston Globe*,
September 27, 1960

After the two change-of-life batting championships, Tom Yawkey was more anxious than ever for Williams to retire. Despite that oft-expressed desire to leave the spotlight, imposed upon him by the world of baseball, Ted could not bring himself to depart.

He had after all, committed himself from the beginning to leave his mark upon the record books. He already had 482 home runs as the 1958 season came to an end and he wanted, he said, to pass Lou Gehrig's mark of 493 before he retired—and, if possible, to become the fourth man in history to achieve a total of 500.

Ted was almost was ready to quit, though, when he learned that the Red Sox would be moving their spring-training headquarters to Scottsdale, Arizona. He had heard, in his travels, that it was almost impossible to work up a sweat in the thin Arizona air, and he was afraid he would never be able to get in shape. He discovered very quickly that his information could not have been more incorrect. He thrived so wonderfully on the dry Arizona air that after a couple of weeks he was in the best shape he had been in for years.

In mid-March, the Red Sox and the Indians were to play a three-game exhibition series in San Diego, Ted's hometown. Since he had not played in San Diego since a barnstorming tour in 1941, he put aside his plans to eschew exhibition games so that he could play once more before a hometown crowd. He arrived in San Diego a day before either of the clubs did to do some advance publicity work. The city opened its arms to greet the man who had become its most famous son. Ted had a great time renewing acquaintances with old friends and schoolmates.

The first two games were played at night. The first night turned out cool and damp, the kind of weather he should never have played in. He stayed in the game for five innings, though, to satisfy the people who had turned out to see him. The next night was even cooler and damper. This time Ted played seven innings. In the final game, played on a warm Sunday afternoon, he played through another seven innings.

With the teams returning to Arizona, Ted was given permission to remain in San Diego for a few more days. Before the Indians left, Frank Lane, their general manager, asked Ted, as a special favor, to try to make one of the upcoming games at Cleveland's own training camp, in Tucson. Ted, who was always fond of Lane, promised that he would.

Although his neck had begun to stiffen up on him, Williams, true to his promise, hopped into his car and drove 150 miles across the desert. He suited up, came to the back of the batting cage, and attempted a couple of warm-up swings. The neck hurt so badly that he didn't even try to step into the cage. "I'm going to have to back out on you, Frank," he told Lane. "I just can't swing at all." "I know you didn't drive 150 miles to back out of anything," Lane told him. "I'm grateful to you for making the try."

At first, his problem was diagnosed as a cold in the neck. It was actually a pinched nerve. Because it was widely believed that Ted had used slight or imaginary injuries to get out of exhibition games for years, the first stories about the pinched nerve were taken, it may be said, with a pinch of salt.

Ted was not alarmed at first, because he was told that the trouble would clear up in plenty of time for him to make the opening game of the season. "It was when it got worse instead of better, and I realized I was going to miss the opener again," Ted said later, "that I began to really feel discouraged."

Shipped up to Boston at the end of March, he was fitted with a thick collar, and told that he would indeed probably miss the opener. He missed much more than that. It was another full month before the collar was taken off, and another ten days before he was able to play.

It was anticipated that he would work his way into the lineup slowly—as he always had in the past—but Ted surprised everybody by asking to be written into the starting lineup as soon as the club came back to Boston. His muscles were still sore, his hands were still blistered, and he bore little resemblance to the Ted Williams whom Boston fans had become accustomed to cheering and booing. He went twenty-one times at bat without a base hit, picked up a couple of hits, then went nothing for sixteen.

He had forgone the slower, surer route because he felt that he was in terrible condition that only the steady, hard competitive play could bring him around. A terrible mistake. The neck bothered him all year. Since he couldn't move his head, he had to stand at the plate facing the pitcher. "I didn't expect to do real good," he said, "but I never thought I'd be that bad."

In mid-June, he was batting .175 (103 – 18). The Red Sox, who had been in fifth place when he returned to the lineup, dropped into the cellar, and for the first time in his life Ted Williams found himself being benched for non-hitting.

He didn't start to hit until after he had failed to make the starting lineup in the All-Star Game again.

And then came a succession of small, nagging injuries to go along with the constant pain in his neck. He skinned the knuckles on his hand sliding. In mid-August, an abscessed tooth knocked him out of a series in New York. By then, Billy Jurges, who had replaced Higgins for the second half of the season, had announced that he was going to "spot" Ted here and there, a nice way of saying that he was being benched again.

In the dog days of August he had always loved in the past, he was deep in another slump. By the last week of August, Ted Williams was batting .233.

He felt old. He was always tired. And, finally, in a night game against Kansas City, he didn't even bother to run back to the Red Sox dugout between innings unless he was due to come to bat. Instead, he took his rest in the Boston bull pen along the left-field foul line.

For the season, he hit only .254. And, despite a final flickering of the flame near the end, he was able to pick up only ten home runs, one short of the number he had needed to catch Lou Gehrig.

As the season came to an end, Yawkey called him to his suite at the Ritz Carlton and told him flat-out that he wanted him to retire. "It hurt me," Ted says, looking back. "I didn't think I was ready to retire. I thought I could still hit. We agreed that we'd see what happened in spring training."

Hurt, yes. Surprised, no. During the season, Yawkey had sent Dick O'Connell to sound him out about becoming the manager. That's the way you do it when you're looking for deniability. You send a third party to ask the man you want to hire whether he would be interested in the job "if it were offered to you." If he turns you down, it is never on the record that the job had been offered. "He told me that he would never give the Boston writers the chance to second-guess him," O'Connell says. "I've never really been sure whether he understood that the job was really being offered to him."

"I knew," Ted laughs. And he also knew why. It was not the first time the job had been tendered. Joe Cronin had offered the job to him during the latter part of the 1954 season. "I said, I don't want to manage. I said, I can still hit. And I proved that for five years. Cronin said absolutely, 'Why don't you take it? The guys all respect you.' They all this and that. They never brought it up again in those five years, but that's the way it all started. And it would have been a terrible mistake."

He would be facing his final year—as he had faced the previous one—with wracking trouble back in San Diego. His brother, Danny, was dying of leukemia, the disease Ted had devoted so much of his time to combating, and his mother—Salvation May of the invincible faith—had broken under the strain of her younger son's obviously losing battle against death and had suffered a complete nervous breakdown.

As the final irony, Danny had straightened himself out after the war and had found work as a contract painter and interior decorator. He had married, he had a couple of kids, and he had reconciled with his older brother.

For at least three years Ted had been chartering planes to fly Danny to Salt Lake City for medical treatment (which puts a different light on those missed appointments in Los Angeles, doesn't it?), and he was making sure that Danny had no financial worries as far as his family was concerned. By 1959, he was also flying back to San Diego himself to tend to the care of his mother and, finally, to move her to a rest home in Santa Barbara (which puts a new light on the early arrival and late departure at that exhibition game in San Diego, doesn't it?).

Danny died in March of 1960, at the age of thirty-nine, while Ted was in training camp. May Williams died on August 27, 1961, in the Santa Barbara rest home.

"Those are just the things that happen in life," is all Ted wants to say. "Sure, I had problems at home trying to help my mother and brother and everybody else who was involved. For sure, it bothered me. I had this responsibility, and I wasn't going to shirk from it, and I really didn't. I did the best I could, and let's let it go at that."

Training camp was sheer torture for Ted. As if it wasn't bad enough to be grieving over his brother and worrying about his mother, he no longer had the support or comfort that had always been provided by Johnny Orlando, the good old friend who had been his confidant from the beginning in all matters concerning his family.

Johnny Orlando had been fired.

Johnny's drinking had got out of hand. No question about it. He was showing up late at the ballpark. He was neglecting his duties. But why now? Why couldn't they have waited one more year, until Williams was gone? Orlando had not only been Ted Williams's pal for twenty years. He had been Yawkey's pal even longer.

Johnny had a flair. He would go striding into a bar where baseball people were gathered and say, "I represent the wealthiest franchise in baseball. Drinks for everybody." And sign Tom Yawkey's name. Why not? He was Yawkey's pal, and he did represent the ball club. A ball team has to entertain people. Yawkey had his own partners buying everybody drinks.

But the Sox didn't tell Johnny he was being fired for being a drunkard. How could they? "Who the hell got him drunk?" Dick O'Connell asks. "Yawkey and Cronin. Tom Yawkey would send him bottles of Old Forester by the carton."

What had happened was that Johnny had been sent to the opening of a baseball library, had bumped into a gathering of wealthy executives in the parlor car on the train, and when he was asked why he was going to St. Louis he had reverted to form. "I represent the richest franchise in baseball," Johnny Orlando had announced. "The drinks are on me." So Johnny was told he was being fired for that.

The writers were told that he was fired for showing up late at the ballpark and for stealing things. "Orlando was a law unto himself," Dick O'Connell says. "There was only one John." He'd run short of dough, get a bunch of autographed balls, and sell them, depending on how much he needed. "I'm with the Red Sox," he'd announce. "I'm stealing baseballs."

"Who gave a damn?" O'Connell says. "If you wanted to look at it that way, it was publicity."

Now, there's no doubt that the Red Sox had every justification for firing Johnny Orlando. They also had every justification to fire Bucky Harris, who was still the general manager. Bucky's only saving grace was that on the rare occasions when he did come in to the office he didn't try to do anything. If Orlando wasn't there to do it, it wasn't going to get done.

But what would have been so terrible about waiting another year? Well . . . Ted had said he'd be making up his mind about returning for another year during spring training, and whatever other reasons Yawkey might have had for firing Johnny Orlando, he wasn't making Ted's return any more attractive for him, was he?

Ted was up in Bangor, Maine, fishing with his pal Bud Leavitt when he was told about the firing. "Ted didn't say anything," Leavitt recalls. "He just went absolutely quiet and solemn, the way he would when he was really upset."

Don Fitzpatrick, who replaced Orlando, had been with the Red Sox for fifteen years, mostly in the visiting clubhouse. He had shagged for Ted in those early-morning batting sessions over the years. But he was not Johnny Orlando, and he knew it. "I think that was probably one of the most difficult periods for Ted, when he found out that Johnny was going to have to go and that he couldn't do anything to save him. It ate at him all year. I was there. I saw it."

Orlando had been so protective of Ted that the sportswriters had come to look upon him, with no affection at all, as Ted's flunky. His Bobo. His paid companion. They did not have a clue about the real relationship, says Fitzie. "Johnny and him had a real genuine love. You know the kind of love I'm talking about. It was a good–bad kind of thing. They blended from the first day."

Ted is more than willing to talk about Orlando. "He would deliver my letters from home, and every one was a problem. He knew all my personal problems. He was a terrific guy, and he loved this game so very, very much, and everybody in it. And he knew all the great players fifteen years ahead of me, and he was my close friend, and he'd always give me something extra. Always be there to tell me everything was going to be all right. And who put the Kid name on me."

When the Kid was riding high and proclaiming himself to be the greatest hitter who ever lived, Orlando would bring him down to earth. "If you'd listen to me," he'd say, "you'd hit .500, not .400." And when Ted was feeling sorry for himself, Johnny would say, "Hey, if you couldn't hit you'd be driving a truck. Who do you think you're kidding?" And then go running down the clubhouse as Williams threw things at him.

In the end, he left the decision on his return up to the Red Sox. When he came to Boston in January of 1960 for the annual contract-signing ceremony, he told Dick O'Connell about his agreement with Yawkey. "But," he said, "if the club doesn't want me, hell, I'll quit." O'Connell, who frankly didn't seem to know what he was talking about, pulled a contract out of his desk. It called for the same $125,000 Ted had received for years, the highest salary in baseball. Ted ripped it up and told him to draw up a new contract for $95,000. He had not come close to earning his salary the previous season, he said, and now he wanted to make amends. "This club has given me the biggest salaries, and the biggest raises, that any player ever had. And now I want to take the biggest cut."

Spring training was sheer torture, and it was made all the more difficult by Billy Jurges's theory that the only way for a man Ted's age to stay in condition was to reach a peak at the beginning of the season and hold it by playing just as often as possible. Even there, Ted fooled him. "The most we can expect from Williams," Jurges had said, at the time of Ted's signing, "is one hundred games. The least is pinch hitting." Ted played in 113 games.

Throughout the training season, Ted seemed to be having so much trouble with his timing that the experts wrote him off, for perhaps the fifteenth time of his career. And so, on his first time at bat in the opening game, Ted Williams hit a five-hundred-foot home run, "possibly the longest of his career"—again—off Camilo Pascual, who was probably the best pitcher in the league. That tied him with Gehrig. The next day, he hit a second homer, this one off Jim Coates, in the Fenway Park opener. That put him ahead. He pulled a leg muscle running out that second homer, though, and when a ballplayer's muscles go while he is doing nothing more strenuous than jogging around the bases, the end is clearly in sight.

It took him almost a month to get back in condition, and then the annual virus attack, coming earlier than usual in the unusually cold weather, laid him low again.

Miserable and drugged when he finally got back into uniform, Ted failed in a couple of pinch-hitting attempts and was just about ready to quit. He started against the Yankees, and Ralph Terry struck him out two straight times. The third time up, the count had gone to 3–2 when Williams unloaded on a waist-high fast ball and sent it sailing into the bull pen in right-center, four hundred feet away.

What developed from there was Ted's greatest home-run spree of his entire career. When he hit his 500th home run, seven days later, it marked his eighth home run of the season, after starting only fifteen games. When he hit his 506th (and eleventh of the year), he had homered once in every 6.67 times at bat.

Ed Rumill, who had become Ted's confidant in the absence of Johnny Orlando, began to express increasing doubts about whether he would be able to bring himself to retire if the season came to an end with Jimmy Foxx's 534 home runs clearly in his sights.

Ted's answer was, "You've been talking about buying a new car, right? I'll tell you what to do. You just bet everybody you know that this will be Williams's last year, and you just keep betting until you've bet enough to buy yourself the car."

Now that he was coming so close to the end, he was growing increasingly bitter about the five years lost to the service. "If you can't be number one," he told Rumill, "what's the difference?"

Despite the triumphs, honors, and records, it was a difficult year for Ted. As Jack Fadden put it, before Ted's last game, "It hasn't been a labor of love for Ted this year, it's just been labor."

He had found it difficult to loosen up even in fairly warm weather, and, to complicate matters he had found it necessary, back in the middle of 1959, to cut out the pregame calisthenics routine he always went through in the clubhouse. The exercising had left him almost too weary to play ball.

It was the accumulation of conditioning over twenty-five years that carried him through.

He had put on enough weight over the winter that running the bases wore him out. His goal was to stay below 212 pounds, and he was on the scales every day. "I'd get to 213 and then I wouldn't eat breakfast, then I'd have a light dinner. The next day I'm still 213. Now, 213 for six-four isn't that bad, but I was not that big-boned a guy for six-four, and I didn't feel as light as I'd have liked to feel. I could still hit. I knew I could still hit. And I did hit. But running around the bases got harder and harder."

He would go back to the hotel before the game, and try to grab a couple of hours of sleep. He was no longer taking fielding practice, or even batting practice. Once the game started, however, he went all out. He was taking the extra base, and he would always just make it. He could make only one good throw a game, and yet at least twice during the season he caught a base runner by faking a throw to third base and then throwing him out as he was trying to scramble back to second.

Still and all, as he had never been hesitant to point out, he was not being paid for his fielding or his base running. Ted Williams had become a living synonym for hitting, and at the age of forty-one, he was still quick with the bat. The payoff, as Ted sees it, for thirty years of constant, disciplined work. "From the day I started until the day I left," he will remind you, "there were two things I always stressed in my mind. Be quick and hang in there. If I had to do it over again I'd have done twice as much work on it in that earlier stage. Not on my build, but most certainly on strengthening my arms and hands."

The neck continued to bother him through the early part of the season, but improved steadily as the season progressed. With his customary spartan resolve, Ted would stand in front of the mirror in his locker every day and adjust the posture of his batting stance to assure himself that no strain was being placed upon his neck nerves. He would stare at himself intently for five minutes, and finally, when he was satisfied that all his visualizations were in place, he would start to swing the towel in his hands as if it were a bat.

On his first time at bat during the game, he would look for an inside pitch between the waist and knees, the only pitch he could swing at naturally and without effort. In the main, though, Ted was more than willing to take the base on balls his first time up. Otherwise, he was pretty much giving it away.

When he strained his shoulder late in August, just as the cold weather hit again, he was just about ready to announce his retirement again. He stayed on for two reasons. Mike Higgins, who had replaced Jurges by then, told him bluntly: "You're paid to play ball, so go out and play." In addition, the Red Sox had two series remaining with both the Yankees and the Orioles, who were still locked together in the pennant race. Ted did not think it fair to eliminate himself as a factor.

The announcement of his retirement came just after the Yankees had clinched the pennant by beating the Red Sox at Fenway Park.

The decision to make the announcement on that particular Sunday had been made four days earlier, at a special meeting that Yawkey had called to decide what job Ted was going to hold to justify the legal requirements of his deferred payments. Ted told Ed Rumill, off the record, that he had been offered the job of general manager—which was probably one of those offers that was made to be turned down. At any rate, Ted had turned it down and expressed a preference for working in player personnel. The announcement stated that he would be reporting to Scottsdale in the spring to serve as batting instructor.

The schedule called for the Red Sox to finish out their last home stand, against Baltimore, on Wednesday, September 26, and then travel to New York for a final series against the Yankees.

Wednesday came on cold and dreary in Boston, a curious bit of staging on the part of those gods who had always set the scene so bountifully for Ted Williams.

Ted came into the locker room at ten-fifty, very early for him. He was dressed in dark brown slacks, a yellow sport shirt, and a light tan pullover sweater, tastefully brocaded in the same color. He went immediately to his locker, pulled off the sweater and strolled into the trainer's room.

The only civilian in the clubhouse when Ted entered was the writer from *Sport* magazine, and he was talking to Del Baker who was about to retire, too, after fifty-six years in the game. Ted looked over, scowled, seemed about to say something but changed his mind. Sure enough, when the man from *Sport* started toward Ted's locker, in the far corner of the room, Ted pointed a finger at him and shouted, "You're not supposed to be in here, you know."

"The same warm, glad cry of greeting I always get from you," the writer said. "It's your last day. Why don't you live a little?"

Ted started toward the trainer's room again but wheeled around and came back. "You've got a nerve coming here to interview me after the last one you wrote about me!"

The man from *Sport* wanted to know what was the matter with the last one.

"You called me 'unbearable,' that's what's the matter."

The full quote, it was pointed out, was that he was sometimes unbearable but never dull, which held a different connotation entirely.

"You've been after me for twelve years, that flogging magazine," he said, in his typically well-modulated shout. "I missed an appointment at some kind of luncheon. I forgot what happened . . . it doesn't matter, anyway . . . but I forgot an appointment twelve years ago and *Sport* magazine hasn't let up on me since."

As always, the man from *Sport* sought to dissociate himself from the magazine by reiterating that he was not a member of the staff.

"Well, when you get back there, tell them what . . ." He searched for the appropriate word, the *mot juste,* as they say in the dugout. ". . . what flogheads they are. Tell them that for me."

The man from *Sport* sought to check the correct spellings of the adjectives with him but got back only a scowl. Ted turned around to fish something out of a cloth bag at the side of his locker. "Why don't you just write your story without me?" he said. "What do you have to talk to me for?" And then, in a suddenly weary voice, "What can I tell you now that I haven't told you before?"

"Why don't you let me tell you what the story is supposed to be?" the writer said. "Then you can say yes or no." It was an unfortunate way to put the question since it invited the answer it brought.

"I can tell you before you tell me," Ted shouted. "No! No, no, no."

Don Fitzpatrick, the clubhouse man, came over with a glossy photo and Ted sat down on his stool, turned his back, and signed it. Then he sat there, his right knee jumping nervously, his right hand alternately buttoning and unbuttoning the top button of his sport shirt.

When he stripped down to his shorts, there was no doubt that he was forty-two. The man once called the "splendid splinter" was thick around the middle. A soft roll of loose fat drooped around the waist.

Tall and handsome though Ted Williams still was, ballplayers age quickly. Twenty years under the sun had baked Ted's face and left it lined and leathery. Sitting there, Ted Williams had the appearance of an old Marine sergeant who had been to the battles and back.

Sal Maglie, who had the end locker on the other side of the shower-room door, suddenly caught Ted's eye. "You're a National Leaguer, Sal," he said, projecting his voice to the room at large. "I got a hundred dollars that the Yankees win the World Series. The Yankees will win it in four or five games."

"I'm an American Leaguer now," Sal said.

"A hundred dollars," Ted said. "A friendly bet."

"You want a friendly bet? I'll bet you a friendly dollar."

"Fifty dollars," Ted said.

Sal took the bet. Projecting his own voice, he said, "I like the Pirates, anyway."

At length, Ted picked up his spikes, wandered into the trainer's room again and, lifting himself onto the table, began to carefully put a shine on the shoes. A photographer proffered a ball toward him and asked him if he would sign it. Ted gazed down at the ball with distaste, then looked up at the photographer with loathing. "Are you crazy?" he snapped. The photographer backed away, pocketed the ball, and began to adjust his camera sight on Ted. "You don't belong in here," Ted barked. And turning to Don Fitzpatrick, he said, "Get him out of here."

As the photographer was leaving, Ted turned toward him and made an obscene gesture. "Get one like this."

The locker room had emptied before Ted began to dress. He did not take batting practice or fielding practice; he made every entrance onto the field a dramatic event. For Ted—despite his protestations—always did warm to the adulation and to the applause. He did not leave the locker room for the dugout until 12:55, only thirty-five minutes before the game was scheduled to start. By then, the Boston writers had gone up to Tom Yawkey's office to hear Jackie Jensen announce that he was returning to baseball.

As Ted came quickly up the stairs and into the dugout, he almost bumped into Bud Leavitt, sports editor of the *Bangor Daily News,* his close friend and fishing companion. "Hi Bud," he said, as if he were surprised to find Leavitt there. "You drive up?"

A semicircle of cameramen closed in around him, like a bear trap, from the playing field just up above. Ted hurled a few oaths in their direction, and as an oath-hurler Ted was still world-class. He guided Leavitt against the side of the dugout, just above the steps, so that he could continue to talk to him without providing shooting angle for the photographers. When the photographers continued to shoot him in profile, anyway, Ted took Leavitt by the elbow and walked him the length of the dugout. "Let's sit down," he said, as he was moving away, "so we won't be bothered by all these cockroaching cameramen."

If there had been any doubt back in the locker room that Ted had decided to run his course to the end, it had been completely dispelled by those first few minutes in the dugout. On his last day in Fenway Park, Ted Williams was clearly resolved to remain true to his own image of himself. To permit no sentimentality or hint of sentimentality to crack that mirror through which he looked at the world and allowed the world to look upon him.

And yet, in watching him, you had the feeling that he was overplaying his role, that he had struggled through the night against the impulse to make his peace, to express his gratitude, to accept the great affection that the city had been showering upon him for two decades. In watching him, you had the clear impression that in resisting this desire he was overreacting and becoming more profane, more impossible, and, yes, more unbearable than ever.

This clash within Williams came to the surface as he sat and talked with Leavitt, alone and undisturbed. For within a matter of minutes, the absence of the limelight began to oppress him. His voice began to get louder, to pull everybody's attention back to him. The cameramen, getting the message, drifted over to him again. Not in a tight pack this time but in a loose and straggling formation.

With Ted talking so loudly, it was apparent that he and Leavitt were discussing how to get together after the World Series, for their annual postseason fishing expedition. The assignment to cover the series for

Life magazine had apparently upset their schedule. After New York, Ted said, "I'll be going right to Pittsburgh." He expressed his hope that the Yankees would wrap it up quick so he could join Leavitt in Bangor at the beginning of the following week.

Leavitt reminded Ted of an appearance he had apparently agreed to make in Bangor. "All right," Ted said, "but no speeches or anything."

A young redheaded woman, in her late twenties, leaned over from her box seat alongside the dugout and asked Ted if he would autograph her scorecard.

"I can't sign it, dear," Ted said. "League rules. Where are you going to be after the game?"

"You told me that once before," she said, unhappily.

"Well, where are you going to be?" Ted shouted, in the impatient way one would shout at an irritating child.

"Right here," she said.

"All right."

"But I waited before and you never came."

Joe Cronin, who had become president of the American League a year earlier, came rolling down the dugout aisle, followed by Joe McKenney, who had just become his assistant. Through Cronin's offices, the local 9:00 news-feature program which followed the "Today" show in Boston had scheduled a filmed interview with Ted. The camera had already been set up on the home-plate side of the dugout, just in front of the box seats. Cronin talked to Ted briefly and went back to reassure the television people that Ted would be right along. McKenney remained behind to make sure Ted didn't forget. At last, Ted jumped up and shouted, "Where is it, Joe, damnit?"

When Ted followed McKenney out of the dugout, it was the first time he had stuck his head onto the field all day. There were still not too many fans in the stands, although far more than would have normally been there to watch a seventh-place team on a cold and threatening afternoon. At first sight of Ted Williams, they let out a mighty roar.

As he waited alongside interviewer Jack Chase, Ted bit his lower lip and looked blankly into space, both characteristic mannerisms. At a signal from the cameraman, Chase asked Ted how he felt about entering "the last lap."

All at once Ted was smiling. "I want to tell you, Jack, I honestly feel good about it," he said, speaking in that quick and charming way of his. "You can't get blood out of a turnip, you know. I've gone as far as I can, and I'm sure I wouldn't want to try it anymore."

"Have we gone as far as we can with the Jimmy Fund?" Chase asked.

Ted was smiling more broadly now. "Oh, no. We could never go far enough with the Jimmy Fund."

Chase reminded him that he was scheduled to become a batting coach. "Can you take a .250 hitter and make a .300 hitter out of him?"

Ted's answer was that you could improve a hitter more than you could improve a fielder. "More mistakes are made in hitting than in any other part of the game."

By then, Williams was completely encircled by photographers, amateur and professional. The pros were taking pictures from the front and the side. Behind them, in the grandstand, dozens of fans had their cameras clicking away too, although they could hardly have been getting anything except the Number 9 on his back.

"All I know," Ted was saying, "is that I'm going to spring training. Other than that I don't know anything."

The interview closed with the usual fulsome praise of Williams, the inevitable apotheosis that leaves him with a hangdog, embarrassed look upon his features. "I appreciate the kind words," he said. "It's all been fun. Everything I've done in New England from playing left field and getting booed, to the Jimmy Fund."

After he had finished, he had to push his way through the wall of cameramen to get to the dugout. "Oh shit," he said. But when one of them asked him to pose with Cronin, Ted switched personalities again and asked, with complete amiability, "Where is he?"

Cronin was in the dugout. Ted met him at the bottom of the steps and threw an arm around him. They grinned at each other while the pictures were being taken, talking softly and unintelligibly. After a minute, Ted reached over to the hook just behind him and grabbed his glove. The cameramen were still yelling for another shot as he started up the dugout steps. Cronin, grinning broadly, grabbed him by the shoulder and pulled him back down. While Cronin was wrestling Ted around and whacking him on the back, the cameras clicked. "I got to warm up, damnit," Ted was saying. He made a pawing gesture at the cameramen, as if to say, "I'd like to belt you cockroaches." That was the picture that went around the country that night, because, strangely enough, it came out looking as if he were waving a kind of sorrowful farewell.

When he finally broke away and ran out to the field, he called back over his shoulder, "See you later, Joe." The cheers arose from the stands once again.

The Orioles were taking infield practice by then, and the Red Sox were warming up along the sideline. Hoyt Wilhelm, the practically unhittable knuckleballer, was fooling around at first base with the second-string infield. "Going to quit us, huh, Ted?" he called out, as he spotted Ted coming up the dugout steps.

"Guys like you did it," Ted called back, smiling broadly. The shared smile that communicates things that nobody outside the small privileged circle of the big-league ballplayer can possibly understand.

Ted began to play catch with Pumpsie Green, the little second baseman who had joined the Sox in July as their first black player. ("He asked me to warm up with him the first day I came here," Pumpsie explained, "and I've been warming up with him ever since. I don't know why.") And, sure enough the cameramen lined up just inside the foul line for some more shots. "Why don't you cockroaches get off my back?" Ted said, giving them his No. 1 sneer. "Let me breathe, will you?"

The bell rang before he had a chance to throw two dozen balls. Almost all the players went back to the locker room. Remaining on the bench were only Ted Williams, buttoned up in his jacket, and Vic

Wertz. One of the members of the ground crew came over with a picture of Ted and asked him if he would autograph it. "Sure," Ted said. "For you guys, anything."

Vic Wertz was having his picture taken with another ground-crew member. Wertz had his arm around the guy and both of them were laughing. "How about you, Ted?" the cameraman asked. "One with the crewmen?" Ted posed willingly with the guy he had just signed for, with the result that the whole herd of cameramen came charging over again. Ted leaped to his feet. "Twenty-two years of this bullshit," he groaned.

The redhead was leaning over the low barrier again, but by now three other young women were alongside her. One of them seemed to be crying, apparently at the prospect of Ted's retirement. An old photographer, in a long, weather-beaten coat, asked Ted for a special pose. "Get lost, Jonesy," Ted said. "I've seen enough of you, you old goat."

Curt Gowdy, the Red Sox broadcaster, had come into the dugout to pass on some information about the pregame ceremonies. "Floggin' cameramen," Ted shouted, to the empty air. The women continued to stare in fascination, held either by the thrill of having this last long look at Ted Williams or by the opportunity of adding a few new words to their vocabulary.

A Baltimore writer came into the dugout, and Ted settled in beside him. He wanted to know if the writer could check on the "King of Swat" crown that had been presented to him in his last visit to Baltimore. Ted wasn't sure whether he had taken it back to Boston with him or whether the organization still had it. "You know," he told the writer, "Skinny Brown is a better pitcher now than he has ever been. Oh, he's a great pitcher. Never get a fat pitch from him. When he does, it comes in with something extra on it. Every time a little different. He knows what he's doing." Still in there stroking to the end. Hector (Skinny) Brown was a slider pitcher.

Waiting in the dugout for the ceremonies to get under way, Ted picked up a bat and wandered up and down taking vicious swings. The photographers immediately swooped in on him. One obliging photographer was taking cameras from the spectators—still and moving picture cameras both—and shooting pictures of Ted for them.

As Ted put the bat down, one photographer said, "One more shot, Teddy. As a favor."

"I'm all done doing any favors for you guys," Ted said. "I don't have to put up with you any more, and you don't have to put up with me."

An old woman, leaning over the box seats, began to wail, "Don't leave us, Ted. Don't leave us."

"Oh hell," Ted said, turning away.

The redhead asked him plaintively. "Why don't you act nice?"

Ted strolled slowly toward her, grinning broadly. "Come on, dear," he drawled, "with that High Street accent you got there."

Turning back, he stepped in front of the man from *Sport,* pointed over his shoulder at the cameramen, and asked, "You getting it all? You getting what you came for?"

"I understand that if you can't make it as a batting instructor, you want to come back here as a cameraman."

"I just want to know what *Sport* magazine thinks I'm going to do," Ted said. "That's what I want to know. What does *Sport* magazine think I'm going to do?"

Speaking for himself, the writer said—having made it clear that as a non-staff member he was not privy to the magazine's thinking—he had not the slightest doubt that Ted was going to be the new general manager.

"*Sport* magazine," Ted said, making the name sound like an oath. "Always honest. Never prejudiced. For twelve years you've stuck it up in me. Go back and tell them they're full of shit. A personal farewell from me to them."

At this point he was called onto the field. Taking off his jacket, he strode out of the dugout. The cheers that greeted him came from 10,454 throats.

Curt Gowdy, handling the introductions, began: "As we all know,

this is the final home game for—in my opinion and most of yours—
the greatest hitter who ever lived. Ted Williams.''

There was tremendous applause.

"Twenty years ago," Gowdy continued, "a skinny kid from San
Diego came to the Red Sox camp . . .''

"Controversial, sure," Gowdy said, in bringing his remarks to a
close. "But colorful.''

The chairman of the Boston Chamber of Commerce presented Ted
with a shining silver Paul Revere bowl "on behalf of the business
community of Boston.'' Ted seemed to force his smile as he accepted it.

A representative of the Sports Committee of the Chamber of Commerce then presented him with a plaque "on behalf of visits to kids'
and veterans' hospitals.''

Boston's paralyzed mayor, John Collins, announced from his
wheelchair that "on behalf of all citizens" he was proclaiming this as
Ted Williams Day. The mayor did not yet know how right he was
going to be.

As Mayor Collins spoke of Ted's virtues ("Nature's best, nature's
nobleman") the muscle of Ted's upper left jaw was jumping, constantly and rhythmically. The mayor's contribution to Ted Williams
Day was a $1,000 donation to the Jimmy Fund from some special city
fund.

Gowdy brought the proceedings to a close by proclaiming, "Pride
is what made him great. He's a champion, a thoroughbred, a champion
of sports.'' Curt then asked for "a round of applause, an ovation for
Number 9 on his last game.'' Needless to say, he got it.

Ted, waiting, pawed at the ground with one foot (just as he had as
a fifteen-year-old junior accepting the player-of-the-year award at Hoover High). Smiling, he thanked the mayor for the donation. "Despite
the fact of the disagreeable things that have been said of me, and I
can't help thinking about it—by the Knights of the Keyboard out
there''—he jerked his head toward the press box, "baseball has been
the most wonderful thing in my life. If I were starting over again, and

someone asked me where is the one place I would like to play, I would want it to be in Boston, with the greatest owner in baseball and the greatest fans in America. Thank you.''

He walked across the infield to the dugout, where the players were standing and applauding along with the fans. Ted winked and went on in.

In the press box, some of the writers were upset by his gratuitous rap at them. ''I think it was bush,'' one of them said. ''Whatever he thinks, this wasn't the time to say it.'' Others made a joke of it. ''Now that he's knighted me,'' one of them said, ''I wonder if he's going to address me as sir.''

In the last half of the first inning, Ted stepped in against Steve Barber, with Willie Tasby on first base and one out. When Barber was born, on February 22, 1939, Ted had already taken the American Association apart at Minneapolis. Against a left-hander, Williams was standing almost flush with the inside border of the batter's box, his feet wide, his stance slightly closed. He took a curve inside, then a fast ball low. The third pitch was also low. With a three-and-nothing count, Ted jumped in front of the plate with the pitch, like a high-school kid looking for a walk. It was ball four, high.

He got to third the easy way. Jim Pagliaroni was hit by a pitch, and everybody moved up on a wild pitch. When Frank Malzone walked, Jack Fisher came in to replace Barber. Lou Clinton greeted Fisher with a rising liner to dead center. Jackie Brandt started in, slipped as he tried to reverse himself, but recovered in time to scramble back and make the catch. His throw to the plate was beautiful to behold, a low one-bouncer that came to Gus Triandos chest high. But Ted, sliding hard, was in under the ball easily.

Leading off the third inning against the right-handed Fisher, Ted moved back just a little in the box. Fisher was even younger than Barber, a whole week younger; when Fisher was being born, on March 4, 1939, Ted was on his way to Sarasota for the second time, widely proclaimed as the Red Sox answer to Joe DiMaggio. Pinning it down exactly, it was the day on which Ted was being checked into a New Orleans hotel with 102 temperature.

Ted hit Fisher's one-and-one pitch straightaway, high and deep. Brandt, in center field, had plenty of room to go back and make the catch, but still, as Ted returned to the bench he got another tremendous hand.

Up in the press box, Jack Malaney was announcing that uniform number 9 was being retired "after today's game." That brought on some snide remarks about Ted wearing his undershirt at Yankee Stadium for the final three games of the season. Like Mayor Collins, Malaney was righter than they knew. The uniform was indeed going to be retired after the game.

Ted came to bat again in the fifth inning, with two out and the Sox trailing, 3–2. And this time he unloaded a tremendous drive to right center. As the ball jumped off the bat, the cry "He did it!" arose from the stands. Right-fielder Al Pilarcik ran back as far as he could, pressed his back against the bull-pen fence, well out from the 380-foot sign, and stood there motionless, with his hands at his side.

Although it was a heavy day, there was absolutely no wind. The flag hung limply from the pole, stirring only occasionally and very faintly.

At the last moment, Pilarcik brought up his hands and caught the ball chest high, close to 400 feet from the plate. A moan of disappointment settled over the field, followed by a rising hum of excited chatter, and then, as Ted came back toward the first-base line to take his glove from Pumpsie Green, a standing ovation.

"Damn," Ted said when he returned to the bench at the end of the inning. "I hit the living hell out of that one, I really stung it. If that one didn't go out, nothing is going out today."

In the top of the eighth, with the Sox behind, 4–2, Mike Fornieles came to the mound, for the seventieth time of the season breaking the league record set by another Red Sox relief star, Ellis Kinder. Kinder had set his mark in 1953, the year of Williams's return from Korea. As Fornieles was warming up, three teenage kids jumped out of the grandstand and headed for Ted. They paused only briefly, however, and continued across the field and into the waiting arms of the park police.

Ted was scheduled to bat second in the last of the eighth, in what was undoubtedly going to be his last time at bat. The cheering began as soon as Willie Tasby came out of the dugout and strode to the plate, acting anxious to get out of there and make way for the main event. Ted, coming out almost directly behind Tasby, went to the batter's circle. He was down on one knee and just beginning to swing the heavy, lead-filled practice bat as Tasby hit the first pitch to short for an easy out.

And now the cheering seemed to come to its peak as Ted stepped into the box and took his stance. Everybody in the park had come to his feet, to give Ted another standing ovation. Umpire Eddie Hurley called time. Fisher stepped off the rubber, and catcher Gus Triandos stood erect. Ted remained in the box, waiting. As if he were oblivious to it all. The ovation lasted at least two minutes, and even then Fisher threw into the continuing applause. Only as the ball approached the plate did the cheering stop. The pitch came in low, ball one. The spectators remained on their feet, but suddenly the park had gone absolutely silent.

If there was pressure on Ted, there was pressure on young Fisher, too. The Orioles were practically tied for second place, so he could not afford to be charitable. He might have been able to get Ted to go after a bad pitch, and yet he hardly wanted to go down in history as the fresh kid who had walked Ted Williams on his last time at bat.

The second pitch was neck high, a slider with, it seemed, just a little off it. Ted gave it a tremendous swing, but he seemed to be just a little out in front of the ball. The swing itself brought a roar from the fans, though, since it was a clear announcement that Ted was going for it all. A home run or nothing.

With a one-and-one count, Fisher wanted to throw a fastball low and away. He got it up too much and in too much, a fastball waist high on the outside corner. From the moment Ted swung, there was not the slightest doubt about it. The ball cut through the heavy air, a high line drive heading straightaway to center field, toward the corner of the bull pen the Red Sox had built for him back in 1940. Jackie Brandt went back almost to the barrier, then turned and watched the ball bounce off the canopy above the bull-pen bench, skip up against the wire fence that rises in front of the bleachers, and bounce back into the bull pen.*

It did not seem possible that 10,454 throats could make that much noise.

Ted raced around the bases at a pretty good clip. Triandos had started toward the mound with a new ball, and Fisher had come down to meet him. As Ted neared home plate, Triandos turned to face him, a big smile on his face. Ted grinned back.

Jim Pagliaroni, the next Red Sox hitter, grabbed his hand as he crossed the plate. Ted ran back into the dugout and ducked through the runway door for a drink of water. When he came back, the batboy was shoving his bat into its hole in the bat rack. Ted told him to take the bat up to Yawkey in his office.

The fans were on their feet again, deafening the air with their cheers. A good four or five minutes passed before anybody worried about getting the game under way again.

When Ted ducked back into the dugout, he had put on his jacket and sat down at the very end of the bench, alongside Mike Higgins and Del Baker. The players, still on their feet anyway, crowded around, urging him to go out and acknowledge the cheers. The fans were chanting, "We want Ted, we want Ted, we want Ted." Umpire Johnny Rice, at first base, motioned for him to come out; Mike Higgins urged him to. Still winded from the quick trot around the bases, Ted just sat there with his head down and a smile of happiness on his face. "Fuck 'em," he said.

---

* My notes at the time read: "The ball cut through the heavy air (it almost had to be low to make it—although you and I know that if the Lord could part the Red Sea for the Hebrews He could part the heavy air for Ted Williams). In the bull pen, the jacketed Red Sox crew are up and screaming. The ball goes over the glove of a leaping figure, bounces off the wall behind the canopy that covers the bench, and you never heard such screaming in your life."

"We wanted him to go out," Vic Wertz said later, "because we felt so good for him. And we could see he was thrilled, too. For me, I have to say it's my top thrill in baseball." Off the record, Wertz said, "I had the impression—maybe I shouldn't say it—that he got as much kick out of refusing to go out and tip his hat to the crowd as he did out of the homer. What I mean is he wanted to go out with the home run, all right, but he also wanted the home run so he could sit there while they yelled for him and tell them all to go to hell."

Mike Higgins had already told Carroll Hardy to take Ted's place in left field. But as Lou Clinton came to bat, with two men out, Higgins said, "Williams, left field." Ted grabbed his glove angrily and went to the top step. When Clinton struck out, Ted was the first man out of the dugout. He sprinted out to left field, ignoring the cheers of the fans, who had not expected to see him out there again. But Higgins had sent Hardy right out behind him. Ted saw him as he turned and ran back in, one final time. The entire audience was on its feet once again, in wild applause.

Since it is doubtful that Higgins felt Williams was in any great need of more applause that day, it was perfectly obvious that he was giving Ted one last chance to think about the tip of the hat or wave of the hand as he covered the distance between left field and the dugout.

Ted made the trip as always, his head down, his stride unbroken. He stepped on first base as he crossed the line, ducked into the dugout, growled once at Higgins, and headed through the alleyway and into the locker room. According to the *Boston American,* he stopped only to tell an usher standing just inside the dugout, "I guess I forgot to tip my hat."

Ted has his own version. "Let me tell you something. When I hit that ball I was obviously hoping it would go, and there it went. Now I have great elation. In my mind as I'm rounding first base, I say, God . . . I thought about my hat, and I thought about it. I hit second base, and I said, no, I'll never tip my hat. And I came into home plate more than ever convinced that I wouldn't. It was that type of feeling. Then when I ran into the dugout, and they're all coming to me and asking me to come on out, come on out, and I didn't do it. That was my feeling going round the bases. Somewhere around hitting second base and going into third, that's where I said No.''

As the other players came filing into the locker room after the game, Ted, who already had his uniform off, shouted, "Lock the fucken door."

"Did it ever occur to you," Vic Wertz said, "that some of us might have people we want to come in here."

Although the photographers were permitted to go right into the clubhouse, the writers were held to the fifteen-minute rule. A Baltimore writer, unaware of the restriction, tried to ride in with the photographers, but Williams leveled that finger at him and said, "You don't belong in here."

Somehow or other, the news was let out that Ted would not be going to New York, although there seemed to be some confusion among the writers about whether it was Williams or Higgins who made the announcement. The official Red Sox line was that it had been understood all along that Ted would not be going to New York unless the pennant race was still alive.

One of the waiting newspapermen, a pessimist by nature, expressed the fear that by the time they were let in Ted would be dressed and gone. "Are you kidding?" Clif Keane said. "This is what he lives for. If it lasted eighteen innings, he'd be there waiting for us. Watch them go sucking up to him."

Ted was indeed waiting at his locker, with a towel wrapped around his middle. The writers approached him, for the most part, in groups. Generally speaking, the writers who could be called friendly hit him first, and to these men Ted was not only amiable but gracious and modest.

Was he going for the home run?

"I was gunning for the big one." He grinned. "I let everything I had go. I really wanted that one."

Did he know it was out as soon as it left his bat?

"I knew I had really given it a ride."

The other players seemed even more affected by the drama of the farewell home run than Ted was. Pete Runnels, practically dispossessed from his locker alongside Ted's by the shifts of reporters, wandered around the room, shaking his head in disbelief. "How about that?" he kept repeating. "How about that?"

As for Ted, he seemed to be in something of a daze. After the first wave of writers had left, he wandered back and forth between his locker and the trainer's room. Back and forth, back and forth. Once, he came back with a bottle of beer, turned it up to his lips, and downed it with obvious pleasure. For Ted, that was almost unheard of. He had always been a milk-and-ice-cream man, devouring them both in huge quantities. His usual order after a ball game was two quarts of milk.

Williams remained in the locker room, making himself available, until there were only a handful of players left. Many of the writers did not go over to him at all. From them, there were no questions, no congratulations, no good wishes for the future. For all Ted's color, for all the drama and copy he had supplied over twenty-two years, they were more than happy to see him go.

When Ted finally began to get dressed, the writer from *Sport* magazine went over and asked, "Ted, you must have known when Higgins sent you back out that he was giving you a final chance to think about tipping the hat or making some gesture of farewell. Which meant that Higgins himself would have liked you to have done it. While you were running back, didn't you have any feeling that it might be nice to go out with a show of good feeling?"

"I felt nothing," he said.

"No sentimentality? No gratitude? No sadness?"

"I said nothing," Ted barked. "Nothing, nothing, nothing!"

Fenway Park has an enclosed parking area so that the players can get to their cars without having to beat their way through the autograph hunters. When Ted was dressed, though, the clubhouse man called the front office in what was apparently a prearranged plan to bring Williams's car around to a bleacher exit.

At 4:40, forty-five minutes after the end of the game and a good hour after Ted had left the dugout, he was ready to leave. "Hey,

Fitzie,'' he called, and Fitzie came around to lead the way. The cameramen—eight of them—came around, too.

The locker-room door at Fenway Park opens onto a narrow alcove, which leads to an outer door, which in turn opens onto the back walks and understructure of the park. It is this outer door which is always guarded.

Waiting in the alcove, just inside the clubhouse door, however, was a redheaded, beatnik-looking young man, complete with the regimental beard and beachcomber pants. He handed Ted a baseball and mentioned a name that obviously meant something to Ted. Leaning over the railing, Ted held the ball against his thigh while he signed. ''How come you're not able to get in?'' he said as he handed the ball back. ''If they let the floggin' newspapermen in, they ought to let you in.'' As he went through the door, trailed by the full squad of cameramen, he called out to the empty air, ''If they let the floggin' newpapermen in, why don't they let anyone in?''

He walked on through the back ways of the park, past the ramps and pillars, at a brisk clip, with Fitzie bustling along trying to stay ahead. Alongside Ted, the cameramen were jockeying for position to snap their pictures. Ted kept his eyes straight ahead, never breaking stride for a moment. ''Hold it for just a minute, Ted,'' one of them said.

''I've been here for twenty-two years,'' Ted said, walking on. ''Plenty of time for you to get your shot.''

''This is the last time,'' the cameraman said. ''Cooperate just this one last time.''

''I've cooperated with you,'' Ted said. ''I've cooperated too much.''

Fitzie had the bleacher entrance open, and as Ted passed quickly through, a powder-blue Cadillac driven by Dick O'Connell pulled up to the curb.

Fitzie ran ahead to open the far door of the car for Ted. Three young women had been approaching the exit as Ted darted through, and one of them screamed, ''It's him!'' One of the others just let out a scream, the kind of a scream one associates with the sighting of a rock star. The third woman remained mute. Looking at her, you had to wonder whether she would ever speak again.

Fitzie slammed the door, and the car pulled away. "It was *him*," the first woman screamed. "Was it really him? Was it *him?*"

Her knees seemed to give way, and her girlfriends had to support her. "I can't catch my breath," she said. "I can hear my heart pounding." And then, in something like terror, *"I can't breathe."* Attracted by the screams or by the invisible vibrations of the grapevine, a horde of boys and men came racing up the street. Ted's car turned the corner just across from the bleacher exit, but it was held up momentarily by a red light and a bus. The front line of pursuers had just come abreast of the car when the driver swung around the bus and pulled away.

There are those, however, who never get the word. Down the street, surrounding the almost empty parking area, were perhaps a hundred loyal fans still waiting to say their last farewell to Ted Williams.

In Boston that night the talk was all of Ted Williams. Only 10,454 had been at the scene, but the word all over the city was "I knew he'd end it with a home run." And "I was going to go to the game, but . . ." With the passage of time, the fans who saw Ted hit that mighty shot now number into the hundreds of thousands. The wind has grown stronger and meaner, and the distance of the blow grows ever longer. Even at the time, many of the reports of the game had the ball going into the center-field bleachers instead of the bull pen.

The seeds of the legend were quickly sown. George Carens, an elderly columnist who had become a shameless sycophant, wrote, "Ted was calm and gracious as he praised the occupants of the Fenway press penthouse at home plate before the game began. Afterwards, he greeted all writers in a comradely way, down through his most persistent critics. In a word, Ted showed he can take it, and whenever the spirit moves him he will fit beautifully into the Fenway PR setup."

Which proved once again that people hear what they want to hear and see what they want to see.

In New York the next day, Phil Rizzuto informed his television audience that Ted had finally relented and tipped his hat after that final home run.

And the *Sporting News* headline on its Boston story was:

Splinter Tips Cap
To Hub Fans After
Farewell Homer

A New York Sunday supplement went so far as to say that Ted had made "a tender and touching farewell speech" from home plate at the end of the game.

All the reports said that Ted had, in effect, called his shot, because it was known that he was shooting for a home run. And who could argue with that? Or wanted to?

So what about it? Had he intended to go on to New York or not? The press release, of Sunday, September 25, is just ambiguous enough to give pause.

The heading reads:

TO BE ANNOUNCED OVER PRESS BOX "MIKE"
AT END OF TODAY'S GAME

President Tom Yawkey of the Red Sox has announced that Ted Williams DEFINITELY is retiring as a player at the end of this season, thus will be playing his final two games here on Tuesday and Wednesday.

But that could be interpreted to mean that they would be the final two games he would be playing "here," meaning in Boston. Or it could be interpreted—if you tried hard enough—to mean that his final two games would be played in Boston.

He had told Bud Leavitt in the dugout that he'd be leaving for Pittsburgh "after New York." But that could be interpreted—if you really wanted to—to mean after the season had ended in New York.

He had not told Don Fitzpatrick not to pack his bags for New York. But that could have been an oversight.

The best evidence is that if he hadn't hit a home run in one of those last three games in Boston he most probably would have gone on to New York.

The best evidence comes from Roy Mumpton. Before the Monday game against Baltimore, Ted had confided to a couple of reporters— Roy Mumpton for one—that he wanted to go out with a home run. And that since the Sox weren't going anywhere, anyway, he was going to leave the game as soon as he hit one.

"That's what he told me," Mumpton says. "And also that he had told Yawkey and Higgins, and they had agreed. In other words, if he had hit a homer in the first inning on Monday, he would have come out of the ball game right there."

He almost did. In the fifth inning of Monday's game he hit a long drive into the wind that hit high off the wall in left center, missing a home run by inches.

All to the good. To have hit a home run in the fifth inning of a desultory Monday game—or, worse, while the Sox were taking a 17–2 beating on Tuesday—would hardly have been going out in style. Aaahh, no, the gods that had always delivered him a script writ large were not going to permit the career of Ted Williams to end with a shrug.

But what if he hadn't hit the home run? Ted says that he told Higgins and Yawkey, after the Yankees clinched the pennant on Sunday, that he would not be going on to New York. But that doesn't mean that the addendum on it wasn't "unless I want to." Because, and here is the final bit of evidence, he had not told Don Fitzpatrick not to pack his bags for New York. Why wouldn't Ted have told him not to bother, unless he was leaving himself the option of deciding after the game?

"If he hadn't hit the home run," Mumpton says, "he would have gone on to New York. I'm sure of that."

Assuming that he was leaving the door open, you could also say that there was tremendous pressure on him not to have to make that decision when he stepped to the plate for what was indisputably going to be his last shot in Boston.

In the end, he did what he did, and what difference does it make? I ended my article on the Kid's last game by writing:

> The epitaph for Ted Williams remained unchanged: He was sometimes unbearable, but he was never dull. And yet, those who saw him go knew that baseball would never be quite the same without him. Boston won't be quite the same either.
>
> Old Boston is acrawl with greening statues of old heroes and old patriots, but Ted left a monument of his own—again on his own terms—in the Children's Cancer Hospital. He left his own monument in the record books, too. He committed himself to becoming the greatest hitter in the game, and for two decades he made the Red Sox exciting in the sheer anticipation of his next turn at bat.
>
> He opened his last season with perhaps the longest home run of his career and he closed it with perhaps the most dramatic.
>
> So the old order passeth and an era of austerity has settled upon the Red Sox franchise.
>
> And now Boston knows how England felt when it lost India.

It still goes.

XIX

The Homecoming

It was the Ted we've all waited to see. There is a joy in living now that wasn't there before. The anger is gone. It was, "It's okay." It was, "Hi, mom, I'm home." What he was really saying was "I always knew you loved me, and I really loved you, too." It was more than a reconciliation; it was a homecoming. The door was open, and there he was. But what a road he had to travel to get there.

—LIB DOOLEY

On May 12, 1991, Ted Williams returned to Fenway Park to be honored again. Unless you believe there is a Divine Hand working these things out, it was only by the sheerest of coincidences that Ted Williams Day in Boston happened to fall on Mother's Day.

It was no coincidence, however, that he was being honored on the fiftieth anniversary of the wonderful season of 1941. Or that it was being held on the day after Ted Williams and Joe DiMaggio, those twin ornaments of the golden age, had brought the curtain down on that era by embracing at home plate.

Nor was it by accident that Ted's son, John Henry, and his daughter, Claudia, the children of his third marriage, were there to see him being honored.

Over the years, Ted had come back to Boston rarely, and then almost exclusively in the service of the Jimmy Fund. The turning point for him had come in 1982, when George Sullivan decided that the time had come to hold Boston's first old-timers' day. "The first player I called was Ted Williams, because without Williams there was no sense." After no more than fifteen minutes of the obligatory moaning and groaning, Ted gave in. "Okay, damnit," he said, with his customary graciousness. "I'll do it."

As long as he was doing it, he stole the show. Not with his bat, but—surprise, surprise—with his glove. The game wasn't a minute old before Mike Andrews blooped a ball to short left field, and Ted came loping in, with that familiar gangling stride of his, coming on . . . coming on . . . coming on . . . and just as everybody was envisioning another broken collarbone, he reached down and made the catch off his shoe tops.

After the game, Ted was ecstatic. "I want to tell you something, you blankety-blank," he roared at Sullivan. "When you called me up a month ago, I didn't want any part of this blankety-blank. When I woke up this morning in the blankety-blank hotel, I didn't want any part of it. I want to tell you now that this is one of the best days of my life."

It marked a turning point in a far more important respect. It was the day on which Ted Williams began to get his son back.

For a man who had always lamented his lack of a close family life while he was growing up and had openly envied those who had one, Ted had managed to come to the sixty-fourth year of his life—the final year before old age sets in, as these things are reckoned at the Social Security office—with no family life to warm his final years.

His three marriages had ended in divorce. Technically, the first marriage lasted eleven years, although to all practical purposes it was over by the time his daughter was born. Two years after his retirement from baseball, he married Lee Howard, a socialite model from Chicago. For both of them it was a second marriage, and it foundered almost from the start. She had been accustomed to a lively social life, and Ted had her buried down in the isle of Islamorada. "He gets up at six in the morning, goes fishing, comes home, and is in bed by nine o'clock," a friend recalls. "During spring training she was so grateful to anybody who came up and talked to her that your heart went out to her." The grounds for divorce were that Ted had "made life unbearable for her" with his "constant obscene criticism." Sounds right. His first wife had divorced him for making her life with him "an intolerable burden and physical impossibility."

In 1968, he married Delores Wettach, who was identified, incorrectly, as an airline stewardess. Ted met her on a plane, all right, but she was not a stewardess; she was a fellow passenger. She was also a former Miss Vermont, a model who had been on the cover of *Vogue*, and a trained nurse. Also an outdoors girl who could fish and hunt—and swear—with the best of them. Literally, a woman for all seasons. In addition, she had never heard of Ted Williams. Who could ask for anything more?

"I thought that would last," says Bill Crowley the onetime Sox publicity man, "because she was not only very attractive but also came across to me as a tough dame." Crowley met her, in a manner of speaking, in the winter of 1969, at the time that baseball was holding its centennial anniversary dinner at the White House. "You had a big head table full of Hall of Famers sitting there, and Williams, who is living right across the street at the Watergate, hasn't shown up." Ted had learned at the last moment that Joe DiMaggio was going to be named the Player of the Century, and even though Ted was getting Hitter of the Century, he had informed his old pal Joe Reichler that he wasn't coming. Reichler, who had become the chief assistant to the baseball commissioner, had come to Crowley for help. "I'm going to call him," Reichler told Crowley. "And Delores doesn't want me to. She's saying, 'To hell with him. I'll take the award.'" What Reichler wanted Crowley to do was to keep her from interfering while he was making the call.

"Dumbest thing I ever did in my life," Crowley says. "I'm wrestling with this woman out in the corridor, and she's using language I had never associated with a lady before. I can hear Joe saying, 'Ted, I don't care that you have to wear a tux. . . . You don't have to wear a tie.' Then he's saying, 'I'll change to a sweater, too, what's the difference? You should be over here.' And she's saying, 'Tell the dirty so-and-so the hell with that, I'll take the award for him.' She's pulling away, I'm trying to hold on to her, and Reichler hangs up the phone and says, 'He's not coming.'"

Delores Williams accepted the Hitter of the Century award for Ted that night, and Bill Crowley decided that she was just the kind of a gal who might be able to handle him.

The marriage lasted five years. John Henry was born on August 27, 1968, three days before Ted's fiftieth birthday, and a daughter, Claudia, came along three years later. Five months after John Henry was born, Ted became the manager of the Washington Senators. He was talked into it against his better judgment, he says, because Bob Short, the owner of the Senators, wooed him, chased him, and wouldn't give up. "Also, I was married to a gal who didn't know anything about baseball, and she thought it would be a great idea.'' In other words, he wanted to impress her. In his first season the Senators improved by twenty and a half games, and Ted was voted manager of the year. But even then, both Ted and his wife had come to realize that his return to baseball had been a terrible mistake.

By the final year of his four-year tenure, Ted was telling a story, with what seemed to be delight but which clearly had a sharper edge to it. Every time he called home, the story went, one of the kids would pick up the phone and ask him where he was, and Ted would say, ''At the ballpark.''

Well, over that final winter he could see that John Henry was getting away with certain things that he didn't like. ''I can see he's going to be a discipline problem. I warned him a couple of times, and finally I gave him a good slap right in the fanny, and the kid looks at me like this''—trembling lower lip—''and says, 'You go back to the ballpark.' That was the identification he had of me. I was the voice from the ballpark.''

It was not an amicable breakup. Delores Williams had come to hate baseball people with such a passion that she did not want her son to have anything to do with them. So strong were her feelings, it was said, that she didn't even want him to play baseball when he visited the baseball camp that Ted had become involved with, going back to his final years in Boston. Under the divorce agreement, she had complete charge of the children's education, and it was clear that she was doing a magnificent job. ''She's a great woman,'' Ted would say. *''Can't live with her,''* he would bellow. ''But, by God, she's a great mother. She's done a great job with those kids.''

It was John Henry himself who began to force the issue when he was thirteen.

He had been four years old at the time of the divorce and he could remember very little about his father. His strongest memory was the month they had spent together in the fishing grounds of Canada when he was ten or eleven. ''My mom had kind of taught me how to fly-cast before I went up, and Dad fine-tuned me. I fly-cast so much up there, I had a groove in my finger where the line rubbed into it." John Henry says he did play a little ball at the baseball camp but lost interest when he was hit twice by pitched balls on the same spot on his thigh. "I was very homesick, and I wanted to go home. I didn't have as much fun as I could have had if I'd been a couple of years older."

He had gone to the Amazon jungle in the spring of 1982 on a school trip—that's the kind of school he was attending—got eaten alive by mosquitoes and came back to Florida early. With a couple of weeks left in the spring break, he joined his father at the Red Sox spring-training camp at Winter Haven, and went running around in a little baseball uniform.

And that brings us back to the first old-timers' game. When John Henry—and it is never John or Johnnie, always John Henry—heard that his father was going to be playing, he asked to be allowed to go down from his home in Putney, Vermont, and watch him. His mother said no, and Ted, as had become his custom, backed her up. The boy asked Johnny Pesky, his godfather, to intercede for him. "For God's sake," Pesky told Ted, "the kid wants to know his father. You've got to let him come down and see you once in a while." They worked it out. John Henry came down, was outfitted with a uniform, and designated the official "junior batboy." His mother came down with him. "I know that for sure," John Henry says, "because she took pictures, which she still has."

It was the first time John Henry had ever been in Fenway Park, let alone in a clubhouse, and from that day he was hooked.

That brings us to Lib Dooley.

Lib Dooley is the number one Red Sox fan. Officially. Her father, a wealthy cotton broker, was one of the original Royal Rooters, going back to the very beginnings of the Red Sox franchise. Lib goes back almost as far.

She certainly goes back to the beginnings with Ted. They had a private sign he'd flash to her in her box when he ran onto the field at the start of every game. A junior high school teacher, she encouraged him to read books. She provided a sympathetic ear. And so, when

John Henry wanted to know more about his father, Lib Dooley was well equipped to provide the institutional memory.

He was fifteen years old when he suddenly asked her, "Was my father really great?"

"You're joking," she said.

When it became clear that he wasn't joking she began to fill him in about his father's career. And about the hammering he had taken from the Boston press.

When she was finished he said, "Do you think I could be a ball-player?"

"Yes," she said. "But you should have started yesterday. Get going, kid."

The way Lib sees it, his mother was wise enough to realize that the boy had reached the age where she was going to have to loosen the reins or run the risk of losing him. "He wants to be with his father," Lib says. "They love each other."

So John Henry went down to Winter Haven and worked out at first base. He had some talent, but it was obvious that he was starting too late. When he was in Boston he'd stay with the Peskys, and in spring training it was Pesky, even more than his father—who would hit grounders to him and work him out. Not only was he starting late, says Pesky, he was starting at a time when he was growing so fast that he wasn't coordinated. Nevertheless, he came to love the baseball environment so much that he would cut his college classes, come down to Fenway Park, and ask the people around the park not to tell his father. He didn't have to worry. They loved him in the Red Sox front office. Everybody loved him. He was the image of Ted at the same age, only taller (he is now six-five) and better looking.

Eddie Kasko, the director of the Red Sox farm system, came across a photograph that had been taken of Ted while he was at North Carolina pre-flight during World War II. A posed shot of Ted, in full football regalia, leaping up as if he is about to throw a pass. Kasko hung the photo, framed, behind his desk, and the first time Ted came in he asked him if he knew who it was. Ted didn't have the slightest idea.

John Henry, who had come walking in behind him, said, "It's you, Dad." How had he been able to tell, asked the astonished father. "It looks just like me," said the son.

The relationship with his son has transformed Ted. On that, everybody is in complete agreement. "Ted has finally become civilized" is the way it's put. "John Henry is the apple of his eye." The father was teaching his son how to fish. (Ted's urge to hunt has diminished with age.) The son was learning new things about his father all the time. "The first thing I learned," John Henry says, "is that when he walks into a room, it's different from when anyone else walks into a room." That's not a bad thing for a father to have his son see.

In May of 1991, John Henry was a senior at the University of Maine, majoring in marketing, and the two were closer than ever. In a manner of speaking, they were in business together. With the explosion of the baseball memorabilia craze and the publicity attending the fiftieth anniversary of his .400 season, the Kid's kid had got his father to agree to put him in charge of exploiting the marketing opportunities. John Henry's partner and mentor was Brian Interland, who is an important enough figure in the recording industry to have a hundred or so gold and platinum records kicking around the house. He is also such an impassioned fan of Ted Williams that his den is devoted to what is probably the largest collection of Williams memorabilia extant.

Brian Interland's relationship with Ted comes under the heading of "A Boyhood Dream Come True." With Brian, it happened twice. As a nine-year-old kid attending a pregame clinic the Red Sox were conducting for Little Leaguers, Brian became one of the three kids plucked out of the stands and brought down to the dugout to have his picture taken with his idol, Ted Williams. The next morning the picture appeared on the front page of the *Boston Globe,* and Brian became a totally committed fan.

Nine years later Brian was a freshman at Northeastern University, working at a major TV station under the university's cooperative program. Ted had just returned to Boston after hitting his five hundredth home run, and the station wanted to do a piece around him to celebrate the event. As it happened, Ted was taking advantage of an off day to work with the kids at his baseball camp, and Brian was tapped to go along with the camera crew and make himself useful. When, at the end of the day, he told Ted about all the statistics he had been keeping on him through the years, Ted invited him to come by his hotel on Sunday morning and show him what he had. "I went down there at eleven-thirty, and he said, 'Jump in the car, Slug, and let's see what you got.' I couldn't believe he was saying it. From that point on, we developed a relationship that changed my life. Gave me confidence that if I could get along with Ted Williams I could get along with anyone."

Through this connection with Ted, Brian got to do the statistics at Fenway Park for Curt Gowdy, and before long he was also keeping the stats for the Celtics, at Boston Garden.

Just as with Bill Starr, who had gone on to become the most successful builder in San Diego, it was his association with Ted Williams that Interland most cherished as he went on to become an increasingly significant figure in the record business. Because of Ted, he rented a house in Islamorada. "I would go down there with my kid, and he'd invite us over to his house for dinner. He'd be buttering my kid's bread, and I'd have a flashback to the Little Leaguer brought down into the dugout, and I'd think, Ted Williams is buttering my kid's bread."

With Ted Williams Day coming up, Interland took a year's leave from his consulting firm to form a company with John Henry, which they called Grand Slam Marketing, Inc. The first item they had come up with was an illustrated T-shirt to commemorate Ted Williams Day.

And so now we have come back to Ted Williams Day. In one respect, the date was, in fact, fortuitous. Ted had already agreed to take part in an old-timers' game—the Upper Deck Heroes of the Past—commemorating the "Wonderful Year of 1941" and starring Ted Williams and Joe DiMaggio. The old-timers' game was scheduled for Saturday, May 11. The Red Sox had also been planning to commemorate the season, later in the year, by holding their own Day for Ted.

Belatedly, Ted agreed. His only stipulation was that he would do both games over the same weekend and with as little hullabaloo as possible.

"He was totally cooperative," Dick Bresciani, the Red Sox publicity man, says. "When he got into town on Friday night, he said that whatever we wanted him to do, he would do. He was fully prepared to wear a uniform, but DiMaggio didn't want to, and Ted didn't want to do anything that might seem disrespectful of Joe's wishes." Ted enjoyed himself immensely, both in the clubhouse and on the field. The current crop of Boston players knew him because he had been the Red Sox batting coach in spring training, off and on, for thirty years (although they did have a disconcerting way of addressing him as Mr. Williams). With the old-timers, it was all laughter and badinage. "I want to thank you, Ted," Tommy Henrich said, as they were assembling for a group photograph in center field. "For what?" asked Ted. "For not calling me Bush," said Henrich. Which happened to be what Ted, as a brash rookie, had called Henrich the first time they met. Everybody who worked at the park in any capacity seemed to be milling around on the field. Ted signed everything put in front of him; posed with anybody who asked.

Joe DiMaggio, however, was nowhere to be seen. The rumor was around, almost to the last minute, that he wasn't coming. Presumably he was peeved at the Upper Deck people for releasing word that he was going to be there before he had agreed to come. As it was, DiMaggio came late and remained up in the Red Sox offices. He looked very frail, and the word was that he was suffering from a depression. He had insisted on massive security to make sure nobody harassed him, and he was whisked away in a waiting limousine as soon as the ceremonies were over. But—and make no mistake about this—it was Joe DiMaggio's presence, together with Ted Williams's, that made the day.

The plan was for the two of them to be brought out through the equipment door in center field on golf carts. A buffet had been set up for them in the equipment area while they waited. As the other old-timers were being introduced, Bill Parillo of the *Providence Journal,* having been tipped off to where they were, went around beneath the stands. "There they were sitting in Joe's golf cart, on a little down-slope, and Ted had his arm around him. If they'd had a photographer there, they would have had one of the greatest pictures ever taken."

Although Parillo knew Ted well, his instincts told him that to intrude on that private moment would be a mistake. So, he stood in the shadows and listened. "Williams was telling him about some of the old-timers who were there. 'Henrich is here, he looks great. Looks tremendous.'" And DiMaggio, looking old and somewhat distracted, would say, "Oh yeah? That right?"

When the time came to introduce them, the grounds keepers began to roll up the door and Ted went back to his own cart. Out of the gate they came, on cue, to be driven off in opposite directions, DiMaggio down the right-field line and Ted down the left-field line. They rode around the park that way, converging slowly toward home plate while the crowd went wild.

When they reached home plate, Ted went over and embraced him. Joe allowed himself to be embraced.

Don Fitzpatrick, who had served as batboy and clubhouse man for both of them, had come running out to the dugout to watch the proceedings. "I was engrossed to where I was living in another era. Teddy seemed to be so happy, he really was, and if you know him you were happy for him, and you're also happy for yourself that you did know him. If you hadn't met him it was something that you really missed. Joe DiMaggio and Teddy, when they hugged each other there were tears in his eyes. Mine, too."

He was not the only one. "Oh, the people in the stands," Johnny Pesky says. "The older people were just crying. I'm getting goose bumps just thinking about it. Here's Ted seventy-two years old, Joe is seventy-six, because Dominic is seventy-four. Bobby is seventy-three and I'm seventy-one. Oh, it was something."

Ted had not only wanted John Henry and Claudia to be there; he had arranged for them to throw out the first ball. As his two children were walking out to the mound, Ted pushed his way to the front of the dugout. "Look out," he said, clearing a path. "I want to see this." Claudia is tall and beautiful. She was educated in boarding schools and was about to go to Paris to study art. Two handsome kids, and they were his. They had both been out the previous day, practicing, and—like any Little League father—he wanted them to look good in front of the crowd.

Brian Interland, as the foremost student of Ted Williams, was watching Ted himself just as intently, and to Interland it was as if Ted were going back and forth through the generations. "It was like he was seeing his father and mother again as he was looking at his kids. Who aren't kids anymore, of course, either."

It was the second time Brian had seen that look that day. While Ted had been in the TV booth earlier in the day, Interland had shown him a picture he had just found of Sam Williams with his second family. Ted looked at the picture for a long time, in deepening silence, and then called John Henry in and told him to find Claudia. "I want her to see her grandfather."

On Ted Williams Day, on Sunday, 33,196 fans turned out. Each of them received a commemorative folder in which was printed a collage of pictures, news clips, and all-purpose memorabilia encompassing Ted's career. The collage had been pasted together by Interland and turned into a finished work by the artist Ray Ward.

It is a mark of what Ted Williams had done that the players treasured the commemorative folder every bit as much as the fans did. When Ted went into manager Joe Morgan's office, such Red Sox superstars as Roger Clemens, Wade Boggs, and Jack Clark lined up outside like Little Leaguers to have Ted autograph it for them. Most of them had more than one folder for him to sign.

Ted has a satellite dish on his house that enables him to watch Red Sox games on cable. For two days he had been able to relate to the players directly by letting them know that he had been staying in touch. "Wade," he said. "On TV, you swung at a three-and-one pitch that was way down and in, and I've never seen you swing at a bad pitch like that on three and one." Boggs knew the pitch he was talking about, all right. He had thought it was going to be a slider, he explained. "And it broke down on me instead."

Players from the visiting Texas Rangers came over and also stood in line to have their folders signed. When Julio Franco (who went on to win the batting championship) came into the office, Ted went into an imitation of Franco's contorted stance, in which the bat is held high and twisted down around his neck. "How the hell do you hit the ball when you get that bat over your head like this?" Then he said, "You do a great job, at that, even though I can't believe you hold the bat that way."

Scott Chiamparino of the Texas pitching staff came over too. On Saturday, Chiamparino had approached Ted, alongside the Rangers dugout, with a picture of Ted, looking unfashionably portly, in a Washington uniform. "Where did you get that lousy picture?" Ted had bellowed. "I'm not going to sign that." This time Chiamparino had a picture of Ted hitting a home run in 1949. "Mr. Williams," he said, "I went down to one of these souvenir places last night, and I got this special." "Okay," Ted said after he signed. "Now, I've been watching your breaking ball. I want you to talk to me about the Bernoulli effect. Remember yesterday I said to you, what is the Bernoulli effect on pitches, and why do they break certain ways? Now, let's get into that." And for the next few minutes the talk was all about wind currents and aerodynamics.

When the last folder had been signed, he went out into the locker room to find Tim Naehring, a rookie shortstop who was in the midst of a godawful 0-for-37 streak. "Hey, everybody goes through these things." Ted told him. "Try to relax. Choke up and try to hit the ball through the middle. That's what I did when I was in a slump. You're a good ballplayer, I've been watching you. Hang in there. You're going to be all right."

Ted hates to make speeches, and because he hates them he prepares them with infinite care. The night before the event, he roughed out an outline of what he wanted to say and asked John Henry to jot down some ideas of his own.

Early in the morning, with John Henry sitting on the edge of Ted's bed, they went over their notes. John Henry's input wasn't really needed. "He showed me his speech—which I still have—and then read it to me." As he was coming to the end, Ted told him, "Right here, I'm going to take a hat, and I'm going to tip it to the fans."

When John Henry told him what a great idea that would be, Ted said, "Don't tell anybody. Just get me a hat."

John Henry: "After all the hustle and bustle of the day, we were on our way out onto the field when he realized that I'd completely forgotten about the hat. So I went back and got one. Then I ran out to him, on the field, and he stuck it in his pocket quick so no one could see it. Then he went on with his speech, and I got goose bumps watching him do it."

In his brief speech, he did two things. He made his peace with the fans, and he did not allow the sportswriters completely off the hook.

Again he was introduced by Curt Gowdy. "Thirty-one years ago," Gowdy began, "I stood here and paid tribute to Ted . . ."

"We'll never see another like him," Gowdy declaimed at the end. "What a career, what a man. Here he is, Ted Williams."

Grinning broadly while he was waiting for the applause to die down, Ted acknowledged the cheers by taking one of those shadow swings for which he was famous. He had worked hard on the speech, and it was well crafted. He started by saying that as a rookie in 1939 he had played his first game against Lou Gehrig. "I was a rookie in right field, and the first ball ever hit to me was a line drive by Lou Gehrig. Very shortly after that, he had to retire because of ill health, and I was there that day when he stood before a huge crowd at Yankee Stadium, and he said that he thought that day he was the luckiest man on the face of the earth, and he was dying, and very shortly after that he did die."

Then the transition from Lou Gehrig Day to Ted Williams Day: "You can imagine today how I must feel, fifty years after being lucky enough to hit .400, and I know fifty years is a long time, but it never seemed very long to me when I was in Fenway Park, and to be here with all the great fans that are here in Fenway Park.''

Next he said, ''I used to get just a little annoyed when some of my teammates would kid me about how lucky a hitter I was, and I didn't mind that because I knew how lucky I was. But when they started writing or when they would even intimate in any way that I was hardheaded, that did bother me a little bit, and it really annoyed me when the Knights''—he pointed in two quick jabs up to the press box— ''elaborated on it in print. That did annoy me a lot.''

He digressed for a moment to express his gratitude, respect, and love for his old teammates sitting behind him.

And then he said: ''I'm especially thankful, though, to have a chance . . . so they can never write ever again that I was hardheaded, never write again that I never tipped my hat to the crowd . . .'' He reached into his pocket, came out with the cap, threw back his head, and laughed. ''. . . because today . . . I tip my hat to *a-a-a-l-l* the people in New England, without question the greatest sports fans on earth.''

As he finished, he turned his head away. ''There were tears shed right there,'' Interland says. ''It was a profession of love on one side and of homage on the other. There is no question but that he was moved at seeing that he still got the same response. And most of the people there had never seen him play.''

About the cap: The first player John Henry had encountered as he walked down the ramp to the dugout was Mike Greenwell, who just happened to be the latest in the line of Red Sox left-fielders that ran from Williams through Carl Yastrzemski and Jim Rice. But that happy little footnote of royal succession faded away when Greenwell's cap turned out to be too small. So did Jody Reed's. Entering the dugout, John Henry approached Jeff Reardon, the ace relief man. ''I was lucky enough to be standing there because I wanted to see the ceremonies,'' Reardon says. ''As his son walked out, he told me that his dad wanted to use my hat. Then Ted put it in his back pocket and sat on it.''

Although Reardon had grown up in nearby Rhode Island, he had

been only five years old when Ted retired, and the historical significance of a tip of the cap from Ted Williams was completely lost on
him. Upon finishing his speech, Ted handed the cap to Bud Leavitt.
"Hey, Bud," Reardon said, "that's my game hat. I'll get you another
one."

He wanted the hat back, Reardon says, because he had a perfect
save record to that point, "and I'm superstitious." It was Fitzie who
told him that the cap had just become too valuable to be worn. And
then had to explain why.

"Ted signed the bill of the cap for me," says Reardon, "and the
next day I had two offers. No way. I have it in my trophy case with
the picture of him waving the hat during the ceremony. I'll never get
rid of it."

At Dick Bresciani's request, Ted had agreed to hold a brief pro
forma press conference before he went down to the luxury boxes to
see Mrs. Yawkey and greet the sponsors of the event and their families. To the surprise of everybody he enjoyed the exchanges with the
sportswriters so much that Bresciani couldn't get him out of there. "I
never saw Ted like this," George Sullivan says. "Bresciani was
literally tugging at his sleeve. After he had put Dick off a couple of
times, he said, evenly, without smiling, 'I'll take five more questions.' And even then he stayed around to talk some more and sign
autographs."

Bresciani had never seen Ted in such a talkative mood, either.
"Having grown up with the stories about the so-called feud with the
media, it was interesting to me that he didn't want to leave. Some of
the writers came up afterward for autographs, and I said sorry, he
didn't have the time, and Ted said, no, no, no, I'll sign them. And he
signed everything they put in front of him."

To George Sullivan, who had seen Ted under far less congenial
circumstances, the press conference was the final stamp Ted was putting on the day. In his speech, Ted had paid both the writers and
himself the respect of not attempting to invalidate their past relationship ("Even today, if you ask Ted he will tell you that he doesn't see

how he could have acted any different''). In his press conference, as Sullivan saw it, he was turning the page on a new generation.

Fourteen months later, he came full circle with another homecoming in San Diego. The occasion was the 1992 All-Star Game, held in San Diego on July 15, and once again the game was to be preceded by an Upper Deck old-timers' game, featuring the appearances of Ted Williams and Joe DiMaggio. Boston had celebrated Ted Williams Day by renaming Lansdowne Street—the historic street behind the left-field wall—Ted Williams Way. The state of California upped the ante by naming a nine-mile stretch of route 56 as Ted Williams Parkway.

To Ted's way of thinking, he was not only rounding out his career by returning to the old hometown but was making his farewell to baseball.

Between the Boston and the San Diego homecomings he had suffered a stroke—not a disabling stroke, but hardly the minor stroke it had originally appeared to be, either.

He had driven down to his secretary's home in the Tampa area on the morning of December 2, a distance of some seventy miles from his home in Citrus Hills, to catch up on a huge volume of mail that had collected. Actually, there had been a failure of communication, and he wasn't supposed to meet her until later that afternoon. ''When I got down there the house was closed, and just about that time I got a headache, and it was quite severe. I always brag that I don't have any headaches, and I still don't. But this was different, and I said I'll check into a motel because I was going to be staying there a couple of days anyway.'' The pain persisted, and he went to a drugstore for some aspirin.

''And I came on back, and I took two, and then I took two more, and then I took two more, and then I realized something a little different was happening to me. I couldn't see very well, and I thought it was something happening in my eye. In fact, I'd lost some of my peripheral vision and I didn't realize it. But I knew I couldn't see as well.'' For the rest of the day and night he did not get out of bed, even to eat.

There is a well-known instinct in humans, not dissimilar to the spawning instinct of the salmon. It goes something like this: *If I'm going to be sick, I'm going to be sick in my own bed.* "It probably wasn't a very smart thing to do, but I felt I could do it, so I got in the car the next morning and drove home." Not a smart thing to have done, it was going to develop, at all.

The next day he went to the hospital to have his eyes examined by an ophthalmologist. A day after that he was in the hospital undergoing treatment for a blocked artery. There still didn't seem to be that much to worry about, though. The loss of peripheral vision was permanent, he was told. Beyond that, he had only to return to the hospital in a month and have the diseased artery reamed out. It wasn't that easy. He had expected to be in the hospital for three days. He was there for more than a week. "The carotid artery, the main artery that goes up to the right side of my head, was pretty nearly totally blocked, and they couldn't go in there with some of this newer procedure and just ream it out. They had to go in there and open it up and scrape it out and clean it out. A very intricate surgical procedure and very, very sensitive. That thing was ninety-five percent blocked, and if it blocks, of course, it completely cripples you. Paralyzes you on the left side . . . or you die." The warning stroke had been, in a manner of speaking, a stroke of luck.

It was going to take a full year, he was warned, before he would be able to get up in the morning without feeling dizzy. "But my vascular system and heart are in great shape. I'm going to be all right, the doctor said. Got to watch my diet and try to lose weight, that's all I can do."

The marketing appearances were cut down and rigorously controlled. John Henry took upon himself the toughest of all tasks, the task of being the rotten kid who says no. But that didn't bother him. "He can be gregarious, and maybe it's not even a job for him to be surrounded by people. But it gets tiring. He just wants to go to bed and relax, wants to go fishing, wants to do what he enjoys."

Fishing is the way they are able to get away and spend some time together. "I'm spending an awful lot of time with Dad now, which is great. One reason we started this company, it keeps him very involved with me, both ways, and Dad enjoys watching me grow up, and I get to enjoy Dad's company.''

When John Henry graduated from the University of Maine at the end of the year, becoming the first member of the Williams family to earn a college degree, Ted wept openly.

Ted has always been able to perform acts of great kindness and charity, but he had always held back from displays of affection. But now he and his son kiss and hug when they part. ''We're so close,'' Ted says. ''God, I enjoy every minute of the time I look at him. He's so bright and honest. And so nice. I want all my friends to get to know him.''

''I want to take good care of Dad,'' John Henry says. ''I'm going to be watching him, making sure he's protected. He's too easy, too nice to everybody. I'm a buffer zone for him.''

The homecoming in San Diego turned into something of a reunion as Ted met with the guys from his old high-school team and took them all out for dinner at a Mexican restaurant. Among the group were Les Cassie and Roy Engle. And Frank Cushing, who had shagged for him as a small kid and become a close friend while they were both in the Marines. And Earl Keller, who had covered him that first year and a half with the Padres. ''I've never forgotten you guys,'' Ted told them. ''I've always loved you.'' His long absences from San Diego, he wanted them to know, had nothing to do with them.

But mostly he was spending his free time retracing his boyhood experiences for John Henry. They went out to Mission Valley, where he had hunted jackrabbits as a kid, and found that instead of the wilderness he had known it was covered by big hotels and golf courses. He showed him North Park (renamed Ted Williams Park at the time of his election to the Hall of Fame). ''John Henry has been extremely interested in everything that has happened to me, as any young fellow would be. Wants to know as much about me as he can. And it's a kick to me.''

The return to San Diego was made particularly memorable by a visit to the old house on Utah Street. And for John Henry that was the best of all.

The house was now owned by a woman from Maine. "I'm Ted Williams," he said as he entered. "I know," the woman said. How could she not know, when he was accompanied by a camera crew from ESPN? They were there, though, only to shoot his entrance. After that, both they and the boyhood friends who had come to the door with him departed, to leave Ted to visit on his own.

When he came out, he could see how disappointed his son was not to have gone in with him. So he went back and asked the lady from Maine for permission to give his son a personal tour.

"I sat back and watched," the Kid's kid says. "Dad was as happy as I've ever seen him at seeing his old buddies again, and there was never a bigger thrill in my life than going into the house where he grew up. I saw his room. I saw where he slept, and I was there with Dad to see it. I had already looked where the field was. The field was his sanctuary, but where it really was was right there in the house. I mean, I saw his roots. And that was tremendous."

Ted saw that, too. "He drooled over every bedroom. He drooled over the little living room. He drooled over everything."

You would have thought Ted would be looking at it through his son's eyes. But that wasn't so. His son, after all, was almost twenty-four years old, four years older than Ted had been when he left to join the Red Sox, and Ted was seeing the nicely kept house through the eyes of the unhappy little kid who still lived inside him.

"I remembered how rundown it was until I made enough money so that I could send home and get it fixed up, and got it fixed up pretty nice, so that I wasn't ashamed to have anybody come into it."

And why not? That little kid had made Ted Williams who he was. "You did all right by me," that kid could well have told him.

All things considered.

Appendixes

APPENDIX A
Career Batting

YEAR	TM/L	G	AB	R	H	2B	3B	HR	HR%	RBI	BB	SO	AVG.	OBP	SLG	PRO	HPB	Pinch Hit AB	Pinch Hit H
1939	Bos-A	149	565	131	185	44	11	31	5.5	145	107	64	.327	.436	.609	1.045	2	0	0
1940	Bos-A	144	561	134	193	43	14	23	4.1	113	96	54	.344	.442	.594	1.036	3	0	0
1941	Bos-A	143	456	135	185	33	3	37	8.1	120	145	27	.406	.551	.735	1.286	3	9	3
1942	Bos-A	150	522	141	186	34	5	36	6.9	137	145	51	.356	.499	.648	1.147	4	0	0
1946	Bos-A	150	514	142	176	37	8	38	7.4	123	156	44	.342	.497	.667	1.164	2	0	0
1947	Bos-A	156	528	125	181	40	9	32	6.1	114	162	47	.343	.499	.634	1.133	2	0	0
1948	Bos-A	137	509	124	188	44	3	25	4.9	127	126	41	.369	.497	.615	1.112	3	2	0
1949	Bos-A	155	566	150	194	39	3	43	7.6	159	162	48	.343	.490	.650	1.141	2	0	0
1950	Bos-A	89	334	82	106	24	1	28	8.4	97	82	21	.317	.452	.647	1.099	0	1	1
1951	Bos-A	148	531	109	169	28	4	30	5.6	126	144	45	.318	.464	.556	1.019	0	0	0
1952	Bos-A	6	10	2	4	0	1	1	10.0	3	2	2	.400	.500	.900	1.400	0	4	1
1953	Bos-A	37	91	17	37	6	0	13	14.3	34	19	10	.407	.509	.901	1.410	0	10	2
1954	Bos-A	117	386	93	133	23	1	29	7.5	89	136	32	.345	.516	.635	1.151	1	4	2
1955	Bos-A	98	320	77	114	21	3	28	8.8	83	91	24	.356	.501	.703	1.204	2	2	1
1956	Bos-A	136	400	71	138	28	2	24	6.0	82	102	39	.345	.479	.605	1.084	1	20	5
1957	Bos-A	132	420	96	163	28	1	38	9.0	87	119	43	.388	.528	.731	1.259	5	5	3
1958	Bos-A	129	411	81	135	23	2	26	6.3	85	98	49	.328	.462	.584	1.046	4	11	3
1959	Bos-A	103	272	32	69	15	0	10	3.7	43	52	27	.254	.377	.419	.796	2	24	11
1960	Bos-A	113	310	56	98	15	0	29	9.4	72	75	41	.316	.454	.645	1.099	3	19	1
Total	19	2292	7706	1798	2654	525	71	521	6.8	1839	2019	709	.344	.483	.634	1.116	39	111	33

Career Batting at Fenway Park

YEAR	G	AB	R	H	TB	2B	3B	HR	RBI	BB	HPB	AVG.	OBP	SLG	PRO
1939	75	277	74	95	169	22	5	14	68	52	2	.343	.450	.610	1.060
1940	76	297	69	101	166	28	5	9	60	47	2	.340	.434	.559	.992
1941	75	243	72	104	186	21	2	19	62	80	3	.428	.574	.765	1.339
1942	75	261	73	93	168	21	3	16	68	64	2	.356	.486	.644	1.130
1946	76	266	74	98	181	21	4	18	69	73	0	.368	.504	.680	1.185
1947	81	277	67	92	176	24	6	16	63	84	2	.332	.490	.635	1.126
1948	66	239	57	88	140	23	1	9	66	66	3	.368	.510	.586	1.096
1949	77	272	87	95	193	27	1	23	86	91	0	.349	.512	.710	1.222
1950	43	160	50	57	118	13	0	16	56	41	0	.356	.488	.738	1.225
1951	73	268	69	108	190	22	3	18	81	64	0	.403	.518	.709	1.227
1952	4	6	1	3	6	0	0	1	3	1	0	.500	.571	1.000	1.571
1953	19	47	10	17	45	4	0	8	18	10	0	.362	.474	.957	1.431
1954	58	186	48	69	129	12	0	16	39	72	1	.371	.548	.694	1.292
1955	54	172	48	67	125	11	1	15	47	52	1	.390	.533	.727	1.260
1956	72	205	39	74	127	19	2	10	43	59	0	.361	.504	.620	1.123
1957	63	206	42	83	138	19	0	12	36	52	2	.403	.527	.670	1.197
1958	66	207	47	68	116	14	2	10	41	57	3	.329	.479	.560	1.040
1959	52	134	14	37	56	10	0	3	21	20	1	.276	.374	.418	.792
1960	60	164	32	54	107	8	0	15	38	47	0	.329	.479	.652	1.131
Tot.	1165	3887	973	1403	2536	319	35	248	965	1032	22	.361	.497	.652	1.150

Career Batting on the Road

YEAR	G	AB	R	H	TB	2B	3B	HR	RBI	BB	HPB	AVG.	OBP	SLG	PRO
1939	74	288	57	90	175	22	6	17	77	55	0	.313	.423	.608	1.030
1940	68	264	65	92	167	15	9	14	53	49	1	.348	.452	.633	1.085
1941	68	213	63	81	149	12	1	18	58	65	0	.380	.525	.700	1.225
1942	75	261	68	93	170	13	2	20	69	81	2	.356	.512	.651	1.163
1946	74	248	68	78	162	16	4	20	54	83	2	.315	.489	.653	1.143
1947	75	251	58	89	159	16	3	16	51	78	0	.355	.508	.633	1.141
1948	71	270	67	100	173	21	2	16	61	60	0	.370	.485	.641	1.126
1949	78	294	63	99	175	12	2	20	73	71	2	.337	.469	.595	1.064
1950	46	174	32	49	98	11	1	12	41	41	0	.282	.419	.563	.982
1951	75	263	40	61	105	6	1	12	45	80	0	.232	.411	.399	.810
1952	2	4	1	1	3	0	1	0	0	1	0	.250	.400	.750	1.150
1953	18	44	7	20	37	2	0	5	16	9	0	.455	.547	.841	1.388
1954	59	200	45	64	116	11	1	13	50	64	0	.320	.485	.580	1.065
1955	44	148	29	47	100	10	2	13	36	39	1	.318	.463	.676	1.138
1956	64	195	32	64	115	9	0	14	39	43	1	.328	.452	.590	1.042
1957	69	214	54	80	169	9	1	26	51	67	3	.374	.528	.790	1.318
1958	63	204	34	67	124	9	0	16	44	41	1	.328	.443	.608	1.051
1959	51	138	18	32	58	5	0	7	22	32	1	.232	.380	.420	.800
1960	53	146	24	44	93	7	0	14	34	28	3	.301	.424	.637	1.061
Tot.	1127	3819	825	1251	2348	296	36	273	874	987	17	.328	.468	.615	1.082

Minor League Totals

YEAR	CLUB	AVG.	G	AB	R	H	2B	3B	HR	TB	RBI	BB	SO
1936	San Diego	.271	42	107	18	29	8	2	0	41	11	—	—
1937	San Diego	.291	138	454	66	132	24	2	23	229	98	—	—
1938	Minneapolis	.366	148	528	130	193	30	9	43	370	142	114	75

All-Star Totals

YEAR	POS	AVG.	AB	R	H	2B	3B	HR	RBI	BB	SO	E	PO	A
1940	LF	.000	2	0	0	0	0	0	0	1	0	0	3	0
1941	LF	.500	4	1	2	1	0	1	4	1	1	1	3	0
1942	LF	.250	4	0	1	0	0	0	0	0	0	0	0	0
1946	LF	1.000	4	4	4	0	0	2	5	1	0	0	1	0
1947	LF	.500	4	0	2	1	0	0	0	0	1	0	3	0
1948	PH	—	0	0	0	0	0	0	0	0	0	0	0	0
1949	LF	.000	2	1	0	0	0	0	0	2	1	0	1	0
1950	LF	.250	4	0	1	0	0	0	1	0	1	0	2	0
1951	LF	.333	3	0	1	0	1	0	0	1	1	0	3	0
1954	PH-LF	.000	2	1	0	0	0	0	0	1	2	0	2	0
1955	LF	.333	3	1	1	0	0	0	0	1	0	0	1	0
1956	LF	.250	4	1	1	0	0	1	2	0	1	0	2	0

All-Star Totals (cont.)

YEAR	POS	AVG.	AB	R	H	2B	3B	HR	RBI	BB	SO	E	PO	A
1957	LF	.000	3	1	0	0	0	0	0	1	0	0	2	0
1958	PH-LF	.000	2	0	0	0	0	0	0	0	1	0	1	0
1959	PH	—	0	0	0	0	0	0	0	1	0	0	0	0
1959	LF	.000	3	0	0	0	0	0	0	0	0	0	0	0
1960	PH	.000	1	0	0	0	0	0	0	0	0	0	0	0
1960	PH	1.000	1	0	1	0	0	0	0	0	0	0	0	0
Tot.		.304	46	10	14	2	1	4	12	11	9	1	24	0

1946 World Series Totals

	AVG.	G	AB	R	H	2B	3B	HR	RBI	BB	SO	E
1946	.200	7	25	2	5	0	0	0	1	5	5	0

APPENDIX B

Ted Williams's .400 Season in 1941

	HOME-AWAY	APRIL			AB	R	H	2B	3B	HR	RBI	BB	SO	HR OFF	
1.000	H	15	*Bos* 7 Was 6	ph	1	0	1	0	0	0	1	0	0		
.500	H	16	*Bos* 8 Was 7	ph	1	0	0	0	0	0	0	0	1		
.667	A	18	*Bos* 3 Phi 2	ph	1	0	1	0	0	0	0	0	0		
	A	19	*Bos* 7 Phi 2	Did not play											
.500	A	20	*Bos* 14 Was 8	ph	1	0	0	0	0	0	0	0	0		
.400	A	21	*Was* 6 Bos 5	ph	1	0	0	0	0	0	0	0	0		
.444	A	22	*Was* 12 Bos 5		4	1	2	1	0	0	2	0	0		First start
	A	23	*NY* 4 Bos 2	Did not play											
.400	A	24	*NY* 6 Bos 3	ph	1	0	0	0	0	0	0	0	0		
	H	25	*Bos* 3 Phi	Did not play											
	H	26	*Bos* 8 Phi 1	Did not play											
.462	A	29	*Det* 5 Bos 3		3	2	2	1	0	1	0	1	0	Gorsica (1)	
.389	A	30	*Det* 12 Bos 8		5	0	1	0	0	0	1	0	0		
		MAY													
.348	A	1	Bos 15 *Det* 9		5	2	1	0	0	0	1	1	0		Low point of season; shut out by Mel Harder and Joe Heving
.307	A	2	*Cle* 7 Bos 3		3	0	0	0	0	0	0	1	0		
.333	A	3	*Cle* 4 Bos 2		3	0	1	0	0	0	0	2	0		
.334	A	4	*Bos* 11 StL 4		5	1	2	0	0	0	2	1	0		
.359	A	7	*Bos* 4 Chi 3		4	2	3	0	0	2	3	1	0	Rigney (2,3)	Wins game w/HR in 11th
.378	H	11	*Bos* 13 NY 5		6	2	3	1	0	0	1	0	0		
.375	H	12	*Bos* 8 NY 4		3	2	1	0	0	0	0	1	0		
.373	H	13	*Chi* 3 Bos 2		4	1	1	0	0	1	1	0	0	Rigney (4)	
.339	H	14	*Bos* 10 Chi 7		5	0	0	0	0	0	0	0	1		
.339	H	15	*Cle* 6 Bos 4		3	2	1	0	0	0	0	2	1		
.333	H	16	*Cle* 9 Bos 3		4	1	1	0	0	0	0	0	0		
.353	H	17	*Cle* 12 Bos 0		5	1	3	2	0	0	1	0	0		2 doubles, single off Feller

DiMaggio vs. Williams
During DiMaggio's
56-Game Streak

	DiMaggio	Williams
	.250	.333
	.375	.286
	.361	.416

			AWAY	MAY		AB	R	H	2B	3B	HR	RBI	BB	SO	HR OFF	
.347	.375	.500	H	18	Det 6 Bos 5	4	0	1	0	0	0	0	1	1		
.342	.350	.411	H	19	Det 4 Bos 2	4	1	1	0	0	1	2	0	0	Gorsica (5)	
.341	.348	.409	H	20	Bos 4 Det 2	3	1	1	0	0	0	0	1	0		
.369	.428	.407	H	21	Bos 8 StL 6	5	0	4	0	0	0	1	0	0		
.371	.438	.387	H	22	StL 4 Bos 1	4	0	2	0	0	0	0	0	0		
.374	.429	.361	A	23	Bos 9 NY 9	3	0	1	0	0	0	3	2	0		
.383	.447	.350	A	24	NY 7 Bos 6	3	3	2	0	0	0	0	2	0		
.404	.488	.341	A	25	Bos 10 NY 3	5	2	4	1	0	0	2	0	0		
.406	.489	.388	H	27	Bos 5 Phi 2	2	1	1	0	0	1	2	1	0	Hadley (6)	
.400	.469	.377			Phi 11 Bos 1	4	0	1	0	0	0	0	0	0		
.409	.481	.375	H	28	Phi 8 Bos 6	5	1	3	1	0	0	0	3	0		
.421	.500	.379	H	29	Bos 6 Phi 4	4	2	3	0	0	1	2	0	0	Knott (7)	16 innings winning HR, one on in 7th
.422	.500	.377	H	30	NY 4 Bos 3	2	2	1	1	0	0	0	2	0		
.429	.510	.379			Bos 13 NY 0	3	2	2	0	0	0	1	1	0		
.431	.507	.369	A	JUNE 1	Bos 7 Det 6	4	2	2	1	0	1	1	1	0	Rowe (8)	
.430	.500	.362			Bos 6 Det 5	5	2	2	0	0	0	3	0	0		
.426	.487	.376	A	2	Bos 9 Det 1	4	2	1	0	0	0	1	1	0		
		.364		3												
.436	.500	.354	A	5	Bos 14 Cle 1	4	4	3	0	0	1	3	2	0	Heving (9)	High point of season
.438	.500		A	6	Bos 6 Chi 3	4	2	2	0	0	1	2	0	0	Rigney (10)	
.433	.487	.368	A	7	Chi 5 Bos 4	4	1	0	0	0	0	0	1	1		
.425	.478	.374	A	8	Bos 5 Chi 3	2	0	0	0	0	0	1	3	0		Ted Lyons stops Ted's streak at 23
.418	.462	.379		10	Bos 3 Chi 0	3	1	0	0	0	0	0	1	1		
		.370														
.409	.445	.375	A	12	StL 9 Bos 4	5	0	1	0	0	0	0	0	1		
.412	.450	.377			Bos 3 StL 2	2	1	1	0	0	1	2	2	0	Niggeling (11)	
.418	.457	.376	H	14	Chi 5 Bos 2	5	0	3	1	0	0	0	0	0		
.421	.463		H	15	Bos 8 Chi 6	3	2	2	0	0	1	1	1	0	Ross (12)	
.427	.468	.368			Bos 6 Chi 4	3	2	2	1	0	0	1	1	0		
				16												

			HOME-AWAY	JUNE		AB	R	H	2B	3B	HR	RBI	BB	SO	HR OFF	
	.461	.422	H	17	Bos 14 Det 6	4	1	1	0	0	1	2	1	0	Thomas (13)	
	.465	.426			Det 8 Bos 5	1	2	1	1	0	0	0	3	0		3 walks, HPB
.364	.454	.419	H	18	Det 5 Bos 2	3	0	0	0	0	0	0	1	1		
.364	.451	.417	H	19	Bos 6 Det 4	3	0	2	1	0	0	2	1	1		
.379	.456	.421	H	20	Bos 4 StL 2	3	1	2	0	0	0	2	1	0		
.395	.449	.417	H	21	StL 13 Bos 9	2	0	0	0	0	0	0	1	0		
.391	.442	.415	H	22	Bos 7 StL 5	3	1	1	0	0	0	2	1	0		
.391	.436	.409			StL 12 Bos 3	3	0	0	0	0	0	0	1	0		
.387	.430	.404	H	24	Bos 13 Cle 2	2	2	2	0	0	1	2	3	0	Bagby (14)	
.384	.435	.408	H	25	Bos 7 Cle 2	3	2	3	0	0	0	2	1	0		
.380	.440	.413	H	26	Cle 11 Bos 8	5	2	1	0	0	0	1	0	0		
.386	.438	.412	A	27	Was 5 Bos 3	3	0	1	0	0	0	0	1	0		
.386	.436	.411	A	28	Was 3 Bos 1	3	0	2	0	0	0	0	1	0		
.383	.438	.412	A	29	Bos 13 Phi 1	4	2	2	0	0	1	2	1	0	Harris (15)	
.377	.427	.406	A		Phi 3 Bos 2	4	0	0	0	0	0	1	0	0		
				JULY												
.380	.422	.402	A	1	NY 7 Bos 2	4	0	1	0	0	0	0	0	1		
.379	.423	.403			NY 9 Bos 2	2	1	0	0	0	0	0	0	0		
.374	.421	.402	A	2	NY 8 Bos 4	3	1	1	0	0	0	1	1	0		
.372	.422	.404	A	3	Bos 5 Phi 2	4	2	2	0	0	1	2	0	0	Dean (16)	
.383	.420	.403	H	5	Bos 5 Was 0	3	1	1	1	0	0	1	1	0		
.385	.418	.402	H	6	Bos 6 Was 2	4	0	1	0	0	0	1	0	0		
.387	.425	.406	H		Bos 4 Was 3	4	2	3	2	0	0	2	0	0		
				10												
.397	.416	.399	A	11	Det 2 Bos 0	4	0	0	0	0	0	0	0	1		Buck Newsom blanks Ted, Sox Ted falls under .400
.397	.414	.397	A	12	Bos 7 Det 5	1	2	0	0	0	0	0	3	0		Ted walks 3 times before popping up. Hurts ankle sliding back to 1b

384

AVG	AWAY	Date	Game	AB	R	H	2B	3B	HR	RBI	BB	SO	HR OFF	Notes
.404	A	13	Bos 10 *Det* 2	Did not play										
.401	A		*Cle* 9 Bos 6	Did not play										
.400	A	14	*Cle* 2 Bos 1	Did not play										
.402	A		*Cle* 4 Bos 1	Did not play										
.408	A	15	Bos 6 *Cle* 2	Did not play										
.412	A	16	Bos 2 *Chi* 1	ph	1	0	0	0	0	0	1	0	0		Sac. Fly to tie game in 8th. Charged with time at bat.
	A	17	Bos 7 *Chi* 4	Did not play										
	A	18	*Chi* 4 Bos 3	Did not play										
.393	A	19	StL 9 Bos 3	ph	0	0	0	0	0	0	0	0	0		
.395	A		StL 4 Bos 3	ph	1	1	1	0	0	1	3	0	0	Niggeling (17)	3-run pinch homer
.395	A	20	StL 6 Bos 3	ph	1	0	1	0	0	0	0	0	0		
	A		StL 10 Bos 0	Did not play										
.396	H	22	*Bos* 6 Chi 2	2	1	1	0	0	1	1	1	0	Rigney (18)	Returns to lineup
.397	H	23	Chi 10 *Bos* 4	5	1	2	0	0	0	0	0	0		
.397	H	24	*Bos* 11 Chi 1	5	1	2	0	0	0	0	0	0		
.400	H	25	*Bos* 10 Cle 6	3	1	2	0	0	1	2	2	0	Hardy (19)	
.405	H	26	*Bos* 4 Cle 3	4	1	3	0	0	0	0	1	0		
.408	H	27	Cle 4 *Bos* 0	3	0	2	0	0	0	0	1	0		
.407	H	29	StL 3 *Bos* 2	3	1	1	0	0	1	2	1	1	Niggeling (20)	
.410	H	31	StL 16 *Bos* 11	3	2	2	0	0	1	4	3	0	Trotter (21)	Grand slam home run
.409	H		*Bos* 4 StL 1	3	0	1	0	0	0	0	1	0		

AUGUST

AVG	AWAY	Date	Game	AB	R	H	2B	3B	HR	RBI	BB	SO	HR OFF	Notes
.412	H	2	Det 6 *Bos* 5	3	1	2	1	0	0	0	1	0		
.410	H	3	Det 6 *Bos* 3	4	0	1	0	0	0	0	1	0		
.407	H	4	Bos 7 Phi 6	2	0	0	0	0	0	0	3	0		3 walks, 2 intentional
.408	H	5	*Bos* 6 Phi 5	4	1	2	1	0	0	2	0	0		
.403	H	6	*Bos* 6 NY 3	3	0	1	0	0	0	0	1	0		
	H		NY 3 *Bos* 1	3	0	0	0	0	0	0	0	1		
.408	H	7	*Bos* 9 NY 5	4	3	3	0	0	1	2	0	0	Gomez (22)	
.407	H	8	*Bos* 15 Was 8	3	2	1	0	0	0	2	2	0		Ends 12-game hit streak

	AWAY	AUGUST		AB	R	H	2B	3B	HR	RBI	BB	SO	HR OFF	
.407	H	9	Was 8 Bos 6	3	1	1	0	0	0	0	2	0		
.411	H	10	*Bos* 7 Was 6	4	0	3	0	1	0	0	1	0		
.410			Was 8 *Bos* 2	3	0	1	0	0	0	0	1	0		
.412	A	11	Bos 8 *NY* 0	1	1	1	0	0	0	1	4	0		4 walks, as N.Y. fans boo Yankee pitchers
.411	A	12	*NY* 4 Bos 0	3	0	1	0	0	0	0	1	2		
.413	A	13	Bos 4 Phi 0	1	0	1	0	0	0	1	4	0		4 walks from Marchildon
.410	A	14	Bos 11 *Phi* 8	5	2	1	0	0	1	3	1	0	Ferrick (23)	
.408			*Phi* 10 Bos 8	4	1	1	0	0	0	0	1	0		
.405	A	15	Bos 9 *Was* 0	2	0	0	0	0	0	0	1	1		7 innings, one walk
.408	A	16	Bos 8 *Was* 6	5	2	3	1	0	0	1	0	0		
.405	A	17	*Was* 6 Bos 2	3	0	0	0	0	0	0	1	0		Shut out by Sid Hudson
.404	A	19	*StL* 3 Bos 2	3	1	1	0	0	0	1	1	0	Galehouse (24)	
.410			Bos 10 *StL* 7	5	2	4	0	0	2	3	0	0	Muncrief (25,26)	3 homers in DH
.411	A	20	*StL* 11 Bos 9	4	3	2	0	0	1	2	1	1	Auker (27)	5 homers in 2 days
.411			*StL* 4 Bos 3	2	1	1	0	0	1	2	2	0	Niggeling (28)	
.414	A	21	Bos 8 *Chi* 5	3	2	2	0	0	0	0	2	0		
.411	A	22	Bos 2 *Chi* 1	2	0	0	0	0	0	1	2	0		2 walks, 106 & 107
.409	A	23	*Chi* 3 Bos 0	4	0	1	0	0	0	0	0	0		
.408	A	24	*Cle* 4 Bos 3	4	1	1	0	0	0	0	0	1		
.404			*Cle* 5 Bos 2	3	0	0	0	0	0	0	1	1		Shut out by Feller. 2 walks
.402	A	25	Bos 1 *Cle* 0	2	1	0	0	0	0	0	2	1		
.404	A	26	Bos 9 *Cle* 4	1	0	1	0	0	0	0	4	0		Walked 4 times by Bagby
.405	A	27	*Det* 6 Bos 3	4	0	2	0	1	0	1	0	0		
.407	A	28	*Det* 8 Bos 7	3	2	2	0	0	1	1	2	0	Benton (29)	
.409	H	30	Bos 12 *Phi* 3	3	3	2	0	0	1	2	2	0	Hadley (30)	
.408	H	31	*Bos* 5 Phi 3	3	1	0	0	0	1	3	1	0	Knott (31)	
.407			Phi 3 *Bos* 2	1	0	0	0	0	0	0	3	0		

AVG	AWAY	SEPTEMBER		AB	R	H	2B	3B	HR	RBI	BB	SO	HR OFF	
.409	H	1	Bos 13 Was 9	3	2	2	0	0	2	4	2	0	Carrasquel (32) Zuber (33)	Walked 4 times in DH 3-run homer in 6th 3 homers and 4 more walks in DH. Takes over lead in home runs
.410	H	3	Bos 10 Was 2	2	3	1	0	0	1	1	2	0	Anderson (34)	
.409	H	3	NY 2 Bos 1	3	0	1	0	0	0	0	2	0		Walked 3 times by Atley Donald
.411	H	4	NY 6 Bos 3	1	1	1	0	0	0	0	3	0		
.409	A	6	Bos 8 NY 1	4	1	1	0	0	0	1	1	0		Loses home run in drive off foul pole
.413	A	7	NY 8 Bos 5	4	3	3	2	0	0	1	1	0		
.412	H	9	Bos 6 Det 0	3	0	1	0	0	0	0	1	0		
.413	H	10	Bos 11 Det 2	4	1	2	1	0	0	3	1	0		
.410	H	12	Bos 5 StL 0	3	1	1	0	0	0	0	2	0		2 walks off Niggeling
.409	H	13	Bos 7 StL 2	1	0	0	0	0	0	0	3	0		3 walks. 2 intentional
.411	H	14	Bos 9 Chi 2	3	1	2	0	0	0	1	2	0		
.409			Bos 5 Chi 1	4	1	1	0	1	0	1	0	1		
.409	H	15	Bos 6 Chi 1	3	1	1	0	0	1	3	1	0	Rigney (35)	
.408	H	17	Bos 3 Cle 2	3	0	1	0	0	0	0	1	0		
.405	H	18	Cle 6 Bos 1	3	0	0	0	0	0	0	1	–		
.406	H	20	NY 8 Bos 1	4	0	2	0	0	0	0	0	–		
.406	H	21	Bos 4 NY 1	3	1	1	0	0	1	2	1	0	Bonham (36)	
.405	A	23	Was 4 Bos 3	3	0	0	0	0	0	0	0	0		Blanked by Dutch Leonard
.402	A	24	Bos 7 Was 2	3	1	1	0	0	0	0	0	0		
.401			Bos 5 Was 4	4	1	1	0	0	0	0	0	–		
.3996	A	27	Bos 5 Phi 1	4	1	1	0	0	0	0	1	–		Falls below .400 for first time since July 25
.404	A	28	Bos 12 Phi 11	5	2	4	0	0	1	2	0	0	Fowler (37)	
.406			Phi 7 Bos 1	3	0	2	1	0	0	0	0	0		

APPENDIX C

Williams's Day-by-Day Record with the Minneapolis Millers, 1938

BATTING AVERAGE	OPP.	AB	R	H	RBI	HR	OTHER EXTRA BASE	
.000	April 16 @ Indianapolis	5	0	0	0			
.000	17	4	0	0	0			
.000	18	3	0	0	1			
.077	19 @ Louisville	1	2	1	1			Walks 5 times, tying American Association record
.167	20	5	1	2	2			
.273	21	4	2	3	2	1, 2	2B	2 titanic inside-the-park HRs, 425 ft. to right and 500 ft. to center
.259	22 @ Columbus	5	1	1	1		2B	
.242	23	6	0	1	0			
.263	24	5	0	2	1			
.256	25 @ Toledo	5	1	1	0		2B	
.250	26	5	1	1	1	3		
.269	27	4	0	2	0		2B	
.303	29 Louisville	4	3	3	4	4		Long HR to right; lands

Date	Opponent	AB	R	H	RBI	XBH/HR	Avg	Notes
30		3	0	1	0	2B	.305	
May 1		6	2	3	6	5, 6	.323	
3	Rain							
4	Rain							
5	Rain							
6	Rain							
7	Rain							
8	Rain							
8	Rain							
9	Rain							
10	Columbus	2	1	0	1		.313	
11		4	1	2	1	7	.324	
12	St. Paul	4	2	1	1	8	.320	
13	@ St. Paul	2	2	1	1		.325	
14	St. Paul	4	1	1	0		.321	
15	@ St. Paul	4	1	1	0		.318	
17	Rain							
18	Rain							
19	Rain							
20	Kansas City	3	0	1	1	3B	.318	
21		4	1	2	0		.326	
22		4	3	2	3	9	.333	2-run HR in last of 11th for 10—9 win

BATTING AVERAGE		OPP.	AB	R	H	RBI	HR	OTHER EXTRA BASE	
.337	22		2	1	1	0			
.337	23	@ Milwaukee	3	1	1	1	10		
.327	24		3	0	0	0			
.330	25		2	0	1	2		2B	
.330	26	@ Kansas City	3	1	1	1	11		
.318	27		4	0	0	0			
	28		Did Not Play						Missed games because of stiff neck
	29	St. Paul	Did Not Play						
	30	St. Paul	Did Not Play						
.328	30	@ St. Paul	3	1	2	1	12		HR on top of Coliseum roof in left-center
.331	June 1	@ Toledo	5	2	2	1	13	3B	
.328	2		4	1	1	1			
.326	3	@ Columbus	4	0	1	1			
.333	4		3	3	2	4	14, 15		
.336	5	@ Louisville	2	1	1	0			
.341	5		4	0	2	2		2B	Doubles in winning run in 9th
.343	6		2	0	1	0			
.350	7	@ Indianapolis	5	1	2	5	16		
.340	8	@ Indianapolis	5	1	0	0			
.338	9		4	1	1	1		3B	
.335	11	St. Paul	4	1	1	0		2B	

		AB	R	H	RBI	Game		AVG
12	@ St. Paul	4	1	2	1	17	2B	.340
13	Toledo	3	2	1	0		2B	.339
14	Columbus	4	0	1	0			.337
15	Wet Grounds							
16	Columbus	3	1	3	0		2B	.349
17	Toledo	3	2	2	2		2B	.354
17		5	3	3	3	18, 19		.361
18		4	1	1	3	20		.359
19	Indianapolis	4	1	1	1	21		.356
19		2	1	1	0			.358
20		4	0	0	0			.351
20		3	1	2	1	22		.355
21	Louisville	2	1	1	0			.357
22		3	1	1	0			.356
23	@ Kansas City	4	1	2	3		3B	.359
24		3	2	1	1		3B	.358
25	@ Milwaukee	4	0	0	0			.352
26		4	0	2	0			.359
26		2	0	0	0			.352
27	Kansas City	5	0	1	0			.348
28		1	1	1	0			.351

Hitting streak extended to 21 games

BATTING AVERAGE		OPP.	AB	R	H	RBI	HR	OTHER EXTRA BASE
.352	29	Milwaukee	5	1	2	3		2B
.350	29		4	1	1	0		
.353	30		4	1	2	1		2B
.354	July 1	@ St. Paul	2	1	1	0		
.354	2	@ St. Paul	3	1	1	2		
.350	3	St. Paul	3	1	0	0		
.344	4	@ St. Paul	4	0	0	0		
	4	St. Paul	Rain					
.343	6	@ Louisville	4	1	1	1		3B
.341	7		4	0	1	0		
.338	8	@ Indianapolis	5	0	1	0		
.336	9		5	0	1	1		
.339	10	@ Toledo	3	2	2	3	23	2B
.333	10		5	1	0	0		2B
.332	11		4	1	1	1		3B
.335	12	@ Columbus	4	1	2	2		2B, 2B
.339	13		5	2	3	4	24	2B 430-ft. grand slam
.336	14	AA All-Star Game	4	0	1	0		
.341	15	St. Paul	3	0	0	2		
.340	16	Louisville	4	0	3	0		
.340	17		4	1	1	1	25	
.340	17		3	0	1	0		
.341	18	Indianapolis	5	2	2	1	26	

.Avg	Date	Opp					Game	2B	Notes
.340	19		4	1	1	1	27		Leads Minneapolis to 9th straight win and into 3rd place
.337	20		3	0	0	0			
.336	20		3	1	1	0			
.338	21	Toledo	2	0	1	0			
.338	22		5	1	2	1	28		
.341	22		3	1	2	0			
.344	23		3	0	2	2		2B	Center fielder makes catch in r.f. while Ted is talking to boy in scoreboard
.344	24	Columbus	3	1	1	3	29		
.350	24		3	1	3	2			
.352	25		4	1	2	1			Loses fly ball because doesn't wear sunglasses and loafs in field rest of game
.354	26	Milwaukee	4	0	2	0			
.353	27		3	1	1	0			
.355	28		4	3	2	2	30		
.354	28		4	1	1	1	31		
.355	29	Kansas City	2	0	1	0		2B	
	30	Rain							
.352	31	@ St. Paul	5	0	1	0	32		
.353	Aug 1	St. Paul	5	2	2	2			
.355	2	@ St. Paul	4	0	0	0			

BATTING AVERAGE		OPP.	AB	R	H	RBI	HR	OTHER EXTRA BASE	
.358	Aug 3	@ Milwaukee	2	1	2	4		2B	Beaned in 5th; taken out of game
	4			Did Not Play					
	5	Rain							
.360	6	@ Kansas City	4	1	2	4	33	2B	
.359	7		4	0	1	0			
.361	7		3	1	2	2	34		
.360	8		4	1	1	4	35		Grand slam HR that provokes bottle-throwing riot by K.C. fans
.358	9	St. Paul	5	0	1	2			
.358	10	@ St. Paul	3	0	1	0			
.358	11	@ Toledo	3	2	1	0			
.359	12		4	0	2	0			
.362	13		5	2	3	0		2B	
.366	14	@ Columbus	4	2	3	0		2B	Hits in 27th straight game
.363	14		3	0	0	0			
.360	15		3	1	0	0			
.362	16	@ Columbus	4	1	2	1	36		
	17	Rain							
.363	18	@ Louisville	4	1	2	1	37		
.362	18		4	1	1	3	38		

Avg.	Date	Opponent					No.	XBH	Notes
.361	19		4	0	1	0			
.360	20	@ Indianapolis	4	1	1	0			
.360	21		3	1	1	1			
.360	21		3	0	1	0			
.359	22	Louisville	3	0	1	2			
.358	23		4	0	1	0			
.360	24		3	1	2	1	39	3B	
.360	25	Indianapolis	3	1	1	0			
.361	26		4	1	2	0		2B	
.363	26		3	2	2	4	40	2B	
.366	27	Toledo	2	2	2	5	41	2B	HR cleared bldgs. on Nicollet & landed in alley between Nicollet and 1st Ave. Walked intentionally with men on base for rest of series
.365	28		1	2	0	0			
.365	28		3	0	1	1			
.366	29	Columbus	2	1	1	0			
.364	29		2	1	0	0			
.367	30		4	2	3	2			Highest avg. of year
.367	30		1	1	0	0			
.366	31	@ Kansas City	3	1	1	0			
.364	Sept 1		3	0	0	0			
.365	2	@ Milwaukee	4	1	2	0			
.366	2		2	2	1	0			
.363	3		4	0	0	0			

BATTING AVERAGE		OPP.	AB	R	H	RBI	HR	OTHER EXTRA BASE	
.362	Sept 4	St. Paul	4	1	1	0		2B	Throws bat after pop foul w/bases loaded and breaks water bottle in dugout
.363	5	St. Paul	4	0	2	0		2B	
.362	5	@ St. Paul	4	0	1	0			
	6	Rain							
.360	7	Kansas City	3	1	0	0			
.359	7		4	1	1	0			Eleven straight games without RBI
	8	Rain							
	8	Rain							
	9	Rain							
.358	10	Milwaukee	4	0	1	1			
.360	10		3	2	2	2	42		Finishes with 8 for 13, 8 RBI in final 2-day doubleheaders
.365	11		4	1	4	4	43	3B	
.365	11		2	0	1	0			

APPENDIX D
Before and After the Elbow Injury

1950 at All-Star Game

AB	R	H	2B	3B	HR	RBI	
268	75	86	22	1	25	83	.321
			(post All-Star Game)				
66	7	20	2		3	14	.303
			final figures				
334	82	106	24	1	28	97	.317

The pre-elbow and post-elbow statistics are, for all practical purposes, the pre-Korea and post-Korea statistics. But not quite.

					PRE-ELBOW						
AB	H	2B	3B	HR	RBI	BB	HPB	AVG.	OBA	SLG	HR%
4489	1574	306	57	290	1121	1174	21	.351	.487	.638	6.68
					post-elbow						
3217	1080	219	14	231	718	845	18	.336	.476	.628	7.18
					final						
7706	2654	525	71	521	1839	2019	39	.344	.4826	.634	6.76

The post-elbow, pre-Korea figures are as follows:

	AB	H	2B	3B	HR	RBI	AVG.	HR%
1950	66	20	2		3	14	.303	
1951	531	169	28	4	30	126	.318	
1952	10	4		1	1	3	.400	
	607	193	30	5	34	143	.318	5.6

Appendix D

In a thumbnail, here are Ted Williams's figures before the elbow injury, before going to Korea, and after his return from Korea.

	AB	H	HR	AVG.	HR%	BB	HPB	OBA
pre-elbow	4489	1574	290	.351	6.68	1174	21	.487
pre-Korea	5096	1767	324	.347	6.36	1327	21	.4834
post-Korea	2610	887	197	.340	7.55	692	18	.4810*

*Take out the 1959 season and his post-Korea OBA is .493.

APPENDIX E: Harold Kaese Records

Batting by Month

YEAR	APRIL					MAY					JUNE				
	AB	H	RBI	HR	AVG.	AB	H	RBI	HR	AVG.	AB	H	RBI	HR	AVG.
1939	32	11	5	1	.344	101	26	31	7	.257	88	28	22	2	.318
1940	43	13	5	1	.302	76	31	16	3	.408	109	32	23	5	.294
1941	18	7	5	1	.389	101	44	22	6	.436	94	35	29	8	.372
1942	52	14	14	3	.269	101	38	41	12	.376	86	28	18	2	.326
1946	52	18	10	1	.346	93	32	27	8	.344	103	38	27	11	.369
1947	38	13	9	3	.342	81	22	20	8	.272	83	24	13	2	.289
1948	32	11	6	1	.344	107	41	36	8	.383	87	40	28	4	.460
1949	36	11	9	1	.306	102	35	32	11	.304	115	35	38	7	.304
1950	20	9	12	3	.450	113	32	29	9	.283	116	40	40	12	.345
1951	37	11	10	4	.297	97	32	32	7	.330	102	37	28	3	.363
1952	10	4	3	1	.400	....	....	....	....		....	....	....	....	
1953	....	....	....	....		....	....	....	....		....	....	....	....	
1954	....	....	....	....		49	20	15	4	.408	38	9	7	2	.237
1955	....	....	....	....		12	4	4	1	.333	63	25	20	8	.397
1956	10	5	3	0	.500	21	5	3	0	.238	91	33	14	2	.363
1957	47	20	8	4	.426	82	33	14	7	.402	95	28	21	9	.295
1958	32	7	7	3	.219	87	25	13	3	.287	84	29	16	5	.345
1959	....	....	....	....		63	12	5	1	.190	70	16	10	4	.229
1960	9	2	2	2	.222	11	4	1	0	.364	76	25	24	11	.329
TOT.	468	156	108	31	.333	1297	436	341	95	.336	1500	502	378	97	.335

YEAR	JULY					AUGUST					SEPTEMBER				
	AB	H	RBI	HR	AVG.	AB	H	RBI	HR	AVG.	AB	H	RBI	HR	AVG.
1939	129	48	28	6	.372	121	35	36	6	.289	94	37	23	9	.394
1940	125	42	21	5	.336	99	35	25	4	.353	109	40	23	5	.367
1941	63	27	19	6	.429	107	43	26	10	.402	73	29	19	6	.397
1942	103	40	15	6	.388	115	38	29	4	.330	65	28	20	9	.431
1946	103	36	29	8	.350	103	28	21	6	.272	60	24	9	4	.400
1947	115	44	29	10	.383	107	41	18	4	.383	104	37	25	5	.356
1948	63	20	12	1	.317	100	32	20	7	.320	110	39	21	1	.355
1949	106	41	25	7	.387	116	47	34	10	.405	86	24	21	7	.279
1950	19	5	2	1	.263	....	....	....	....	....	61	16	11	3	.262
1951	99	30	20	7	.303	119	36	18	6	.303	77	23	18	3	.299
1952	....	....	....	....	....	....	....	....	....	....	....	....	....	....	....
1953	....	....	....	....	....	42	18	17	7	.429	49	19	17	6	.388
1954	104	40	29	11	.385	99	33	24	7	.333	96	31	14	5	.323
1955	92	27	23	10	.293	88	34	26	6	.386	65	24	10	3	.369
1956	102	36	23	7	.353	88	29	15	8	.330	88	30	24	7	.341
1957	84	37	21	9	.391	93	33	14	4	.355	19	12	9	5	.632
1958	90	28	21	6	.311	62	23	15	4	.371	56	23	13	5	.411
1959	71	21	16	3	.296	55	13	9	2	.236	13	7	3	0	.538
1960	73	23	12	5	.315	83	26	20	6	.313	58	18	13	5	.310
TOT.	1541	545	345	108	.354	1597	544	367	101	.341	1283	461	293	88	.359

YEAR	OCTOBER				
	AB	H	RBI	HR	AVG.
1948	10	5	4	1	.500
1949	5	1	0	0	.200
1950	5	4	3	0	.800
TOT.	20	10	7	1	.500

This appendix was compiled from materials in the Harold Kaese collection at the Boston Public Library by Mark Shreve and Dick Johnson. It first appeared in *Ted Williams: A Portrait in Words and Pictures*, by Dick Johnson and Glenn Stout, published in 1991 by Walker and Company.

Appendix E

Career Batting Before and After the All-Star Break

YEAR	BEFORE					AFTER				
	AB	H	HR	RBI	AVG.	AB	H	HR	RBI	AVG.
1939	258	79	12	70	.306	307	106	19	75	.345
1940	267	92	11	52	.345	294	101	12	61	.344
1941	237	96	16	62	.405	219	89	21	58	.406
1942	262	91	18	80	.347	260	95	18	57	.365
1946	274	95	23	71	.347	240	81	15	52	.338
1947	225	69	15	48	.307	303	112	17	66	.370
1948	263	102	16	72	.388	246	86	9	55	.350
1949	289	94	20	85	.325	277	100	23	74	.361
1950	268	86	25	83	.321	66	20	3	14	.303
1951	267	91	16	76	.341	264	78	14	50	.295
1952	10	4	3	1	.400			Did not play		
1953			Did not play			91	37	13	34	.407
1954	120	44	8	34	.367	266	89	21	55	.394
1955	99	39	12	30	.394	221	75	16	50	.339
1956	155	57	5	30	.368	245	81	19	52	.331
1957	248	85	20	45	.343	172	78	18	42	.454
1958	226	71	14	45	.314	185	64	12	40	.346
1959	152	33	5	18	.217	120	36	5	25	.300
1960	123	42	14	33	.341	187	56	15	39	.299
TOT.	3743	1270	251	937	.339	3963	1384	270	902	.349

Game-Winning Home Runs

1939

1. May 9 at St.L., with 2 on in the 10th off Harry Kimberlin to win 10–8.
2. July 2 vs. N.Y., with 2 on in the 7th off Lefty Gomez. Final score 7–3.
3. August 19 at Wash., grand slam in the 9th off Pete Appleton to win 8–6.
4. August 28 at Clev., with 2 on in the 8th off Mel Harder to win 6–5.
5. August 29 at Clev., grand slam in the 5th off Harry Eisenstat. Final score 7–4.
6. September 10 at Phil., with 1 on in the 9th off Chubby Dean. Final score 10–7.

1940

1. June 16 at Chi., solo HR in the 12th off Ted Lyons to win 4–3.
2. July 5 at Wash., with 1 on in the 5th off Walt Masterson to win 9–4.

1941

1. May 7 at Chi., solo HR in the 11th off Johnny Rigney to win 4–3.
2. May 27 vs. Phil., solo HR in the 3rd off Bump Hadley. Final score 5–2.
3. May 29 vs. Phil., with 1 on in the 7th off Jack Knott. Final score 6–4.
4. June 6 vs. Chi., with 1 on in the 3rd off Johnny Rigney to win 6–3.
5. June 12 at St. L., with 1 on in the 3rd off Johnny Niggeling to win 3–2.
6. August 31 vs. Phil., with 2 on in the 6th off Jack Knott. Final score 5–3.

1942

1. May 2 vs. St.L., with 1 on in the 9th off Eldon Auker to win 11–10.
2. May 16 at St.L., with 1 on in the 9th off Bob Muncrief to win 4–2.
3. May 29 at Phil., with 2 on the 1st off Russ Christopher to win 14–2.
4. June 24 at Det., solo HR in the 7th off Virgil Trucks to win 1–0.
5. August 15 vs. Wash., with 1 on in the 3rd off Hal Hudson. Final score 2–1.
6. September 6 vs. Phil., with 1 on in the 8th off Lum Harris to win 8–7.
7. September 13 at Chi., with 1 on in the 7th off Buck Ross. Final score 6–1.

1946

1. May 2 vs. Det., solo HR in the 10th off Tommy Bridges to win 5–4.
2. May 22 at Clev., with 1 on in the 12th off Peter Center. Final score 7–4.
3. June 6 vs. St.L., with 1 on in the 7th off Ox Miller to win 5–4.
4. July 7 at Wash., with 1 on in the 3rd off Sid Hudson. Final score 11–1.
5. July 14 vs. Clev., with 2 on in the 8th off Joe Berry to win 11–10 (3rd HR of game).
6. July 30 at Clev., solo HR in the 4th off Steve Gromek to win 4–0.
7. September 13 at Clev., solo HR in the 1st off Red Embree to win 1–0.

1947

1. May 6 at St.L., with 2 on in the 11th of Fred Sanford to win 6–5 (HR off Jack Kramer tied score in 9th).
2. May 16 vs. St.L., grand slam in the 5th off Walter Brown. Final score 12–7.
3. May 18 vs. Det., with 1 on in the 9th off Virgil Trucks to win 5–4.
4. June 4 at St.L., solo HR in the 6th off Bob Muncrief. Final score 5–2.
5. July 16 at Chi., with 1 on in the 3rd off Red Ruffing. Final score 7–2.
6. July 26 vs. St.L., with 1 on in the 1st off Cliff Fannin. Final score 12–1.
7. August 2 vs. Det., with 1 on in the 1st off Virgil Trucks to win 2–1.
8. September 27 at Wash., with 2 on in the 1st off Walt Masterson to win 6–1.

1948

1. August 27 vs. Chi., with 2 on in the 6th off Marino Pieretti. Final score 10–5.
2. August 29 vs. St.L., with 2 on in the 1st off Karl Drews. Final score 10–2.
3. October 2 vs. N.Y., with 1 on in the 1st off Tommy Byrne. Final score 5–1.

1949

1. May 18 vs. Chi., with 1 on in the 3rd off Marino Pieretti. Final score 7–4.
2. May 28 vs. Wash., solo HR in the 5th off Dick Welteroth. Final score 5–4.
3. May 30 vs. Phil., with 1 on in the 8th off Carl Scheib. Final score 4–3.
4. June 24 vs. St.L., with 2 on in the 1st off Joe Ostrowski. Final score 21–2.
5. July 16 at Det., with 1 on in the 1st off Virgil Trucks. Final score 11–1.
6. September 21 vs. Clev., solo HR in the 7th off Steve Gromek. Final score 9–6.

1950

1. May 5 vs. Chi., with 1 on in the 7th off Billy Pierce. Final score 5–2.
2. May 16 at Det., with 1 on in the 3rd off Art Houtteman. Final score 6–1.
3. June 28 at Phil., with 1 on in the 8th off Lou Brissie. Final score 6–2.

1951

1. May 6 at St. L., solo HR in the 10th off Lou Sleater. Final score 5–4.
2. May 21 vs. Clev., with 1 on in the 7th off Gene Bearden. Final score 9–7.
3. May 27 vs. Wash., grand slam in the 3rd off Julio Moreno. Final score 7–1.
4. June 17 vs. St.L., with 1 on in the 1st off Al Widmar. Final score 3–0.
5. September 5 at N.Y., solo HR in the 3rd off Vic Raschi. Final score 4–2.
6. September 14 vs. St.L., with 1 on in the 2nd off Al Widmar. Final score 9–6.

1952

1. April 30 vs. Det., with 1 on in the 8th off Dizzy Trout. Final score 5–3 (Williams's farewell day before Korean War duty).

1953

1. August 19 vs. Phil., with 1 on in the 7th off Charlie Bishop. Final score 6–4.
2. August 31 at Clev., with 2 on in the 7th off Mike Garcia. Final score 6–4.
3. September 17 vs. Det., with 1 on in the 8th off Ned Garver. Final score 2–1.

1954

1. August 6 at Balt., with 1 on in the 10th off Bob Chakales. Final score 3–1.
2. August 11 vs. Wash., with 1 on in the 1st off Connie Marrero. Final score 10–1 (hit another in the 3rd).
3. September 3 at Phil., with 1 on in the 3rd off Arnie Portocarrero. Final score 11–1 (HR #362, which passed Di-Maggio).

1955

1. June 10 at Det., with 1 on in the 3rd off Duke Maas. Final score 5–2 (hit HR in the 1st, also).
2. June 21 vs. Det., with 2 on in the 8th off Ned Garver. Final score 5–4.
3. July 29 vs. Det., solo HR in the 1st off Jim Bunning. Final score 5–0.
4. July 31 vs. Det., grand slam in the 4th off Ned Garver. Final score 8–3.
5. August 15 vs. Wash., grand slam in the 2nd off Ted Abernathy. Final score 8–4.
6. August 27 at Det., grand slam off Al Aber in the 9th to win 4–3.

1956

1. July 8 vs. Balt., with 1 on in the 1st off Ray Moore. Final score 9–0.
2. July 17 vs. K.C., solo HR in the 6th off Tom Gorman. Final score 1–0 (HR #400).
3. July 26 at K.C., with 1 on in the 10th off Bobby Shantz. Final score 5–3.
4. August 5 at Clev., solo HR in the 6th off Bob Lemon. Final score 2–1.
5. August 8 vs. Balt., solo HR in the 6th off Connie Johnson. Final score 7–2

(fined $5,000 for spitting the day before).
6. September 1 vs. Balt., with 1 on in the 8th off Morrie Martin. Final score 4–2.
7. September 8 at Balt., with 2 on in the 1st off Billy Loes. Final score 5–1.
8. September 11 at Chi., solo HR in the 5th off Bob Keegan. Final score 5–3.
9. September 25 vs. Wash., with 2 on in the 2nd off Pedro Ramos. Final score 10–4.

1957

1. May 7 at Chi., with 1 on in the 9th off Dick Donovan. Final score 4–3.
2. May 8 at Chi., solo HR in the 3rd off Bob Keegan. Final score 4–1.
3. June 2 at Wash., with 2 on in the 8th off Pedro Ramos. Final score 5–3.
4. June 13 at Clev., with 2 on in the 5th off Early Wynn. Final score 9–3.
5. July 14 vs. N.Y., with 2 on in the 2nd off Don Larsen. Final score 6–4.
6. July 28 at Det., solo HR in the 7th off Jim Bunning to win 1–0.
7. September 21 at N.Y., grand slam in the 2nd off Bob Turley. Final score 8–3.
8. September 24 at Wash., solo HR in the 4th off Hal Griggs. Final score 2–1.

1958

1. May 22 at K.C., grand slam in the 4th off Jack Urban. Final score 8–5.
2. June 26 at Clev., solo HR in the 9th off Cal McLish. Final score 2–1.
3. June 29 at Det., with 2 on in the 8th off Bill Fischer. Final score 10–7.
4. July 19 vs. Det., with 1 on in the 12th off Hank Aguirre to win 7–6.

1958 *(cont.)*

5. July 29 at Det., with 2 on in the 11th off Bill Fischer. Final score 11–8.

6. August 8 at Clev., with 1 on in the 9th off Gary Bell. Final score 3–2.

7. September 28 at Wash., solo HR in the 7th off Pedro Ramos. Final score 6–4.

1959

1. May 30 vs. Balt., with 1 on in the 7th off Jerry Walker. Final score 8–3.

2. June 27 at Clev., with 1 on in the 5th off Jim Grant. Final score 6–4.

3. August 12 at Det., solo HR off Don Mossi in the 4th. Final score 7–1.

1960

1. June 17 at Clev., with 1 on in the 3rd off Wynn Hawkins. Final score 3–1 (HR #500).

2. June 19 at Clev., with 1 on in the 7th off Jim Perry. Final score 7–1.

3. August 20 vs. Balt., with 2 on in the 6th off Chuck Estrada. Final score 8–6.

4. September 17 at Wash., with 1 on in the 6th off Pedro Ramos. Final score 2–1.

Home Runs vs. Opponents

YEAR	G	TOT	H	A	AT BALT.	AT CHI.	AT CLE.	AT DET.	AT K.C.	AT N.Y.	AT PHIL.	AT ST.L.	AT WASH.
1939	149	31	14	17	—	2	3	4	—	1	2	4	1
1940	144	23	9	14	—	3	1	1	—	4	2	2	1
1941	143	37	19	18	—	3	1	3	—	0	4	7	0
1942	150	36	16	20	—	1	2	5	—	4	4	4	0
1946	150	38	18	20	—	2	4	6	—	2	3	1	2
1947	156	32	16	16	—	1	0	1	—	2	5	5	2
1948	137	25	9	16	—	3	3	1	—	3	2	2	2
1949	155	43	23	20	—	6	2	6	—	1	1	4	0
1950	89	28	16	12	—	0	1	3	—	3	3	2	0
1951	148	30	18	12	—	1	1	1	—	1	4	2	2
1952	6	1	1	0	—	0	0	0	—	0	0	0	0
1953	37	13	8	5	—	0	2	0	—	0	1	0	2
1954	117	29	16	13	1	3	1	4	—	1	3	—	0
1955	98	28	15	13	2	1	2	4	2	1	—	—	1
1956	136	24	10	14	2	1	4	1	4	0	—	—	2
1957	132	38	12	26	0	5	6	5	4	3	—	—	3
1958	129	26	10	16	0	1	3	5	2	2	—	—	3
1959	103	10	3	7	0	2	2	2	1	0	—	—	0
1960	113	29	15	14	0	0	5	3	2	2	—	—	2
TOT.	2292	521	248	273	5	35	43	55	15	30	34	33	23

New York Yankees

YEAR	TOTAL					HOME					AWAY				
	AB	R	H	HR	RBI	AB	R	H	HR	RBI	AB	R	H	HR	RBI
1939	60	19	21	6	17	30	14	11	5	12	30	5	10	1	5
1940	68	17	24	6	14	32	8	13	2	5	36	9	11	4	9
1941	68	23	32	2	14	35	13	16	2	6	33	10	16	0	8
1942	77	14	23	6	16	39	6	11	2	7	38	8	12	4	9
1946	69	18	13	3	10	35	11	8	1	5	34	7	5	2	5
1947	74	11	17	2	7	38	8	8	0	3	36	3	9	2	4
1948	83	16	29	5	30	42	8	16	2	21	41	8	13	3	9
1949	78	17	30	5	18	43	11	17	4	10	35	6	13	1	8
1950	59	18	20	4	16	31	12	13	1	10	28	6	7	3	6
1951	67	12	24	3	13	45	9	18	2	11	22	3	6	1	2
1952	Did not play														
1953	17	2	8	1	6	10	2	5	1	5	7	0	3	0	1
1954	57	18	23	3	15	24	9	9	2	8	33	9	14	1	7
1955	36	4	13	2	4	15	2	7	1	3	21	2	6	1	1
1956	56	3	11	1	6	31	3	8	1	5	25	0	3	0	1
1957	53	10	24	6	13	32	6	17	3	6	21	4	7	3	7
1958	42	10	19	3	13	28	6	12	1	7	14	4	7	2	6
1959	31	5	12	1	8	20	3	10	1	8	11	2	2	0	2
1960	40	7	14	3	9	30	4	11	1	5	10	3	3	2	4
TOT.	1035	224	357	62	229	560	135	210	32	135	475	89	147	30	94
	AVG. .345					AVG. .375					AVG. .309				

Philadelphia Athletics
(1939 – 1954)

YEAR	TOTAL					HOME					AWAY				
	AB	R	H	HR	RBI	AB	R	H	HR	RBI	AB	R	H	HR	RBI
1939	83	28	39	6	24	46	15	23	3	15	37	13	16	3	9
1940	90	23	33	4	23	48	12	17	2	13	42	11	16	2	10
1941	63	19	28	8	22	28	9	13	4	11	35	10	15	4	11
1942	75	21	21	10	29	35	11	11	6	15	40	10	10	4	14
1946	70	17	19	3	13	29	4	5	0	4	41	13	14	3	9
1947	69	22	22	9	22	34	9	12	4	12	35	13	10	5	10
1948	69	15	25	2	9	39	8	14	0	3	30	7	11	2	6
1949	76	19	26	5	20	35	14	11	4	14	41	5	15	1	6
1950	31	10	13	5	18	9	5	5	2	7	22	5	8	3	11
1951	69	18	26	7	24	31	13	12	3	12	48	5	14	4	12
1952	1	0	0	0	0	1	0	0	0	0					
1953	9	2	4	2	3	5	1	2	1	2	4	1	2	1	1
1954	63	20	25	5	17	29	8	12	2	7	34	12	13	3	10
TOT.	768	214	281	66	224	369	109	137	31	115	409	105	144	35	109
	AVG. .366					AVG. .371					AVG. .352				

Kansas City Athletics
(1955 – 1960)

YEAR	TOTAL					HOME					AWAY				
	AB	R	H	HR	RBI	AB	R	H	HR	RBI	AB	R	H	HR	RBI
1955	58	14	26	4	12	29	7	14	2	8	29	7	12	2	4
1956	57	10	21	6	13	27	3	8	2	4	30	7	13	4	9
1957	60	19	26	7	14	28	8	13	3	8	32	11	13	4	6
1958	66	10	23	4	16	30	6	9	2	9	36	4	14	2	7
1959	47	4	12	1	6	25	1	6	0	1	22	3	6	1	5
1960	39	8	12	3	13	13	5	5	1	7	26	3	7	2	6
TOT.	327	65	120	25	74	152	30	55	10	37	175	35	65	15	37
	AVG. .367					AVG. .362					AVG. .371				

Baltimore Orioles
(1954 – 1960)

YEAR	TOTAL					HOME					AWAY				
	AB	R	H	HR	RBI	AB	R	H	HR	RBI	AB	R	H	HR	RBI
1954	44	8	11	5	8	20	6	7	4	6	24	2	4	1	2
1955	32	9	10	5	10	18	7	6	3	8	14	2	4	2	2
1956	65	17	26	5	21	32	11	16	3	11	33	6	10	2	10
1957	66	8	23	1	7	27	5	9	1	4	39	3	14	0	3
1958	43	6	11	0	4	24	5	5	0	2	19	1	6	0	2
1959	26	4	10	1	6	12	3	5	1	3	14	1	5	0	3
1960	34	8	11	3	11	24	5	8	3	9	10	3	3	0	2
TOT.	310	60	102	20	67	157	42	56	15	43	153	18	46	5	24
	AVG. .329					AVG. .357					AVG. .301				

Cleveland Indians

YEAR	TOTAL AB	R	R	HR	RBI	HOME AB	R	H	HR	RBI	AWAY AB	R	H	HR	RBI
1939	77	14	18	4	23	41	8	7	1	11	36	6	11	3	12
1940	77	17	23	3	17	39	10	14	2	12	38	7	9	1	5
1941	58	22	24	3	9	38	14	18	2	6	20	8	8	1	3
1942	71	27	25	4	20	34	13	10	2	8	37	14	15	2	12
1946	78	20	30	11	28	39	13	20	7	18	39	7	10	4	10
1947	66	15	18	0	4	34	8	6	0	3	32	7	12	0	1
1948	87	23	33	5	23	43	12	15	2	12	44	11	18	3	11
1949	81	11	25	3	18	38	8	14	1	10	43	3	11	2	8
1950	44	8	11	4	10	20	6	7	3	5	24	2	4	1	5
1951	94	12	24	3	19	52	8	16	2	11	42	4	8	1	8
1952	Did not play														
1953	14	6	5	5	9	8	3	3	3	5	6	3	2	2	4
1954	47	7	16	3	9	24	4	10	6	6	23	3	6	1	3
1955	56	9	12	5	15	34	4	8	3	6	22	5	4	2	9
1956	56	16	22	4	15	37	11	15	0	6	19	5	7	4	9
1957	57	22	27	9	20	30	11	14	3	8	27	11	13	6	12
1958	69	10	22	3	7	34	5	12	0	8	35	5	10	3	4
1959	41	5	8	2	3	20	1	3	0	3	21	4	5	2	3
1960	54	9	18	8	16	32	5	10	3	6	22	4	8	5	10
TOT.	1127	253	361	79	265	597	144	202	36	137	530	109	161	43	129
	AVG. .320					AVG. .338					AVG. .304				

Detroit Tigers

YEAR	TOTAL					HOME					AWAY				
	AB	R	H	HR	RBI	AB	R	H	HR	RBI	AB	R	H	HR	RBI
1939	80	19	24	4	21	36	7	10	0	7	44	12	14	4	14
1940	73	18	27	1	15	45	10	17	0	8	28	8	10	1	7
1941	74	21	25	5	19	36	7	12	2	9	38	14	13	3	10
1942	80	20	31	7	22	37	9	16	2	9	43	11	15	5	13
1946	77	28	30	10	21	39	16	12	4	7	38	12	18	6	14
1947	82	13	27	4	19	40	7	15	3	9	42	6	12	1	10
1948	66	17	20	2	12	29	9	12	1	5	37	8	8	1	7
1949	96	32	33	10	25	46	15	16	4	13	50	17	17	6	12
1950	49	10	12	5	14	26	3	7	2	7	23	7	5	3	7
1951	76	10	19	2	12	39	3	12	1	7	37	7	7	1	5
1952	3	1	2	1	2	3	1	2	1	2					
1953	8	1	3	1	3	4	1	1	1	2	4	0	2	0	1
1954	58	15	19	5	16	28	7	6	1	3	30	8	13	4	13
1955	53	20	22	8	24	27	12	11	4	13	26	8	11	4	11
1956	60	8	19	2	8	32	3	10	1	4	28	5	9	1	4
1957	64	16	23	6	11	36	7	13	1	4	28	9	10	5	7
1958	63	15	16	6	15	28	8	7	1	4	35	7	9	5	13
1959	46	7	11	3	11	23	2	4	1	3	23	5	7	2	8
1960	59	10	23	6	13	28	3	10	3	7	31	7	13	3	6
TOT.	1167	281	386	88	283	582	130	193	33	111	585	151	193	55	162
	AVG. .331					AVG. .332					AVG. .330				

Career Batting vs. Opponents
Chicago White Sox

YEAR	TOTAL					HOME					AWAY				
	AB	R	H	HR	RBI	AB	R	H	HR	RBI	AB	R	H	HR	RBI
1939	84	13	24	2	9	40	9	13	1	2	44	4	11	1	7
1940	88	23	30	3	13	44	10	14	0	2	44	13	16	3	11
1941	69	17	26	7	17	42	11	17	4	9	27	6	9	3	8
1942	71	8	17	2	13	40	3	9	1	7	31	5	8	1	6
1946	76	13	22	2	14	40	5	12	0	8	36	8	10	2	6
1947	80	20	29	6	15	44	12	13	3	10	36	8	16	1	5
1948	58	10	27	4	31	29	4	13	1	18	29	6	14	3	13
1949	87	30	31	12	39	36	14	12	6	21	51	16	19	6	18
1950	44	14	15	3	10	19	10	9	3	10	25	4	6	0	0
1951	73	18	25	5	18	42	13	20	4	15	31	5	5	1	3
1952	Did not play														
1953	18	4	8	1	5	7	2	4	1	3	11	2	4	0	2
1954	60	9	19	5	12	32	6	12	2	4	28	3	7	3	8
1955	38	7	12	1	8	12	4	5	0	1	26	3	7	1	7
1956	55	6	19	1	6	24	2	8	0	2	31	4	11	1	4
1957	63	9	21	6	13	25	3	11	1	4	38	6	10	5	9
1958	68	12	21	2	9	31	8	11	1	4	37	4	10	1	5
1959	46	3	8	2	5	18	1	4	0	2	28	2	4	2	3
1960	47	8	10	3	7	23	3	6	3	4	24	5	4	0	3
TOT.	1125	124	364	65	244	548	120	193	31	126	573	104	166	34	116
	AVG. .324					AVG. .352					AVG. .290				

St. Louis Browns
(1939–1953)

YEAR	TOTAL					HOME					AWAY				
	AB	R	H	HR	RBI	AB	R	H	HR	RBI	AB	R	H	HR	RBI
1939	91	20	32	5	32	41	8	12	1	9	50	12	20	4	23
1940	89	20	29	3	13	45	11	12	1	7	44	9	17	2	6
1941	61	17	26	9	26	33	7	13	2	11	28	10	13	7	15
1942	75	21	34	6	23	41	13	18	2	15	34	8	16	4	8
1946	72	22	34	5	18	47	13	27	4	12	25	9	7	1	6
1947	82	31	39	11	33	48	17	22	6	19	34	14	17	5	14
1948	62	20	26	4	13	20	7	7	2	4	42	13	19	2	9
1949	79	20	28	6	26	38	10	13	2	15	41	10	15	4	11
1950	60	17	24	6	23	22	9	9	4	12	38	8	15	2	11
1951	74	18	24	5	16	34	13	13	3	11	40	5	11	2	5
1952	Did not play														
1953	9	0	0	0	0	9	0	0	0	0					
TOT.	754	186	296	60	223	378	108	146	27	115	376	98	150	33	108
	AVG. .393					AVG. .386					AVG. .399				

413

Washington Senators

YEAR	TOTAL AB	R	H	HR	RBI	HOME AB	R	H	HR	RBI	AWAY AB	R	H	HR	RBI
1939	90	18	27	4	19	43	13	19	3	13	47	5	8	1	6
1940	76	14	27	3	18	44	7	14	2	13	32	7	13	1	5
1941	63	16	24	3	13	31	11	15	3	10	32	5	9	0	3
1942	73	28	35	1	14	35	16	18	1	7	38	12	17	0	7
1946	72	24	28	4	19	37	12	14	2	10	35	12	14	2	9
1947	75	13	29	2	14	38	6	16	0	8	37	7	13	2	6
1948	84	23	28	3	9	37	9	11	1	3	47	14	17	2	6
1949	69	21	21	2	13	36	13	12	2	8	33	8	9	0	5
1950	47	5	11	1	6	33	4	7	1	5	14	1	4	0	1
1951	78	21	27	5	24	34	11	17	3	14	44	10	10	2	10
1952	6	1	2	0	1	2	0	1	0	1	4	1	1	0	0
1953	16	3	9	3	8	4	1	2	1	1	12	2	7	2	7
1954	57	16	20	3	11	29	8	13	3	6	28	8	7	0	5
1955	47	13	19	3	10	37	11	16	2	8	10	2	3	1	2
1956	51	11	20	5	13	22	6	9	3	11	29	5	11	2	2
1957	57	12	19	3	10	28	2	6	0	3	29	10	13	3	7
1958	60	12	23	8	21	32	9	12	5	14	28	3	11	3	7
1959	35	3	8	0	4	16	2	5	0	4	19	1	3	0	0
1960	37	8	10	3	4	14	4	4	1	1	23	4	6	2	3
TOT.	1093	172	387	56	231	552	145	211	33	140	541	117	176	23	91
	AVG. .354					AVG. .382					AVG. .325				

Season Home/Away Averages and Miscellaneous Season Highs

YEAR		HR	AVG.	HIT STREAK (GAMES)	HITLESS STREAK (GAMES)	HIGH RBI	HITS (SINGLE GAME)	PERFECT DAYS AB	GRAND SLAMS
1939	H	14	.343	12	4	6	4(3×)	5	2
	A	17	.313						
1940	H	9	.340	11	3 (0-19)	4	4(2×)	4	1
	A	14	.348						
1941	H	19	.428	23	2 (0-7)	4	4(4×)	8	1
	A	18	.380						
1942	H	16	.356	15	4 (0-15)	7	3(17×)	5	1
	A	20	.356						
1946	H	18	.368	10	4 (0-12)	8	4(2×)	8	2
	A	20	.315						
1947	H	16	.332	9	4	5(2×)	5	8	1
	A	16	.355						
1948	H	9	.368	16	3 (0-10)	7	5	9	0
	A	16	.370						
1949	H	23	.349	12	2(3×)	7	4	1	1
	A	20	.337						

YEAR		HR	AVG.	HIT STREAK (GAMES)	HITLESS STREAK (GAMES)	HIGH RBI	HITS (SINGLE GAME)	PERFECT DAYS AB	GRAND SLAMS
1950	H	16	.356	12(2×)	3	7	4(2×)	1	1
	A	12	.282						
1951	H	18	.403	10	4 (0-14)	5	4(3×)	2	1
	A	12	.232						
1952	H	1	.500	—	—	—	2	1	0
	A	0	.250						
1953	H	8	.362	12	3 (ph)	4(2×)	4	5	0
	A	5	.455						
1954	H	16	.371	14	4 (0-17)	5	5	7	0
	A	13	.320						
1955	H	15	.390	9	3 (0-10)	6	4	3	3
	A	13	.318						
1956	H	10	.361	7(3×)	3 (5 ph)	4(4×)	4(2×)	10	0
	A	14	.328						
1957	H	12	.403	17	2	5	4	11	1
	A	26	.374						
1958	H	10	.329	6	3 (0-9)	7	4	4	2
	A	16	.328						
1959	H	3	.276	4	4 (0-17)	3	3	11	0
	A	7	.232						
1960	H	15	.329	7(ph)	6	6	3(6×)	2	0
	A	14	.301	2(st)					

Projected Career Statistics

Had Williams played in the 727 games he missed while in the Marines his career totals and all-time rank would be as follows:

	CAREER TOTAL	CAREER RANK	PROJECTED TOTAL	PROJECTED RANK
Games	2,292	63rd	3,017	6th
At Bats	7,706	100th	10,149	12th
Runs	1,798	13th	2,301	1st
Hits	2,654	48th	3,496	6th
Doubles	525	19th	692	5th
Triples	71	—	93	—
Home Runs	521	10th	686	3rd
Extra Base Hits	1,117	10th	1,471	2nd, by 6
RBIs	1,839	11th	2,242	2nd
Total Bases	4,884	13th	6,433	2nd
Walks	2,019	2nd	2,659	1st
Strikeouts	709	—	934	99th
Stolen Bases	24	—	32	—
Grand Slams	17	—	22	2nd
Average	.344	6th		
On Base Percentage	.483	1st		
Slugging Percentage	.634	2nd		

417

Batting Average vs.
the Yearly Batting Champion

1939	Joe DiMaggio	.381
	Jimmie Foxx	.360
	Luke Appling	.348
	Bob Johnson	.338
	Hal Trosky	.335
	Charlie Keller	.334
	Red Rolfe	.328
	TED WILLIAMS	.327
1940	Joe DiMaggio	.352
	Luke Appling	.348
	TED WILLIAMS	.344
1941	TED WILLIAMS	.406
1942	TED WILLIAMS	.356
1946	Mickey Vernon	.353
	TED WILLIAMS	.342
1947	TED WILLIAMS	.343
1948	TED WILLIAMS	.369
1949	George Kell	.3429
	TED WILLIAMS	.3427
1950	Billy Goodman	.354
	TED WILLIAMS	.317 (89G, 106 – 334, DNQ)
1951	Ferris Fain	.344
	Minnie Minoso	.326
	George Kell	.319
	TED WILLIAMS	.317
1952	Ferris Fain	.327
	TED WILLIAMS	.400 (6g, 4 – 10, DNQ)
1953	Mickey Vernon	.337
	TED WILLIAMS	.407 (37g, 37 – 91, DNQ)
1954	Bobby Avila	.341
	TED WILLIAMS	.345 (117g, 133 – 386, DNQ)
1955	Al Kaline	.340
	TED WILLIAMS	.356 (98g, 114 – 320, DNQ)
1956	Mickey Mantle	.353
	TED WILLIAMS	.345

1957	TED WILLIAMS	.388
1958	TED WILLIAMS	.328
1959	Harvey Kuenn	.353
	TED WILLIAMS	.254 (69–272, DNQ)
1960	Pete Runnells	.320
	TED WILLIAMS	.316 (98–310, DNQ)

Years qualified for the title	12
Years as batting champion	6
Second	3
Third	1
Fourth	1
Seventh	1
Disqualified from	7

When he qualified he was beaten out by only twelve players in his career.

Career MVP Balloting

1939

J. DiMaggio, N.Y.	280
J. Foxx, Bos.	170
B. Feller, Clev.	155
TED WILLIAMS	126

1940

H. Greenberg, Det.	292
B. Feller, Clev.	222
J. DiMaggio, N.Y.	151
B. Newsom, Det.	120
L. Boudreau, Clev.	119
J. Foxx, Bos.	110
TED WILLIAMS (15th)	16

1941

J. DiMaggio, N.Y.	291
TED WILLIAMS	254

1942

J. Gordon, N.Y.	270
TED WILLIAMS	249

1946

WILLIAMS WINS MVP	224

1947

J. DiMaggio, N.Y.	202
TED WILLIAMS	201

1948

L. Boudreau, Clev.	324
J. DiMaggio, N.Y.	213
TED WILLIAMS	171

1949

WILLIAMS WINS MVP	272

1950

P. Rizzuto, N.Y.	284
B. Goodman, Bos.	180
Y. Berra, N.Y.	146
G. Kell, Det.	127
B. Lemon, Clev.	102
TED WILLIAMS (23rd)	7

1951

Y. Berra, N.Y.	184
N. Garver, St.L.	157
A. Reynolds, N.Y.	125
M. Minoso, Chi.	120
B. Feller, Clev.	118
TED WILLIAMS (13th)	35

1953

A. Rosen, Clev.	336
Y. Berra, N.Y.	167
M. Vernon, Wash.	162
M. Minoso, Chi.	100
V. Trucks, Chi.	81
TED WILLIAMS (26th)	1

1954

Y. Berra, N.Y.	230
L. Doby, Clev.	210
B. Avila, Clev.	203
M. Minoso, Chi.	186
B. Lemon, Clev.	179
E. Wynn, Clev.	72
TED WILLIAMS	65

1955

Y. Berra, N.Y.	218
A. Kaline, Det.	201
A. Smith, Clev.	200
TED WILLIAMS	143

1956

M. Mantle, N.Y.	336
Y. Berra, N.Y.	186
A. Kaline, Det.	142
H. Kuenn, Det.	80
B. Pierce, Chi.	75
TED WILLIAMS	70

1957

M. Mantle, N.Y.	233
TED WILLIAMS	209

1958

J. Jensen, Bos.	233
B. Turley, N.Y.	191
R. Colavito, Clev.	181
B. Cerv, K.C.	164
M. Mantle, N.Y.	127
R. Sievers, Wash.	95
TED WILLIAMS	89

1959

N. Fox, Chi.	295
L. Aparicio, Chi.	255
E. Wynn, Chi.	123
R. Colavito, Clev.	117
T. Francona, Clev.	102
TED WILLIAMS (26th)	2

1960

R. Maris, N.Y.	225
M. Mantle, N.Y.	222
B. Robinson, Balt.	211
M. Minoso, Chi.	141
R. Hansen, Balt.	110
TED WILLIAMS (13th)	25

APPENDIX F
Lifetime Records

BATTING AVERAGE

Ty Cobb	.367
Rogers Hornsby	.358
Joe Jackson	.356
Ted Williams	**.344**
Tris Speaker	.344
Babe Ruth	.342
Harry Heilmann	.342
Bill Terry	.341
George Sisler	.340
Lou Gehrig	.340

HOME RUNS

Hank Aaron	755
Babe Ruth	714
Willie Mays	660
Frank Robinson	586
Harmon Killebrew	573
Reggie Jackson	563
Mike Schmidt	542
Mickey Mantle	536
Jimmy Foxx	534
Ted Williams	**521**
Willie McCovey	521

HOME RUN PERCENTAGE

Babe Ruth	8.50
Ralph Kiner	7.09
Harmon Killebrew	7.03
Ted Williams	**6.76**
Dave Kingman	6.62
Mickey Mantle	6.62
Mike Schmidt	6.61
Jimmy Foxx	6.57
Hank Greenberg	6.37
Willie McCovey	6.36

RUNS BATTED IN PER GAME

Lou Gehrig	.92
Hank Greenberg	.92
Joe DiMaggio	.89
Babe Ruth	.88
Jimmy Foxx	.83
Al Simmons	.82
Ted Williams	**.80**

Hack Wilson	.79
Bob Meusel	.76
Hal Trosky	.75

WALKS

Babe Ruth	2056
Ted Williams	**2019**
Joe Morgan	1865
Carl Yastrzemski	1845
Mickey Mantle	1734
Mel Ott	1708
Eddie Yost	1614
Stan Musial	1599
Pete Rose	1566
Darrell Evans	1564

WALKS RATIO

Ted Williams	**20.76**
Max Bishop	20.42
Babe Ruth	19.67
Eddie Stanky	18.80
Ferris Fain	18.70
Gene Tenace	18.31
Roy Cullenbine	18.03
Eddie Yost	18.01
Mickey Mantle	17.63
Charlie Keller	17.14

ON-BASE PERCENTAGE

Ted Williams	**.483**
Babe Ruth	.474
Lou Gehrig	.447
Rogers Hornsby	.447
Ty Cobb	.432
Jimmy Foxx	.428
Tris Speaker	.427
Ferris Fain	.425
Eddie Collins	.424
Max Bishop	.423
Joe Jackson	.423

SLUGGING AVERAGE

Babe Ruth	.690
Ted Williams	**.634**
Lou Gehrig	.632

Jimmy Foxx	.609
Hank Greenberg	.605
Joe DiMaggio	.579
Rogers Hornsby	.577
Johnny Mize	.562
Stan Musial	.559
Willie Mays	.557

PRODUCTION

Babe Ruth	1.163
Ted Williams	**1.116**
Lou Gehrig	1.080
Jimmy Foxx	1.038
Hank Greenberg	1.017
Rogers Hornsby	1.010
Mickey Mantle	.979
Joe DiMaggio	.977
Stan Musial	.977
Johnny Mize	.959

WALKS, SEASON

Babe Ruth, 1923	170
Ted Williams, 1947	**162**
Ted Williams, 1949	**162**
Ted Williams, 1946	**156**
Eddie Yost, 1956	151
Eddie Joost, 1949	149
Babe Ruth, 1920	148
Eddie Stanky, 1945	148
Jim Wynn, 1969	148
Mickey Mantle, 1957	146
Ted Williams, 1941	**145**
Ted Williams, 1942	**145**

ON-BASE PERCENTAGE, SEASON

Ted Williams, 1941	**.551**
Babe Ruth, 1923	.545
Babe Ruth, 1920	.530

Ted Williams, 1957	**.528**
Ted Williams, 1954	**.516**
Babe Ruth, 1924	.516
Mickey Mantle, 1957	.515
Babe Ruth, 1924	.513
Babe Ruth, 1921	.512
Rogers Hornsby, 1924	.507
Ted Williams, 1942	**.499**
Ted Williams, 1947	**.498**
Rogers Hornsby, 1928	.498
Ted Williams, 1946	**.497**
Ted Williams, 1948	**.497**

SLUGGING AVERAGE, SEASON

Babe Ruth, 1920	.847
Babe Ruth, 1921	.846
Babe Ruth, 1927	.772
Lou Gehrig, 1927	.765
Babe Ruth, 1923	.764
Rogers Hornsby, 1925	.756
Jimmy Foxx, 1932	.749
Babe Ruth, 1924	.739
Babe Ruth, 1926	.737
Ted Williams, 1941	**.735**
Babe Ruth, 1930	.732
Ted Williams, 1957	**.731**

PRODUCTION, SEASON

Babe Ruth, 1920	1.378
Babe Ruth, 1921	1.358
Babe Ruth, 1923	1.309
Ted Williams, 1941	**1.286**
Babe Ruth, 1927	1.259
Ted Williams, 1957	**1.259**
Babe Ruth, 1926	1.253
Babe Ruth, 1924	1.252
Rogers Hornsby, 1925	1.254
Lou Gehrig, 1927	1.240

From *Total Baseball* by John Thorn and Pete Palmer.

APPENDIX G
Chronology of Career with Red Sox

Dec. 1, 1937, Sox obtain Williams from San Diego

Feb. 7, 1938, Ted's parents demand a $5,000 bonus from San Diego as a condition of their son's reporting to the Red Sox

March 3, 1938, Eddie Collins pays the money and signs Ted to a Sox contract

April 17, 1938, farmed to Minneapolis

April 1, 1939, throws ball over stands during exhibition game in Atlanta and taken out of game

April 19, 1939, hits two of the longest homers in Detroit history

August 8, 1939, falls behind Foxx in RBI race, loafs, and is taken out of game

Sept. 30, 1939, Babe Ruth terms him "rookie of the year"

Aug. 14, 1940, calls Boston "lousy" sports town, asks to be traded, hates Fenway Park and fans, calls $12,500 salary peanuts, later denies story

Sept. 24, 1940, one of four Red Sox to hit 2 homers in the same inning in Phila.; pertinence of this is what Ted did hit from August 14 to end of year

July 6, 1941, wins All-Star Game with 9th inning home run

Sept. 28, 1941, goes 6 for 8 to finish season with batting average of .406

Feb. 13, 1942, classified 1A by Minnesota draft board

March 16, 1942, Ted's classification to 3A because he supports his mother

April 14, 1942, hits three-run homer first time up in season's opener, adds two RBI singles

May 22, 1942, enlists in US Naval Air Corps

July 1, 1942 (or is it July 22?), fined $250 by Joe Cronin for loafing, yanked out of lineup in fifth inning against Washington. Hitting .336 and leading league in homers and RBI. Apologizes, admits he was wrong. Lets fans get under his skin.

July 14, 1946, Cleveland manager Lou Boudreau invents Williams Shift after Ted clouts three homers

Oct. 1, 1942, wins first Triple Crown

Oct. 14, 1946, Sox lose World Series to St. Louis Cards with Ted hitting only .200 (five hits). Named League's MVP.

Dec. 8, 1942, inducted into Navy, assigned to US Naval aviation Preliminary Ground school at Amherst

May 4, 1944, marries Doris Soule of Princeton, Minn.

Jan. 2, 1946, returns from service, vowing no more feuds with writers or with the fans in Fenway Park left field stands.

October 1, 1947, wins second Triple Crown, loses MVP to Joe DiMaggio by single vote

January 28, 1948, fishing in Florida when daughter is born at Richardson House, Boston; flies in five days later

Oct. 1, 1949, wins MVP, his career high in RBI with 159 plus 43 home runs

Jan. 16, 1950, signs contract for $125,000

May 10, 1950, drops fly, booed by crowd, replies with vulgar gestures and spitting

July 14, 1950, fractures left elbow in All-Star Game

March, 1951, criticizes Red Sox spirit in radio broadcast, praises that of Yankees, and says he won't play exhibitions. "He's not bigger than baseball," says manager Steve O'Neill.

Nov. 16, 1951, Lou Boudreau says Ted on trading block, offered to four AL teams. "If the time has come for me to leave Boston," says Ted, "then the time has come for me to leave baseball."

December 12, 1951, Boudreau reverses himself, says, "We won't trade Williams."

Feb. 7, 1952, Marine Corps announces Williams will be recalled to active duty for two years, probably in May

April 2, 1952, passes physical at Jacksonville, Florida, navy base and will report for active duty on May 2

April 30, 1952, final appearance before heading for Korea hits 2-run homer to win game

May 3, 1952, starts active duty at Willow Grove, Pa.

Dec. 2, 1952, becomes partner in Southern Tackle (Fishing) Distributors of Miami

Feb. 4, 1953, arrives in Korea and assigned to first Marine Air Wing

Feb. 16, 1953, lands jet fighter safely after being hit by Red ground fire that sets plane on fire

April 27, 1953, second brush with death when right wing of his Panther jet is smashed by flak.

June 28, 1953, ordered back to US.

July 10, 1953, released by Marines

July 14, 1953, tendered ovation as he throws out ball at All-Star Game in Cinci

July 29, 1953, signs Red Sox contract and starts working with Red Sox

August 6, 1953, makes pinch hit appearance against Marlin Stuart of Browns and pops up

August 9, 1953, hits pinch home run at Washington

Sept. 27, 1953, finishes season with batting average of .407 for 37 games

Jan. 24, 1954, wife sues for separate support

March 1, 1954, breaks collarbone first day at Sarasota, pin inserted in shoulder

March 9, 1954, operated on for broken collarbone, has pin put in shoulder to hold bone together

March 16, 1954, discharged from hospital. Says it's "up to God" when he will be able to play

April 10, 1954, "This is my last year," says Ted in *Saturday Evening Post* article

May 7, 1954, first start at Detroit. Hits two homers, a double, five singles and collects seven RBIs in doubleheader as Sox lose both games

June 15, 1954, goes out of lineup for three weeks with virus infection in right lung, bordering on pneumonia

Sept. 4, 1954, hits 362 homers to pass DiMaggio in all-time ratings

Sept. 27, 1954, officially "retires" from baseball. Hits .345 with 29 homers

May 9, 1955, Ted's wife wins divorce and is awarded $50,000 and $125 a week

May 13, 1955, signs Red Sox contract for reported $80,000, says he "missed baseball" more than he thought

May 24, 1955, first game back from retirement, gets first of 28 homers for season

July 1, 1955, plagued by back trouble

Dec. 24, 1955, league announces Ted topped sluggers with .703 percentage

March 14, 1956, calls draft boards, politicians, and baseball writers "gutless"

April 18, 1956, out of lineup with bruised tendon in right instep from slip in shower room.

May 29, 1956, returns to lineup in New York after missing 33 games

July 17, 1956, hits 400th homer; beats KC 1–0

August 7, 1956, fined $5,000 by Cronin for spitting in 1–0 win over NY, walked in 11th

May 17, 1957, fined $25 for bat-tossing incident

June 14, 1957, becomes first American Leaguer ever to hit three home runs in a game twice in one season. Drives in five runs against Indians

Sept. 23, 1957, ties record by hitting four home runs in four consecutive times at bat

Appendix G

Sept. 29, 1957, wins batting crown with .388

Oct. 17, 1957, slugging crown with .731, highest in majors in 16 years.

Nov. 23, 1957, Mickey Mantle named AL MVP, Mantle completely flabbergasted that Williams was bypassed

Jan. 10, 1958, named outstanding male athlete for 1957

Feb. 6, 1958, signs Sox contract for reported $125,000

July 23, 1958, spits after fans booed, is fined $250

Sept. 21, 1958, hurls bat in anger for letting called third strike go by, but hits Mrs. Gladys Hefferman. League fines Ted $50

Sept. 28, 1958, wins sixth AL batting crown and second in a row with .328 average

March 30, 1959, enters hospital for treatment of neck ailment that threatens to end his playing career. Has to wear cervical collar

April 8, 1959, is discharged from hospital, but must rest before playing again

May 12, 1959, goes hitless as he returns to game, but fans give him huge ovation

June 14, 1959, benched by Mike Higgins for not hitting

June 16, 1959, offers to retire and is turned down

July 19, 1959, reoccurrence of neck injury

August 27, 1959, quoted as saying "I've had it."

December 17, 1959, tells Miami judge he received only $60,000 salary from Sox in 1959, not $125,000 as was guessed by informed circles. Difference, of course, is in deferred payments.

June 17, 1960, hits 500th homer against Cleveland

August 10, 1960, hits 512th and 513th homers in Cleveland to become third ranking home run hitter in baseball history behind Ruth and Foxx. Announces he'll retire at end of the season

August 14, 1960, voted Player of the Decade by the *Sporting News*

Aug. 20, 1960, hits two three-run homers at Baltimore

August 26, 1960, strains shoulder

Sept. 25, 1960, announces he will finish his playing career on Sept 28

Sept. 28, 1960, hits home run on last time at bat

Index

Index

Index

Index